Just Do It

JUST DO IT

The Nike Spirit in the Corporate World

Donald Katz

ADAMS MEDIA CORPORATION
Holbrook, Massachusetts

Frontispiece photo copyright ©1994 by David Madison
Portions of this work were originally published in *Sports Illustrated*.

Published by Adams Media Corporation
260 Center Street, Holbrook, MA 02343
by arrangement with Random House, Inc.

ISBN 1-55850-479-6

Printed in the United States of America.

J   I   H   G   F   E   D

Library of Congress Cataloging-in-Publication Data
Katz, Donald R.
    Just do it : the Nike spirit in the corporate world / Donald Katz.—Updated ed.
    p.   cm.
    Includes index.
    ISBN: 1-55850-479-6
    1. Nike (Firm)—History.   2. Sporting goods industry—United States—
History.   3. Sports—United States—Marketing.   I. Title.
    HD9992.U54N555   1995
    338.7'6887'0973—dc20   94-46830
                                                                       CIP

This publication is designed to provide accurate and authoritative information with
regard to the subject matter covered. It is sold with the understanding that the publisher is not engaged in rendering legal, accounting, or other professional advice. If
legal advice or other expert assistance is required, the services of a competent professional person should be sought.
    — From a *Declaration of Principles* jointly adopted by a Committee of the American
            Bar Association and a Committee of Publishers and Associations

Book design by Lilly Langotsky

This book is available at quantity discounts for bulk purchases.
For information, call 1-800-872-5627 (in Massachusetts, call 617-767-8100).

Visit our home page at http://www.adamsmedia.com

For Bill Grant

1923–1993
Cavaliere del Lavoro

Preface

When I first approached Nike founder and chairman Phil Knight with the idea of writing this book, he said no.

I had suggested telling the Nike story via a description of the company on the move through 17 months of glory and panic and fervid economic activity—between the Summer Olympics of 1992 and the beginning of 1994. Nike's remarkable, private way of company life and its highly charged means of achieving a ubiquitous connection to the world outside would surely allow such a text to transcend a straightforward description of one of the most successful enterprises of recent times. The book could offer insights into the burgeoning business of sports and the world of sports superstars. By letter, phone, and in person, I persisted—positing to Knight that a description of the special rituals and practices that are used to project the Nike brand into the world would cast light onto the whys and wherefores of the culture of selling called marketing.

The book could describe the trick of creating the kinds of jobs people really want in an advanced economy. Nike was becoming something of a model of the global, postindustrial enterprise. "That's the problem," Knight eventually replied, cutting off the pitch in midstream. "We've already taught the entire sports and fitness industry how to do what we do. Now the deal for us is coming up with the next big idea. Our competitors already just follow our lead. Why should we let everyone else know how we do it?"

For want of a snappier reply, I contended that because of *ix*

DONALD KATZ

Nike's particular history and anthropologically sui generis corporate culture, any attempt to copy Nike was bound to miss the essential alchemy—the trick of injecting the surfeit of passion the people of Nike put into their business processes and their shoes. "The Republic of the Philippines has the same constitutional blueprint as the United States," I continued, feeling thin ice underfoot. "And the Philippines has hardly turned out to resemble the motherland."

Knight laughed and said no once again.

At that point—the summer of 1993—I had already completed a manuscript for a *Sports Illustrated* article about Nike that was to be published soon. Two weeks before the article was scheduled to appear, Phil Knight changed his mind and said that he'd decided to let me back inside the company.

The timing of the decision was entirely typical of Knight's unconventional management style. On one hand, Knight remains one of the least accessible CEOs among all the largest companies—one of the "reclusive billionaires" so often wondered about in the press. On the other, he agreed to let me head out to Asia with open access to Nike's global chain of command before he knew how I'd treated the company in *SI*. Other executives might have waited the two weeks until the magazine article hit the stands.

Along the Nike trail I met line workers gluing shoes together in one of the thousands of factories rising from the dust by the week in Southern China. I spent time with inner-city retailers in Newark, N.J., mall store proprietors in California, and retailers in running stores all over the country. I met hundreds of Nike customers who regard stores bearing Nikes as museums or churches. I talked basketball, baseball, and tennis with various Nike sports heroes—Michael Jordan, Bo Jackson, Charles Barkley, Andre Agassi, and Alonzo Mourning were all particularly helpful—and I got to know a great many Nike employees, most of whom, at first, thought I would never "get it," because they thought others who'd tried to describe Nike's separate way of life had failed.

After many months of observation and travel, I came to see that Nike is at once a state of mind and an intricate network connecting far-flung economic nodes. The company courses along like some revved-up latter-day descendant of the subdivided labor and economic activity described in Adam Smith's

The Wealth of Nations. Once you've become Nike-minded, the company's influence becomes perceptible in every vista.

I had previously spent a long time inside another famous American company that also became a way of life for its employees. I wrote a book during the mid 1980s about the end of the separate society inside Sears, Roebuck. That book described the consummate company of the era in which a generation of World War II veterans transferred their battlefield loyalties to great American corporations, believing that their victories would never end. Nike, with its hipness, quality-of-life appurtenances, massive cultural sway, and global army of true believers, appears as an idealized, if extremely introverted corporation of the post–World War II generation. In a time of vanishing personal identification with companies and the general assumption that every American will have several different careers, most Nike employees clearly imagine themselves to be elite functionaries of a company cast as a movement.

Over the course of the months I conducted research for this book, I observed Nike's hypertrophic growth rate slow for various external environmental reasons, and also for reasons that Knight believed were due to flaws in the creative machine. Professional investors stepped back all at once from Nike's high-flying common-stock shares, and Knight's more than 25 million shares of Nike shed over a billion dollars in value. The diminution of his personal net worth relegated him to the thirty-second minibiography in the "over $1,000,000,000" category of the fall 1993 *Forbes* 400 list. At the end of one four-day run when the Nike share price lost fifteen dollars and Knight's shares lost close to $390 million in value—a sum surpassing that spent on Nike's legendary TV advertising over the past two years—Knight observed that the loss was no less "surreal" than the market gains that had turned his five-hundred-dollar investment in Oriental track shoes into one of the world's great fortunes.

Mistakes were made during my time of watching Nike work, in particular a botched Nike-sponsored high school basketball tournament for future stars that threatened the eligibility of the kinds of athletes Knight reveres. But rather than closing the door, Knight made sure I understood how the setbacks made him feel. Though he had vowed after a spate of traumatic layoffs in 1986 and 1987 never to break up the Nike family again, in September 1993 Knight let me watch him try to explain to employees why job cutbacks were necessary.

DONALD KATZ

My questions often indicated that the book would include the company's blemishes and inconsistencies, but Knight never balked at offering answers. He seemed to realize that an honest portrait of a company in motion must include such errors and setbacks and even—though I understand it was not easy for him to convey it—the corresponding psychological torment and emotional pain.

All of this, Knight seemed to believe, was important for a book seeking to reveal the rewards and trials of the creation and constant re-creation of a company that, as Knight put it one day, is "about much more than business—a company with a soul."

Contents

Just Do It

PROLOGUE: CHICAGO

October 1993

Along the slender thoroughfare called West Illinois Street, a long line of television vans idled noisily with their microwave saucers thrust skyward as if to catch the October night. Under a forty-foot-high portrait of Michael Jordan flying toward a basketball net, a crowd of crestfallen fans milled in front of the Chicago restaurant that bears Jordan's name.

Twelve hours earlier, "the most illustrious athlete of his generation," as more than a few journalists described him in funereal tones that day, had decided to back away from an image grown too large and demanding, from the psychic debilitations of a life lived always on stage, and so to retire from the public playing of a game that until quite recently he'd envisaged as his last true refuge.

Chicago's grieving dominated the ten o'clock news. After the minicam crews reported from the corner of West Illinois and La Salle Streets—buttonholing loiterers and passersby to ask them how it felt to hear Jordan say that it was time to "move beyond games," as he phrased it, and to "disappear"—somber graphics began long expositions upon Chicago's Loss and the Era of Air Jordan. One channel flashed a simple black-bordered salutation: "Good-bye Mike."

Inside Michael Jordan's Restaurant, surrounded by numerous cocktails and plenty of fried crab cakes, and in the company of a dozen friends, the young retiree—dressed in an elegantly draped green silk shirt and billowy pleated slacks—glanced up at a nearby television screen from a table designed for tall people **3** where a game of gin rummy was in progress. The announcer covering the evening's important baseball play-off game was once again averting between innings to a report about Jordan's decision to retire from professional basketball. A clip of the morning press conference was shown, and then sound-bite elegies were offered up by several of Jordan's fellow athletes.

As the others in the tiny, suburban-den-like retreat grew quiet, Jordan gazed back at the cards in one of his huge, soft hands and smirked. Then he lifted his glass toward the friends assembled in the private enclosure built into the back of the second-floor dining room and pointedly rolled his eyes.

Most of the men inside what regulars at the restaurant call Michael's room started to laugh.

Jordan had already told each of them that he wanted them to be happy. Some of the friends—particularly the old boys in from North Carolina—seemed distraught when they'd arrived at his house earlier in the day, but Jordan had asked them to understand that quitting basketball was the only way he could get free.

The members of Jordan's tiny circle of old buddies who'd known him for many years, his "boys," the "crew" that "keeps me from going crazy," as Michael once noted—Fred, André, Dog, Wes, and his college roommate Buzz Peterson—were all in attendance. The two grizzled-looking men playing gin with Jordan at the table in the middle of the room were members of the security team at the Chicago Stadium, off-duty Federal Drug Enforcement Agency officers who, over the recent years of public stress, had also served—as mood and circumstances so required—as late-night Falstaffs to Jordan's increasingly impacted desire to occasionally play Prince Hal.

And there were three Nike guys there who'd flown in from Oregon at Jordan's request: Howard White, the Nike pro basketball manager, sat a few feet away from his famous friend in one of the overly deep chairs designed for basketball players. Howard and Michael traded stories, and as was their daily habit, they exchanged friendly, down-home jibes.

Though not a tall man, Howard White was a talented guard at the University of Maryland back in the early 1970s and was even drafted at graduation to play as a pro. But bad knees led to a coaching job and then to one of the sporting world's more prominent insider positions as overseer of Nike's mammoth marquee stable of professional basketball talent—the "consul-tants," as the players' endorsement contracts have it.

4

During the nine years of Nike and Michael Jordan's simultaneous and symbiotic rise to preeminence, Howard White—"Michael's guy," in Nike parlance—had either seen Jordan or talked to him by telephone almost every day. Howard tended to refer to Michael Jordan as M.J. or M. or, for some reason known only to them, as Slim—though Howard, with his broad Southern inflection, said, "Slee-im."

Next to White on one of the couches arrayed around the dimly lit room sat Tinker Hatfield, the lean and soft-spoken former world-class pole-vaulter who'd designed eight of the ten generations of Jordan's meticulously wrought basketball shoes—a new pair of which Jordan had ceremoniously unboxed and laced up before 667 regular season games, 111 play-off contests, and innumerable exhibitions and practices. When the late-night phone call from Nike chairman Phil Knight had come two days earlier, Tinker was still in his home studio in Portland. After a long, creative struggle, he had just completed drawings for the tenth permutation of the Air Jordan basketball shoe.

"Bring your overnight bag to work tomorrow," Knight said in his typically cryptic manner, though Hatfield could tell something was wrong. "We're going to Chicago."

Knight, as was his habit, sat out at the far nimbus of Michael Jordan's circle of manly support that evening. He wore a wrinkled green business suit—the wrinkles having become something of a trademark over time—and he clutched one stem of his ever-present wraparound sunglasses in his hand.

Over the years since he first began selling imported track shoes out of the back of his 1964 Plymouth Valiant, Phil Knight has worn various hairstyles. At one point the look was reminiscent of Little Lord Fauntleroy, then of the Beatles in the early days, and then of a fifteenth-century monk, but sitting in the restaurant with a drink in one hand and sunglasses in the other that evening—with his longish, reddish-blond curls, close-cropped beard, and extravagantly designed eyewear—Knight looked for all the world, at the age of fifty-five, like some prosperous, if mellowed, rock-and-roll star.

Few of the people who have worked beside Knight during his rise to corporate power, to huge wealth and unwelcome fame, have the slightest idea what he wants or thinks, but Howard White and Tinker Hatfield could tell that Knight was still thinking sadly about the end of a golden run during which Nike had been "reinvented," as Knight so often described the years since

Michael Jordan came into his life. Knight was pondering the end of a stretch of time only nine years long, during which he and Michael Jordan and many other Nike guys (" 'Guys' is generic around here," as Knight commented one day) had conspired so profoundly to mark the general culture that, through their labors, Nike had altered the look and sound and feel and even the abiding fantasies of everyday life.

During the past nine years, the relationship of the billionaire businessman, Phil Knight, and the basketball wizard, Michael Jordan, had become epical—the source of many additions to both business and sports folklore. The skinny kid out of Brooklyn and North Carolina, cut from the team during his first high school tryout, who went on to redefine athletic prowess, partnered for the greater span of his singular career with a very good middle-distance runner from Oregon who, from a business school thesis, built one of the only large organizations in the world still run by its founder and who managed along the way to create a private pantheon of beloved sports heroes perceived by a generation of young people as some superhuman team.

Around the time Michael Jordan became a Nike guy, Phil Knight finally had begun to apply in full measure his hunch that if a company could somehow manage to project everywhere his own incorrigible sports-fan's urge to ascribe glory to gifted athletes, the results could be magical. If the general public could be helped to imagine great athletes as he imagined them—as having implications of the very best that the human spirit had to offer—then those athletes would become heroes like the heroes of old . . . like heroes in books. And the people would come to these heroes and listen to what they had to say, Knight believed, because superior athletic ability speaks to everyone's belief in some primordial capacity for a kind of true greatness that has been obscured over time by expediency and disappointment and the general clutter of contemporary life.

People don't concentrate their emotional energy on products in the way fans abandon themselves to the heroes of their games. But great products that were necessary to great athletic figures, Knight reasoned, could create customers who were like fans. "Nobody roots for a product," Knight would say; the products needed to be tethered to something more compelling and profound.

The remarkable and strangely muscular business culture Knight had created outside of Portland, Oregon, was built upon his similar belief that an economic organization—cast as a team on a roll—could also aspire to some elevated definition of greatness.

By the time all of these ideas began to be enchained as corporate process during the middle of the 1980s, Nike was a slightly countercultural, decidedly down-in-the-dumps, somewhat cash-strapped running-shoe company at the far end of a jogging boom. Industry experts and securities analysts agreed that Nike had "run out of feet."

At the time, few Americans outside circles of serious college basketball fans had heard of the slender rookie out of North Carolina named Jordan. But during the spring of 1985, millions of prime-time television viewers saw a basketball roll quickly across an urban court toward a handsome kid in very baggy shorts. He easily caught the ball with the toe of one of his Technicolor shoes and flipped it into his hands. Then the kid began to move across the blacktop to the keening sound of jet engines revving to take-off. By the time the engines roared at critical scream, he was aloft, his arms and legs splayed in a slow-motion tableau so magically vivid and elongated that children who couldn't generate the vertical leap sufficient to turn a doorknob were invited to climb right inside the moment.

Michael Jordan stayed in the air with his legs apart for the last ten seconds of the commercial, fusing spectators who had never been to a basketball game with an abiding fantasy of athletic virtuosity—the testimonial comprised of nothing more than Jordan's ability to fly like a bird and the implication that the padded technologies bound to his feet had something to do with his agility and his grace.

The Nike commercial—"Jordan Flight"—was replayed often in 1985 as Michael Jordan became ever more famous as Air Jordan, the Nike guy who could fly. Almost immediately there ensued a nationwide Air Jordan basketball shoe shopping spree replete with long lines, hoarding, sales far above the retail price, secondary street markets, traumatic disappointments over the limited supply, and the general aura of buying panics inspired by impending national disasters or wars.

For the following eight years—as Nike's ad budget swelled from under $20 million to well over $150 million—new Nike commercials projected billions of Michael Jordan "impressions" with each new selling season. A gifted young ad copywriter named Jim Riswold, who as a child was mesmerized by the little

7

bubbles of humanizing data included on his baseball cards ("Ed loves to go fly-fishing in the off-season. . . . Bob likes to build model airplanes"), fielded Knight's prescription for a fantastical superhero mythos predicated on Jordan's breathtaking physical gifts and adorned him instead with an incongruous capacity for good-guy self-effacement, with an attendant sense of style reeled in from the farthest edge of urban hip, and with the best of all good hearts.

Often made in collaboration with the filmmaker Spike Lee, Riswold's award-winning commercials projected Jordan's beautiful smile and the sweet and pliant personality of every child's imaginary best friend. The economy and power of Nike's signal-making connected to Michael Jordan had indeed helped make Jordan a hero in the oldest sense of the term, and the hippest of the hip, too. Nike commercials took on the insidious, mantra-like quality of popular songs. Viewers waited for them and wanted to see them again and again.

A year before Michael Jordan phoned Phil Knight to say he'd lost the fire he needed to proceed, *Newsweek* magazine published a list of the one hundred most influential people in all of American culture and Jim Riswold's name was on the list. By then, it had become difficult to locate a three-year-old—or, for that matter, a Trobriand Islander or an Inuit hunter on the tundra—who couldn't explain that Michael Jordan is a Nike man.

"What Phil and Nike have done," Jordan mused four months before he retired, "is turn me into a dream."

By early 1993, one of every three pairs of athletic shoes sold in the United States were Nikes. There was, by then, a discernible Nike way of shoe design, marketing, advertising, and corporate governance. There was a more widely understood Nike mystique, a Nike irreverence and a special Nike strain of the myraid intricacies of cool.

Competitors in the booming $60-billion domestic industry based around making and selling goods connected to sport feared and envied the bound-for-glory, winning-team ethic powering the hero-machine in Oregon. Many of them began to call Nike "the cult." Knight's team, "the family"—growing in size by close to 40 percent each year, to a force of almost ten thousand true believers by 1993—all but breezed through the macroeconomic recession that dampened most corporate performances during the late 1980s and early 1990s. During the six years before Michael Jordan retired, the company's yearly sales expanded from one billion dollars to just under four billion, and profits rose by over 900 percent.

An independent "brand-power survey" indicated that in a perfect world the shoes that 77 percent of American boys between 18 and 25 wanted in 1993—as opposed to ones they actually had or could afford—were Nikes. Word of the arrival of a new Nike design in a local shoe store is often anticipated for weeks and has been known to depopulate a school long before the final bell. Six years into the reinvention, young American shoppers outside most any school yard were able to name more than a dozen new Nike models released within the past two months. Many of them were able to refer to the shoes according to Nike's six-digit Stock Keeping Unit number stamped on the side of the shoe boxes.

While Phil Knight and Michael Jordan toasted the past and talked of old times in Chicago, many young people all over the consuming world were asleep and dreaming in Nikes. In a relatively short amount of time, highly designed athletic shoes became objects that conjured a yearning and fascination that for much of the century—during industrial capitalism's more robust moments—had been inspired by cars. Nike still receives dozens of drawings each week from children who understand the technicalities of heel counters, air bags, crash pads, and functional grooves in the way many of their fathers understood high-rise cam shafts and four-barreled carbs. Kids attach "death ray ejectors" and any number of buttons and levers to their own designs for new Nikes and then mail them off to Knight's headquarters in Oregon. "The New Air Jet, just $303!" one eight-year-old scrawled across the bottom of a drawing of a combination basketball shoe and tactical assault weapon that still hangs near one Nike designer's drafting table.

The name-brand athletic shoe might seem an unlikely seminal artifact of these last years of the twentieth century, but that is clearly what the shoes have become. These innovative, technical, but ultimately simple inventions have spawned the same sorts of abiding popular obsessions and powerful, high-profile companies inspired in the past by the airplane, the automobile, and the computer. From a once-homogeneous stew of mass-produced canvas and rubber simplicities, Nike has managed to so distinguish its nine hundred different seasonal offerings that one hundred million pairs of Nike shoes were sold during the fiscal year ending in the late spring of 1994—two hundred pairs for every minute of every day.

When a small Nike outlet opened in Shanghai, China, in January 1993, hundreds of Asian residents of a burgeoning global marketplace of similar popular desire—a technology-born force connected with the passions that had obliterated so many political barriers during the years of Nike's reinvention—waited in the dark for hours to be first among the billion to own Korean- or Indonesian- or Chinese-manufactured all-American Nikes. Nike managers in Beaverton, Oregon, were not shocked by the crowds that stormed the tiny store, because in 1992 a survey conducted in the People's Republic resulted in a report that Chinese schoolchildren believed the two most famous men in all of world history were the revolutionary hero Zhou Enlai and Michael Jordan of Chicago, Illinois.

At the time Jordan called him with his shocking news, the dream-maker, Phil Knight, had recently been named "the most powerful man in sports" by *The Sporting News.* He had appeared on the cover of *Sports Illustrated,* his bearded face obscured by the dark, wraparound Oakley shades. Though already a hero to thousands of young entrepreneurs launching their own businesses every year and the subject of countless formal case studies pored over by future MBAs, Knight was now being likened to Horatio Alger, to Howard Hughes, and he was portrayed by some as a dark plunderer who had invaded and sullied sport in the name of profit.

On one hand, Nike was studied as one of the premier corporate practitioners of the art and science of marketing, and on the other, the company was constantly attacked by labor groups, sports purists, and journalists, and by securities analysts and professional investors who had always wondered if Knight's golden ride was a fad.

In March 1986, Nike was featured in a *Business Week* cover story about America's new "hollow corporations." As nothing more substantial than a marketing and design firm that ceded its manufacturing offshore to low-overhead foreign factories, Nike, the widely discussed article posited, was an example of "a new kind of company," a "disaggregated" enterprise that was contributing to the progressive gutting of the American industrial corpus. The *Business Week* article began with a quote from Akio Morita of Sony: This "hollowing of American industry," Morita warned, meant that "the U.S. is abandoning its status as an industrial power."

But within just a few years, Nike was being hailed as the very model of a global corporation of the postindustrial future. Just before Jordan retired, the trade magazine *Brand Week* observed that in only five years Nike had transformed itself from a "discomfited, internally ravaged No. 2 in the athletic footwear industry" into a "global megabrand" alongside Sony and Coke. With its special ways of distributing something less palpable and more meaningful than shoes, Nike could "rewrite the rules of marketing," the magazine augured.

While Sony scrambled during 1993 to relocate its own production base to the same Asian nations where Nike shoes had been made for years, Nike was portrayed as having hit upon a way to provide a large number of decent and desirable jobs in an economy in which job creation had not proven easy for big corporations to do. During 1992, Nike's domestic corps of designers, computer operators, marketing specialists, and other office employees expanded more quickly than the similarly expansionist and Pacific Northwest–based software creators at Microsoft.

Nike images carried by new technologies had by the early 1990s colonized psyches and created brand loyalists throughout Asia, Europe, and South America. One of every five pairs of Nikes was now sold outside of the United States, and Knight believed half of the company's revenues would someday come from sales outside the American market.

Not far from Michael Jordan's downtown restaurant, over on North Michigan Avenue, a 68,000-square-foot expanse of pure retail theater called Nike Town was drawing some 12,000 visitors every day. The store looks much more like an athletic shoe and sports museum than a store—with a basketball court, white statues of Michael Jordan and other Nike athletes, giant tanks full of tropical fish, and vivid Nike imagery built into every wall and even the floors. As soon as Nike Town opened during the summer of 1992, it passed the Lincoln Park Zoo, the Shedd Aquarium, and the world-renowned Art Institute to become the single most popular tourist attraction in the Chicago area, a Nike place in a Nike city.

Along with Jordan, almost every one of the other world champion Chicago Bulls were prominent Nike guys, too. Nike hero Bo Jackson played baseball on the South Side for the White

Sox, and the combined cultural power of Jackson, sports, and Nike inspired the illustrious Chicago Symphony to promote the advent of a recent season with the slogan "Bow Knows."

When the Bulls won their third straight National Basketball Association title in June 1993, the most popular line imprinted on caps and sweatshirts was a play on Nike's famous call to arms of the reinvention years: "Just Did It" went the variant apothegm, "Again and Again and Again."

From the Chicagoan's perspective, Nike was much less a global enterprise run by a billionaire in Oregon than Nike was Michael and Bo and Nike Town and Just Do It. In the jampacked terraced bar on the main floor of Michael Jordan's Restaurant, where patrons face seventeen contiguous television screens showing looped footage of Jordan and the Bulls in action, a television-sized backlit rectangle on one side of the screens displayed the elegant "Jump Man" Air Jordan silhouette, and on the other side was the bright red and white Nike logo.

But when the crowd downstairs saw a clip of Jordan celebrating the Bulls' third world championship and they heard him say, "And I'm sure we'll be back for a fourth," they all began to moan.

That morning Michael had said he wanted to step over the top of the mountain of his own image and disappear over the other side, and all of Chicago—like Nike—seemed on the verge of being very much diminished.

"Come on now, P.K.," Howard White said to his glum-looking boss after the big Nike Gulfstream G-3 had landed in Chicago that morning. "Michael and Nike, they're like two parts of the same thing. Michael can become any dream there is. He's not gonna fade away."

But Knight had watched with concern as Jordan had become increasingly withdrawn ever since the Barcelona Olympics fourteen months earlier. He'd heard Jordan talk about losing touch with the joy of the game, and he'd seen him become enraged when the spotlight brought criticism of his love of gambling.

When Jordan's father, James, was murdered in July, Knight, Howard White, and Tinker Hatfield had all gone to the funeral in North Carolina, and Knight assumed Jordan's decision to retire was, in some part, the result of a lasting depression caused by this loss.

Knight got out of a limo in front of Jordan's home in suburban Highland Park, thirty miles north of Chicago, and he watched the endless stream of gawkers circle the little cul-de-sac leading up to the house. Fans came and left flowers, signs, basketballs, and other devotional items on the Jordans' lawn so often that his home sometimes looked like a shrine. Jordan's five-year-old son, Jeffrey, was due to enter a local nursery school, but first $300,000 worth of high-tech security gear had to be placed inside the school by Jordan's own security team.

Knight had been thinking for months about the price Jordan paid for being so much the hero, and now, not for the first time, he wondered if perhaps the icon-making had gone too far.

Air Jordan shoes and apparel sales accounted for some $200 million of the $4 billion in Nike sales, but for all of the commercial ramifications, the worst of it for Knight was the loss of what he called "the artistic thing"—the beauty of the ride he and Michael Jordan had taken together—and the loss of the opportunity to continue to watch Jordan so dominate a game and freeze the best in lasting stasis that he made basketball look like art.

Jordan greeted Knight, and the Nike contingent joined a small group of tense and morose-looking friends in the living room. "I see one tear outa any of you guys," Jordan said, glaring at some of his North Carolina buddies, "and I'll kick your ass."

The group departed for a press conference that interrupted the regular television viewing of hundreds of millions of people around the world.

Knight was taken aback by Jordan's apparent euphoria when the friends returned to his house.

"Phil," Jordan said, his handsome smile wrapped up around the sides of his face, "you've gotta listen to what happened to me in California two weeks back. I played golf, and then I went riding on this rented bike around Laguna Beach. And I'm riding along with my pilot and this guy who works for Gatorade, when we see eight guys playing some serious half-court pick-up ball near a school."

Jordan went on to tell Knight that after a brief discussion, one of Jordan's golf party—a white man far from conversant with the street protocols requisite to "getting next" (securing the right to play the winner of a four-on-four basketball game), dismounted and wandered onto the cement court, saying something to the *13* effect of "Excuse me, fellows, but I'm here with Michael Jordan, and we'd very much like to take on the winner of your basketball game."

"Get the hell off the goddamned court, man," one of the players barked.

"Apparently, they won't let us play, Michael," the pilot reported to Jordan, who was still astride his bike and chortling beneath his bike helmet and dark sunglasses.

"You have to go to the edge of the court and say 'Next,' " Jordan explained.

The four winners of the game had their backs turned when Jordan took off his helmet and walked onto the court. Finally turning to face their next opponents, each of the four young men suddenly froze, their mouths all similarly agape. Then they all began to take slow steps backward.

After what seemed a very long silence, by far the shortest and roundest player spoke up. "Man, I've wanted a piece of yo' ass for about five years now," he said. "So let's get to it."

"So the eight of us, we just played and played," Jordan told Knight. "We whooped and laughed and just played like crazy. Word got around and pretty soon five hundred people were standing around the court, but you know what, Phil?" Jordan said, his deep voice softening. "That game just might have been the most fun I've ever had playing basketball."

Then Jordan looked directly at Knight. "Ya see, it's just that I don't have anything left to prove."

Knight nodded as if he understood, but in truth, the idea of having nothing left to prove was something he could only contemplate as the most abstract of suppositions. There were $2 billion of unrealized sales sitting out there in the world, Knight would say. And there were potential customers who knew what Nikes looked like and what they "meant" but couldn't get at them yet. There were competitors coming at the company from all sides, and there were institutional investors who perceived each lull in Nike's rapid growth as the beginning of the end.

Perhaps it was the difference between the will to always win that causes business empires to rise and the will to win that creates sporting majesty, but Knight couldn't begin to imagine having nothing left to prove.

Later that night, after several hours of drinking and talking the strangeness and sadness out of the day, some of the friends gathered in Michael Jordan's back-room retreat began to get pretty rowdy. By then, Tinker Hatfield had his notepad out, and he and Howard White were working Knight over as Jordan encouraged them eagerly from the side. "A Jordan golf shoe is a natural," Hatfield said. "A casual line . . . an entire company: Brand Jordan."

"Can you imagine M. running a company?" Howard White teased. "He'd fire everybody's ass the first day. Who could work for him?"

They all laughed.

An exhibition basketball tour of Europe was discussed, as was a Nike-sponsored string of Michael Jordan sports camps for kids who couldn't get out of the city on their own.

At one point, Jordan said, "I don't want anybody to know this in case it doesn't work out, but one thing I plan to do is try to make the White Sox next season. I'm gonna start training pretty soon with some coaches in a field house around here, and then I'm going to Florida a month before spring training."

The Nike guys just looked back at him. They could tell he was serious.

Tinker Hatfield looked at his watch and said he had to phone a shoe designer he was trying to hire away from Adidas, Nike's longtime competitor and now a demonized force inside Nike because an ex-Nike insider had taken over and vowed to crush Nike as Nike had the Adidas empire.

"Michael, you talk to him," Knight urged. "Close the deal for us."

So the young Adidas designer, a hopeless basketball fanatic, found himself talking to Michael Jordan, "on one of the most historic days in the history of sports," as the young man would later tell family and friends until they were sick of the story.

"I can't believe they haven't hired you yet," Jordan said. "Cause when these guys want something, it's usually right there."

BARCELONA

August 1992

During the late Olympic summer of 1992—just days before the superstars of the American basketball team were expected to easily trounce all comers and claim their gold medals— the most casual of sports fans and news-on-the-hour regulars learned that certain members of the vaunted "Dream Team" seemed bent on denigrating one of the most hallowed rituals in all of sports. This, the news reports said, because of their preference in footwear.

Officials of the United States Olympic Committee announced that if Michael Jordan, Charles Barkley, David Robinson, John Stockton, Scottie Pippen, and Chris Mullin—Nike endorsers composing half of the American team—did not relent and wear the official, American flag–bedecked awards ceremony jackets also bearing the emblem of Reebok, the athletic-shoe company against which Nike had conducted a holy war for much of a decade, the players would not be allowed atop the medals stand when some 600 million television viewers in 193 countries heard the "Star-Spangled Banner" begin.

But Michael Jordan and the other Nike guys on the Dream Team refused to budge. "We won't wear Reebok," Jordan said.

As news of the standoff spread, phone calls began to pour into Nike headquarters in Oregon. By 1992, Nike had become one of those rare corporations that members of the public think to call on the telephone for reasons not connected to the products Nike sold. A recent magazine-based advertising campaign featuring lengthy, often poetic messages addressing the feelings and passions of American women had inspired thousands of phone calls to the World Campus in Beaverton. Many of the callers wanted copies of the ads for their refrigerators and bulletin boards, and others simply wanted an anthropomorphized Nike to know how the ads had touched them.

But almost every telephone call inspired by the burgeoning Dream Team affair in Barcelona at the twenty-fifth Olympic Games indicated that the Nike public believed the company was orchestrating an impending embarrassment, and that—this time—the shoe warriors had simply gone too far.

Here, after all, was a sports moment meant to reside above the marketplace, an event indicative of sport's traditional purity of purpose: the flag unfurled and the national anthem on the public-address system, the tears of young athletes glistening in the arc lights. And yet certain ostentatiously remunerated basketball players seemed willing to deny the nation this experience because of loyalty not to the flag, to the "glory of sport" or "honor of our teams," as the Olympic oath has it, but to a company in Oregon that markets their shoes.

Charles Barkley—soon to become the star power-forward of the Phoenix Suns, and a veritable Tocqueville when moved to observe a complex social phenomenon and distill its essence—managed to underscore the perception that mammon was about to triumph over patria in Barcelona by proclaiming that he had no less than "two million reasons not to wear Reebok." As a result of his "marriage," as they say in the world of modern sports marketing, to Nike, Barkley was being paid a million dollars as an annual guarantee. Charles would also be paid a million more dollars over a year by Nike pursuant to his contractual right to 2 percent of the net wholesale price of the popular Nike Air Force basketball shoes he wears.

"These days," Barkley reflected not long after the Olympics ended, "you play a sport very well and that takes you to a certain level by itself. But Nike can take you way beyond that. Nike has helped me make a whole lot of money, and I'm not about to forget it."

If Barkley had more than two million reasons to refuse to be a human billboard for Reebok in Barcelona, then Michael Jordan—with his much larger guarantee and his 5 percent of the wholesale price of every pair of Air Jordans sold—was in the process of accumulating some twenty million reasons to remain loyal to Phil Knight and Nike over the course of 1992.

All of this was occurring in an era when most Americans had come to accept that Michael Jordan, Bo Jackson, and Michael Jackson shared a great deal more than aspects of their proper names—an era in which most children realized that Jordan sits on the bench wearing a hat bearing Nike's famous logo not only to keep his head warm; when the sports pages of metropolitan newspapers have come to resemble the business pages of the recent past; when the business pages look like the sports pages of old; and when player salaries are divided by batting averages like earnings divided by outstanding shares. But Phil Knight still sensed that the Reebok warm-ups controversy could become a problem. This was the kind of controversy that could loosen Nike's special hold on the popular imagination.

Knight had decided not to go to the Olympics, though he could have gone to the restless capital city of the Catalans and sat beside sheiks and prime ministers in the front rows. "Too many people come up to me at the track-and-field events I love to watch," he said when he decided not to make the trip. "The Olympics have actually become kind of a pain for me."

Knight usually loves to go to track events, and he enjoys watching tennis. Students of Nike who are aware of Knight's extremely introverted nature are occasionally shocked to see him stand up during tennis matches to yell and scream like a hockey fan at rinkside—occasionally during moments of general silence. But for the most part, Knight is famous for not showing up where he might be expected, and since actually being there for the big game or the annual trade show is so essential to others who work for businesses connected to sports, he had managed to underscore his power over the years through the simple act of staying away. The constant refusals to be interviewed or appear at the right business roundtables have given rise to general characterization of Knight as shy—though few observers think the Nike chairman's reticence compromises the man's fervid determination to win each and every game he plays. Knight tends to end his rare exhortations of the Nike troops with two words: "Let's win." He directs a company named not for the Greek goddess overseeing sport or play but for the goddess of victory.

And from the first time he heard about the impending public relations fiasco in Barcelona, Knight realized that the medals-stand outfit battle was one Nike could not win, except in the most Pyrrhic way. But he also realized that the problem was going to be very difficult to fix, since it involved the will and competitive resolve of Nike's own "ultimate warrior" and in-house Superman, Mr. Jordan.

When the broad sheaves of computer printout bearing one-line conversation summaries had been generated by the stream of angry phone calls coming into the 800-number operators over in the Mike Schmidt Building, Knight thought back to an evening he'd spent with Jordan five weeks earlier, when Jordan was in Portland with the Dream Team for the Tournament of the Americas, a phase of the Olympic team qualification process.

Before Knight and Jordan went out for a lengthy pasta dinner at Pazzo, the wood-lined restaurant in downtown Portland's Vintage Plaza Hotel, the Dream Team had humiliated the Cuban squad in what would turn out to be the only game the assembled superstars would play at anything above half-speed.

The Dream Team was the slam dunk of basketball squads, and as much fun as the best players in the world were having sharing the same colors, they all knew that they'd been assembled to dazzle and sell. There was never a hint of doubt that they would win.

Jordan had originally told Knight that he didn't want any part of a professionalized Olympic competition. "It's for the kids," he'd said. "I have my gold medal already from eighty-four."

"I don't want you to play anyway," Knight had replied.

"Why's that?" Jordan asked.

"Because I'm afraid it will shorten your career."

The American representatives to the *Federation Internationale de Basketball*—FIBA—the world basketball-governing body that had made pro players eligible for the Barcelona games, had actually voted against sending in America's famous pros, but the representatives from other countries wanted the basketball explosion on an international level to continue, and they were more than willing to sacrifice their own teams if the American superstars who appeared in those commercials would be willing to play.

The Boston Celtics' star Larry Bird, had originally agreed that younger players should compose the American team, but then both Bird and Jordan got phone calls from Magic Johnson urging them to play. Johnson had recently revealed that he was HIV positive. He said that Barcelona might turn out to be his on-court swan song.

After squashing Cuba, Jordan told Knight over dinner that **19**

Dave Gavitt, the president of the USA Basketball organization responsible for drafting the pro Olympians, had taken him aside in the locker room after the game.

"So he tells me that we have to wear these special warm-ups on the medals stand that have a Reebok emblem on them," Jordan said. "He said not our shoes, just these special outfits."

"What did you say?" Knight inquired.

"I said, 'Ya know what, Dave? I have a real big problem with this. All of us on this team are hired guns, so let's not pretend we're anything else. All of us have endorsement deals with different companies. How can you have gone and sold these rights and expect us to wear these things?' "

Gavitt, the senior executive vice president of the Boston Celtics and a respected figure in both amateur and professional basketball circles, had tried to explain that the marketing of the medals uniforms was done separately from the official USA Basketball paraphernalia. But Jordan told Knight that Gavitt appeared to understand his position and had vowed to "fix the problem."

"Good going, Michael," Knight had said—though looking at the computer printouts reporting the content of phone calls and watching the news, Knight now fervently wished he'd said something less rousing to his most famous part-time employee.

According to Howard White and the other Nike people working in Barcelona, Jordan noticed that the Reebok warm-ups problem had not been fixed while reading a legal document he was handed during the team's overseas flight. Included in the text of the Olympic Code of Conduct was a description of what would happen to an Olympian who commits a felony during the games, a pledge not to use drugs, and a formal agreement to wear the official awards suit.

"I'm not stepping up on any platform in Reebok," Jordan reiterated to Gavitt, and he proceeded to cross out and initial the offending clause.

A discussion ensued among the other players on the plane, and soon, most of the other Code of Conduct documents were amended in ink, this—Olympic Committee officials later said—for the first time anyone could recall.

A few days later, on a flight headed for Barcelona from the Dream Team's first European stop, Monte Carlo, Gavitt told Jordan and the others that they simply had to wear the Reebok sweats if they wanted to formally receive the gold medals they would surely win.

Jordan was furious when he bounded off the plane in Barcelona. "I'm not wearing outfits that say Reebok," he said into the inevitable circle of reporters.

"Me neither," Charles Barkley chimed in.

And so something of an international incident had commenced, and Heather DeDona and Lisa McKillips—who deflect all but the most pressing requests for Philip Knight to establish personal contact with the non-Nike world—began to field calls from various senior Olympic officials in Barcelona.

The Dream Teamers did relent during their game against the Angolan team by allowing the African squad to score 48 points to their own 116. The Angolans had scored only 1 point against the Dream Team during the Americans' early 46-point run, so the guys decided to lope. Charles Barkley distinguished himself during the contest by elbowing an Angolan player half his size. Charles later told reporters that the African athlete, who flew into the air as if he'd been hit by a car, "probably hadn't eaten in a few weeks."

Knight took a phone call from Dr. Harvey Schiller, the former sports-marketing-minded commissioner of the intercollegiate Southeastern Conference and the current executive director of the United States Olympic Committee. Schiller was calling from Barcelona to ask Knight to please call off his boys.

"I'm continuing to do what I can," Knight said. "But the truth is, I can't do much at all."

"The Olympic Committee and the press are all acting like I have a magic wand," Knight complained to Nike's thirty-five-year-old VP for corporate communications, Liz Dolan, after Dolan called Knight to talk damage control from Barcelona. "This is getting serious," Knight said. "We have to get to Michael."

Despite Michael Jordan's atavistic incapacity to back away from anything that looked remotely like a competitive challenge, it did seem entirely logical to most observers that if anyone could call Jordan off the attack, that person was Phil Knight. That residents of the Nike-conscious public even perceived Phil Knight and his company to be in control of public events in Spain was *21* also not difficult to understand, grand orchestrations having become one of Nike's many fortes.

Bo Jackson often says that he will never forget the day the piece of modern marketing lore called the "Bo Knows" campaign began: "I was about to step to the plate from the on-deck circle at the 1989 All-Star game when I looked up and saw a plane flying over the ballpark trailing a huge Bo Knows banner. Then I looked up into the stands and all I could see were Bo Knows signs and people putting Bo Knows hats on their heads."

So Bo went to bat and homered massively, the celebration later fading into a commercial break premiering the soon-to-be unavoidable "Bo Knows" television ad campaign. The timing of the commercial was no more a part of an advertising strategy than Bo's home run, but it looked as if the whole thing were part of a Nike master plan.

"For a very long time after that," Jackson recalls, "turning on the television was like looking into a mirror. It all broke around me like a sudden storm. It was everywhere. Suddenly everyone knew me. Everything changed."

Nike sends employee teams storming into a city to stage elaborate multimedia sound-and-light shows replete with dozens of Lycra-clad models dancing around a hotel room for the benefit of three or four magazine editors. Long before industry trade shows begin, railroad cars and semis full of Nike personnel and millions of dollars worth of Nikeabilia arrive to assure the company's continued image of world dominance and a knack for controlled orchestration of events.

Though Knight says he rarely thinks about the power implicit in his control of the Nike machine, he was startled by the preponderance of Nike imagery covering the city of Melbourne when he attended the 1992 Australian Open. "I turned one corner, and there, stretched across one of the biggest buildings in Melbourne, across the whole skyline it seemed, was a huge 'Just Do It' banner," he recalled. "And I stopped and let myself feel the enormous thrill."

Where other sports apparel and equipment companies offered hospitality suites in Barcelona, Nike personnel had converted a nightclub next to the Torre Catalunya Hotel into an elegant ring of quiet, enclosed "pods" where athletes and other VIPs could relax and chat. The place was laden with fax machines and phones and mountains of food and, as always, lots of athletic clothing and shoes to give away. A local cinema had been secured for a media event featuring Jordan, Barkley, the Ukrainian pole-vault master Sergei Bubka, and other Nike track-and-field stars.

Before the twelve hundred reporters filed into the movie theater, Michael Jordan arrived at the Nike Barcelona outpost. Security personnel created a cordon around one of the pods, where Jordan sat down with Howard White and Steve Miller, the recently elevated Nike director of sports marketing and the general overseer of the Nike stable of stars.

Now forty-seven, Miller had already been a Detroit Lion, the athletic director at Kansas State University, a college and high school track coach, and Nike departmental overseer of the company's many track-and-field relationships. A preternaturally extroverted man, he seems to have met every coach in North America at some point. With his squarish haircut, head, and squared broad shoulders, Steve Miller looked like a prototype of the tough but caring coach he had been. When Miller had been hired to run the world's largest sports-marketing organization less than two years earlier, Knight said, "You've got the best and the worst job in the company. It's the best because you can just about do anything you want in this business. It's the worst, because I'm gonna be watching you every step of the way."

So much of Nike's public presence is hitched to the abbreviated half-lives of its athletes—to their health, performance, personal rectitude, and continued popularity—that staying on top for Nike had come to mean establishing a presence at every draft of amateur talent in every sport and every tournament. Every team had to have Nike players, so Steve Miller ran a department of more than sixty sports-marketing specialists, each of whom was expected to know everything going on inside their respective games.

"The PR side of this is impossible to win," Miller said to Jordan.

"Hey, we're partners," Jordan replied, looking at his friend Howard White. "We spend a lot of time talking about ethics and pride. This is about ethics and pride to me. Way I look at this, we oughta battle this one out . . . together."

But as the Olympic games progressed, even as Team Nike continued to rack up more medals than would be collected by the entire Unified (formerly Soviet) Team, efforts to control the fallout from the medals ceremony affair were getting nowhere.

Several American sportswriters who cover the NBA walked

into the Barcelona office of United States Olympic Committee PR man Mike Moran. The journalists reiterated Michael Jordan's and his teammates' refusal to wear the medals outfit, and Moran quoted the Olympic Code of Conduct and went on to remind the writers that the money Reebok had paid the USOC supported athletes who might not have millions of dollars. The money went to fencers and wrestlers who in the past had had to "crawl under chain-link fences at night to train, who worked long hours behind lunch counters, and whose parents made extreme sacrifices to support their children's determination to compete."

Press reports soon carried word that Mike Moran of USOC had in effect called Michael Jordan and the other Nike holdouts greedy.

Many Nike employees were deeply hurt by the perception that the company was stage-managing the controversy in Barcelona, that an overt lust for market share was causing Nike to act in ways inimical to the best interest of sports. Even employees still working as trainees knew that the whole pious idea behind Nike from the beginning had been to build a pedestal for sport such as the world had never seen. Nike was nothing if not "an athlete's company," an organization by and for athletes.

"The athlete," Knight repeated often, "remains our reason for being." Nike's customers were all "athletes," too. If this classification served to create a pipeline for fantasies connecting elite athletes and the consuming public, if it served to honor the customer—the statement was less than technically true in light of research that showed that, at most, 40 percent of Nike shoe buyers used the shoes for their intended sport—the vision also telegraphed a corporate desire to create covenants between customers and a special company cast as a haven for people who identify completely with athletes and sports.

When Phil Knight started Nike, the dominant athletic-shoe corporation was the German firm Adidas, inventors of the modern soccer boot and other sports-specific footwear. In the view of Nike's antiestablishment founding fathers, Adidas was an elitist organization that was deeply entwined with the corrupt and aristocratic international sports authorities of the day. The Adidas guys were "sports bureaucrats" who wined and dined league officials and international fat cats.

The early Nike guys, on the other hand, were athletes—almost all of them competitive long-distance runners at first—and via their own athletic pursuits, the young company acquired a decided preference for athletes over teams or the rule-makers controlling sport. There was an internal obsession with "authenticity." The company would be dedicated to the proposition that authentic athletic desires would help create authentic products for authentic athletes. The cause of the individual athlete would become the company's cause.

"Michael Jordan holds us to our values," Nike executives—most of whom have never met him—would often say. The company exists, one formal statement of collective purpose proclaimed, to "enhance people's lives through sports and fitness." Over and over again they proclaimed that Nike's success was predicated upon a shared commitment to "keeping the magic of sport alive."

Sports-marketing specialists estimated that by the 1990s fully seven times as many athletes were parties to working agreements with Nike as with any other company. Over half of the NCAA championship basketball teams of the past ten years had worn Nikes, and more than sixty big-time colleges were "Nike schools"—this, in most cases, because their coaches were Nike coaches. Well over 200 of the 324 NBA players wore Nike shoes, over 80 of them by contract. Two hundred seventy-five pro football players wore Nikes, as did 290 major-league baseball players.

By the summer of 1992, Nike had so masterfully connected its business aspirations to customers, sports, and high-profile athletes that the revenues the company would report at the end of the fiscal year in late May of 1993 were as large as those garnered from TV deals, tickets, and retailed paraphernalia by the National Football League, National Basketball Association, and major-league baseball combined.

Three months before the Olympics, an interviewer from the *Harvard Business Review* asked Phil Knight why Nike used so many athletes to support company initiatives.

"Because it saves a lot of time," Knight said. "You can't explain much in sixty seconds, but when you show Michael Jordan, you don't have to."

Many of the business activities conducted by Nike were designed to help build a given sport. Anything that was good for sports, Knight often said, was good for Nike. Sports had arguably surpassed popular music as the captivating medium most essential to being perceived as "young and alive," and sports, as never before, had so completely permeated the logic of the market-place in consumer goods that by 1992 the psychological content of selling was often more sports-oriented than it was sexual.

That members of the public could interpret Michael Jordan's loyalty to the corporate cause as bad for America and bad for sports testified to Knight's constant warning that the company's special relationship to all the pathos and nobility of athletics was forever vulnerable. Unlike automotive or computer dynasties—but just like sports dynasties and batters on hitting streaks—Knight argued that shoe empires would tend to ascend to extremely brief, Icarian moments near the sun.

He believed that the modern athletic-shoe empires—drawn together from fragments of much older shoe, clothing, and sporting-goods industries—had risen and fallen through the post–World War II era according to natural cycles. "First Converse had its day, then Adidas, then Nike. The cycle took us from zero to a billion dollars in a short time, and suddenly Reebok had its years in the sun. Then Nike was reinvented during the late eighties, and now we're back on top."

Knight believed that there was even a relationship between the vicissitudes of Nike's influence and the cyclical shape of its premier athletes' careers. Even before the time of global hero-creation—when Nike athletes were a few track stars and a small group of basketball players—the fortunes of company and athletes seemed to be tied.

"And everything happens faster now," Knight would continue. "In this business, every six months is like a new life. We can't take our eye off the ball, because if we lose it in the next six months, we'll have a son-of-a-bitch of a time getting it back. It's just so fragile. We have to reawaken the consumer every six months. So everybody around here has to want the ball in the closing seconds. Everybody needs to win."

Talk to a Nike manager about the company's "ownership" of 75 percent of the market in shoes with cleats on the soles or 40 percent of the running-shoe market or 65 percent of the huge market in basketball shoes (the company's other basketball "sub-brands" besides Air Jordan—the Barkley-connected Force shoes and the popular Flights—accounted for the sale of many more basketball shoes than Converse and Adidas combined), and he or she will invariably interrupt and soberly intone, "It's borrowed. No market in this business can be owned."

· · ·

The profits available to those who would artfully entwine products and sports are often said to have been discovered first by a St. Louis brewer named Chris Von de Ahe, who was so struck by the congruence of baseball fans and alcohol-related thirst that, in 1881, he purchased the St. Louis Brown Stockings so he could sell his beer in the stands. By 1992, 150 MBA programs and law schools over the country offered extensive sports-marketing courses or degrees. Hollywood entertainment lawyers continued to leave their firms to become highly paid sports agents or sports marketers for Nike or one of the other more than four thousand separate companies spending billions of dollars on some manner of sports marketing. Statistics collected at the end of 1992 by International Events Group, Inc., would show that $2.1 billion was spent by North American companies on sponsorship of specific sports events—the figure dwarfing the $254 million spent on "causes" by corporations and the $233 million spent on the arts.

Though participation in and observation of sports had exploded during the eighties, the sports-marketing expansion was in large part a pragmatic reaction to the expense and relative inefficiency of traditional advertising. Sports endorsements, licensing deals, promotional tie-ins, and sponsorships were now perceived by marketers whose products and services were not remotely connected to sports as a way to achieve a more direct connection to the consumer's elusive will to spend.

One study of the invasive force of sports marketing in 1986 emanated from an analysis of the value of the sugar substitute NutraSweet's position as sole sponsor of the United States Figure Skating Association. NutraSweet's television ads were blacked out during a skating event in selected markets, and yet the study showed that most viewers of the event were still quite sure that they'd seen NutraSweet commercials during the broadcast anyway. The past association of company and event had branded popular perception. Nike marketers enjoyed pointing out that the vast majority of people attending the 1984 Olympic Games in Los Angeles thought Nike was an official sponsor— this because of all the Nike billboards observable all over the city—though Converse was in fact the corporate sponsor.

No scoreboard, dasherboards around a hockey rink, sweatband, blimp, scorer's table, courtside folding chair, plastic water bottle, or half-time extravaganza now remained unclaimed by the forces of sports marketing. Events were sliced into "sports moments" and sold off as frameable parts. The kickoffs beginning National Football League halves were often sold separately to corporate sponsors. So was the announcement of the starting line-ups before hundreds of televised contests. The photograph on the back of the Kellogg's cereal box depicted not just world-class American bike racers but the winner of the Kellogg's Tour of Britain, the winner of the Thrift Drug Classic, the winner of the Nissan Tour of Ireland, and even the "Motorola Cycling Team Doctor." Kayak racers and competition snow-boarders now wore patches and color combinations indicative of contractual corporate support that was formerly accorded only a handful of the most colorful tennis stars.

Michael Jordan talked of his "portfolio"—a welter of business agreements that, to Phil Knight's chagrin, now included seven- to eight-figure endorsement and licensing deals with more than fifteen different enterprises (this, according to Jordan's agent David Falk, the result of a "consolidation process" that had brought the number of deals down from eighteen).

Though a relative saturation of the United States market for athletic goods and apparel was achieved during the late 1980s, the sports-marketing generals looked out at a world more girdled by new telecommunications capacity every day. They watched capitalism—or at least rampant consumer desire—emerge from the end of the $10-trillion Cold War, and they saw a thousand potential brushfire wars over product and brand suzerainty where forces arrayed behind competing ideologies had stood in opposition before.

And Nike, by force of Knight's perception of the global continuum of sports, was already out there and heavily armed. "To paraphrase Willy Sutton," Knight would say when questioned about the deployment of his "global power brand," "we're going out into the world because that's where the feet are."

Nike had begun propelling its sophisticated imagery into the European marketplace in 1985. In the Netherlands and in France, certain models of the Nike Air Max running shoe were already essential accoutrements of generational definition for European teens. Though the most recent Air Max retailed for 299 Dutch guilders in Amsterdam—over $155—the shoes are as indispensable to large numbers of young people along the canals as bell bottoms were in the San Francisco Bay area of twenty-five years ago.

By the summer of 1992, the Nike International division was fielding over forty applications a day from citizens of the former Eastern Bloc who wanted to open up Nike distributorships in nations where Nike had come to represent sports and irreverence and cool. Nike's president, a former Kennedy White House and Boston lawyer named Dick Donahue, was stunned not long after the Olympics ended when a kid in Buenos Aires, Argentina, asked him if Chicago Bulls and Dream Team star Scottie Pippen was wearing a new shoe. Nike had sent Pippen the latest prototypes dreamed up by the designers in the Michael Jordan Building on the Nike World Campus in Oregon only ten days before Donahue left for South America.

Three years earlier, the mention of Air Jordan had caused participants in focus groups in Osaka and Tokyo, Japan, to giggle, because Jordan rhymed with the Japanese word for "joke." But now Air Jordan was the number one shoe in Japan. A single television advertising onslaught in 1989 had elevated Nike from relative obscurity to the number two most desired American brand among teenagers in Japan—the number one spot going to Coke.

Few people working for Nike had been more carefully tutored in the Nike way of playing out Knight's competitive urgencies than Michael Jordan. From Jordan's perspective, his job in Barcelona was to vanquish the competition—which included "grinding down Reebok," as Nike's forty-one-year-old general manager Tom Clarke had put it before the games began. Jordan had seen Knight's own ferocity of competitive impulse up close for years now, and he'd never seen Knight or Nike back away.

Basketball, the Nike strategists believed, was on its way to dislodging soccer as the world game, and the Dream Team at the Olympics would be the best chance to show power basketball to the world. A year earlier, Michael Jordan was part of a Nike marketing caravan that had traveled through Europe. Several months later, it was difficult to find a wall or street lamp in Munich that failed to announce the imminent arrival of Nike stars Charles Barkley and Scottie Pippen for a colorful pre-Olympic festival of slam dunks and exhibition basketball.

During the year preceding the Olympics, Nike's international sales had increased by over 33 percent, and the European market share controlled by Reebok and Nike combined was approaching 50 percent of total athletic-footwear sales, up from just 5 percent a decade earlier. In an effort to grab 10 percent more of the market during 1993, Nike's ad planners had earmarked $50 million for European spending—for "investment," as the ad dollars were now perceived by the Nike marketing gurus in Beaverton.

The sports marketers at Reebok, Nike's estimable competitor from Massachusetts, had not a single endorsement athlete on the Dream Team. Reebok still had invested massively in the Olympic buildup, outspending Nike to produce a television campaign depicting American track-and-field athletes Dan O'Brien and Dave Johnson as two modern gladiators, pitted in Olympic contests that would discern who was the "greatest athlete in the world."

The winner, the commercials promised, would emerge in Barcelona, but Dan O'Brien had a terrible day during the Olympic trials and failed to make the team. *Sporting Goods Business* magazine's survey of industry retailers and manufacturers could locate only one respondent who knew Dan or Dave's last name—and when the would-be Reebok star, Dave Johnson finally competed inside Montjuïc Stadium in Barcelona, he would wear Reebok shoes and official USA track-and-field clothing prominently sporting the Nike name and logo as part of yet another multimillion-dollar sponsorship agreement.

Everything had gone according to plan, but now, as Knight looked on with frustration, the Great Satans of Reebok were getting millions of dollars of free publicity from the networks and newspapers, all of it generated by a four-cent, two-inch strip of cloth that said Reebok.

But Reebok was only one of the big-time brand-name combatants involved in the Olympic marketing firefight. Nike was also jostling for position on the global basketball stage with the aspiring global power brand known by the initials "NBA."

Three days before the basketball finals, Harvey Schiller of the Olympic Committee met with Dave Gavitt of USA Basketball to discuss the Dream Team uniform impasse. The men emerged with a press release that proclaimed that while all members of the U.S. team must wear the Reebok-made uniforms, "some players may choose to wear the awards suit in a manner that does not reveal any commercial identification. . . . However, in no instance will the uniform be defaced," Gavitt's statement decreed, "or covered by any other material."

Though it was Dave Gavitt who had demanded that Jordan

and the others wear the outfits, he and other USA Basketball functionaries in Barcelona were extremely critical of intimations by Olympic officials that the Dream Teamers were greedy. Gavitt was being assisted in Barcelona by Russ Granik, the number two USA Basketball executive and the deputy commissioner of the NBA. As thousands of business-minded sports fans all over the world knew, when the Nike Dream Teamers and various USA Basketball officials squared off, USA Basketball was an NBA sub-brand for Olympic purposes, and the NBA and Nike had been warring over the profit potential of pro basketball and the control of certain players' services for a long time.

The more-than-$800-million Nike basketball shoe business was around the same size as the NBA in terms of revenue. On a far more personal plane, the entrepreneurial wizard behind Nike—Phil Knight—and the entrepreneurial wizard behind the resuscitation of the National Basketball Association—forty-nine-year-old former attorney David Stern—had for years been locked in what everyone in the sports and sports-business worlds perceived as both an overt power struggle and an indirect contest over who would be known as the smartest sports-business figure of them all.

Eight years earlier, when David Stern became commissioner of the NBA, professional basketball was widely predicted to become the first major professional sport in America to simply close up shop. Seventeen of the twenty-three pro teams lost money in 1984, and the general image of the sport was overshadowed by player drug use, terrible labor relations, and an assumed absence of future marketability that was often attributed to the "blackness" of the urban game.

But then David Stern turned pro basketball into what Knight and many others see as the best-run sport. Stern built new alliances with team owners and the NBA players association. Game attendance increased until tickets were hard to come by in almost every NBA town, and television viewership increased each year—in part because current Dream Teamers Larry Bird and Magic Johnson arrived to help in 1979 and Michael then soared onto the scene during the mid 1980s. During Jordan's first year, the Chicago Bulls franchise was valued at $18.7 million. Nine years later it was worth $190 million.

Pro basketball's revivification is historically analogous to the rebuilding of scandal-ridden and far-too-unsophisticated pro baseball between the World Wars. A strong commissioner,

Kenesaw Mountain Landis, employed public relations techniques to install the game as the "national pastime," and the true
meaning of baseball was successfully personified by the Michael
Jordan of baseball—George Herman "Babe" Ruth.

David Stern, like Knight, perceived sports as an unbreakable
chronological and geographical continuum, as a highway broad
and strong enough to carry thousands of salable things. "At some
point," Stern had said during a speech to an American Marketing Association gathering before the Olympics, "the Cosby
Show will stop, even in reruns. But I promise you the Boston
Celtics will open the season."

Though Stern got most of the general notice for the sudden
hipness and success of pro basketball, many in the industry believed Knight and Nike had shown Stern how to turn the boys
into icons fit for a sports-minded time. The best television teaser
spots starring Jordan and the others did seem to replicate the
vigor of Nike's famous commercials. And it was Nike that had
most profitably demonstrated that once the new heroes were
created, the things they wore and talked about would become
desired by millions.

Nike had been allied with Michael Jordan in battles with the
league since the fall of 1984, when Stern had invoked a league
"uniformity of uniform" clause to ban Jordan from wearing his
new black and red Air Jordan shoes. Nike immediately fired
back with the first Jordan commercial. The spot was shown in
test markets, and it depicted the twenty-year-old rookie as a
glowering and dangerous presence for the last time. Jordan aggressively slammed a basketball from one hand to the other as a
voice intoned: "On October fifteenth, Nike created a revolutionary new basketball shoe. On October eighteenth, the NBA
threw them out of the game. Fortunately the NBA can't keep
you from wearing them."

By the end of the 1980s, the NBA had moved heavily into
product marketing. Almost every Nike employee could by then
recite the elements of sacrilege entailed in the way Jordan's face
was being exploited by others. There was even a Jordan puppet
beer-can cooler ("You bent back Michael's head . . . and it was
for beer!") and an absurd caricature of Jordan on the NBA Prop-
erties T-shirts.

The thirty-six-year-old Nike sports-marketing director at the
time, Fred Schreyer, had moved to Beaverton, Oregon, from
Los Angeles and a partnership in one of the big entertainment-

oriented firms. In August of 1989 Schreyer phoned Jordan's agent David Falk to point out that the NBA Player's Agreement included a little-known clause by which players could formally "opt out" of the licensing program. When the collective bargaining agreement between players' representatives and the league had been struck, there was little thought about selling several hundred million dollars' worth of NBA goods, so the amount the players were making from the goods was minimal.

Two years after Falk had told the NBA of Jordan's desire to "opt out," Jordan finally announced that he was "taking back his face." He would transfer the rights to his likeness and name to the company that was so instrumental in making Michael Jordan universal. Several other players also opted out of the NBA licensing agreement and reclaimed their images, but Knight and his sports marketers believed that the only reason most NBA players didn't reclaim the rights to profit from their images was that those images were so poorly tended and protected by the army of sports agents who, in Knight's estimation, seldom understood the complexity of marketable celebrity.

By the NBA All-Star game in 1992, Nike and the league were still going at it. A staff of sixty full-time marketing specialists now retailed NBA faces, names, logos, and gear, whereas a single individual had done so before Stern took the helm. "Licensed" NBA-sanctioned team jackets and shirts had become part of the omnibus youth uniform that began on the ground with Nike shoes, but Michael Jordan's face was missing from the caricature T-shirts retailed at the All-Star game. If disappointed fans asked why, they were told that Nike was flexing its corporate muscles again.

It had often come to Knight over the past few years that one of the only other people in the business who understood that marketing was the key to the health of a modern professional sport—and that agents had become inimical to the best interests of the game—was David Stern.

Knight could often be heard to complain that the sports agents striking endorsement deals for athletes were mucking up the business. "The agents came out of a time when someone making a hundred thousand dollars was a well-paid athlete," he'd say. "Agents were just fringe lawyers or guys with a huge passion for a sport, like Mark McCormack with golf. From those hundred-thousand-dollar NBA contracts, the agent got four thousand. But now you've got one-hundred-twenty-thousand-dollar agent fees for a single team contract, and for a million-dollar endorsement, the agent gets up to twenty percent. The incentive to fragment an image is huge, and when you split it up too often nobody wins."

Sports agents across the ethical spectrum suffered from an image problem not unlike personal injury lawyers. The word "agent" was often abjured in favor of "athlete representative," or, since a large number of the two hundred or so more prominent sports agents had gone to law school, "lawyer." Even "sports lawyer" was invoked.

David Falk, who was occasionally referred to among sports insiders as the "agent from hell," often reminded writers and new acquaintances that Michael Jordan referred to him as his attorney. "It's a mark of respect," Falk would add.

Knight was not in the least bit pleased to observe the way Falk had managed the progressive dilution of Michael Jordan's Nike-engendered public presence by the prominent additions to his "portfolio," as Jordan called the agglomeration of Gatorade, Wheaties, Chevy, Hanes, and even a Ball Park Franks endorsement deal. Coca-Cola and McDonald's had had Jordan under contract before he was a superstar, but only Nike had invested the creative energy and financial resources required to create Air Jordan. By 1992, Knight believed that Michael Jordan was no longer, in sports-marketing nomenclature, "clean."

It seemed that David Falk always had some angle to play when he broke the news of another deal—the CEO of one company was an old North Carolina Tar Heels guy; "Michael wanted to do this deal because it's in Chicago"—but Knight saw Jordan as manipulated and significantly devalued by association with underwear and hot dogs.

Then came the evening when Knight stared at his television screen and watched Andre Agassi, a Nike guy since he was a sixteen-year-old wild kid whom no other company would touch, pumping Canon cameras. Andre tipped down his sunglasses, looked into the camera, and with a knowing smirk, said, "Image is everything."

Knight flipped.

Agassi was particularly precocious in his understanding of the power of an image, but to go public with such an analysis was crazy. "This is a one-hundred-and-eighty-degree turn away from our own imagery!" Knight fumed. "Here we work like crazy to convey that performance, not the image, is everything.

Andre wins more grand slams than Ivan Lendl at the same age, and yet everyone thinks he's a loser now because he lost three grand slams. How many did Lendl lose before he won one? Six or some damned thing. This 'image is everything' is hurting him and it's going to hurt us."

So before the Olympic summer began, a new control mechanism was created by Nike, and at the end of June the new system was publicly unveiled during the annual drafting of college basketball players by NBA teams. Shortly after Georgetown University's star center, Alonzo Mourning, was selected as the second draftee, a reporter asked Alonzo who he would be working for during the coming season—the young Charlotte Hornets team that had just drafted him or Nike.

"I work for Nike," Alonzo said.

And the sports-business grapevine coursed with news that Phil Knight was at it again.

It turned out that Mourning—a young man whose glower often masked a handsome face and an infectious smile—and another young star, the leaping "Mini-Michael" from USC, Harold Miner, had signed revolutionary agreements in which Nike would pay them guaranteed sums not just to endorse shoes and apparel but also to play basketball. As part of Knight's desire to extend control, the new Nike sports-management division run by Fred Schreyer would manage Mourning's contract with the Hornets, his financial affairs, his public image, his ancillary marketing agreements, and even his charitable work.

For all the notoriety Alonzo Mourning had accrued as a child basketball prodigy—as a high-profile college superstar playing for Nike coach John Thompson at Georgetown University and as a surefire multimillion-dollar pro basketball draftee—as long as Alonzo could remember, he had perceived a business association with Nike as the means by which a gifted player would finally transcend the hardwood courts and the sports pages in a single bound. Now that he was with Nike, young Alonzo said in a dreamy, deep voice, "I'll be a household name."

Knight never denied that the new management program was designed to increase Nike's control over a sports-marketing system he believed the company had helped create and perfect. And though agents had the most to lose from Nike's sudden move into player management, David Stern realized that when the Nike players came to negotiate their new contracts, the balance of power would be substantially altered.

Stern had come to Beaverton in late April, 1991, to enlist Phil Knight's help in drafting the best of the pros to showcase the future world game in Barcelona. Stern sat across a long conference table in a room near Knight's office atop the John McEnroe Building. He personally assured Knight that despite a standing agreement that made Converse the official shoe of USA Basketball, the Dream Team stars would not be expected to wear Cons in Barcelona.

By mid-July, USA Basketball had already sold twenty-three licenses granting the right to produce Dream Team shirts, watches, mugs, and other items. Thirteen corporations were on board as official sponsors (Nike being prominently absent from the list).

But the medals-stand outfits were not among the items sold off by USA Basketball. It turned out that other powerful marketing organizations were more central to the awards-suit impasse than Nike or the NBA. By far the most prominent brand symbol (as a fellow from the Grey advertising agency employed by the International Olympic Committee called it) on display in Barcelona were the five interlocking Olympic rings. Twelve companies had paid $30 million each to be official Olympic sponsors (Nike passed), and others had paid at least $6 million to "bolt the rings," as marketers said, to their products.

At one point during the selling festival in Spain, a British athlete named Daley Thompson had trooped around the infield before a day of track-and-field competitions in a T-shirt that said THIS SPACE FOR RENT.

Though Jordan held Gavitt and the league responsible for the Reebok warm-ups snafu, it was actually a quirk of the Olympic brand marketing system that had led to the conflict. The United States Olympic Committee had showered all of the American athletes with thousands of dollars worth of sponsored goods— casual clothes, coats, rings, bags, cosmetics, and enough other stuff to fill a footlocker—but the only garment the athletes were required to wear by Olympic dictum was the awards suit. The awards suit, it turned out, was marketed not by the U.S. Olympic Committee but by the much snootier and less easygoing International Olympic Committee—an assemblage of the sorts of "aristocrats" Nike people were taught to detest. And the American team's awards suit had become commercial space bought and paid for by Reebok back in 1988.

• • •

"This is all about control," Knight fumed as the controversy persisted.

For over a year Knight had been spending time pondering his belief that Nike's future plans required an increased level of control. Knight was being constantly forced to acknowledge how much easier it had been when Nike was an entrepreneurial association of renegades. "We were the underdogs for so long there," he'd say. He talked about the importance of the global-scale Nike learning to "fight a little less with the authorities" and seeking to "make peace with the leagues." And yet, if the Nike, Inc., of 1992 had been a twenty-year-old boy instead of a large commercial organization, a lingering authority problem would still have been a reasonable diagnosis—the residual penchant for irascible knee-jerk behavior and bloody-minded adventures being a legacy that was difficult for Nike's leaders to leave behind.

Michael Jordan had every reason to believe that his associates at Nike would revel in the controversy he was perpetuating in Spain. Jordan had spent years observing that while Nike people on one hand proclaimed a corporate mission designed to protect those weighty values that allow athletics its pious references and high-Puritan platitudes, they also subscribed to another equally essential aspect of the corporate ethos that elevated iconoclasts and individualistic athletes with big-time attitudes above any sport, governing body, league, or team.

Nike executives loved athletes such as the combustible tennis players Ilie Nastase and John McEnroe. The McEnroe some observers perceived as spoiled and immature was in fact an antielitist thorn in the side of an aristocratic tennis establishment from the Nike perspective; "Mac" was a fearless athlete who set new standards of "intensity and the desire to win," as Knight phrased it, that still symbolize the fierce spirit of competitive drive referred to inside Nike as the company's special "fire."

A Nike athlete like the Atlanta pro football and baseball player "Neon" Deion Sanders, who sometimes jumped up and down on top of first base while the pitcher was trying to concentrate and who did weird butt-twitching dances in the end zone, acted in a tradition harking back to Nike football player Lester Hayes, who reached inside opponents' helmets and slapped them in the face. Charles Barkley, who during the previous NBA season had called the city where he'd played—Philadelphia—"racist," also behaved well within a bad-boy-with-attitude Nike tradition.

The kinds of athletes that embarrass grown-ups were entirely acceptable Nike guys.

To be a Nike guy, you did not necessarily have to be sweet, squeaky-clean, or even in nominal control of your mouth or your fists, but you did have to "get it," as they say on the Nike World Campus—which can mean various things not unconnected to a basic respect for Nike's heritage and a fervid unwillingness to lose. As Michael Jordan knew well, the Nike heritage included an "attitude" and a taste for a good fight.

Nike's annual report issued that summer—a document of a tradition as bland as a phone book—all but dripped with their corporate attitude. It presented profit-and-loss graphs as murky expressionist paintings. The text mocked conventional wisdom (Knight often ironically used the phrase "conventional wisdom", invariably noting that he considered the phrase "an oxymoron") in light of the recent triumphs of various Nike athletes: "No one will ever break [Bob] Beamon's long-jump record at sea level. Andre Agassi can't win on grass. Nolan Ryan is too old. . . . A black man can never be a good company spokesman in white America. The rest of the world has caught up with the USA in basketball."

But recently Knight had observed that each time Nike ventured out to protect its lead, the corporate imperatives, rangy company traditions, and the popularly perceived purities connected to sport all seemed to collide. There had even arisen, during the recent years of the company's surging business performance and more palpable dominance of the sports industry, an identifiable constituency that hated Nike—not in the way rabid fans loathe the other team, but in the way people say they hate evil. At some point during the corporate rise corresponding to Michael Jordan's success curve, a discernible anti-Nike critique had emerged within the Nike-watching community. The "Nike attitude," born so specifically of antiestablishment, baby-boom impulses, was portrayed as corporate arrogance—even as the empire-crumbling flaw of hubris—by certain purists protective of the egalitarian superiority of amateur and noncommercial sports. Among the regular Nike critics were numerous sportswriters whose moral tone marked them now as latter-day Cromwells of the back pages. As so much entertainment journalism had lost its critical edge and become integrated as part of the industry's publicity infrastructure, some sportswriters had maintained a critical perspective predicated on the belief that sports and business should remain as separate as church and state.

The members of the small coterie of crusading sportswriters that offered Nike as an example of what was wrong with sport did not question the morality or the artistic disadvantages of professionalizing violin-playing or painting, but the enmeshing of sports and commercial-culture-inspired moral outrage—especially in light of the clearly persuasive force the combination was capable of generating on human will.

But the thing that was so unsettling about the phone calls coming in to Nike headquarters during the Olympics was that most of the callers were Nike customers who seemed this time to have bought the anti-Nike line.

"It's as if we've become a discrete set of values for our consumers," Nike's chief of public perception, Liz Dolan, complained after Barcelona. Tens of thousands of brand loyalists had called Nike to say that ads or shoes or even inspired posters had changed their lives. Letters circulated in Beaverton from citizens claiming that they finally left abusive husbands or even achieved heroic rescues from burning buildings just because Nike had injected "Just Do It" into the zeitgeist. "But because we're connected to sports," Dolan complained, "our success is perceived as something bad. If a computer company in Silicon Valley grew so quickly that profits had doubled by the year and had delivered buckets of money to shareholders, the public would be thrilled. But for us, it's different."

"Everybody loves success," McEnroe once scoffed. "But they hate successful people."

"We were the up-and-comers once and everybody liked us," Knight observed after the Olympics ended. "Then we became number one and everybody started shooting. It's not just because of our connection to sports. It's also because there's a flip side to all the emotion we generate and the tremendous well of emotions we live off of. Somehow, emotions imply their opposites, and at the level we operate, that reaction is much more than a passing thought."

The emotion made possible the progression from company ethos to sports to individual athletes to customer creation. The emotion was woven deeply into everything about Knight's aspirations, and the emotion was laced into Nike's special vision of   **39** corporate organization, the requirement of constant internal change, the fierce view of competition, the marketing philosophy, the ads, and the products. It was the emotion—the Nike spirit, the composition and maintenance of which so many outside the company regarded as a trade secret—that had made objects bearing the Nike logo on the heel or breast pockets such universal objects of desire.

And that emotion was what the competition feared, what they found almost impossible to replicate, and so it was one of the things they mocked and derided. Nike was "the cult." Nike was the company that wanted to subordinate the best of sport to profit.

Knight's global sports-marketing efforts gave rise to fears that Nike would never stop until it had vertically integrated all of sports, until it controlled all the games. After Nike players there would be Nike teams and Nike leagues and even Nike sports. "They'll make them up," one competitor contended. "Like in that movie, *Rollerball*."

By the end of the Barcelona summer, Knight realized that Nike was fast becoming a lightning rod for all of the popular ambivalence about the general convergence of American business and American sports. Nike stood in for all the encroaching uneasiness over the way sports had come to so preoccupy public consciousness and discourse. The backlash emanated from a lasting intellectual distrust of sports still characterized by T. S. Eliot's famous decrying of the "decadent athleticism" of American culture; and the critique drew force from both the Victorian view of sport as an avoidance of sober virtue and from the radical view of sport as a barbiturate capable of clouding the fervor of the people and making them item-starved and bargain-hungry.

Knight worried about the way momentary setbacks requiring moral reconsideration were coming on faster and more furiously all the time. He had looked on while Michael Jordan took a lot of heat after he chose to play golf and vacation with his family instead of going to meet President Bush at the White House after the Bulls won their first championship in 1991. William Faulkner had refused an invitation to dine at the White House with John Kennedy because it was "too far to go for dinner," and yet his reputation for intellectual and creative seriousness was only enhanced. But American sports heroes were Americans of another sort. Inventors fighting to protect their patents were individualists bucking the bureaucratic status quo, but Jordan's decision to secede from the collected caricatures on the All-Star T-shirt was perceived as tantamount to an absence of patriotism. And still, during each month of the summer of 1992, hundreds of babies were given the first and middle names "Michael Jordan." At a Nike press gala held in a huge and ornate Barcelona movie theater, it was a Japanese reporter who rose to ask, "Mr. Jordan, how does it feel to be God?"

"Guess we can't lose now," Charles Barkley jibed from the side. Barkley was then asked what he saw when he looked at Michael Jordan. "Just a black, bald-headed millionaire," he replied.

Jordan grinned his famous grin and deflected the God question, but over the months that followed Barcelona, Jordan would join Knight in wondering if, as Knight put it, "the hype had finally gone too far."

"Do I think Nike creates images for athletes that exceed their capacity to perform as athletes—or as real people?" Knight was to muse after the Barcelona crisis finally passed. "Well, my short answer is yes, but it's not just us. It's TV that really defines these athletes. We just expand on the image. But perhaps our efforts do combine with the power of television to come together and create something that nobody can live up to."

By the end of the summer, it had occurred to Phil Knight that perhaps the sheer force of Nike's image-making had created expectations capable of blindsiding the company. This was particular cause for concern because Knight—as all who know him will confirm—is a man who must always see what's coming at him.

Howard White left the Nike encampment for the Ambassador Hotel off the main drag of Las Ramblas, where members of the Dream Team had been granted special permission to lodge away from the fifteen thousand other athletes occupying the Olympic Village. By midafternoon on the day of an eight P.M. Dream Team appearance, the hotel was completely surrounded by thousands of onlookers held back by hundreds of policemen, who waited to observe the American players simply traverse the sidewalk between the hotel entrance and a waiting bus.

"It's like traveling with twelve rock stars," the Dream Team coach, Chuck Daly, complained later in the day.

Festooned with a half-dozen necklaces bearing various security passes and identification tags, Howard White waded through the crowd to Jordan after discussing the impending fiasco with Steve Miller and Liz Dolan.

White tried to convey to his longtime friend that Knight thought this time it might be wise to pull back, to just go ahead and wear the Reebok awards-ceremony garb on Sunday.

"Well, then I guess Phil doesn't realize how loyal I really am," Jordan replied, frowning. "What's happening here?" Jordan inquired, staring at Howard White, who used to check out the women who flocked to Jordan during his rookie year, trying to discern potential gold diggers. "Isn't Phil gonna back me up on this?"

As reports appeared in a Salt Lake City newspaper quoting L.A. Gear endorser Karl Malone and Nike's John Stockton ("In a million years there's no way I'm not going up there") as disagreeing with the hard-line point of view, Howard White called Knight. "M. wants to know why we're not backing him on this," White said. "He seemed disappointed. You know Michael. It's that ultimate warrior stuff. Shit's black or shit's white. There's no gray at all. He says the NBA hired him—like a gunfighter—and they should have known that there were limits to what he'd do."

International news wires carried reports that NBA commissioner David Stern had criticized comments about the Dream Team made by Mike Moran of the United States Olympic Committee, who was described on the wire as a "low-level public relations official." Stern said that Moran had "issued an ultimatum and our guys didn't like it, so they decided to have some fun with it. . . . Our players always intended to come here, represent their country, win the gold medal, and represent the U.S. at the medal ceremonies."

Not long before the final game on August 8, Michael Jordan read a somewhat legalistic-sounding memo from Knight that affirmed Nike's position that wearing the prescribed medals-stand uniform would not violate the Nike athletes' contractual agreements.

Jordan knew that he was about to play a basketball game in which he was not Jordan of Chicago or even Jordan of the NBA. He was the greatest of all the global gunfighters in a world at comparative peace. He was Jordan of the great big marketplace-to-come in Barcelona, and to be forced to pretend otherwise amid the elaborate jockeying for strategic position that was the Olympics of 1992—as Howard White conveyed to his boss—made Michael Jordan "plenty pissed."

In Barcelona, "a ticket to the basketball awards ceremony" had by now become the standard reference to the increasingly expensive and hard-to-come-by ticket to the final game.

The Dream Team members gathered once more before leaving the hotel to finally decide what was to be done. Though Gavitt's statement had proscribed covering the medals uniform, Jordan now argued for taping over the Reebok tabs on the jacket and pants. Magic Johnson was strongly supportive of Jordan's view even though he'd become fed up with his own shoe endorsement company—Converse—because they'd failed to help him step up into the light as Nike had done for Michael and Charles.

While Michael Jordan's son, Jeffrey, played one-on-one against John Stockton's son on the miniature basketball court set up inside the players' lounge in the hotel, some members of the team argued that Gavitt's reference to wearing the awards suit "in a manner that does not reveal any commercial identification" was best addressed by rolling the collars of the jackets back until the Reebok emblem was obscured.

"Let's get some safety pins," someone said.

"Don't you think things have gone too far to back away?" Jordan asked David Falk.

"The point is to make your statement," Falk said. "I think there's a better way to do this."

As the music blared on the loudspeaker system in the arena, the roaring crowd greeted the smiling and waving Croatian team the American squad had just beaten by thirty-two points.

Then, to rising cheers, Magic Johnson led the Dream Team onto the floor. Johnson had joined the others in rolling back the collars of their red-white-and-blue jackets and pinning them near the shoulders. The huge V created on the players' chests and the bulkiness of the rolled collar were reminiscent of the way motorcycle riders wore their leather jackets in the earliest biker films.

If any of the hundreds of millions of people tuning in bothered to get up close to the screen and squint—as the leaders of Reebok were undoubtedly doing in and around Stoughton, Massachusetts—they could just about make out a Reebok patch visible on most of the players' pants ("I never viewed the incident as a businessman," Reebok CEO Paul Fireman would later claim. "I looked at it as an American, as someone seeing another level of societal breakdown—greed and personal desires being chosen over the patriotic and global values we ought to have").

"From the start," NBC announcer Marv Albert intoned, "they called them . . . the Dream Team."

Magic Johnson had come out waving an American flag above his head, but now that Michael Jordan had appeared—looking serious and blowing bubbles with his chewing gum—the crowd could see that he, and then Charles Barkley, had carefully arranged American flags around their necks and secured them with safety pins so as to cover even the little Reebok emblem on their pants.

Barkley stood atop the stand just a few feet away from Karl Malone of the Utah Jazz. If Charles was indeed the most celebrated power-forward playing the game, then Malone matched or possibly even exceeded Barkley in the realm of pure talent. And yet Malone could still walk down a crowded street and pass unnoticed by children and football fans. There were no Karl Malone simulated-bald-pate skullcaps on the market, and Malone could not be found cavorting with dancing girls or battling Godzilla in outrageous tongue-in-cheek commercials like those that had made Barkley famous in places where the annual per-capita income barely exceeded the cost of a pair of Nike shoes.

Charles certainly had a ready-for-media face and a late-night-talk-show mouth, but the projection of his image was a function of the shoes he wore. Karl Malone had the talent to be a hero of Nike proportions, but he'd signed with another company.

Barkley threw kisses from the stand, and eventually even Michael Jordan began to grin. Jordan stood between Scottie Pippen and Clyde Drexler, with Old Glory over one shoulder. The flag concept was apparently David Falk's contribution, but the idea was suggested so close to game time that only three flags could be found.

Jordan later said he figured nobody would question the patriotism of a man literally draped in the flag. But people did. Letters complaining that wearing a flag was unAmerican arrived at both the Nike and U.S. Olympic Committee headquarters. Citizens who seemed unaware of the logo battle that had preceded the medals ceremony were offended by the flag being turned into clothing and associated with a mere game.

JUST DO IT

Dave Gavitt was philosophical as the incident at Barcelona finally passed into sports-hype history. "Michael was nothing but a superstar through the whole thing," Gavitt said. "And Phil Knight did everything he could to help. But you've gotta say one thing about those guys at Nike—like 'em or not—they march to the beat of a very separate drummer."

It was never quite clear which members of the Dream Team went home without their Olympic awards suits, but maintenance personnel cleaning up the arena on the final day of the 1992 games reported that several red-white-and-blue jackets with "USA" on the front and matching blue warm-up pants had been found between some benches on the locker-room floor.

BEAVERTON I

January 1993

O n a cold day in early January, Phil Knight's elegant jet-
black Acura NSX sports car, sporting a license plate that read
NIKEMN, growled through the Oregon morning. The car thundered up over a bridge ten miles west of Portland spanning
Route 26, shot past a trailer park on the left, and then cornered
aggressively into a gap in the grass-covered earthen wall surrounding the corporate Xanadu called the Nike World Campus.

Knight pulled into his parking space not far from the John
McEnroe Building and began to unfurl from the high-tech
cockpit of the automobile, an appropriately Asian rendition of
an otherwise less efficient and far more expensive Italian car.
Knight readily admits to having a "thing" about cars. He's not
into collecting them as such—though he does own a Lamborghini Diablo and also a Ferrari Testarossa he was just holding on
to until the resale prices went back up . . . and he did have a
Porsche until he racked it up last year.

Knight says he only likes cars that go fast. "I get sleepy going
slow. Fast is safer for me," he said, smoothing down an Italian-
looking, well-wrinkled business suit. "I've collected eighty-five
speeding tickets over years of staying wide-awake at the wheel."

Through the nearly horizontal, knee-high windshield of the
Acura, a yellow Post-it note could be seen stuck to the rearview
mirror. The printing on the note clearly explained how Knight
might locate a garage door opener less than a foot away from the
mirror and even how to operate the device.

46   Knight's management of his electronic and voice-mail mes-

sages is a simple task, because no one who knows him would ever leave a message. They all understand that Knight is incapable of navigating the worldwide Nike E-mail system to retrieve a message. And since Knight hardly ever wants to hear from someone he doesn't already know, he sees no reason to alter a serviceable status quo.

Every so often he does feel moved to type out a letter on one of the hundreds of Apple PowerBook laptop computers that are almost as ubiquitous around the World Campus as Nike gym bags. He will peck out the letter and then walk the PowerBook out to one of his secretaries so the communication process can proceed.

"It's a good thing I didn't dream about the computer business," Knight said as he stepped onto a silvered, wood-plank walkway in front of a stand of tall pine trees. "I'm still utterly mystified by a light bulb going on. I'm what you'd call a complete technologic and mechanical klutz."

Then Knight flashed a huge grin that extended up under the jagged perimeters of his ever-present Oakley sunglasses, the aerodynamic, ellipsoidal geometry of the patented heater lenses reflecting in Terminator-silver hues a panoramic span of one of the most renowned workplaces in the world—a seventy-four-acre shrine to quality of life and athletic pursuits, contrived as a company town.

Beyond a marble fountain leading back from forty-eight flagpoles bearing the flags of only half the nations where Nike conducts business, young employees of the company could be seen walking quickly to work beneath covered sidewalks that connect the McEnroe Building to the Alberto Salazar Building, the Dan Fouts Building, the Michael Jordan Building, the Bo Jackson Fitness Center, and several other glass-walled office structures commemorating the life's work of individuals in some cases no more than thirty-five years old.

Alberto Salazar—at once a Nike legend and a current full-time employee of the sports-marketing department—won the New York City Marathon in 1980, 1981, and 1982, golden years for the upstart shoe gang from Oregon and the international running boom Nike helped create. Dan Fouts was a talented quarterback who was willing to wear and promote a strange-looking pair of Nike shoes with soles shaped like waffles back in 1972, the year the Nike name was first unveiled, so **47**

Fouts—like Michael and John and Bo—was also honored with a building bearing his name.

The reasonably scaled buildings were set close to a perfectly still seven-acre man-made lake. On the far side of the lake, along broad, redbrick walkways and past numerous sculptures and austere stone benches, there is a thoughtful and secluded Japanese garden. Many stands of tall trees dot the campus grounds, most of them crisscrossed by tanbark-covered ribbons of jogging trail.

None of the young soldiers of Nike who casually passed the chairman with brief smiles or nods wore a business suit and tie like the boss, and some of the men had very long hair by corporate standards. At least half of the employees power-striding across the corporate quad carried an accessory bag that said "Just Do It" or "Nike" on the side, and many of them seemed to be wearing extremely interesting shoes cooked up in the Nike labs—exotic sports sandals or advanced prototype footwear that in a few cases wound up around the lower part of their legs like the thongs of Roman centurions.

Nike executives can occasionally be spied "on campus," as they always say in Beaverton, wearing two entirely different shoes—which fellow employees are sure to notice, because in Nikeworld, everyone says hello and then, as if by autonomic impulse, stares down at the other person's shoes. At first, visitors tend to believe they've dropped something or perhaps spilled during breakfast.

Nike employees refer to the world outside the campus as "the biosphere" or "the real world." "Beyond the berm"—a reference to the close-cropped grass wall, atop which the kinds of serious runners who don't wear socks can be seen chugging along at any hour of the day—there is the America Nike serves and "enriches" through sports and fitness. Inside the berm is Nikeworld, where almost everyone is fit and healthy, where nobody can ever smoke, where the corporation pays employees a fee to ride bikes or in-line skate to work instead of driving, and where it's quite all right to go on over to the Bo Jackson Fitness Center and work out for two hours at lunchtime—because your entire department will probably be at work until nine at night, grinding out the metaphoric yardage for the good of the company cause.

Knight stopped to read a flyer in the lobby of the McEnroe Building that called for "fit, muscular, and toned men and women who excel in the sport for which they are hired" to report for a test photographic shoot connected to a coming promotional campaign. Knight laughed and walked toward the elevator wondering aloud if there was a room on campus "big enough to hold 'em all."

The average age of a Nike employee has risen over the past five years to thirty-one, and company personnel specialists report that the majority of the some forty thousand job applications received during 1992 were from people much younger than that. The Nike Joan Benoit Samuelson Center, named for the distance runner who won the first women's marathon at the 1984 Olympics, is occasionally referred to as the "student union building," and when plans were made for baseball legend Nolan Ryan's visit for the dedication of the Nolan Ryan Computer Services Building, corporate event planners decided to guarantee at least one intimate gathering during the attendant celebrations by restricting attendance at one party to those Nike employees over forty.

One of the many high-quality documentary videos Nike produces for internal viewing includes the serial observations of "What it's like to work at Nike" from one youthful and attractive Nike talking head after another. At one point, the camera frames a very blond young woman, the light reflecting off her big, perfect smile as she wrestles with the enigma: "Working at Nike?" she sighs. "It's li-i-i-ke—"

Suddenly other faces and voices cut in with answers. Working at Nike is like:

". . . a factory for fun."

". . . like finals night."

". . . being in a playground."

". . . coming down the face of a wave."

Then, just as suddenly, the blond employee reappears with her own analysis. It's kind of like a symphony, she reflects: ". . . There's moments when it's soft and . . . subtle. . . . And then . . . there's times, when . . . it will crescendo into a great, powerful moment!"

Without ever having to pass outside the berm, Nike employees can get a haircut, do their laundry, get a massage or a complete fitness evaluation, buy Nike products, and even shop in a store clearly stocked with the kinds of items appreciated by spouses and children who haven't seen a long-laboring loved one in awhile. Carloads of Nike children can be seen being hauled past the Mike Schmidt Building and around the Fouts

Building on their way to the progressive play programs offered at the Joe Paterno Day Care Center.

Despite the startling youthfulness of the corporate scene, innumerable employees talk of having been reborn at Nike after abandoning less fulfilling ways of life. "I taught English. . . . I'm a reformed accountant. . . . I pitched for the LA Dodgers for a while. . . . I was drafted by the San Diego Chargers, but then I blew out my knee."

Among them are dozens of former lawyers who once wrote Nike's briefs, former editors of ski magazines and shoe industry trade magazines who once wrote articles about the company, former politicos (Neil Goldschmidt, the former governor of Oregon, used to work for Nike), and a lot of former vagabonds, overaged surfers, and ski bums ("More than a few people here worked at the Mangy Moose bar in Jackson Hole or one of the hotels in Sun Valley," one manager noted). One employee, David Rikert, is a former Harvard Business School teacher who wrote one of the many Harvard case studies about Nike's unique ways of doing what it does.

Many former professional athletes, former Olympians, near-Olympians, all-Americans, and one-time collegiate competitors of considerable prowess work on every floor of every building. In addition to the distance great Alberto Salazar, Rudy Chapa, another world-class runner who occasionally beat Salazar during their college days, also works in sports marketing. Company road races and bike races are often won in near world-class times, and it is actually difficult to find an employee without some stellar moments in his or her competitive past and at least one current participatory-sports obsession for which he or she is "in training"—in some cases twice a day.

One of Knight's possible heirs-apparent—not that Knight has any intention of backing away in the near future—was a forty-two-year-old former track coach with a Ph.D. in sports-related biomechanics, Tom Clarke. Clarke often manages to complete two full-scale long-distance training runs every day.

Most of the work spaces inside the campus buildings are so heavily adorned with Nike and general sports imagery that the walls are reminiscent of the walls in the frat houses that house the campus jocks. There are volleyball posters, Charles Barkley Born to Be Wild posters, Mary Joe Fernandez tennis posters, posters of sinewy women sitting on weight benches, Jim Courier tennis posters, and cutouts of Bo Jackson holding a dumbbell in a way that made his bicep bulge like a grapefruit. Sports mugs, sports equipment, and other sports paraphernalia sit on every surface, and sports clothing hangs from nearby hooks.

Professional athletes still in the prime of active careers are universally dazzled by the Nike World Campus. The Atlanta Braves and Atlanta Falcons multisport star, Deion Sanders, had recently come to Beaverton for a day but had ended up staying for three days, working out for hours in the beautiful gym at the "Bo" and hanging out with Nike designers to talk about sports gloves that will protect his fingers when he slides into second base. Deion and the designers also discussed new shoes that would replicate the effect of the yards of tape Sanders always wrapped around the outside of his football shoes and socks (the habit, called spatting, is anathema at Nike, because the logo must be visible on TV).

Bo Jackson loves the campus scene so much that he says he wants to retire to Beaverton and a job at Nike. ("Yeah, well Bo's crazy," Michael Jordan said when he heard this. "No way *I'm* retiring to Beaverton, Oregon.")

Nike employees are proud of their collective knack for staying cool when Jordan, Sanders, Agassi, Jim Courier, Nike baseball star Ken Griffey, Jr., and other members of the consultancy gang are on campus. Famous athletes can work out on one of the three sprawling floors at the Bo or have a sandwich in the big, circular cafeteria in the Benoit Samuelson Building without being bothered. NBA teams visiting Portland to play the Trail Blazers often hold pregame shoot-arounds in the Nike gym, and even Converse and Reebok athletes are welcome.

After several rounds of grueling interviews, a recent candidate for an important job managing Nike's new "environmental action team," a former Reagan administration official with both a PhD in a relevant field of science and a law degree, was told by a member of the selection committee that he had just one more question: "Who's Deion Sanders?"

"Well, I don't really know," the candidate replied.

And that was the end of that.

On the walls of the covered arcades connecting the signature buildings on the World Campus, there are rows of bronze plaques bearing images in bas-relief of athletes whose greatness has been less than fully recognized outside Phil Knight's and Nike's particular vision of the lasting nobility of sport. Along the Nike Walk of Fame, Charley Lau, the batting coach, shares a place with even lesser-knowns: triathletes, forgotten Jamaican sprinters, local-hero college coaches, and wheelchair road racers. Lots of tough-guy athletes such as Franco Harris, of the Pittsburgh Steelers of the glory years, and the lineman Lee Roy Selmon ("Son of a sharecropper . . ." begins the typically elegiac inscription on his plaque) are up on the wall. Company wags will sometimes note that the sculptor who does the faces on the "Walk of Noses" has managed to cause the physiognomy of young Andre Agassi to closely resemble the strikingly different visage of Chicago Bulls forward Scottie Pippen. But everyone inside the berm seems to know that understanding the Walk of Fame is connected to understanding the Nike mindset, the fundamentals of "the Nike heritage," as Knight calls it. Employees who want to excel at Nike must understand what makes people able to cry and scream with pleasure while watching a game. They must be bull-moose fans—like Phil Knight.

The soaring athleticism of the campus scene has caused one or two students of the Nike culture to posit that if company officials ever decided to partake of the corporate vogue in random employee drug testing, they might consider testing for steroids. The sports-mindedness of the corporate culture means that nonjock employees feel they must follow teams and scores as a matter of protective coloration. Basic salutations between employees almost invariably include give and take about contemporary sporting events and players' performances, usually with information only carried in the finest print on the sports pages.

Unlike so many other businesses in which sporting metaphors have become part of the everyday managerial vocabulary—"quarterbacking" a committee and the like—Nike *is* a gigantic, multifaceted sports metaphor. Entire careers are envisaged as extended sports moments. Work weeks and fiscal quarters are all imagined as increments upon a game clock, as portions of the season's perpetual big game.

And as of the beginning of 1993, everyone inside Nike knew that the head coach of the company had been crowned "the most powerful man in sports."

Four months after the jangling events in Barcelona, the annual *Sporting News* magazine's list of the "one hundred most powerful people in sports" was published with Knight's grin and sunglasses on the issue's cover. Knight had ascended to the top of the most powerful list from seventy-fourth place a year earlier.

Last year's "most powerful" had been David Stern, who had fallen behind Knight on the new list to the number two spot. Dave Gavitt, president of USA Basketball, was number eight.

The Sporting News's editors reported that it wasn't really the size of Nike that made Phil Knight so powerful; it was his ability to "effect change across a broad spectrum of sports." In a long article accompanying the coronation, the measure of Knight's authority seemed to have been derived from the sheer number of other individuals he had managed to terrify or infuriate over the previous year. The U.S. Olympic Committee, the NBA, and basketball fans living in Charlotte, North Carolina, were all numbered on a long list of offended parties.

Charlotte Hornets fans only became aware of the new Nike sports-management program that had so shaken the sports-marketing establishment when it came time to negotiate Alonzo Mourning's contract. "Mourning Won't Sign: It's the Shoes" read one headline in The Charlotte Observer. Another story reported that Mourning might indeed never play for the Hornets because of the years of financial security Nike had already provided him. One local fan wrote to the newspaper, claiming that Nike's $16-million five-year salary and endorsement guarantee with the brilliant young center had "taken the spirit out of the game."

As the fans fumed and the sports-marketing industry looked on, David Falk—who had been asked to negotiate with the Hornets on Nike and Mourning's behalf, since Nike was not accredited as an agent with the NBA—argued that Charlotte had better give in to his demands for a better contract, because Nike's largess had secured Alonzo's immediate future whether he played basketball or not.

Hornets president Spencer Stolpen and team owner George Shinn countered with their own hunch that Nike's leaders would be less than pleased with Falk if he fixed it so their expensive endorser didn't play basketball at all. The fans weighed in with strong opinions expressed in newspaper and local televised sports reports, and Knight was told that talk of a Hornets-organized local boycott of Nike products was in the air.

Knight, who was known to respond energetically to threats, inventoried the situation, and on opening day, Alonzo still refused to play. Knight had by then received a personal appeal by phone from the Hornets' player personnel director, Dave Twardzik, who formerly played for the Portland Trail Blazers and was a Nike endorsee. "No, Dave," Knight said, clearly enjoying the company's ability to increase a player's leverage, "Alonzo will decide when he has a fair deal."

In the end, the final contract more than compensated for Nike's guarantee, and Mourning joined his team—vowing to "work hard and let Nike do the rest"—during the fifth game of the NBA season.

It was around that same time that Deion Sanders took a ride in the Nike-financed plane between Pittsburgh, where Deion and the Atlanta Braves participated in a National League play-off game, and Miami, where, the next day, Deion and the Atlanta Falcons played a football game. Sanders then was flown back for another baseball game, though he actually spent all of the game on the bench. Atlanta Braves officials, local fans, and various national sports journalists seemed to disapprove.

CBS sportscaster and former player Tim McCarver said on the air that it was "flat-out wrong" to do such a thing, so ever-playful young Deion—while his teammates on the Braves celebrated their seventh game victory in the clubhouse—dumped three huge buckets of cold water on McCarver's head, right there in front of the whole baseball-loving nation.

Several of the subsequent press reports indicated that Nike and "the most powerful man in sports" paid Sanders a huge bonus only if he participated in two professional sports.

This was not the case, but Nike was once again perceived to have been stage-managing the episode—even by insiders. On the morning of Deion's cross-disciplinary doubleheader, Atlanta Braves president Stan Kasten—ostensibly Sanders's boss—phoned then Nike sports-marketing director Fred Schreyer to ask if Deion indeed planned to fly to Miami after the baseball game to play football. If he did have such plans, Kasten continued, would Nike be willing to stop him?

When Nike president Dick Donahue—true to the feisty corporate tradition—was asked about the company's reaction to Deion dumping water on McCarver, he quickly responded, "What's wrong with that?"

By the end of November, Nike's rising public profile was attended by the rise of another, albeit more rarefied, measure of the public perception of the company's power. The value of Nike shares on the New York Stock Exchange had risen precipitously by then to a historic high of $90¼ per share on November 24—this from a low during the dark days of late 1984

of less than $6⅝ a share ($3¼ adjusted for an intervening split).
New investors continued to be drawn to Nike's 1992 return on
investment, a rate more than double the average American corporation, and sales during the second quarter of the 1993 fiscal
year that ended in late November were up by 18 percent over
the previous year.

The company had a strong and conservative balance sheet—
which professional investors only seem to like when things are
going very well—and a worldwide brand presence increasingly
compared to Coca-Cola's global sway. There was explosive
market-share growth abroad—sales had grown by 345 percent
in the Netherlands through the fall, by 181 percent in Italy, and
by 155 percent in Spain. A firm grip was still held on a third of
the huge American market in athletic footwear, and—if all the
"most powerful" stuff was accepted as true—Nike had something of a choke hold on the global sporting mechanism that
each day so many more CEOs at other companies were asking
consultants and other specialists to explain to them.

And then, the formal investment analyses and trade press reports would continue, there was Nike's corporate leadership, the
team lead by the "marketing genius" who also owned one third
of the company himself. Knight took the teasing about being
"the most powerful man in sports" in stride and sloughed off the
genius bit with a smirk. He said he had seen the stock price
dance rings around the true health and future prospects of the
company from the beginning, so it was hard to put much store in
that either.

Nike stock traded at a considerable discount to the measurable
fact of its business strength at times, and then at a large premium
of the true state of affairs at other times. Nike's stock price, like
everything else connected to the company, seemed to fly up and
down upon a contagion of feelings and emotions. The vicissitudes of the price in some part reflected the fact that analysts and
traditional investors were never quite sure how to classify or
analyze Nike's value. Many Wall Streeters who "covered" the
company regarded Nike's distinctive corporate ways and products as part of the fashion industry, and thus as the most successful company growing out of an athletic-goods explosion that
could be a passing fad.

Even during the price run-ups, Nike usually sold at a 20–30
percent discount of the average Standard & Poor's 500 multiples.
"Part of the problem is that this sports and fitness industry just

isn't a great industry yet," Knight would say. "It will be, but right now it's not great yet."

As *USA Today* and other publications weighed in with articles on the sports pages in the wake of *The Sporting News*'s ordination, most of them wondering if perhaps Nike had become "too powerful" for the good of sports, Knight spent much more time worrying about the future of a company that was growing well beyond his own grasp or even his capacity to see all of Nike from atop the heap. Knight seemed to wrestle every day with his ambivalence over Nike's size. "As you get bigger, you do have to tone down your entrepreneurial instincts," he said at the beginning of the year, sounding less than resolved. "But you have to do it in a way that doesn't put out the fire."

The young media entrepreneur Chris Whittle had come to Beaverton a few months earlier to pitch Knight on Whittle's controversial Channel One, advertising-supported video news programs for school classrooms. As Whittle liked to do as part of his pitch, he sought to demonstrate his understanding of Nike by offering his own compressed history of the company, from the time of Knight's grad school idea to that of its current position of dominance.

". . . And now," Whittle concluded, "you are the Goliath of the industry."

"But we will always," Knight said, speaking up for the first time during the meeting, "behave like David."

"Sometimes I get reports," Knight said that day, in front of the elevator in the lobby of the McEnroe Building. "I'm told that people around here say 'Phil Knight is our Walt Disney—except he's not dead yet.' Guess it's kind of a compliment and kind of an insult at the same time."

And with the slightest nod, Knight stepped into the elevator and went to work.

Around the running track at the University of Oregon, Phil Knight answered to the trail hand or trapper's name of Buck.

Buck Knight was a runner. He ran very fast middle-distance races during the last years of the 1950s, a time in which most team-sport athletes regarded running a long way as fast as you can as decidedly unglamorous and slightly strange. Knight was a very good runner who happened to be a member of a track team that possessed considerable glamor and some of the fastest middle-distance runners in the world.

Knight once ran a 4:13 mile. He once ran on a University of Oregon four-mile relay team that included a future world record–holder, and the team set a Drake relays record. But for the most part Knight remained one of the squad runners who excelled by force of commitment and tenacity. Knight had learned to hate losing in high school. He was cut from the freshman and junior varsity basketball teams, but through "evolution of my attitude," as he puts it now, he learned to keep other players from getting around him and finally made the team as a senior.

Knight was the guy on the track team who was always ready for the dozens of six A.M. uphill four-hundreds required by his mentor, the famed Oregon and future Olympic team track coach, Bill Bowerman.

Bowerman was a country boy even by midcentury Oregon standards. He'd learned about coaching track from Bill Hayward, an Oregon coach and teacher for forty-four years, another country boy who believed that the storied tradition of Oregon road runners had something to do with the weather. Hayward made extra money during the summer breaks by traveling the fairs and picnic grounds of rural Oregon offering to race quarter horses for money.

Except for regularly railing on about the "arrogant bastards" who ran the American Athletics Union and generally ranting about "people who like to sit on their butts and watch life go by," Bowerman was known as a man of very few words. An Oregon runner once asked him to please explain the secret of improved performance.

"Run faster," Bowerman said.

While attending the annual Rose Festival in Portland one Sunday, Bowerman ran into another stern and demanding man known for his carefully culled conversation, the publisher of the *Oregon Journal* newspaper, Bill Knight—who was in the company of a pale high school track star named Buck.

Bill Knight had worked for a Portland law firm before being hired as the chief attorney and business manager of the *Oregon Journal*. Eventually he became the publisher. Though his tough, "European-style" father didn't say much, Buck Knight knew he was expected to go east to college and then to enter some established tributary of the social and economic mainstream. But Buck Knight went to Oregon to run for Bowerman, a tough, European-style coach who dispensed approbation carefully if at all.

Knight was stunned not long after meeting Bowerman when an Oregon runner blasted through a long-standing record time, crossing the finish line to the screaming adulation of the famously emotional Oregon track fans. The victorious athlete came up to Bowerman, but Bowerman continued to walk right by him. "Nice race," he said without turning his head.

Bill Bowerman spent all of his free time pondering ways to help his athletes excel. He'd developed training protocols such as interval runs years before they were adopted as standard procedure, and he spent long days pulling apart clunky track shoes and trying to build his own shoes in the hope of making them lighter and more comfortable.

Bowerman began his reign at Oregon in 1947, right after "World War II ruined the track shoe business." He thought the Wilson and Spaulding companies made decent enough shoes until they converted production to the war effort, so Bowerman decided to learn to make shoes himself. One shoemaker tried to convince the coach that making shoes took years of study and apprenticeship, but a maker of spiked logging boots in Eugene taught him in a day how to cut out and sew up a shoe.

Bowerman would count the number of strides his runners needed to cover a mile, and he figured that if he could trim only an ounce from the weight of their shoe, the effect would be to free his boys of some 550 pounds over the course of a race. "A shoe must be three things," he'd preach. "It must be light, comfortable, and it's got to go the distance."

Bowerman's athletes would find him mixing vats of tar or grinding up tires retrieved from the local dump for an endless series of experiments that eventually led to the first all-weather surface for running tracks.

"The man was obsessed," Knight recalls.

Knight says that Bowerman appeared to him then as "part genius, part madman," and when Knight was assigned a term paper for a course in small business management at the Stanford University graduate school of business (he'd majored in journalism at Oregon but didn't like the pay-scale horizon involved), he found himself returning to Bowerman's belief that the then state-of-the-art track shoes manufactured by Adidas were simply not good enough—especially in light of the high price the German shoes commanded.

The professor teaching the small business course, Frank Shallenberger, was one of the only members of the Stanford B-school faculty who didn't believe his purpose was to transform students into omnibus general managers fit to inherit control of the great corporations of the day. Shallenberger only taught in Palo Alto a few hours each week, because he spent the rest of his time tending, buying, and selling young bu nesses. In 1962, people like Shallenberger were still known as small businessmen, the term "entrepreneur" having yet to come into vogue within the popular business culture of the time.

"It's a personality thing," Shallenberger would tell Knight. "People are kind of bent one way or the other. Go into the lunchroom and see the guys eating alone. They're the ones who are going to start their own businesses."

Knight's first pair of serious racing shoes had born the hallowed triple-stripe insignia of Adidas. The shoes were the then-freshman Oregon runner's prized possessions for a long time, but when Shallenberger assigned his class the task of imagining a new business and describing its purpose and basic marketing plan, Knight thought about his beloved Adidas spikes and drew upon two separate memories to come up with a plan. One recollection was of Bowerman's constant dissatisfaction with running shoes—Adidases included. The other was his memory of a discussion he'd overheard between professional newspaper photographers at the *Oregon Journal*. Knight remembered the staffers debating whether or not some of the new and much cheaper Japanese Nikon-brand cameras would ever displace the legendary and expensive Leicas from Germany.

Knight wrote in his paper that despite Japan's reputation for shoddy product, if a low-cost Japanese producer could make high-quality running shoes, the price differential would open a market niche.

Shallenberger was impressed with the idea, but Knight still went on to major in accounting, and after graduation he went back to Oregon and a job with Coopers & Lybrand, a Big Eight firm that had a Portland office. Though he'd acquiesced to his father's rarely expressed but clearly delineated desire that he partake of a traditional career path, Knight did take himself on something of a *Wanderjahr,* a summer trip around the world, in 1963, with a stop in Japan. Knight climbed Mount Fuji with the other tourists, but he also took a side trip to the inland port city of Kobe, where he garnered the courage to present himself as a shoe salesman to the managers of the Onitsuka Company, producers of running shoes that were sold under the brand name Tiger.

"These shoes aren't half bad," Bowerman said after Knight showed him the Tigers he brought home. "How 'bout letting your old coach in on this?"

Knight was so transported by the rare approval implied by Bowerman's suggestion that he could barely respond. "Bill," he managed. "There's nobody I'd rather do this thing with than you."

Knight can't put it all in psychological perspective now, but he's sure the assassination of John Kennedy inspired his resolve to exit the endless rut he perceived as his own future as an organization man. "It was a time when a lot of young men, for the first time, said 'What's the point?' " he recalls now. "I got my ass chewed at work for staying home to watch the funeral. I guess you'd call it a moment of alienation."

Bowerman and Knight each invested five hundred dollars in one thousand pairs of Tiger shoes, and Knight began haunting high school track meets on weekends and days off from his accounting job during 1964, retailing the light and comparatively cheap shoes out of the back of his car. He stored the inventory in his mother's laundry room, and by the end of the first year, Blue Ribbon Sports—the name Knight came up with a few seconds after the Onitsuka managers asked him the name of the company he represented—had sold eight thousand dollars' worth of track shoes—which the company founders immediately plowed back into an order for another 3,500 pairs of shoes.

To his father's extreme chagrin, Knight quit his day job and began to run the little shoe company out of a storefront hole-in-the-wall next to the Pink Bucket Tavern in working-class Portland. He remembers once sticking colored pins all over a wall map of the United States so that an important visitor who could have helped expand his selling range would think that Knight knew what he was doing. But the guy never called back.

"It's a good business idea," Knight would say to his father.

"You're just screwing around," his dad would scoff.

Bill Knight had provided a five-thousand-dollar letter of credit early on—when he still thought the adventure would be a passing, youthful diversion—but as the business began to grow and Phil came back in search of the financial guarantees necessary to raise more capital, his father said, "You can cross me off that list right now. I don't intend to go down this particular road."

While still working with the shoes only part-time himself, Knight had hired a full-time salesman, a competitive runner from California named Jeff Johnson. In a glass case in the Nike museum at the World Campus there sits a grainy, uncaptioned photo of Jeff Johnson during his first year on the job, in which he looks to be all of fourteen. Johnson had a degree in anthropology from Stanford at the time, but he was not unlike other intercollegiate-level long-distance runners in that he didn't see how he could ever hold down a real job and still continue do the one thing that really mattered in life—which was to run.

"It was really a way to continue a lifestyle and still make a living," Knight says now.

"And it was a way to remain a running geek, a person who didn't have a chance to fit in," Nelson Farris adds. Farris is one of the few "Nike originals" still working for the company. He talks about the early days as part of the official training spiel presented to new employees. "A serious runner was the very definition of a social outcast during the early nineteen-sixties," Farris says. "In those days it was true geekdom."

Knight's guys were all humanities majors just trying to avoid the real thing. Not one of them came from the tribal interior of the largely New England–based American shoe industry. All they knew was how shoes were supposed to feel and that—as Bowerman said—the good ones would help you win the race. Farris and Jeff Johnson and the others who came to join Phil Knight's burgeoning association of geeks recall that the Adidas representatives at track meets would come by their card tables full of Tiger shoes and laugh at them.

In 1966, Bowerman shipped the Onitsuka Company one of his own designs for a new kind of running shoe, with a soft nylon upper instead of a leather one. Bowerman had cooked up some sort of cushioning compound for the shoe that ran from toe to heel. The resulting shoe—the Cortez—was a big hit in local track circles in the Northwestern states.

Knight borrowed various parts of ten thousand dollars; Bowerman came up with another ten, and they proceeded to browbeat a Portland banker into coming up with one hundred thousand dollars to invest in new inventory. "Dear Sir," Knight wrote in a letter to track coaches and other potential customers. "The world's great imitators, the Japanese, have entered a brand-new field—track shoes. Their low cost of labor has already broken up the domination of the Germans in cameras and the Greeks in shipbuilding; now they are going after the track-and-field market which the Europeans have had to themselves for so long." Oregon coach Bill Bowerman, Knight wrote, choosing not to refer to their business connection, was one coach who'd decided to order his $6.95 running flats "exclusively through Blue Ribbon Sports."

During 1969, the boys and the coach sold a million dollars worth of shoes, and by 1971—still dependent on a somewhat shaky relationship with Onitsuka and fearing that the Japanese company might award distributorships to more seasoned sellers—Knight decided it was time to give some of the shoes a new name and decorate them with a separate symbol or trademark. Shortly thereafter, during a fitful dream, the image of Nike came to Jeff Johnson—who by then had begun to design innovative new shoes for the company in the Bowerman tradition. Nike, the winged Greek goddess of victory, was of a time when the images of beautiful gods were wrought from heroic representations of real people. Nike implied a sporting spirit of the democratic past, and besides, Johnson argued more pragmatically to Knight—who had himself come up with Dimension Six, a name that drew much derisive laughter and comment from the other geeks—some of the best and most memorable names in American business had only one or two syllables and included seldom-used letters like "X" and "K"—"Look at Xerox. Look at Kleenex," Johnson said.

The first Nike shoes, marked with an amorphous symbol that looked like a fat checkmark or some warped and slightly psychedelic half moon (the image, contrived by a local Portland design student, became known inside the company as the Swoosh) debuted at the Olympic trials in Eugene in 1972. All forty-five employees of the company were in attendance.

Knight and Bowerman sold $3.2 million worth of shoes that year. Their profits doubled over the previous year, and were to at least double during each of the next ten years, too.

Never once did the relationship between Bowerman and Knight become a partnership of equals. The exacting coach would scream at Knight all the time—usually about technicalities of the shoes—and Knight would drive away and wait for the coach to cool off. "It wasn't easy because I was always in a position of proving my worth, like a freshman runner. But I also knew his motives were always sincere. He would never sell me out."

This is not something he would attribute to almost anyone else he's known. "The feelings there are unique," Knight says now.

Pictures of Bowerman and other indices of his powerful presence can still be found all over the walls of the World Campus. Bowerman's quotes grace countless company documents, and Knight honors the old coach by regularly repeating the vice chairman of the board's maxims. But the Nike historical figure whose memory and mythos evokes the most palpable emotion among Nike veterans is that of another Bowerman protégé, the magnificent and famously free-spirited distance runner Steve Prefontaine.

Inside the museum rooms of the Steve Prefontaine Center, set beyond the marble fountain in front of the campus, a life-sized bronze statue of the mustachioed Oregonian runner in full gallop, his long hair flying back with the wind, resides in a sun-filled atrium. Visitors stare into display cases holding the yellowed molds upon which Bowerman made Prefontaine's customized shoes, and there is a letter in a display case from the American Athletics Union—the AAU—warning the irascible, charismatic athlete to take the word "Nike" off of his shirt, because it violated official rules, the likes of which Prefontaine violated all the time. "Pre" had been running in Adidas shoes, and like all of the premier runners back then, he took a little bit of under-the-table money from the German firm to allow himself the freedom to train. From the most senior Olympic officials to local track coaches, the payments to elite runners were accepted but never acknowledged. But Knight offered Prefontaine five thousand dollars, aboveboard, in exchange for wearing Nike shoes and a competition shirt that said NIKE.

The directors of the AAU did not approve, and sports bureaucrats all around the world were displeased at the sight of the hypocrisy of the payment system being brought into the light.

But it was the early 1970s by then, and Prefontaine wasn't much "into" established authority. One day in Bakersfield, Bowerman had told him to run a lengthy, five-thousand-meter race.

"I don't run three-mile races," Prefontaine said, turning his back.

"Well, you sure will today," Bowerman said.

Pre ran the race and won, but Bowerman would always remember the interchange, because nobody else had ever talked to him like that.

Knight and Prefontaine felt comfortable sticking it to the AAU, because Bowerman had indoctrinated all of his runners to believe that the AAU leadership was comprised of "a bunch of rich old farts—aristocrats looking for free trips."

Nike adopted Bowerman's view, and when Knight and some of the other Nike guys asked Prefontaine what he wanted to do about the AAU warning, Pre agreed, saying, "Screw 'em."

A small book inside one of the display cases in the museum lies open to Prefontaine's final notation in his last training journal. There is also a moving letter of condolence written to Pre's parents after his death in a car crash in 1975. Prefontaine won almost every race he ran under Bowerman, and he held seven American records by the time he died at the age of twenty-four. Bowerman says that he's still not seen Pre's equal in his events.

If Phil Knight is Nike's own Walt Disney, then Steve Prefontaine—forever running fast, with Sgt. Pepper sideburns, irreverent and twenty-four and essential to the ritual and ancestor worship that stokes the Nike corporate fires—lives on like Nike's very own James Dean.

"To many he was the greatest U.S. middle-distance runner ever, but to me he was more than that," Knight intoned in a voice thickened with emotion during an in-house film begun in September 1992 for the company's upcoming twentieth-anniversary festivities. "Pre was a rebel from a working-class background, a guy full of cockiness and pride and guts. Pre's spirit," Knight said while Pre ran in the front of the pack on the screen, "is the cornerstone of this company's soul."

Not long after Pre died, much less serious athletes began to hit roads and trails all over the country in running shoes.

Back at the beginning of 1964, Bill Bowerman had visited New Zealand. While on a hilly run during the trip, Bowerman watched one old man or middle-aged female runner after another pass him by with ease. It turned out that they'd all become involved in programmatic, easygoing running sessions. The half-speed training pace was called jogging.

By the end of the year, Bowerman had begun light jogging programs for noncompetitive runners in Eugene. *Life* magazine ran a picture and a bit of news about coach Bowerman's slowest runners, and in 1967 Bowerman coauthored *Jogging: A Physical Fitness Program for All Ages.* The book became a best-seller.

The following year, an Air Force doctor and marathoner named Kenneth Cooper wrote a book that retrieved the adjective "aerobic" from its simple biological reference to the presence of oxygen and repositioned the term as a means of remaining healthy forever.

Then in 1972, Frank Shorter electrified sports fans and adorned long-distance running with a new aura of romance when he won the marathon as a member of Bowerman's 1972 Olympic team in Munich.

Knight's jocks had always subdivided the general, nongeek populace into those who participated in life—the runners—and those who liked to watch. But now jogging and other amateur aerobic pursuits were luring previously sedentary Americans over to the other side. A flourishing new market became available to a company making innovative and comfortable shoes that addressed the obvious inefficiencies of traditional canvas and rubber sneakers, inadequacies that became readily apparent to any jogger capable of running more than a mile.

Around that time Bowerman had an epiphany at the kitchen table while his wife was at church. He was staring at the waffle iron when the idea hit him so hard that he forgot to spray the inside of the family waffle iron with the greasy release compound he used to make his molds. He stuffed the waffle iron full of modeling clay, but then he couldn't get the clay out without a pliers. Then he drove to the store and came home with six new waffle irons, disappeared into his basement, and went to work.

The result was a black, waffle-shaped sole that made the new bright blue, yellow-Swooshed Nikes brought to market in 1977 feel like bedroom slippers.

Citizens who could barely run out of the path of an oncoming vehicle suddenly wanted to jog around the neighborhood in a pair of bright blue Nikes. A year or two earlier, Nike was generally thought outside circles of cinder track to be the name of a company based in Japan. Nike was widely thought to rhyme with "Mike." But now, in every park across the republic, people could be seen trudging along in nifty new Swoosh-marked impact-absorbing pillows for the feet.

Magazine articles and television reports weighed in, and very quickly the idea of exercise and game-playing ceased to be something the average American did for fun. One ran for long life, for health, or for a toned body suitable to the imminent halter-topped and stretch-panted aesthetic. Those at one with the ethos celebrated the movement of limb, and they sought the daily racing of their hearts in pursuit of a new liberation of spirit. This was especially true of those hailing from the mammoth postwar generation from which Nike was constructed, a generation composed of citizens often frustrated in their more cooperative liberatory efforts before self-discovery appeared to loom just a few miles down the road.

"When I run the roads, I am a saint," wrote the running guru Dr. George Sheehan in a best-selling book. ". . . I am Thoreau, the solitary seeking union with the world around him."

Physical self-improvement and health became the basis of the new secular religion, and Nikes became the chalices and rosaries of choice. "One thing that all consumers share is a fear of death," the current Nike director of advertising, Scott Bedbury, mused one day in Beaverton. "Nike rose up by force of that fear and a host of other human longings that seemed universal."

To this day, numerous students of the sports and athletic-shoe businesses claim that Nike started the fitness revolution. "We were at least right there," Knight says. "And we sure rode it for one hell of a ride."

During the last half of the 1970s, Nike's sales grew from $10 million to $270 million. At decade's end, one out of every three Americans owned a pair of running shoes, and half of all running shoes sold were Nikes.

The company made all sorts of other athletic footwear, too, and a few relatively prominent—or at least high-potential—professional athletes began to wear Nike shoes. Some members of the LA Lakers and Boston Celtics basketball squads could even be seen on television wearing Nikes. A few of them, to Knight's nervous elation, even came to visit Nike's chief sports fan at his house.

One night, amid the Nike hypergrowth of December 1977, Phil Knight walked into his father's house while Bill Knight watched the last of the ten o'clock news. Despite all of his son's success up to that point, Bill Knight had yet to ever once back away from his contention that his son was just "screwing around with his life" by selling shoes.

Knight sat down near his father, who turned to him and said that he'd just witnessed a horrible event replayed on the news.

Apparently a scuffle had broken out during an NBA game between the Houston Rockets and the LA Lakers. A full-scale melee had ensued during which mild-mannered Rockets player and early two-thousand-dollar-per-year Nike endorser Rudy Tomjanovich had run toward the brawl to try to make peace. A player for the Lakers named Kermit Washington paused in his pounding of a Rockets player named Kevin Kunnert long enough to think that six-foot-eight-inch "Rudy T" meant to attack him. Kermit brought his fist up from the floor and punched Tomjanovich in the face with such force that Rudy actually lofted backward into the air and landed on his back, blood flowing everywhere out onto the floor. Tomjanovich had survived—which surprised many of those watching the replay that night—though he missed the fifty-nine games remaining in the season, recovering from several bouts of reconstructive facial surgery.

"I was sure he was dead, Buck," Bill Knight said in his even voice. "It was probably the most horrible thing I've ever seen in sports." After a pause, Phil thought he saw a strange light in his father's usually unreadable eyes. "And Buck," Bill Knight said with great energy, "you shoulda seen the close-up on Rudy's shoes!"

Knight remembers the evening as the first and last time his father indicated that his chosen calling might not, in the end, have been a mistake.

During the late 1970s, after Blue Ribbon Sports was retired in favor of renaming the company for the word on most of the shoes, Nike introduced a cushioning system for the midsole that was based on a fat-moleculed "supergas" trapped inside a polyurethane bag whose molecular pores were too small for the gas to get out. The gas would not sustain life, but still, over the course of several years, it became known as Nike Air.

The shoes had already become fixed in the public imagination as tools in aid of a general return to health, but now, as the desire for things "high-tech" invaded most consumer market products, Nike became known for the first overtly high-tech shoes. The popular new products became even more widely prized during the early 1980s when the look of athletes in participatory gear became part of the new fashion uniform, quickly becoming as culturally and generationally specific as wing tips and rep ties had been in the past. Women casting off the orthopedic nightmares called high heels were soon seen striding to and from work in Nikes.

During the first year of the new decade, Nike dislodged Adidas from its dominance of the American market—a feat judged unthinkable by industry pros only five years earlier. *Forbes* magazine asked 150 junior high students in Dallas to name their favorite athletic shoe in 1981, and each and every one of them said Nike.

At the time, life inside the company was still dominated by a rogue spirit drawn from Prefontaine and Bowerman's antiauthoritarian impulses, from a shared determination to work day and night for the sake of the company cause, and from an equally impressive commitment to never becoming so self-serious and businesslike as to lose sight of the importance of having a good time. In the exhaustive, unauthorized corporate history covering Nike's formative years called *Swoosh,* authors J. B. Strasser and Laurie Becklund detail beer bashes, selling demonstrations that employed a hashish pipe, a lot of passing out and throwing up, and even a case of executive bed-wetting performed in pursuit of separating the company from staid and gray corporate traditions. "Managers drank and danced and closed the bar every night. Even the heads of the company wore jeans and played Frisbee on the big green lawns," Strasser and Becklund wrote.

In 1982, Harvard professor Terrence Deal and McKinsey & Company consultant Allan Kennedy lobbed the term "corporate culture" into an increasingly self-conscious public debate about America's then-faltering managerial class and the lack of "competitiveness" demonstrated by the larger American firms. By then Nike had a corporate culture that more than once had caused the company to be characterized as "the *Saturday Night Live* of the *Fortune* 500." *Swoosh* includes a photo of Phil Knight during the "halcyon days"—his own reference to the ten years subsequent to Steve Prefontaine's death—arriving at a corporate event in drag.

Just after the *Forbes* 1982 Annual Report on American Industry had marked Nike as the single most profitable company in America over the previous five years, the Nike forces assembled at the annual sporting-goods industry trade show in Munich, West Germany, determined—this time—to demonstrate Nike's grown-up and sober determination to dislodge Adidas from its continued domination of the international market.

The plan included a formal, Adidas-style banquet that would demonstrate Nike's sophistication, but the event wasn't an hour old before the dinner degenerated into a schnapps-snorting bacchanalia capped by pitchers of beer being poured on guests' heads and a mass food fight featuring those very heavy, deep-fried *knödel* potato balls—and more than a bit of the traditional throwing up.

Fortune magazine estimated that Adidas was a $2-billion company worldwide at the time. The nonshoe apparel revenues generated by the German shoe empire were greater than Nike's total sales. Nike's goal of passing Adidas and becoming number one in the world, the *Fortune* writers predicted around the time of the Munich food fight, "is probably unattainable."

Nike had become a publicly traded company by the end of 1980, and Phil Knight had instantly become one of the richest men in the world. Knight thought it appropriate to raise capital in the public marketplace back in 1975, but by then the company had become embroiled in a lengthy series of highly politicized wars with customs and trade officials. A powerful lobby called the Rubber Manufacturers Association, supported by Converse and other traditional rubber and canvas sneaker makers, had called for heavy duties on Nike shoes and other imports as way to stem the flight of American shoe jobs.

Nike did have factories in Exeter, New Hampshire, and Saco, Maine, but a lot of the shoes still came from the Orient. No high-tech athletic shoes were made in the United States, Nike's lawyers and hired lobbyists argued, because traditional American manufacturers, as in the auto industry, never invested to keep their plants at the cutting edge.

But the company faced customs duties of up to 10 percent of the wholesale price on shoes that were "like or similar" to those made in the United States. One customs claim for retroactive payment involved more than a billion dollars. Knight decided to put going public on hold until the various claims and counterclaims were finally resolved.

Company shares initially went out at $5.50 apiece, a price high enough to make Knight superrich and a dozen key employees instant millionaires, too. Another dozen early investors in Blue Ribbon Sports—mostly middle-class families from Portland and Eugene—had put ten to twenty thousand dollars into Nike debentures when Knight sought to raise two hundred thousand in operating capital. The local investors who'd pitched twenty thousand dollars into the young enterprise now owned public shares worth $15 million after the initial offering; those families that retained their shares until the week when Buck Knight was named the most powerful man in sports would hold Nike stock worth close to $100 million.

Bowerman was also a multimillionaire after the offering, though for much of the next twelve years he complained that being rich was just a "pain in the ass," because "parasites" were always approaching him for money. Bowerman was not nearly as rich as Knight, because he'd reduced his ownership to 2 percent of the company by selling Knight his shares. There had come a point when signing his name to documents that included personal guarantees for millions of dollars worth of loans had made Bowerman uncomfortable. "I've actually got some assets to protect," he told Knight—who had none outside the business. "I want to get out. This thing is successful enough. I eat three meals each day, and I just want to be comfortable. So how much you want? Buy it all if you like."

"No way," Knight said. "You have to keep some of it."

Knight had divvied up some of Bowerman's shares and distributed them to certain members of the Nike team. Suddenly Nike millionaires in jeans and running shoes could be spotted in the Nike lunch room and in the downtown bars in Portland.

Knight says he knew that going public would change life inside the company, but he wasn't sure how. But it wasn't long before some of the millionaire pioneers—the anthropology majors and English majors who'd for so long envisaged Nike as an underground movement successfully masquerading as a business—sensed that the change meant it was time to leave.

"I felt useless," Jeff Johnson recalls. "I had been elevated about forty levels above my proper place—designing and selling shoes. I was being wheeled out for corporate dog and pony shows like some museum piece: 'And here's our first employee!' "

So in 1983, Johnson—then forty-one years old—left, followed over subsequent years by several other of the original employees. Johnson went to live in rural New Hampshire, where he coached track and collected books. He says he always looked up to Phil Knight as a second father, though he already had a father he loved and respected. Johnson wonders now at his own regard for Knight as a paternal presence, because he and Phil were only four years apart in age and because—for all of the nearly twenty years they worked together—Knight never invited him over for dinner or even had very much to say.

Johnson comes back to Portland every now and again to tell young employees what Nike was like at the beginning. He runs along the Jeff Johnson Trail, which curls everywhere through the grounds of the World Campus, and hangs out with Nelson Farris and some of the other old-timers who've hung on.

The street running along the berm in the front of the campus is called Bowerman Drive, and Bowerman, now eighty-two, still comes to the campus for board meetings and throws shoes up on the scales, barking at designers about the "damned shoes being too heavy" ("He won't be happy until we can figure out how to get spikes onto a runner's bare feet, or until the things just float away," one browbeaten designer complained).

Bowerman doesn't tend to make it through all of the various committee meetings when the board of directors convenes, because he gets too tired and bored. He also limps along now with braces on his lower legs, this because of the years of "killing myself slowly," as he puts it, "sniffing glue." A few years earlier Bowerman began to lose the power in his legs, and his hearing and sight were going, too. He was diagnosed as having ALS—Lou Gehrig's disease—but a trip to the Mayo Clinic indicated that he didn't have the disease after all.

Bowerman reported to an orthopedist in Eugene who knew Bowerman and his habits that the Mayo team couldn't figure out what was going on. The doctor suggested an analysis of the glues and solvents Bowerman used to cobble shoes in a small closet at home. The old-fashioned solvents turned out to include n-hexane, a substance that causes narapathy, dissolving the nerve coating like the old shoe- and hat-making benzene compounds that gave rise to the phrase "mad as a hatter."

Bowerman has little time for irony, though he does add, "And I wasn't even getting high" to his telling of the story.

Knight says that his liaison with Bowerman "was less a partnership than the relationship of a father and a son." Knight allows that he finds himself missing the early days, but he bridles at the implication in *Swoosh* that he cast off several former friends and colleagues out of, at best, some Machiavellian impulse, and at worst because of a certain heartlessness. "Of the dozen people involved," Knight snapped when the accusation came up, "eleven left of their own choice. The real reason they left is because they were entrepreneurs who didn't want to parcel out decision making. It really bugged them."

One author of *Swoosh* was the wife of one of the millionaires who left—the Nike marketing specialist, Rob Strasser—and the other writer was her sister.

Knight admits that he posted Strasser in Europe not long before he left the company in late 1986 because he was getting "sick of him . . . but then I think he was sick of me too," Knight adds.

"I never liked that Strasser," Bowerman scoffed. "One time he said he wanted to talk to me and walked around a big table to sit real close. 'If you wanna talk to me,' I said, 'just get on over on the other side of this table. I don't even like you.' "

"They were all millionaires, so they didn't have to put up with the frustrations of a transition to a managed company," Knight said, standing up from behind his desk and putting on his sunglasses. "I'm still here because I don't have a choice. All my eggs are in this basket. I can't just pick up and leave."

In front of the entrance to Knight's office suite atop the McEnroe Building, there looms a strangely massive bronze statue of a cartoonishly formidable chest and buttocks. The statue speaks of nothing but raw and untamed manly power, like some parody of classical images of the goddess Nike.

Knight's suite is divided by rice-paper-style walls and includes glass display cases full of oriental objects, gifts from his thirty years worth of business relationships in the Far East.

The displays of sporting images observable on every other wall in Nikeworld—twenty-foot-high hyperreal photos of tennis balls buried in racquet strings; famous grimaces enlarged a thousand times—suddenly cease at the entrance to Knight's office, where blond wood, black lacquer trim, and elegant wall sconces take over.

Visitors to Knight's lush outer office are asked to remove their shoes, but this bit of Oriental propriety rarely comes up, because the number of times Knight invites someone into the outer office can be counted off on his two secretaries' hands at the end of the year. He meets employees and outside visitors in a private conference chamber next to his office called the Wimbledon Room, where the sole indication of commercialism is a tiny sculptural piece of rock shaped like a Nike Swoosh.

Fellow officers of the company know not to wander into the outer office, but one day Knight caught Oregon senator Mark Hatfield standing, without permission, in the middle of the outer office. "Over here," Knight barked at the startled senator, pointing at the Wimbledon Room. Eventually he relented and told Hatfield to take off his shoes.

The senior managers of Nike all realize it would be pointless to try to find Knight in the outer office anyway, because he spends all his time in his inner office, a room accessible through a sliding door in the back of the outer office that most of Knight's associates of twenty years have never seen. Tinker Hatfield is one of the only Nike employees to ever enter the inner office. He and Michael Jordan were once ushered together into a room that felt strangely unbusinesslike and serene. The inner office was fitted out with a geometric stone fireplace and delineated by redwood beams. There was a huge television, connected to a sports-grabbing satellite dish on the roof, and dirty running clothes were piled on the floor near piles of articles and papers.

"The outer office only exists because the architects thought they were designing an office suite for a normal person," one senior executive quipped.

"It was designed to be a ceremonial office, but I don't like the room and I don't like ceremonies in my office," Knight explained. "Once you let people in your office, they'll come in and out all day long. I need to think. The office thing is an aspect of style."

From the hallway near the huge bronze buttocks that employees can be seen patting as they pass in a gesture less suggestive than sporting—as in "nice play"—visitors to the third floor of McEnroe can gaze past a sitting room where one of Knight's secretaries works and see Knight shuttling back and forth very quickly, like the target in the proverbial shooting gallery. Senior Nike executives often see him moving back and forth like this, because those who need to talk to Knight before closing deals or signing off on important decisions— even the president of the company, Donahue, who works across the central atrium; the general manager, Tom Clarke; the chief financial officer; the head of investor relations; and the others—tend to come and hang out in the hall area to see if they can catch Knight on the fly.

Requests for formal meetings with Knight are almost always

denied. On the other hand, Knight appears unannounced in managers' offices all the time. If they aren't there, he has been known to read the papers on their desks.

If a colleague does manage to intercept him, Knight usually avoids direct eye contact until the conversation warms up. He tends to speak in rapid-fire bursts, often punctuating phrases with a little humming noise or a laugh, as if he's already become bored by a listener's effort to catch up with his galloping cogitations.

Knight manages the Nike empire by nuance—a raised eyebrow here, the jingle of keys in his pocket there, a yawn. Gnomic half-pronouncements are offered after periods of distant contemplation, often at Knight's mountain retreat near Sunriver, Oregon.

Last year, a rough-hewn line of outdoor, cement-court basketball shoes was suddenly created and brought powerfully to market by Nike because Knight, considering a similar new product from Reebok, wrote "I think we should respond to this" on one of those little yellow Post-it notes and stuck it on VP Mark Parker's desk.

"Most people think it's a combination of his father and Bowerman," one Nike veteran observed. "All that unsaid stuff makes for a man who also leaves a lot unsaid."

"It's definitely true that some of my instinct toward a low profile must be genetic," Knight mused as he took long strides along the Walk of Fame on the way to lunch. "But some of it also has to do with something Bowerman taught me: Always let your performance talk for you."

Knight doesn't run in races anymore, and he says he covers his three- to five-mile runs at a leisurely pace. But Knight's wife of twenty-four years, Penny, was in training to run a marathon later in the year. Penny Knight was at one time, years ago, Phil Knight's student in an accounting class he taught at Portland State. When the company was still very small, Penny did the books, "though she's been replaced by fifty million dollars' worth of computing machinery," as Knight often reminds her. "For a long time," Knight continued, "Penny has put up with my absences and personal idiosyncrasies—and I am a person with personal idiosyncrasies.

"I just hope she gets through the race," he said. "Otherwise she'll have to run another one. It's like living with some champion athlete. She gets all cranky about getting to sleep and gets mad if I move around in bed. But I'm the last one who can say anything about it, so I just zip it up and count the days."

Knight's own extremely competitive nature still comes out on the tennis court these days. He likes to play for money, and he hates to lose. Pro tennis veterans Bobby Riggs and Pancho Segura recently took on Knight while in California. The first day, Knight and a partner beat the visiting pros, but the next day—the stakes elevated—Knight realized he'd been hustled when his team could barely get a point. He tried to hide his irritation. "Bastards took five hundred bucks off me," he still growls upon recalling the loss. "Two old guys—just kicked my ass."

Professional tennis players like Andre Agassi who have played doubles with Knight are often shocked by how seriously he takes the game. "He clearly likes to win," Agassi has observed.

Knight is famous, even among young employees afraid to approach him and say hello, for sponging anywhere from twenty-five cents to twenty dollars off of Nike employees and never paying it back. He is also known—ironic though it is in light of the way the world of big-money sports is in some significant part his own creation—for hating to negotiate. Knight calls the cross-table give-and-take reported each day in the world's business pages haggling. "I simply find the whole thing demeaning," he admits.

But this one absence from Knight's own array of competitive specialities is more than compensated for by a huge Nike sports-marketing department and by the presence on campus of one of the only figures other Nike employees considered more mysterious and unusual than Knight: the infamous former sports agent and, according to some, Knight's unlikely alter ego, Howard Slusher.

Slusher, who is known far and wide in the sports world as "Hold 'em out Howard" or "Agent Orange" (the latter reference pertaining only in part to Slusher's red hair) is a fifty-three-year-old native of the tenement streets of the Williamsburg section of Brooklyn who spent his childhood fantasizing about the lives of baseball heroes like Augie Galan and the Boston Red Sox star Johnny Pesky. Slusher was small and only pretty good at stickball, but he still dreamed about big-time sports and regarded sports as "the path away from the streets."

As a university student, Slusher came upon the classic sociological study of the role of play in a culture, Johan Huizinga's

Homo Ludens, and the book changed his life. Huizinga contended that the increasing absence of the playful invention, spontaneity, artlessness, daring, and "gladness" of games from other aspects of modern culture had caused sports and athletes to become more important in response. Slusher's fascination with the beauty of people at play and the glory of great athletes led to graduate study and a doctoral thesis that compared cognitive behavior and normative responses in an effort to discern whether or not athletes operated in a subculture. Slusher wrote a book called *Man, Sport, and Existence: A Critical Analysis* while teaching courses in the philosophy and psychology of sports at the University of Southern California in Los Angeles. He also taught an easier introductory course popular with USC's many jocks, and after Slusher added a law degree to his academic credentials, some of those jocks came back and asked their former professor to help them by looking over contracts they'd received from various professional teams.

Though many young sports agents believe Howard Slusher began the modern era of sports representation, Knight says that Howard's salient contribution was to "turn haggling into an art form." It was Slusher who added the phrase "withholding of professional services" to the sports negotiation lexicon and so changed forever the balance of power between the best athletes and recalcitrant owners of teams. Slusher represented stars like quarterback Dan Fouts and the balletic receiver Lynn Swann, but he always sought out the linemen, who were forever selling themselves short at contract time. At one point during the mid 1970s, Slusher represented nineteen members of the powerhouse Pittsburgh Steelers team and was several times called "the most powerful man in sports." He managed to get "no cut" clauses in players' contracts. In 1980, a basketball player named Gus Williams refused to play for all of the ensuing pro season at Slusher's insistence, and the next season Williams came back with a contract that more than made up for his year of rest.

By then, people recognized Howard Slusher in airports. "Howard Slusher," a flight attendant checking his ticket said one day, "are you the dick my husband's always talking about?"

Knight met Howard Slusher in 1975 when he came to Portland to negotiate a shoe endorsement deal for Paul Westphal, a former USC student, then a "sixth man" for the Boston Celtics, and currently Charles Barkley and the other Suns' coach in

Phoenix. Slusher, a short man who has a very high, raspy voice and at that time weighed nearly three hundred pounds, sat down to negotiate with Knight and Rob Strasser at nine A.M. By eleven A.M., they'd struck a three-year, $75,000 shoe deal for Westphal.

Knight wandered away from the table at one point, and Slusher said to Rob Strasser, "What's with that hair? Is that fake hair? The guy looks like an albino." When Knight returned, Strasser told him, "Mr. Slusher has some questions about your hair, Phil."

Over lunch, Strasser and Knight asked Slusher what he would like to do in Portland before his plane took off at one o'clock.

"What I'd really like to do," Slusher said, "is sit here and get five thousand dollars more out of you two."

"That's crazy," Knight barked. "This deal is closed."

But after an hour of excruciating badgering, Knight caved in, and Slusher had Westphal's five thousand dollars.

Slusher got up from the table and turned to leave, and Knight turned to Strasser: "I want you to hire that son of a bitch," he said.

Slusher agreed to come on board, but only as a part-time employee. He said he still had clients to care for and wasn't suited to the full-time regimen anyway.

Nike employees who hit the road with Slusher would invariably come back with new tales of the man's incredible chutzpah. If all the room were booked at a Hilton, Slusher would inquire what the manager would do if Conrad Hilton showed up and asked for a room. "I'd find him a room," the manager would eventually admit after being worn down by Howard's talking.

"Well, I'll take his room tonight," Slusher would say.

One time some football players Slusher was representing in Buffalo watched their agent secure the grand ballroom of an overbooked hotel. Three cots were wheeled into the ballroom, and Slusher worked the price down below that of a single.

Knight would send Slusher parachuting into the final moments of long negotiations that had nothing to do with sports. One time when Knight heard that the company across the table had amassed a veritable army of New York lawyers for the next round of talks, he was heard to say, "Who cares how many assholes they bring? We've got Howard."

Slusher eventually let most of his outside work go so he could spend most of his time with Nike. This, Howard says, was because he saw Phil Knight as "a hero" and as a man "who was very much alone."

"It was widely perceived that Phil Knight had a grand design that was about money, but I could see that he could have been much richer than he was. He was the lone runner. He loved athletes, and he loved the games. I'd dealt with hundreds of leaders in the business of sports who couldn't have cared less about the game and who, in fact, loathed the athlete. You think Tom Landry of the Dallas Cowboys loved athletes? The man ended hundreds of athletic careers every year by waiving players and not even saying good-bye.

"Knight chose the athlete over the organization, over the machine. He was antibureaucratic. He loved the act of play. The man was a hero but so much alone that he needed someone like me."

Slusher has never understood why Knight fails to understand the obvious difference between haggling and negotiation. Slusher can recall only one incident when he thought Knight began to understand the beauty of negotiation. He and Knight were waiting for connecting flights at Narita airport in Tokyo when Knight realized he was on a different flight and had five hours to spare. Knight said he was going to rent a car and drive out to see the new Japanese Disneyland that had opened a month earlier. But he soon returned looking disappointed. "I don't have an international license so they won't rent me a car."

"Well shit, take a cab," Slusher said.

"I went and asked and you know how much they want? A hundred and fifty dollars for the ride."

Slusher couldn't believe it. And what he couldn't believe about the situation had nothing to do with the juxtaposition of $150 and Phil Knight's net worth: "There must be four hundred cabs out there," Slusher said, looking out the window. "The last cab in that line will be here for days. Go to the last guy in line and offer him a third of that to take you."

"Really?" Knight said.

A minute later Knight returned to get his bag. He looked thrilled. "This shit really works," he said.

But for the most part, Howard Slusher believes that the hero, Phil Knight, is kind of gullible and naïve and in need of constant protection ("The man doesn't even lock his car!" Slusher will protest).

For his part, Knight is appreciative of Slusher's loyalty and endlessly entertained by Howard's personality. Slusher has become close to Penny Knight and the rest of the Knight family, and over the past year of turning from a very large person into a very skinny one, he had become Penny Knight's running partner and was committed to finishing a fall marathon race.

"The guy has tons of emotional things going on you just don't see in other places," Knight said as he strolled across the campus. "He's a total tough guy with an intricate value system. And he's entirely mistrustful. One morning I came in to work and I said, 'Hi Howard. Good morning.' And he snaps back at me. 'Good morning? Good morning? Don't you think I know what you *mean* by that?' "

Knight once sent Slusher out to renegotiate some Asian factory deals, and Slusher came back to report his gut feeling that two Nike contacts on the scene were taking bribes.

Knight said that the employees in question were "good Oregonians"—"Oregonian" being a compliment in Knight's view of things—but it was later discovered that Slusher was right.

"He can sense that kind of stuff, because he doesn't trust anybody and because he's got every hang-up in the book," Knight said fondly.

Knight was so sure that his jocks and Oregonians would be eaten alive by the kinds of big-time contractors bidding to build the World Campus during the last of the 1980s that he set Howard on them to "fight for every nickel"—which Slusher did to the point, in one case, of legal action. The large man-made lake ringed by cherry trees and sculptures is unofficially known on campus as Lake Slusher.

Many employees conjecture that the reason Slusher has remained a consultant or "special assistant" all these years is that the arrangement allows Knight to pay him many hundreds of thousands of dollars each year without having to report his salary in SEC documents.

"He just can't bring himself to have a full-time job," Knight explains. "Howard's no team player—which is what's really needed around Nike these days—but he's also the kind of guy a company like this needs sometimes. Besides, Howard is almost as hopeless a sports fan as I am."

Knight walked into the crowded, skylit company cafeteria, and hundreds of employees suddenly hushed. He continued past **79** walls covered with framed *Sports Illustrated* covers featuring Nike athletes, going back to a cover depicting Prefontaine—"America's Distance Prodigy"—coming across the finish line in the summer of 1970. Knight once said that the company's relationship with premier athletes addressed the fact that while an internal ad page of *Sports Illustrated* could be had for fifty thousand dollars, the cover remained unpurchasable. And yet each of the framed covers on the cafeteria wall showed a prominent Nike logo, or at least the Swoosh emblem on shoes or clothes.

Knight met up with another of the more worldly, loquacious, and sports-obsessed Nike guys whose company he clearly enjoys: Michael Doherty, Nike's creative director of film and video, who waited for the boss in the Boston Deli restaurant beyond the cafeteria. Howard White was there, too. Michael wore a typical work uniform—khakis and a pullover sweater—but Howard was wearing a nifty burnt orange leather sport coat and a brilliantly colored necktie that had drawn sarcastic commentary all morning.

The Boston Deli is wood-paneled and ringed by a shelf displaying battered football helmets representing most of the professional teams. The three walls of the Deli that face a serving area decorated with suspended garlic and salamis are covered with photographs. One photograph shows Slusher weighing at least three hundred pounds, but most of the others are stock publicity shots of the sort handed out by athletes and famous entertainers. The entertainers—Michael Jackson, Billy Crystal, the cast of *Cheers,* Ed Begley, Jr., and dozens of others—all seem to have offered some kind of handwritten ode ("I like Nike." "Thanks for Making It Easier to Just Do It") and many of them begin "Phil" or "For Phil . . ."

Knight admits he's hardly met any of the nonsports celebrities that cover the walls in several different campus locations. Nike has for years maintained a promotional office in Culver City, California, its sole purpose being the dissemination of free shoes and goodwill to entertainers and entertainment executives. If Nikes are thought by some critics of the popular culture to be inordinately powerful indications of status for inner-city youth, then it must also be noted that the capacity to land a shipment of free Nikes from the Culver City office is a measure of celebrity status in Hollywood on a par with good seats at certain restaurants or awards ceremonies. On any given day Meryl Streep and her kids can be spotted being fitted out in one corner of the

Culver City showroom while the members of a band such as Metallica wait patiently across the way.

The Nike Entertainment Promotions crew—known as "Hollywood Promo" on campus—jockeys, as do employees of many other consumer products companies, to get hold of early versions of movie and television scripts in order to get Nikes onto the screen. Over the coming months, Murphy Brown's new baby would sport Air Jordan stuff, Whitney Houston would exercise in Nike gear in *The Bodyguard,* the young hero in *Free Willy* would bound around in a big black pair of Nikes, and Demi Moore would wear a pair of Tinker Hatfield's Air Huarache shoes in *A Few Good Men*—all because of the work of Nike troops in Hollywood.

During the coming week, to Knight's considerable bemusement, the front page of the *Los Angeles Times* would report a startling new business alliance connecting "the world's biggest shoe manufacturer" and "Creative Artists Agency, Hollywood's most aggressive talent firm." The article would claim that the "unusual multimillion-dollar bid to create a global sports entertainment business" would bring together "two of the business world's most innovative but secretive executives. Nike founder and chairman Philip H. Knight and CAA chairman Michael S. Ovitz function almost exclusively behind the scenes, and both have well-documented propensities for cultivating relationships with powerful figures outside their fields."

Knight knew that Ovitz had built his business from a time during the mid 1970s when he and his young partners' wives answered the phones. The man whose agency represented Tom Cruise, Steven Spielberg, Barbra Streisand, and Sylvester Stallone was said to be an exercise nut who claimed that his management style was drawn from "Eastern thought and Western team sport." Knight also had observed that CAA had transcended the role of traditional talent agents, moving into movie production and even the T-shirt business and other product-oriented ventures.

Knight hadn't known what to expect from Ovitz, but from the first time he met him, during the Tournament of the Americas games when Michael Jordan first told Knight about the Reebok uniforms, "the most powerful man in sports" decided he liked "the most powerful man in Hollywood" just fine.

"I'm crazy about him," Ovitz reported after the deal was struck. "Phil's decent, normal, simple, and easy to deal with." **81**

At the first strategy meeting in Los Angeles, Nike sports marketer Steve Miller was stunned by what utter jocks the famous agent and his minions seemed to be. Miller had been in the business long enough to know that the one thing all famous athletes dreamed of being was a famous movie star and the thing entertainment celebrities dreamed about was being a jock, but some of Ovitz's guys were able to talk insider sports like sports pros.

At an early meeting, Ovitz talked about a coming entertainment and technological frontier built on communications advances. Ovitz said he believed a new world of "software possibilities" connected to sports would be made because of the new technologies. He argued that Nike and CAA should collaborate on a project that would put both companies out ahead of the technological curve. Knight, though decidedly nontechnological, was impressed.

In a media world changing by the day with the advent of such innovations as interactive television and the possibility of hundreds of new channels, Knight and several of his younger managers had already envisaged the Nike of the future as "an experience company." Nike's relationship with sports in general and with the lion's share of those athletes who had become as famous or more famous than most movie stars had already positioned the company as a leading supplier of the "software" of the coming digital age.

An alliance with director George Lucas's Lucasfilms to develop futuristic sports entertainment had already been made, and there was talk on campus of a Nike theme park loaded with digitized virtual-reality booths in which participants could virtually experience the best golf holes in the world or go one-on-one with Jordan, and of customers being able to race Alberto Salazar on a virtual running track in a retail store. "Retailing and entertainment are moving together," Knight said. "If you look at our Nike Towns, at the talent we have, and at the new sports agency business, you can see new directions."

Howard Slusher could lately be heard to say that Nike's competition in the future would be Disney, not Reebok. But Knight considered Howard's supposition a "stretch."

CAA had already shaken up the advertising and professional marketing establishments by launching media consultation and marketing deals with Coca-Cola and Apple Computer. Commenting on the new CAA-Nike alliance, *Advertising Age* had referred to CAA as the imminent "advertising agency of the future."

Of the twenty-five ideas on the table when Knight, Slusher, Steve Miller, Tom Clarke, and Mark Parker, the general manager who handled design and retail, had gone to CAA headquarters in LA for a December meeting, only one was selected for immediate action.

Knight had been dreaming about a Nike-sponsored series of college football events leading up to a final play-off between the two best teams—a college Super Bowl . . . a "Nike Bowl"—for years. College football gate receipts and television revenues were down at the end of 1992, and though college football mavens still postured about their sport as the kingpin of collegiate games, the popularity of college basketball had actually eclipsed football. Ovitz and Knight agreed that part of the problem was the way college football ceded the airwaves to pro football between Thanksgiving and the often uninspired pairings of the New Year's Day bowl games. College football needed "a big kick in the ass" by the end of 1992, the new allies agreed, and CAA and Nike would work to provide it.

Since a college Super Bowl would probably entail NCAA approval, a formal plan of action was required to address the labyrinthian processes by which the NCAA made decisions affecting nearly nine hundred universities. Ovitz and CAA agreed to handle the television side of the deal, and Nike would begin to galvanize its old-boy network of coaches and athletic directors.

The goal of Project Victory, as it was code-named, was to present a plan to a powerful NCAA committee of college presidents—the Presidents Commission—that was due to meet in Kansas City in June. A resolution from the Presidents Commission would be required to take the idea to a vote of the 144 NCAA "1A" colleges that would be eligible to play in the tournament. The Presidents Commission had voted against a similar idea in 1989, so the effort to lobby the right coaches, athletic directors, college presidents, and NCAA officials would have to be incessant and energetic. Knight assigned Howard Slusher to the case.

The working arrangement, from Knight's perspective, was far from "going Hollywood," but Knight was impressed by Mike Ovitz's expansionist aspirations. He was also amused by the press reaction to the CAA move. "Nike is absolutely drunk with success," the president of the Burns Sports Celebrity Service, David Burns, was quoted as saying in the *Los Angeles Times*. "I think this will help them dominate for years to come."

Over lunch in the Boston Deli that day, Mike Doherty was jabbering away about the previous evening's sports contests with Knight and Howard White. Doherty represented Beaverton's own little piece of Hollywood style. His team in the Mike Schmidt Building created elaborate films and videos for Nike in-house employee conclaves and external marketing events, but before that, Doherty was the talent coordinator for *The Merv Griffin Show*. He also produced the quiz show *Jeopardy* for a time, and for a while he ran a bar in Carmel, California, owned by Clint Eastwood. Doherty came to Nike in 1982 and set to the work of making some fourteen hundred films in the company's state-of-the-art production facility, most of them strangely evocative works that mixed the dramatic musical scores and ethereal imagery of rock videos with deeply emotive, often slow-motion sports highlights cut from miles of the best game footage.

At the 1992 rallying of the troops to celebrate the twentieth anniversary of the launch of the Nike name, a Doherty production ended with Knight, returned and standing alone at the hallowed running track at the University of Oregon, his hands in the pockets of a Nike baseball jacket. Knight gazed toward the infield, clearly listening to a whispered soundtrack: "If you build it, they will come," the line from the movie *Field of Dreams*.

"It's not like you're ever short on emotional material because you've got sports," Doherty said while Knight ate his smoked turkey sandwich and yogurt. "I can build a whole show around a shoe."

Knight sat with his back to a huge seven-foot-wide and eight-foot-high television screen positioned next to a large photograph of the great, balding quarterback, Y. A. Tittle. As if on cue, a Nike commercial appeared during a break in the sports event playing on the huge screen. It was one of the newer Nike Outdoors spots composed of artistically refracted images of a young athlete sprinting through wet riverbeds set in some lush backcountry.

The outdoor market, some eighteen million American hikers, all the mountain bikers, and other members of a huge "down set"—those given to spending hundreds of dollars each year on items stuffed with down or made out of a variety of high-tech, semipermeable, all-weather membranes—had already provided Nike with some $140 million worth of business during the previous year. The hybrid marketplace of fitness aficionados and backpacker types required an entirely new marketing vision, and Knight was pleased with how quickly former employees of state-of-the-art technical gear manufacturers and even retailers from outdoor specialty shops in Denver and Boulder, Colorado, had been drafted to the cause.

Howard White and Doherty stared past Knight's curls, aglow before the big screen, at the commercial.

"Kind of a Big Brother moment," Doherty said quietly.

An employee stopped by the table to report that a newspaper in Phoenix had taken to reporting Charles Barkley's thoughts about life in a separate box every morning. The previous day, Barkley had been asked what he would have liked to have been if he hadn't become a basketball player.

"A porn star," Charles had replied.

Then the lunchtime conversation turned to personal fantasies—all of them about sports. Doherty said that in his dreams he is occasionally Dwight Clarke of the San Francisco 49ers, the wide receiver who snared "the catch" to win the NFC championship game in January, 1982. "Montana to Doherty," the forty-nine-year-old image-maker mused unselfconsciously and with dreamy eyes.

"Well, I don't have sports fantasies," Howard White proclaimed. "That's one of the reasons I can deal with my guys."

"What about you, Phil?" Doherty asked.

"Oh, I don't know," Knight said uncomfortably, picking his sunglasses up from a spot next to his yogurt. "I guess it'd be winning the fifteen-hundred-meter race at the 1964 Olympics. But the thing is, fantasies like this, they've all changed since I was a kid. They've become more accessible because of communications, but sometimes I don't know if they run as deep as they did for me.

"When I was growing up around here, I believed the greatest baseball player in the history of the world was a guy named Johnny Pesky, the shortstop for the Portland Beavers. He went on to play for the Red Sox, but such was the extent of my world that Pesky was my man. Only by listening to the radio did I even realize there were some relatively inconsequential teams playing out in Brooklyn and New York and Boston. *85*

"Now the experience of sports is everywhere. It's all-encompassing, and instantaneous. It's right there beside you from cradle to grave . . . the culture of the world." Knight paused, the others at the table clearly lacking a quick response to this rare moment of public reflection offered by their famously reflective but introverted leader.

"But, yeah," Knight said as he stood up to leave, "I think it would definitely be that fifteen-hundred-meter run in 1964."

Out on the huge playing field behind the Bo, a maniacal game of Ultimate Frisbee was being played during working hours by dozens of Nike "Ekins," who were in Beaverton for a few days of meetings. The young Ekins—which, many of them seem embarrassed to admit, is taken from "Nike" spelled backward—coursed back and forth across the field as the chaotic, football-like competition progressed, sometimes running very fast and crashing into each other at high speed.

The Ekins are Nike's circuit-riding technical experts. The program was begun in 1981 as a way to institutionalize the enthusiastic personal connection to retailers that Knight, Jeff Johnson, and others had established during the early days. Ekins will cover hundreds of miles in a week, stopping in at store after store to offer clinics and explain technical details about the ever more complex shoes. The Ekins are known among the twelve thousand retail outlets Nike serves to have nothing to sell, though they tend to work day and night, like the most driven salespeople.

Internally, the Ekins serve as the resident wild things of the latter-day company culture. Most of them are in their mid or late twenties, and if any of the fifty or so Ekins are less than completely committed to personal fitness and competitive sports, they certainly hide it.

Many of the Ekins wear a ritual tattoo shaped like a Nike Swoosh. The tattoos were mostly implanted during mass visits to tattoo parlors during the quarterly Ekin gatherings held in various parts of the country. The Swoosh is usually applied to the calf, though some are drilled into skin near the groin, at the top of the leg. "So when you're running in a pair of split-legged running shorts," one young Ekin explained, "the Swoosh shows every time you take a stride."

"There's a whole lot of employees at this company who don't have platelets in their blood," Knight's assistant, Lisa McKillips once observed during one of Michael Doherty's films. "They have little Swooshes."

"The Ekins epitomize the original lust," a Southern California-based Ekin named Duke Stump proclaimed. "We are that passion from the early days, and we're the eyes and ears of the company too. While others are buzzing around headquarters, we're out there with the customer. If we all look athletic, then that's because we represent the most athletic of all the brands there are."

Solid and blond, Duke Stump played professional ice hockey in Sweden for several years before deciding that a young man can be asked to take only so many bus rides across the tundra. He worked in a sporting-goods retail outlet and often fantasized about joining Nike as an Ekin—the jobs being like full scholarships to Ivy League schools to the huge number of ex-college athletes and sports-related retail employees who understand the status the position implies. Many of the young Ekins have tasted the nine-to-five life in other employment spheres, and so, one after another, they tend to claim they have the best job in the whole world—the modern career as an extended sports moment.

Aside from riding his circuit, Duke still finds time to train for triathlons. He was soon to compete in a "half–Iron Man" competition that included a 1.1-mile swim, a 56-mile bike race, and a 13-mile run. After that, he was shooting for a full Iron Man race in August.

"I feel like I'm part of an amazing tradition as an Ekin," Duke Stump said with sincerity. "We like to say that Phil Knight was the first Ekin."

Knight accepts the "first Ekin" association enthusiastically, and he halfheartedly even contends that he would have a Swoosh tattooed on his body if he was an Ekin today.

Knight worries constantly that the kind of damn-the-torpedoes enthusiasm the Ekins represent is becoming increasingly difficult to retain as the company grows larger, more global and far-flung. His concern led to a recent attitude survey conducted by the James H. Joerger firm, but the results revealed Nike to have the highest level of corporate loyalty and acceptance of company policy and style the national firm had ever recorded. A forthcoming *Business Week* survey would rank Nike thirteenth for "most improved productivity" among all the Standard & Poor 500 companies.

The corporate "we" is used in place of "I" with regularity inside Nike, even as the corporate "we" is lost at most other companies. The loyalty quotient is such that ex-Nike employees who leave for other shoe companies tend to become instant nonpersons with an old Soviet completeness. A majority of Nike employees claim to have never read the who-did-what-to-whom early-days chronicle *Swoosh,* this as a matter of company loyalty. The book, coauthored by Rob Strasser's wife, was said to reflect Strasser's viewpoint. Rob Strasser was now a consultant to Adidas USA—once the demonized competitors, before Reebok came to the fore—and though he used to be Knight's friend, he was now his enemy. So those who had read *Swoosh* tended to keep it to themselves.

The pervasive Nike mindset and the long hours have probably contributed to the tremendous number of Nike in-house marriages, relationships, and affairs, and the distinct possibility that Nike ex-husbands and ex-wives will end up at the same meeting or company function.

"It's a cult," the visiting Ekin Duke Stump noted before returning to the Ultimate Frisbee field. "But it's a great cult."

"There's no shoe school out there to create talent that can understand what we need to do," Knight said as he passed by the Ekins at play. "And there's certainly no other company that we considered very well managed to draw upon. Nobody else has defined the good management of the large, global sports-and-fitness company. So it has to happen here."

During orientation, new employees receive lists of Nike values: Be flexible and adaptive. Stay lean and mean. Challenge the status quo. Accept that Nike is a big company (but that doesn't mean we have to be slow). Use structure to promote innovation. Manage with courage. Fight any feeling of entitlement. Be humble. We are not preordained to be #1. Live off the land."

"There are only three things that can kill this company," Tom Clarke told a group of managers attending a Nike education program. "Arrogance, entitlement, and bureaucracy."

Some senior Nike managers—notably the president, Dick Donahue—actively disagree with Knight's belief that only those Nike employees who've grown up inside the company can ever "get it" well enough to be leaders. But Knight can think of only two employees of the company who still call him Buck. And one of them, Nelson Farris, is ostensibly employed to convey to new employees how things were when the company was a slightly organized way to avoid a real job.

Knight was told that, after a recent showing of one of Doherty's celebrations of the Nike way, several young employees had been heard wondering who "that runner was, the dude with the long hair."

The dude turned out to be Prefontaine.

Knight knew that the Nike family that was being exposed to a regular diet of the never-quit pronouncements of Bowerman and athlete-against-the-powers-that-be renditions of the Nike ethic was dominated nine-to-one by employees who weren't even on the payroll when Michael Jordan arrived and who, for the most part, were children when Steve Prefontaine was killed in 1975. And even if the high spirit can be transplanted between generations, there is still the issue of company size.

Only seven years earlier, Phil Knight stated that "some company will become the IBM of the sports-apparel industry within the next five years," but now that Nike logos marked the landscape far more prominently than images wrought by IBM—now that Nike had indeed risen above all the other organizations connected to sports as an unavoidable presence and often fearsome power—the corporate quest involved how not to become the floundering IBM of the sports-and-fitness business.

Knight gazed into the coming year and saw Nike's strategies consistently rubbing up against a public sense of the "good of sport." He saw the rapidly expanding global reach of the company possibly dissipating the heat of Nike's special corporate culture. The looming risks of growing larger included the possibility of "smothering," as the organizational theorist Kenneth Boulding once wrote all corporations eventually will, "the very things the organization was created to embody."

But then Knight had always said that the grasp of any company—even one that had managed to capture so much of the pathos, and even the moral force, of athletics and then brilliantly reify that passion as pairs of shoes—was bound to be fragile. All he could think to do was control what could be controlled and never stop looking for the next "big idea."

Knight could abstract his sense of the corporate future, but he **69** could also only see it all as personal. "I worry over it like I worry about my kids. . . . I can't break the power of the connection any more than I can stop worrying about my two kids—and they're grown up now. There's just too much emotion involved. I'll never quit worrying about Nike, and we'll never stop needing to win."

ATLANTA

February 1993

"**N**eon" Deion Sanders slouched in a chair on the ten-yard line of Honolulu's Aloha Stadium, yawning so long and loud into the microphone clipped to his luminous red-and-blue outerwear that the sound technician on the scene was moved to adjust the volume. Deion was heavily accessorized on this morning of February 7, Pro Bowl day in Hawaii. He sported very dark sunglasses heavily trimmed with gold, a large gold bracelet, gold rings bigger than his knuckles, a weighty encampment of gold earrings, and a white fresh-from-the-box cap trimmed only with a tall and slender Nike Swoosh.

On the ground below Deion's chair was a pair of high-tech shoes from the Deion-endorsed Air Diamond Turf line, some quarter million of which were due to be shipped to stores during the coming June. The shoes were extremely flashy-looking gold mesh, jet-black, red, and white creations that the designers and developers in the Michael Jordan Building had cooked up and launched onto an internal Nike fast-track called the Quick Strike program. The designers were inspired to create the shoe after considering Deion's signature eighteen-karat jewelry and the fact that he mentioned to them during a visit to Beaverton that one thing he truly loved was a black Lamborghini.

"I'm so tired, man," Deion said, before the marketing presentation began, glancing up at the stadium's Jumbo Vision screen, where a huge "You Gotta Believe"—the Deion-slogan Nike marketers had seized upon as a serviceable tagline for their incipient "new-age athletic hero"—flashed on and off next to a clock that read seven 7:57 A.M.

Sanders fiddled with his earpiece and microphone and said that the sound gear reminded him of his bygone days as a cashier at a drive-through fast-food outlet. "Worked a Bojangles," he said, before yawning like a man yodeling to the faithful from atop a minaret. "But mini-i-mum wage didn't cut it," Deion continued. "I wanted"—another yawn—"big things, the finer things in life."

Sanders—who had just completed a very successful season playing cornerback for the Atlanta Falcons—was only signed up to be a Nike endorsement athlete during the spring of 1992. The Nike dream-makers, Deion said, "waited for me to mature."

"I'm Tom Phillips!" an enthusiastic voice suddenly reported in Deion's earpiece, causing the athlete's head to jerk back as if he'd suddenly smelled something unpleasant. "I'm the category marketing manager for cross-training!"

The youthful and bearded Phillips—a Nike management star who also served as the category marketing manager for the company's $500 million line of kids shows—spoke to Sanders from the Nike booth at the annual Super Show, held each February in Atlanta, Georgia.

As Phillips went on to tell his audience in Atlanta about Nike's corporate desire to "satisfy all the needs of its athletes," to render them as "something more than figureheads . . . part of a big family effort," Deion Sanders woke up and began to assemble a presence suitable to the moment. By 1:05 P.M. in Atlanta—8:05 A.M. on the clock in Honolulu—when Tom Phillips introduced Deion Sanders, "by satellite," to a handful of elite conventioneers among the 95,977 who'd gathered in Atlanta, Sanders's boyish grin was duly affixed.

Deion understood that when the red light went on it was showtime in Nikeworld, and by the time it lit up, he was suddenly smiling and laughing and more than ready to explain that "playing two sports makes me feel like a kid, just like kids who play their sports all year round." He proclaimed that his approach to sports was "not about makin' a lot of money. It's about having fun." He said that he believed in his heart that "you got to look good to play good," and that "Nike is a lot like Deion." Deion raised a half-clenched fist to shoulder height, and then he said, "You gotta believe."

•   •   •

Outside the multimillion-dollar separate world that sixty-five Nike employees unpacked from four railroad cars and numerous semis four days earlier, the annual sports bazaar organized by the National Sporting Goods Manufacturing Association sprawled out for miles. Amid the more than 8600 different display booths, dumbbell shaped water bottles were given away and "Buns of Steel" videos competed with Lava Buns seat warmers, designed for those cold days in the stands. Over twenty different sports energy drinks were on display near a new hockey puck product replete with a speedometer built into one facet ("If I'd had one of these when I was playing," read the statement-of-the-obvious "endorsement" on the package by retired hockey great Bobby Hull, "I would have known how fast my shot was").

In-line skaters flew through the air, dozens of bodybuilders flexed, and rock climbers scaled the eighty-foot climbing wall rising above one of the central Super Show thoroughfares. Miss Fitness USA—Marla Duncan—was available for autographs in booth 1244-7N, and cheerleaders from the Atlanta Hawks, Dallas Cowboys, and even the University of North Carolina all milled around, also available for autographs but essentially present for effect. Reggie Jackson, Magic Johnson, Mickey Mantle, Joe Namath, and thirty-five other stellar retirees sat in front of huge lines with pens in hand.

All of the hallways and even the playing field of the Georgia Dome, located at one end of the sprawling Georgia World Congress Center, was given over to participants in the trading-card and sports collectibles industry, a niche in the sports marketplace that had grown from less than $50 million in total sales to over $1.5 billion over the past decade. So much focus had been brought to bear by the new industry on the value of hoarded images of sports celebrities printed on small cardboard rectangles—and so rapidly had open markets and price-setting mechanisms accrued to so many other tradable items over the same period of time—that children with official trading-card price guides protruding from the back pockets of their jeans had become part of the endemic still-lives observable in school yards and playgrounds all over the United States.

The Atlanta Super Show covered twenty-five acres, and everywhere participants looked—more evident than any other single sporting thing—there were shoes. Organizers would later claim that a billion dollars worth of business was transacted over the four days of the show, and the majority of that business involved shoes.

"Seen Nike yet?"

"Been to Nike?"

"Does this badge get me into Nike?"

"When we think of the next step we have to make," said the man from Rollerblade, Inc., the eponymous leader of an in-line skating boom that has tripled the number of its acolytes to an estimated 9.8 million in just three years, "we think of doing it like Nike, of using TV."

"We will pass Nike by within two years!" asserted Reebok CEO Paul Fireman at a press conference. But then in April of 1992, Fireman had said Reebok would overtake Nike in 1993.

Nike ads dominated displays on walls at the Atlanta airport baggage area. Nike images lined billboards along Interstate 85 on the way into town. Nike shuttle buses ran around downtown Atlanta, saving show participants the hassle of finding a taxi.

At a previous Super Show, the Nike tour de force included the construction of a Greek temple, with columns, statuary, and a tuxedoed gentleman playing a white grand piano at the entrance to the booth. For 1993, Gordon Thompson, the former architect and now director of Nike Design (Image Division), had directed his team to turn a fifty-thousand-square-foot ballroom at the Atlanta Omni Center into an unimpeachable visual statement that Nike was indeed "The #1 Sports and Fitness Company in the World."

That phrase—The #1 Sports and Fitness Company in the World—vaulted in huge capital letters across the bottom of an escalator leading up past glowing pillars wrapped with bright color photographs of sporting scenes. Each column was crowned by a huge clear globe Gordon Thompson had designed just for the show. Each globe was lit from below, etched with the shapes of the continents, and emblazoned—from sea to sea—with a gigantic NIKE.

On opening day a large and angry crowd encircled the guards at the bottom of the escalator leading up to the separate plateau of the Nike booth. The crowd extended back along either side of the escalator, where portholes had been cut into walls that were also covered with etched templates of the Nike world. Inside each porthole, different films showed athletes and children in motion on behalf of individual Nike product categories.

Buyers in the middle of the bad-tempered crowd holding up

red badges, and retailers and consultants flashing theirs, surged toward the guard desk to complain and even scream at members of the security force. The officials tried to explain that only the orange-badged financial analysts and purple-badged members of the press were ever allowed into Nikeworld on the first day of the Super Show.

Those allowed to ascend to the top of the escalator stepped off before a dazzling show of vivid photographs drawn from Gordon Thompson's carefully curated "Nike image bank." The pictures coruscated in rapid-fire sequence across a screen running the length of a huge black-walled foyer. The glowing sconces designed to match the globe-covering theme shed just enough light to cause the entryway to resemble the trendiest new restaurant in town—not unlike Gordon Thompson's design for one of the most beautiful restaurants back in Portland, the ocher, black, and copper-surfaced outpost called Zefiro. Gordon had somehow fit the Zefiro project into his seven-day weeks designing things for Nike. He owned a piece of the restaurant, which was always heavily booked, even amid a local culinary explosion that has covered downtown Portland with dozens of hip restaurants offering a hundred creative variations on grilled Chinook salmon, local mushrooms, and when in season, the fattest and sweetest berries in North America.

Thompson is a slight and dapper thirty-two-year-old, a Nike guy of only four years, and—luckily, in terms of his own ability to assimilate at Nike after leaving a high-paying design job back in Los Angeles—a former intercollegiate tennis player with "a pretty horrible competitive streak." He left a stellar career in design, which had taken him to work in New York, London, Paris, and Hong Kong, to join the image masters in Beaverton, Oregon.

Gordon sees both irony and purpose in the Nike engine of things hip being stationed "as far as you can get from the epicenters of cool." Beaverton's lack of urban cultural clutter, Gordon contended at the Super Show, allowed him and his designers to concentrate their energies. It was Thompson who designed the Nike retail extravaganzas that had since become the Nike Towns—"part 1939 World's Fair, part theater," as Gordon imagines them—in Portland and Chicago.

Just before coming to Atlanta, Thompson mentioned to a fellow passenger on a plane flight headed to Chicago that he had in fact designed the Nike Town on Michigan Avenue, and he was *95* immediately surrounded by passengers who wanted to meet such a man.

Thompson's knack for grand conceptions had allowed him to thrive inside the culture of risk-taking at Nike. One time, for a company sales meeting, he ordered an entire purple room to be constructed from the cosseting, wetsuit-for-the-feet neoprene/ Lycra spandex material used in Nike's Dynamic Fit liners. The room gave everyone a headache because of the color and the smell, but the audacity of the venture was a hit.

Gordon was on his way to one of the top ten or twelve jobs at Nike by the time of the Super Show, managing a huge creative staff. "But I want you to stay away from numbers," Knight had said as Thompson's responsibilities began to multiply. "You just keep on drawing, Gordon."

Nike executives, who had shed T-shirts and jeans and the odd urban-stubble beard for clean shaves and Armani suits, greeted the reporters and Wall Street VIPs at the top of the escalator in the huge round lobby Thompson had devised. The booth was full of gentle music, pin-spot lighting, and benches that were lit from below filled with examples of the same "visible air" that cushions the shoes. Some 4,500 square feet of blond, highly polished hardwood flooring had been unloaded from the boxcars. Numerous conversation booths, display pods, and large private conference rooms were everywhere to be found inside the mazelike Nike outpost. There was a big VIP conference room, and the "Phil Knight Room" was for technical demonstrations.

But the dominant feature of the Nike booth was a gigantic central turntable mounted with rows of terraced seating. "Think Carousel of Progress—Disneyland, circa 1967," Gordon said, climbing up onto the carousel.

Since orders for the majority of Nike wares due to be sold in the fall of 1993 had been placed at least a month earlier and, in some cases, the shoes had already been made, Thompson's mission in Atlanta was about the sanctity and the energy of the image. The environment had to become a statement. Newer Nike dealers were in town from Europe and Asia, where sophisticated selling displays were not an important part of the retail tradition. The booth was a way to show them how merchandise could become props inside a spectacle. Visitors could be helped to understand the discrete images of Nike's different "consumer segments"—Men's Fitness, Women's, Kids', Outdoor, Men's

Sport, et cetera—which had become so essential to the marketing focus during the reinvention phenomenon of the last six
years.

"This space is different from anything these people will find
. . . out there," Gordon Thompson said, waving the back of his
hand down toward thousands of booths representing companies
that Thompson considered still mired in a ham-fisted and une-
volved aesthetic of athletic goods design.

"The music, the fact that it's not so bright in here. It's all
different," he said. "You can see people calm down when they
get here. I try to play on peoples' senses. At one time I thought
Nike's image was essentially about glamor; now I understand
that it's really about romance."

After the media and Wall Street VIPs settled into the seats on top
of the giant carousel, the lights went down and the turntable
rotated the visitors into position. Everyone stared up at the inner
face of a towering, circular projection screen that was positioned
above a sprawling banner bearing the now venerable Nike slogan, "There Is No Finish Line."

After a loud drumroll, a series of everyday faces appeared on
the screen, and Nike employees took turns proclaiming "Nike's
all about being number one. . . . Nike allows you to be your own
person."

"Pushing the limits," said a middle-aged woman with close-
cropped hair, her eyes cast toward the firmament. "Trying
things that haven't been done before."

The close-ups and one-liners continued until a young man in
a baseball cap said, "It's the one shoe you can depend on." Then
a very heavily muscled fellow with a long body and long face
said, "You feel like you're part of the family."

If some of the securities analysts and reporters in for the show
didn't recognize the baseball player Ken Griffey, Jr., and David
Robinson of the San Antonio Spurs, there was also John
McEnroe, Bo Jackson, and finally, Michael Jordan: "Nike's
gonna be on top forever."

Now the screen flashed another face, a somber-looking guy in
wraparound sunglasses. He spoke unusually deliberately, like
someone telling himself all the while to slow his patter down.
"It's a company," Knight said, "in a position to say that the
future is unlimited."

The assembled Nike-watchers all knew that this was the closest Knight would get to the Super Show. Knight had become a high-profile no-show at the Super Show. As with Nike's recent announcement that no Nike booth would be constructed at another industry gala in Chicago later during the year, Knight's absence was interpreted in the industry as another way in which Nike distinguishes itself from the herd.

The lights went back on in the booth, and young Nike marketing managers and dozens of athletic-looking models continued the careful choreography of the show. Smoke descended from the ceiling, aerobic dancers danced, and a rappeller came down a wall. The carousel spun while consumers on the screen above testified to the way their lives were changing—marathon runners with families and new jobs who'd had to modify the pace; young mothers bored with their workouts. And Nike, as luck would have it, had products, a customized sensibility, and even a vocabulary of strenuousness and achievable freedom that might address these alterations of habit.

At one point, a Nike old-timer of thirty-seven, Tom Hartge, stood before the crowd holding a strange shoe that looked like the hoof of some great purple, silver, black, and deep green beast.

"The Air Carnivore," he said. "Vegetarians beware."

Hartge, as he's known on campus since everyone abjures his first name, is a serious marathon runner and so pure a Nike believer that colleagues count him as one of the employees who "embodies the heart and soul of the company." Hartge—pronounced "Har-chee"—watches the sports marketers in McEnroe warily at times, always wondering if Nike will remain true to the lower-level hardworking athletes that "made the company great." So complete is Hartge's company identification that he refuses to drink a specific beer made in one of the many local Portland microbreweries because the brewery was partially owned by Rob Strasser, the Nike apostate who abandoned the fold back in 1987 and then offered his considerable skills as a consultant to Adidas. Hartge reads all the arcane track magazines and sometimes trains along the Jeff Johnson running track twice in a day, without socks.

"The most distinctive performance-oriented cross-trainer we've ever done," Hartge continued during his presentation of the Men's Fitness line, holding the great green shoe in his right hand. "The fit of a running shoe, the lateral stability of a basketball shoe. Not a tame shoe, the Carnivore proves that Nike is still leading the industry in cross-training footwear."

And the music rose up, the carousel began to move, the smoke obscured the view again, and another vivid scene amassed before the mesmerized crowd.

Exhibitors at the Super Show are not allowed into the booths of competing manufacturers (though a year earlier one Nike employee who knew him fairly well reported that Reebok leader Paul Fireman sneaked into the Nike booth wearing someone else's credentials—an assertion Fireman denies), but word still filtered back to the Nike troops manning the booth about items competitors had brought to the show. Nike managers knew that L.A. Gear was promoting a new "technological innovation"—a little red light set into the heel and connected to a lithium battery. The light flashed every time the shoe struck the ground.

There was general amusement at the thought of the shoe fakers at L.A. Gear showing, once again, that their technical expertise was nothing but gimmickry. "Nike's technology—it's *real*," one of the talking heads from the Nike Sports Performance Laboratory had enthused during the first part of the show back in the Nike booth.

L.A. Gear was also bringing to market an "Encapsole Air" sole and a neoprene "Sock-fit" system that Nike soldiers perceived as attempts to cash in on Nike technology and a spring-loaded heel gizmo called the Catapult that, trade analysts would later report, few of "the kids" approaching "the walls" inside American athletic-shoe outlets accepted as real.

L.A. Gear charged into public view in 1985, just as Phil Knight's crusaders were suffering the first significant setbacks in the company's history, the time of business reversals and emotional trauma commencing in the mid 1980s that is officially referred to during the orientation program for new Nike employees as "the transition."

In 1985, L.A. Gear sold just $11 million worth of shoes that were, from the Nike perspective, simply phony. But it was the mid 1980s, when authenticity had little to do with the financial services scene, so L.A. Gear went public in 1986.

The company immediately launched an extensive national athletic-shoe advertising campaign on television, and by 1989, **99** the price of L.A. Gear stock, adjusted for a split, had risen from $3 per share to $50. In 1990, sales rose to $820 million.

"If you're talking performance shoes," the chief financial officer said at the time, "you need only one or two pairs. If you're talking fashion, you're talking endless pairs of shoes."

Fashion—the very noun is all but officially proscribed inside Nike. Fashion, a phenomenon devoid of larger values and implying whim instead of abiding passion, was the antithesis of authenticity.

Only Knight ever seemed to use the word "fashion" ("We say design instead"). Fashion—especially before the transition years of the mid and late 1980s, was thought to be only a by-product of technical and innovative mastery inside the company. Whereas some 80 percent of athletic shoes are thought to be used for activities other than the purpose of their design in the general marketplace—usually they were used for walking around—Nike's more dedicated, sports-specific users composed 40 percent of their purchasers.

L.A. Gear was just a marketing organization, in the Nike view—"totally L.A." and without anything of substance to market. After he left, one of two entrepreneurs who started the company would later in 1993 market a new product called Brewski, a beer packaged for the toga party set.

L.A. Gear had recently stopped growing, and 1992 revenues were half of total sales in 1990. A little over a year before the Atlanta Super Show, out of cash and sitting on millions of pairs of unsold shoes, new investors had installed a turnaround artist—in fact, the author of a book called *The Turnaround Prescription*—the former Revlon and Reebok executive, Mark Goldston.

Goldston had been involved in the launch of the Reebok Pump, and he was quite excited about the new lighting technology in his shoes. Goldston said he imagined that the shoes would soon be fitted with microprocessors and accelerometers. They would make great noises and provide information. "The visual drama is as important as the authenticity," Goldston believed.

But his company hadn't shown a hint of profit in two years, and many industry-watchers in Atlanta wondered if L.A. Gear—still the third-largest shoe company in the domestic industry—would eventually die. The struggling company was nearly twice the size of Converse (inventors of the basketball shoe in 1908) and fourth-ranked Asics (a descendant of the Onitsuka Tiger brand Knight used to sell), and it was much more than twice the size of Adidas USA (connected to the German inventors of the modern soccer boot in 1949).

But L.A. Gear was only one sixth the size of Reebok—inventors, as a British company then called Foster & Sons, of the track-and-field shoe, in 1900—and the struggling company was one tenth the size, in terms of sales, of Nike.

Most Nike managers in Atlanta tended to avoid anything beyond the most casual contact with the managers working for competitors. This was sometimes difficult for company veterans, because—as with General Motors, Sears, and IBM in their respective heydays—ex-Nike employees had seeded the entire athletic-shoe industry.

Jim Moodhe was Nike's first sales manager and one of the original wild and crazy Nike guys who became instantly rich the day Phil Knight became much richer. Moodhe retired from Nike only a year after the public offering, at the age of thirty-four, to drive race cars and pursue other adventures on a short but pressing list of "Walter Mitty dreams." Moodhe got burned badly in the ski business, came back to shoes, and eventually became the president of Guess Athletic, one of a dozen or so niche brands that reside on the tier below Nike and Reebok.

Instead of offering Deion by satellite or Bo Jackson, who would arrive, in person, at the Nike booth on the last day of the show, the Guess booth featured a model named Anna Nicole Smith, the Jayne Mansfield look-alike from the Guess Apparel ads and the soon-to-be-crowned Playmate of the Year. "From the crumbs that fall off Nike's plate you can catch three hundred million to four hundred million dollars' worth of yearly sales—which isn't half bad," Moodhe said as Smith, dressed in a gold lamé blouse, leaned over to sign calendars. "I'm looking to sell as many shoes in a year as they sell in a month. The trick is to find a particular niche where they don't dominate."

"Given our size, we're frankly nothing more than a minor annoyance to Nike or Reebok," read a new full-page magazine ad for New Balance, one of the other niche players in the athletic-shoe field. "The question is, what are you to Nike or Reebok?"

Fila, an Italian company until recently associated with the gin-and-tonic, après-tennis-on-the-veranda look, was said to be gleaning funds from a recent public offering in Europe for a full-scale incursion into Nike's hero business. The new Fila look on display at the Super Show "read" urban streets. It read young males who play basketball and think Michael Jordan and Charles Barkley are gods. Steve Miller and the Nike sports marketers were watching Fila and other niche competitors, because they expected certain smaller companies to bid for the endorsement services of one of the several college basketball stars who would be drafted into the pros at the end of the coming June.

"They learn by watching us," Knight explained one morning in Beaverton. "And I don't worry about any one of them. It's all of them trying to grab a piece at once that makes this all so interesting."

Though most industry insiders in Atlanta had expected it to happen for some time, the Super Show scene was set abuzz by the announcement at a press conference that former Nike VP Rob Strasser would become the CEO of Adidas USA. The German-based Adidas would purchase Strasser's Portland-based Sports Incorporated for a rumored $15 million, and Strasser would join the board of the company he once, as Phil Knight's close associate, had vowed to "tear down to the last sport shoe on the streets of Berlin." Strasser would be joined in his crusade to revive Adidas's fortunes by Peter Moore, who designed Nike's first- and second-generation Air Jordan shoes before he left to form Sports Incorporated with Strasser in 1987.

Adidas in February of 1993 was but a shadow of the company that had lorded over the athletic shoe and international sports scene for much of the post–World War II era. Jesse Owens had run his famous race in front of Hitler in shoes that were crafted by the gifted cobbler Adi Dassler, of Herzogenaurach, Germany, and then brought to the markets by Adi's brother, Rudolph. After the war, the Dassler brothers had a falling out and rarely spoke or even looked at one another again—even during the vicious courtroom battles that followed.

Rudolph went to the other side of Herzogenaurach and started to make shoes under the brand name Puma, and Adi merged his own nickname and a bit of "Dassler" to form Adidas. Adidas soon offered soccer boots in a variety of configurations that could be fitted with dozens of different cleat styles. In 1954, it was widely believed among athletes and soccer fans that the German squad's triumph over Hungary during the World Cup competition that year was due to Adi Dassler's turf-gripping shoes.

The designers at Adidas wrote the first book on the idea of having one shoe for one sport, and by 1972, the year the Nike brand was born, the company so dominated international competition that more than eight of ten medal winners at the Montreal Olympics wore Adidas gear. For years, young runners like Phil Knight and Jeff Johnson heard stories from coaches like Bill Bowerman about a sinister shoe company that made payments to athletes, kept files on international officials, and generally stood astride the sporting landscape with imperialist sway.

Adi Dassler died in 1978, and his son and business heir, Horst, died in 1987. Three years later, Nike surpassed the worldwide sales of Adidas shoes and apparel, as the once-dominant company shriveled into decline. The chic and sport-minded French industrialist Bernard Tapie, a ubiquitous name in Paris gossip columns, managed to pick up control of Adidas for a mere $289 million. But he would soon relinquish control of the unprofitable company after suffering the humiliation of resigning from the French cabinet amid accusations that he had pocketed $2.5 million paid to one of his companies by Toshiba. In early April, Adidas would be taken over by a new group of investors led by Robert Louis-Dreyfus, the chief executive and financial force behind the recent expansion of the British-based Saatchi & Saatchi advertising and marketing company.

Adidas now controlled only 3 percent of the American market, compared to Nike's 33 percent, and the company had replaced its American chief manager three times before Rob Strasser's ascension.

Inside the drama- and intrigue-riddled gathering in Atlanta, the announcement of Rob Strasser's new job was made more poignant because it was widely believed that the huge, bearded Nike veteran and Phil Knight—once his friend—now loathed each other.

Rob Strasser was a Berkeley-trained lawyer and a member of the hard-living Nike inner circle. He was sometimes called "the fat guy" inside Nike, until a newspaper article written at the very beginning of the 1980s called Strasser "the man who saved Nike." Colleagues wore T-shirts to work that said THE MAN WHO SAVED NIKE after that, but after he left, Strasser, Knight believed, had somehow forgotten the irony with which they'd both regarded the savior label at the time, and Knight deeply resented the way Rob had accrued so much credit for Nike's success to his résumé.

In the last part of *Swoosh,* the history of Nike co-written by Strasser's wife, Knight is quoted as saying to Strasser, "If I have to have a friend, it's you." But, from now on, every move the two companies made would be perceived as part of a plot line rife with revenge and ego.

"I certainly don't recall saying, 'If I have to have a friend it's you'—not as such," Knight said before the Atlanta show began. "But it's true there was a time when we really were good friends. But we split during the 1980s and Rob just continues to over-state his role. He took a long sabbatical in the fall of 1986, and then he left for good in June of 1987, and it's interesting to see that when he left Nike, sales were down two hundred million dollars, and after he left they began to rise—to eight hundred million and then up to close to four billion."

Knight tended to become quiet and hesitant when Strasser's name came up, and Strasser would sputter with emotion if asked to talk about Knight. Strasser would say he didn't want to talk about Phil, but then he would—at length and with ire.

The Nike blood feud with Reebok—and Knight's personal antipathy toward its founder and CEO, Paul Fireman—is so intense and pervasive that Michael Jordan admits that he found himself zeroing in with special intensity upon Reebok players such as Dominique Wilkins, Shaquille O'Neal, and Shawn Kemp during a game. "But this thing between Strasser and Phil," Jordan said of the two men, both of whom had been present at his signing as future king of the Nike guys, "it's very big and very deep. It clearly involves things that I can't even begin to understand."

"I know they're not what they once were," Jeff Johnson observed from his retreat in New Hampshire when one of the other Nike originals called him with news of Strasser's move. "But Adidas people were the Huns. I would starve to death before I'd work for Adidas."

It was generally acknowledged inside the sports and sport business worlds that Phil Knight and Nike had the power to block a specific small competitor's every move if a concentration of resources was brought to bear. But Knight didn't show his hand very often, so everyone in Atlanta agreed that it was going to be quite something to see if Nike and little Adidas, two of several sports companies run by force of powerful personalities, would soon go to war.

• • •

Over at booth 5100-E—a busy but traditional trade show display presented by Reebok—the company VP for production, the VP of design, research, and development, and the VP of sports marketing were only a few of the ex-Nike people now employed by the "R company."

"As soon as you leave Nike you really get a lesson in friendship," said John Morgan, Reebok VP of product marketing and a Nike manager for some fourteen years. "People I worked with, some of them personal friends, turn their heads when I see them in the hallways. Some of my closest friends in the company don't even return my phone calls anymore. It's crazy because when you boil it all down, what we do is just about sneakers."

Since no right-thinking Nike soldier would ever say such a thing—or even utter the word "sneaker"—it was clear that John Morgan had gone over to the other side.

Nike people tend to think of Reebok people as willing to sell anything to anybody. They will "open anyone"—which means that Reebok is willing to sell to those low-service mass merchants and no-service discounters where customers can't possibly be taught to understand or appreciate the shoes. The Reebok marketers are occasionally called P & G types in Beaverton, which implies that they study statistics-laden research reports based on decades of borrowed behavioral science instead of bringing goods into specific markets because they are inspired by and true to a long history of service to athletes.

One of the few employees of Nike who worked for Reebok in the past is Kevin Paulk, the Beaverton-based "developer" whose job included shepherding the green Air Carnivore Tom Hartge had just unveiled through all fifteen months of its production process. Paulk admitted that each time he was asked to describe his personal goals as part of the employee review process during his first three years at Nike, he wrote that his goal was to "stop being the Reebok guy."

At Reebok headquarters in Stoughton, Massachusetts—a workplace not without its own sense of pride, esprit de corps, and allure (in 1992, twenty thousand people applied for a job among fewer than four thousand workers)—Nike people are thought to be naïve and unreconstructed Oregonian-style jocks who are so caught up in their famous heritage and cultlike culture that they have lost the ranginess necessary to be true entrepreneurs. "They run a good and effective business," Paul Fireman contended after the Super Show was over. "But they demonstrate the symptoms of a real cult—they isolate themselves in a compound."

Fireman, a college dropout and former salesman, got the idea of acquiring the right to sell Reebok shoes in the United States at a Chicago trade show during the running-boom year 1979. "I was leaving a family business and I didn't have the credentials to do anything important," Fireman recalls. Reebok was just an $800,000 maker of custom athletic footwear at the time, originally—as Foster & Sons of Great Britain—the company that shod the 1924 British Olympic track team recalled so evocatively in the 1981 movie *Chariots of Fire.*

When the movie came out, Fireman's plan to sell expensive Reebok running shoes had not panned out so well. But two years later, Reebok came out with a flimsy, snow-white shoe of wrinkled leather—a cross between a sneaker and a dancing shoe—called the Freestyle. As soon as Fireman saw the soft leather wrinkled at the toe, he realized that women might equate the look with the finest soft leather gloves and handbags. But by then the humiliated Asian factories had figured out how to get the wrinkles out of the process, and it took six months for them to figure out how to get the wrinkles back in.

Fireman hit upon a brilliant marketing strategy that included simply giving the shoes away—as Tylenol is handed out to patients in the hospital—to the thousands of new "aerobics instructors" suddenly drawing women to the health clubs and dance studios that were opening all over the country.

Rob Strasser was heard at the time to proclaim that "Nike will never make shoes for those fags who do aerobics." But Nike managers, sitting in airports or walking along urban streets and staring—as they all do—at the feet shuffling by, began to see a lot of flimsy Freestyles. Mick Jagger wore Freestyles. Movie stars wore them, too.

Until 1983, fashion-conscious and sports-conscious consumers of both sexes preferred running shoes, but with the advent of aerobics, women quickly acquired an athletic activity that was not some tamed permutation of the games men could be seen performing on television. Reebok latched on to the sea change just as speciality retail chains such as Foot Locker and Athlete's Foot began to double and triple their number of outlets. The results of so many forces coming together at once created an instant shoe empire.

Reebok's sales proceeded to grow from $1.5 million in 1981

to $1.4 billion in 1987, in percentage terms surpassing Nike's record growth rate. In 1986, when Nike spent over $64 million on advertising and Reebok spent less than $16 million, Reebok moved up even with Nike in terms of sales, and in 1987, the R company completely passed Nike by. The stylistically rough-hewn Fireman was suddenly mentioned as a "marketing genius" in sentences shared by Knight, and his name was invariably listed among the most highly paid executives in the world. Fireman's salary and benefits still ranked high on the annual *Forbes* list of most luxuriously remunerated executives: In 1993, they would report that over the past five years Fireman had been paid over $45 million in compensation. He owned close to $585 million worth of Reebok stock, with another $16.6 million worth of unexercised options.

After falling to number two, Knight and Nike managed to regroup, reinvent, and then storm back to dominance of the industry, but not before Reebok's dizzying rise had knocked some of the freewheeling child out of the company. Bowerman's Lombardiesque observation that "Nobody ever remembers number two" became a battle cry at Nike after Reebok became number one, and much of that youthful, "we don't need to be a real company to succeed," damn-the-torpedoes élan was replaced by a grimmer and more strategic determination to never get blindsided again.

Knight is still resentful over the losses suffered during Reebok's rise. "We simply make better shoes than Reebok," Knight had said when his turnaround began. "The most innovative piece of R and D equipment they have is the copy machine!" Paul Fireman was installed as a semi-official devil figure inside Nike, and he remains a dark presence there to this day. To Knight, Fireman was a late entry and something of a faker, a capricious pretender. Reebok people don't really care about sports. To them—Nike dogma has it—it's just business.

"Well I don't think of myself as just a shoe guy," Fireman says. "But I also don't think of myself as a big-time presence in sports. That's foolish."

Most Nike employees believe Knight truly loathes Fireman for Reebok's part in causing setbacks so briefly terrifying and destabilizing that six years ago Knight agreed to lay off several hundred members of the company family.

Four hundred employees were laid off at first, and then, in 1987, 275 more were cast away. Mention of the layoffs causes **107**

Nike veterans to bow their heads. "Reebok was God's way of telling us that we'd gotten off track," said David Kottkamp, the tall former Portland politico who runs Nike's burgeoning international division.

"Nothing marks Phil's psyche more than the fact of those layoffs," added corporate president Dick Donahue, who stood at Kottkamp's side.

Though Knight can be heard to tell employees that he "hates Paul Fireman," he will also talk about the larger cycles of shoe empires and blame himself for backing away from hands-on management of the company in the mid 1980s—just when the billion-dollar sales threshold was reached and employment growth was skyrocketing—and thereby losing sight of the rim.

"We should have planned for that transition, but we didn't," Knight says.

He can also talk for hours about the obfuscations of customer desire caused by the near-religious belief that shoes for the best athletes would always be the shoes the people would buy.

But when Fireman comes up, Knight's jaw sets and his voice falls into a lower "must-win" range.

Knight holds Reebok and Fireman in some part responsible for the 1990 call to boycott Nike products by the Chicago-based civil rights group, Operation PUSH. The Reverend Jesse Jackson sent a fax to Knight after giving a morning address in which he announced that his organization had begun to look into the relationship of Nike to its customers and employees hailing from the black community. In the fax, Jackson wondered if Knight was coming to the annual industry trade show convening the next day in Chicago, so that perhaps the two men could meet.

Knight said he wasn't coming, but that the company's recently appointed president, Dick Donahue, would be there if Jackson wanted to get together. The Chicago meeting was pleasant enough. Jackson did not attend, but a representative, the Reverend Tyrone Crider, asked for figures reflecting Nike's employment of minorities and other numbers indicating the balance of sales and marketing expenditures derived from and directed to minority citizens. The request list included information about Nike's bank accounts and investments.

Donahue agreed to take the list back to Oregon.

The meeting was adjourned, and Donahue opened the door to find a wall of microphones and cameras waiting. At the end of the surprise question-and-answer session, Donahue was asked to name the highest-ranking black manager inside Nike, and he had to admit that he could not.

Back home, Knight, Donahue, and Liz Dolan thought about the requested list of intimate corporate details, and they decided to ask Operation PUSH to provide concomitant lists of statistics about their own operation.

Communications subsequently broke down, and PUSH called for a nationwide Nike boycott. The group demanded that Nike give out contracts to minority businesses and jobs to blacks in proportion with the business it did in black communities. PUSH officials claimed that Nike was a company run by white males that had no black vice presidents or board members—which was true. Ministers who supported the PUSH boycott claimed from their pulpits that Nike sold 40 to 45 percent of its products to inner city youths, though Liz Dolan and her public affairs team countered with publicly available sales records that indicated 13 percent of the company's sales were made to minority consumers.

Georgetown University basketball coach John Thompson intervened, and Knight agreed to meet Jesse Jackson at the longtime Nike coach's office in Washington, though Knight says his one quid pro quo was that the press not be notified.

During the meeting, Knight thought that Jackson was intent on getting him to steer Nike advertising business to specific, African-American-run Chicago firms.

Knight said that Nike did use one minority-run ad firm and that they had a formal working relationship with Spike Lee, noted African-American filmmaker.

But Jackson said this wasn't enough.

Knight pointed out that minority employment had grown from 11 percent to 14 percent over the course of the previous year and was getting better all the time.

Jackson said that wasn't good enough either.

Knight looked at Jackson's shoes.

"Cole-Haans?" Knight asked, referring to the New England–based make of top-of-the-line men's and women's dress shoes.

"Always," Jackson said.

The meeting adjourned, and Knight was infuriated to find another media wall blocking his way outside Thompson's office.

"Well, one thing we can assume is that Reverend Jackson

DONALD KATZ

intends this boycott of Nike to apply to everyone but himself,"
Knight said. "Because he showed up at this meeting wearing
shoes made by a company Nike happens to own."

Knight couldn't decide if he thought it racist or naïve of Jackson to equate Nike's many black endorsers with target-selling to
blacks. White as Nike was ("Oh, it's pretty white," Howard
White agreed outside the Bo one day. "Sometimes I get off a
plane in Chicago or Los Angeles and I think, 'Where'd all these
other black folks come from?' "), everyone who knew Knight
believed that it had never crossed his mind to hire athletes because of their race. In fact, Knight's obsession with the best of all
athletes ran against conventional wisdom. During the 1970s, it
was well known among sports agents and product marketers that
only white spokesmen were thought capable, by corporate leaders, of moving product. Every city had a beloved African-American athlete figure, but not until Michael and Bo had a black
athletic hero become a corporate star.

John Thompson and Michael Jordan issued statements in support of Nike's good intentions, and Bo Jackson submitted a
statement that attacked PUSH so specifically that it was judged
too incendiary to release ("What the hell did PUSH ever do for
my family?" was among the least adamant lines from Jackson's
expletive-strewn response).

On September 17, 1990, around twenty-five PUSH supporters came to Oregon to protest at Nike headquarters and stage a
demonstration at the annual shareholders' meeting.

But by then, opinion polls indicated that the general public
supported Nike three to one, and Nike's advance orders for the
coming quarter were up by nearly 40 percent.

The boycott was judged a failure, but John Thompson was
soon named to the Nike board (Reebok appointed a black director around the same time). Minority employment has continued
to grow to an official level close to 20 percent, though the fact is
hard to discern walking around the World Campus ("That place
makes Disneyworld look like a crackhouse!" comedian Jerry
Seinfeld quipped after a visit inside the berm).

Knight and Dick Donahue firmly believe that the protesters
who twice came to Portland on PUSH's behalf had plane tickets
indirectly financed by Reebok. During an August 1990 gathering of Nike coaches held at Carmel Valley Ranch in California,
Knight publicly referred to the presence of "Bo Knows Apart-

heid" signs during Nelson Mandela's visit to Boston as part of
Reebok's anti-Nike campaign.

Paul Fireman says that Knight is wrong about his company's
involvement.

Some Reebok employees could be heard talking at the 1993
Super Show about their concern with delivery schedules, and it
was said along the broad hallways of the Omni Center that Paul
Fireman had been so displeased with the basketball line for late
1993 that he had ordered it reconstructed at the last minute.
Nike is thought throughout the industry to be the more professional operation, and, as central as Knight is to the force and
meaning of the elaborate Nike culture, Nike is generally
thought to possess a much stronger and more stable tier of middle managers. Fireman is generally thought to be less obsessed
than Phil Knight, a better one-on-one salesman, and far less reflective. Longtime industry-watchers often talk of the differences between Knight's and Fireman's styles as brought out by
their distinct reactions to a Sears, Roebuck promotional adventure of several years earlier. Knight and Fireman were both
shocked and offended to discover that Sears had offered cut-rate
Nikes and Reeboks to customers on the back of cereal boxes—
in the commercial space usually reserved for plastic rings and
personalized coffee mugs.

Fireman was enraged by Sears's unilateral decision to deni-
grate the Reebok brand with a cereal box promotion, so he
informed Sears that in the future the retailer must purchase an
entire year's worth of Reeboks in the first quarter of the fiscal
year—a condition that remains part of the relationship of the
two companies to this day.

Knight was also enraged by the decision to devalue the Nike
brand. He called a press conference and announced that Nike
would henceforth do no business at all with Sears, and when
Sears sent a contingent of top managers to Beaverton in an effort
to make peace, Knight wouldn't even acknowledge that the executives were in town.

Mike Ovitz had recently told Knight that CAA was constantly
being dogged by the other big, diversifying Hollywood talent
agency, International Creative Management. "But that's good,"
Knight said. "Competition like that can be helpful."

Asked if the ritual demonization of a competitor—a visceral
antipathy widely believed inside a company to emanate from the

leader's deepest personal feelings—might be a serviceable corporate-management and morale-building tool, Phil Knight's grin spread up under his sunglasses. "Yeah sure," he said. "Especially when it's real."

Amid all the competitive fury, Nike and Reebok had still grown up to be symbiotic codominators of the $11-billion athletic shoe and apparel industry. Nike dominated 33 percent of the market by having its way with men and athletes, and Reebok swelled via its popularity among women.

But now both companies were set to invade the other's core strength. Nike was charging full force into Reebok's franchise with American and European women, and Reebok—like Fila and Adidas—was going after boys who love games.

During 1992, the recently named president of the Reebok sports division, Roberto Muller, admitted that a boy who was serious about his basketball or an athlete who "wanted to wear a badge" would not choose to buy Reebok shoes. But Muller vowed to change all of that.

Muller was well known to Nike in the past as the president of Pony. Back in 1982, Muller had tried to lure away an early Nike endorsement athlete named Darryl Dawkins, known as "Chocolate Thunder" around the NBA at the time. The raid was only half successful in that Darryl went out to play with a Nike shoe on one foot and a Pony shoe on the other.

Just before "Super Show" (industry regulars often omit the article), it was announced at a banquet in Moscow attended by Boris Yeltsin that Reebok would sponsor and provide apparel for twenty different Russian sporting federations and the Russian Olympic team, the agreement to last through the 1996 Olympic games in Atlanta. Reebok also bought the rights to supply the U.S. Tennis Association National Team, and the company now boasted that eighteen prominent pro baseball players were now wearing Reebok spikes, as were several big-name football players.

And as Phil Knight was reminded too often, as far as he was concerned, Reebok had Shaq. Giant cardboard cutouts of the huge Orlando Magic rookie stood at the entrance to the company's booth in Atlanta, and Shaquille O'Neal commercials had aired alongside Air Jordan spots during the recent Super Bowl. Jordan cavorted ironically with Bugs Bunny and Porky Pig, playing the wise-guy superstar who's paid "one bazillion simoleons." Shaq starred in a tongue-in-cheek commercial featuring basketball legends Kareem Abdul-Jabbar, Bill Russell, and Bill Walton, who each offered manly sports platitudes—the attitude being recognizable to the most casual observer of Nike commercials as a Nike ad in Reebok shoes. The Reebok VP for advertising, Dave Ropes, said that Shaq is "a star that you might expect to see in Nikes . . . in Reeboks."

"It's the convergence bit," Dick Donahue said in the lobby of the Nike booth. "If they get up close enough to us, then perhaps people will be confused. Pepsi's been at it with Coke for years."

"Nike blew it. They had the chance to drive a nail into Reebok's coffin," said John Miller, the VP for sports programming at NBC and a longtime student of pro basketball and the shoe wars. "They really should have gotten Shaq."

But over at the Nike shrine, at the top of the escalator, it was universally understood that young Shaq was, quite simply, no Nike guy. Nike could indeed have signed the number one draft choice of the previous June if money and promises were all that were entailed, but young Shaq had not proven himself to be amenable to a Nike connection. Shaq didn't "get it."

Only six or seven elite college players are invited to tour the World Campus, meet Phil Knight, and hear an elaborate multimedia marketing rendition of their own foreseeable futures. Only Shaquille O'Neal had ever showed up on campus in a Reebok jacket. And only Shaq had yawned during the presentation and demanded to be as front and center inside the Nike stable as Michael Jordan.

Since Nike can control the general corporate endorsement drill, O'Neal was asked to come to Beaverton after he had visited Converse, Reebok, and any other companies of a mind to shift investment priorities in the direction of the seven-foot, one-inch, over three-hundred-pound future star. The Nike dealmakers always like to be last, unless they believe a preemptive arrangement is in the cards.

Howard White, Fred Schreyer, and the other stable-drafters and athlete tenders could also assume that given the opportunity and the same contract, an athlete turning pro would almost automatically choose Nike. Jimmy Jackson, the fourth pick in the NBA draft in which Shaq and Alonzo Mourning were picked first and second, had already phoned Howard White while still on his tour of other shoe companies before Shaq came to town. "Come on man. I bought your guy's program years ago. Nike brought me up. So why don't you just let me come on board without all this traveling around?"

Jackson signed a five-year, $850,000 endorsement deal—less than Converse had put on the table. His agent then proceeded to go into negotiations with his future team, the lowly Dallas Mavericks, implying that he didn't care if he had to hold out for a good deal because Nike was behind Jimmy . . . even though the contract said Jackson had to actually play to get his shoe money.

Before extending an invitation to a player, the marketing team used its connections with college and high school coaches to find out what they could about "the kids" (all young athletes in the sports-marketing world are called "the kid") demeanor and family background. In Shaq's case, the Nike basketball managers knew he came from a close family dominated by his father, an army sergeant named Phil Harrison. The assumption in Beaverton was that Harrison would be a military dad on the order of Ambrose Robinson, San Antonio Spurs center David Robinson's father, who was an obvious stabilizing force in his son's life.

But Shaq's father turned out to be much different. Phil Harrison seemed angry and volatile from the start. He had fire in his eyes.

Also along for the visit to Beaverton was one Lenny Armato. Young Shaq was widely known in sports-marketing circles to have been "tied up" for some time in a private "total career management" program operated by Armato, who preferred the term "manager" to "sports agent," and who was also president of Management Plus Enterprises. Everybody in the McEnroe Building already knew Leonard Armato. He had represented Kareem Abdul-Jabbar for a while as well as the talented center Akeem (until he changed it to Hakeem) Olajuwon, whom Howard Slusher admits was the player he told Knight to draft back in 1984 instead of the Jordan kid.

At one point in the past, Leonard Armato had advised L.A. Gear executives that if they wanted to muscle in on Nike's athlete and grassroots coaching stable, they should apportion some of the tremendous amount of money they'd made toward signing up college coaches nearing the end of their contracts with other shoe companies. Often working on a "percentage of budget" arrangement that was perceived throughout the industry as a 10 percent finder's fee ("It wasn't that simple," Armato says), Armato began drafting talent.

Much of the sports industry stood by, dumbstruck by a deal that seemed to encourage Armato to expend as much L.A. Gear money as possible, while Armato hooked some lesser Nike coaches. He signed up LSU and Converse basketball coach Dale Brown to a contract worth several hundred thousand dollars, and Brown told his star sophomore center that he would be wearing different shoes during the coming season. The center was an outgoing giant of a kid everyone called Shaq.

Agents and sports-marketing executives who met O'Neal while he was an undergraduate—a time when Leonard Armato was becoming close with Shaq's parents—were struck by how much time he'd already spent pondering his commercial future. Shaq had observed the explosion of the sports-marketing scene ("He took sports-marketing courses," Armato says) and the rise of Michael Jordan, and he'd decided that rather than becoming a part of several varied corporate marketing strategies, an array of companies might be assembled as part of a brand presence that was he. Consumer products companies would become part of Team Shaq, rather than the other way around. "We're looking for consistency of image," Armato would say as he began collecting the team on Shaq's behalf. "Like Mickey Mouse."

Even before Shaq arrived in Beaverton, Howard White, Fred Schreyer, and the others believed they would be meeting with the first rookie they could remember who didn't think that Nike was the only place a future superstar should be.

Still wearing—without explanation—his Reebok jacket, Shaq, Armato, and Shaq's father all listened to the Nike presentation, and Phil Harrison continued to glower. Then Armato responded. He said that while they didn't expect Shaq to be "as big as Michael right away," they also did not intend to take a backseat to David Robinson, Barkley, or any of the others as part of the Nike Air Force or Air Flight line of basketball shoes. They expected a signature shoe immediately and a national commercial by the coming October, when Shaq would have been playing pro basketball for only a few days.

"It's interesting that you seem less intent on how Shaq is used than when he'd be used," ad director Scott Bedbury said to Armato.

Before this first phase of the meeting was over, Shaq and his father simply got up and left the room, as if the whole thing had become a bore.

After the presentation and a short return to neutral corners, *115* the negotiating phase of such encounters would usually commence.

Schreyer and Howard White huddled briefly.

"He doesn't want to be here," Schreyer said. "I'm not into throwing out a number that will help him get more out of somebody else."

Schreyer had already said to Knight that he thought Shaq would probably cost at least a million a year over several years.

White agreed with Schreyer and added that word along the grapevine was that Team Shaq wanted a total endorsement package, from an accumulated list of companies, of $50 million over several years, and nothing less.

Shaq was taken across campus to tour the Bo, and, as was tradition, few passing Nike employees allowed themselves to stare—though some employees did turn to see if it really did say Reebok on the huge kid's back, just like everyone on campus was saying.

"We see great things here for Shaq, and we think you know what Nike can do for an athlete," Schreyer said to Armato and Harrison when the meeting reconvened. "But we don't think Shaquille really wants to be here, so rather than making an offer, why don't you just throw out the number in your head and we'll give a quick yes or no."

At this, Shaquille's father—who is much smaller than his son at six foot five and only 250 pounds—stood halfway up, his eyes wide with fury. "What is this shit!" he bellowed. "You dare to bring us here and—why? why!—because my son wears a Reebok jacket, you dare to question his desire!"

Harrison railed on and the visit was ostensibly over, and White and Schreyer were left to wonder if perhaps Shaq had wanted to be a Nike guy after all.

But Team Shaq and the can of worms that many others in the sports business world soon knew to be his dad ("He doesn't have the discipline or support to handle the adulation about to come his way," Knight commented when he agreed to pass on Shaq) went on to sign a complex arrangement with Reebok that would pay him about $15 million over five years, depending on shoe sales and other factors. Shaq also signed a $13-million deal with Pepsi, and deals with Kenner toys, Spaulding, and Scoreboard trading cards that would be worth close to $25 million more.

Over the course of the basketball season, Shaq would do a rap album, appear in a movie, "write" a book about his twenty-year-long life, and when his commercial began to air, nobody in the sports business world was surprised to see the old sergeant Phil Harrison on the screen, too. Everyone on the World Campus immediately began to hope the very worst for Shaquille O'Neal. He had just appeared in an ESPN documentary about the building of the Team Shaq "cross-marketing" phenomenon, and the film showed Shaq back on the Nike World Campus, leaving the gym on the third floor of the Bo after the Orlando Magic team came to practice before a game against the Trail Blazers. Shaq was chanting "Air Out, Pump Up," the anti-Nike Reebok slogan. Young Shaq—as every Nike secretary or sales rep from Beaverton to Okinawa would tell you—was no Nike guy.

"He's not a Nike guy because they don't have him," barked the ex-Nike grassroots basketball man and promoter—the colorful and wild-mouthed "ex–Las Vegas gambler," as he was too often described—Sonny Vaccaro. "What's a Nike guy? They got Nike guys in prison too, you know. This Nike guy stuff is just bullshit."

In December of 1992, two months after Shaq began to accomplish slam dunks in unprecedented numbers and to eventually shatter backboards as a member of the Orlando Magic, a group of twelve- to thirteen-year-old boys visiting the Universal Studios theme park in Orlando were asked if they wanted to come into a room and talk about athletic shoes. The boys were not told which company the two young market research specialists represented, but they were all shown a black, white, and aqua basketball shoe. "If you saw this Shaq shoe in the store," they asked the boys, "would you buy it?"

Several of the boys moved in close, and some—most of them Floridians—said they surely would.

"Now let's talk about celebrities—famous people," a young British market researcher said to the kids. "Who comes to mind?"

"Michael Jordan!" yelled half the kids. "Scottie Pippen," said several others. "Charles Barkley!" said another, and the rest of the boys all agreed. "Chris Mullin . . . David Robinson . . . Andre Agassi . . . Yeah, Andre Agassi!" the boys all cheered.

From the back of the room, the parents of the boys could see the two researchers look at each other and roll their eyes. *117*

As the boys left, they were all handed little key chains and pens that said Reebok on the side.

"We don't have the guys to get us that exposure and it's damn irritating," a Reebok executive had complained to a writer for *Ad Week* during 1992.

But now Reebok had a guy. By February of 1993, there were babies being named Shaquille all over America.

"You rolls the dice and you take your chances," Knight mused in February. "Five years from now, maybe I will say we should have gotten Shaq. I am the guy who said a college player named Magic Johnson's professional future was in doubt because he was a player without a position. We didn't have Magic and we didn't have Bird," Knight said with a grin. "And we still did pretty well."

On the afternoon of the second day of the Super Show, the Nike encampment burbled with ironic and derisive asides: "Maybe we should throw out some rose petals," Dick Donahue said. "His Excellency, Prince Juan Antonio Samaranch, one of God's noblemen, is coming to pay us a visit."

Though Nike had grown larger and more powerful than any of the governing associations, leagues, or teams it occasionally finds itself set against, the thoughtfully tailored, utterly patrician—some would say regal—president of the International Olympic Committee was still perceived inside the booth as representative of a manner of authority Phil Knight and others at Nike found difficult to stomach.

The seventy-two-year-old Samaranch was known to often characterize the International Olympic Committee as the guiding force behind a "social movement" or as "the world's leading moral authority on competitive sport." He was called upon to eulogize Horst Dassler in 1987, when the Adidas leader died at the age of fifty-one.

During the past Christmas season, Knight had sent senior Nike managers and others he knew a copy of an old-fashioned muckraking tome about the International Olympic Committee called *The Lords of the Rings: Power, Money and Drugs in the Modern Olympics,* authored by Vyv Simson and Andrew Jennings, two British investigative reporters. The book portrays Samaranch as the head of a corrupt and secretive club. Horst Dassler appears as a shadowy, power-mad close associate of the Spanish

IOC president and as the main force behind a commercialization of the Olympics that, the authors argue, involved as many large and small bribes as there were aboveboard sponsorship payments by companies seeking to get closer to the Olympic brand.

Still at heart a track-and-field man in the Bowerman tradition, Knight found it difficult to mask his contempt for one member in particular of Samaranch's International Olympic Committee, an Italian "aristocrat" named Primo Nebiolo, who was also president of the International Amateur Athletics Federation, the organization that controlled international track competition. In Knight's view Nebiolo was a geopolitical power broker who was bad for sports and specifically bad for track and field, a sports category that had been sitting dead in the water in comparison to other athletic pursuits for years.

Nike is often mentioned when the marketing woes and declining popularity of the track-and-field scene come up. During the late 1970s, Nike established a training organization called Athletics West in Eugene, Oregon, a refuge where Olympic contenders and athletes who had graduated from college could continue to train. Nike advertisements in track-and-field and running magazines have long been acknowledged to be as much a way to support the sport's means of communications as ways to sell gear—the retailing of spiked racing shoes having become so nominal to the larger selling scene as to only remain important to the company out of respect for the past.

Those who talk about reviving track and field and reinfusing the events with a new media allure tend to look to Nike as the only organized force that can do the trick. The company did make a long-term commitment to underwrite the American international track program, and at an early 1992 meeting in Beaverton, officials of the stodgy-sounding Athletics Congress, or TAC, were presented with a nifty new logo cooked up by Nike Design, and a new name, USA Track and Field.

Over the next few weeks, Nike would begin the public process of making the American Olympic gold-medal winner in the four-hundred-meter race, Quincy Watts, a household name— but only in Europe. A commercial called "Don Quincy" would soon air all over the much more track-attuned Continent, in which an operatic Viking king would offer Quincy Watts his very large wife in exchange for a pair of Nikes ("The super-cushioned wife for your super-cushioned Air Max shoes" was the rough translation of the Italian). At the end of the commercial, the overfed soprano wife would sing "Quin-cy!" as Watts sprints away from the deal.

By early summer, European fans would be chanting "Quincy" from the stands at track meets, but Quincy Watts was simply not famous enough in his own country to warrant the cost of playing the commercial in American markets. The track-and-field events of the Barcelona Olympics had rated below swimming events among American TV viewers, and there was such desultory interest in the coming late-summer track-and-field world championships in Stuttgart that NBC would decide, for the first time, not to carry the event.

While Knight blames many of the deficiencies of the track-and-field scene on the stodgy bureaucrats who run the sport, he does admit that the Nike machine could probably organize the forces necessary to repopularize track and field in the United States by repackaging the whole thing, but he says the money required to turn track and field around "could never justify the return."

But Nike nevertheless ends up in the middle of the international track scene all the time. The greatest runners and jumpers still number among its endorsers, and the company is regularly, in some way, at odds with the kinds of officials who used to make Bowerman so mad, or is at odds with athletes for failing to fight the track establishment.

In the fall of 1990, another of the best American four-hundred-meter specialists, the world record–holder in the event, Butch Reynolds, had been banned from competition by Nebiolo's International Amateur Athletics Federation after failing a test for proscribed performance-enhancing drugs. Reynolds claimed the test had been incorrectly administered. The gifted sprinter said he was innocent of the charge, but he was still dropped as a Nike endorsement athlete. Every Nike endorsement contract contains a clause that allows the company to cut and run if "the value of the consultant's endorsement is impaired by the commission of any act that shocks or offends the community, or which ridicules public morals and decency." The contract also permits the company to drop an athlete banned from competition for using drugs.

So Nike dropped Reynolds—who hired a lawyer and spent over two years protesting the legality of his suspension up through the American court system.

Reynolds was deeply hurt by Nike's lack of support, though Steve Miller says he tried to figure out a way to get Butch back into the program when Reynolds earned the right to compete again during the spring of 1992. But the nature of the new deal implied to Reynolds that his Nike contacts thought he was guilty, so no agreement was reached.

The perception among Reynolds's supporters and among others in more elite track-and-field circles was that Nike's lack of support for Reynolds, a man, in Phil Knight's own estimation, of Nike-like tenacity who gave up years of competition and the Barcelona Olympics fighting the powers that be, juxtaposed unflatteringly with Nike's handling of similar accusations of drug use against the German sprinter Katrin Krabbe. Nike had purchased Krabbe's entire formerly East German track club, and when Krabbe tested positive for performance-enhancing drugs, Steve Miller had rushed off to Germany to manage damage-control duties, stood by the runner's contract, and even paid for her legal defense. When Krabbe was banned anyway, Nike did drop the blond, blue-eyed sports heroine and obvious conduit to a huge East German market where Nike International hoped to sell a lot of shoes.

But by then some observers were saying that the difference between the two cases was that a handsome, world-class African-American four-hundred-meter runner and Nike guy could be easily replaced by another handsome, world-class African-American four-hundred-meter runner and Nike guy. Inside Nike, the two incidents were simply not the same, and race was never consciously part of the applicable decision-making. By the time the Krabbe situation came up, the company had more experience in pursuing steroid cases, and that incident had taken place in a Third World country where testing protocols were questionable. Knight had even entertained a more-than-passing notion that Adidas had something to do with the failed test. And there was also the considerable difference between Butch's $85,000-per-year deal and the much-larger cost of Krabbe and her club's endorsement.

Nike executives had rooted for Butch Reynolds throughout his legal wars, and they closely followed his progress when he started racing again. The Nike track guys all knew that Butch was badly hurt by being cut away from "the family," and they tried to assure him and his agent that it had nothing to do with race. Sometimes these things were, first and foremost, about business.

When the smiling and nodding Juan Antonio Samaranch breezed through the Nike booth, Dick Donahue was standing next to Steve Miller. Both men smiled broadly in the direction of the IOC entourage.

"Wish Butch was here," Donahue said to Miller through his half-smile. "I wish Butch was here to hand His Excellency a copy of that damned book."

"I really want to stop fighting so much with governing bodies and leagues," Knight had told his senior managers after Barcelona. "It's easier to fight with them when you're the little guy. Even though we still think the old way, being number one means that you simply can't fight all the time. So let's start waiting for the big fights."

So the stately president of the International Olympic Committee strolled through the colorful pods of Gordon Thompson's temporary Versailles, nodding and smiling, and the Nike troops stood by, dutifully nodding and smiling right back.

If the authorities who officially manage sports have never been entirely popular inside Nike's own circle of power, then various members of the professional investment community have often felt that Nike people have regarded them in the same way.

"They're just plain cocky," said one money manager before catching the Nike show inside the booth in Atlanta. "Sure they're the best. But American Express was the best company in its field too, and all of a sudden a bunch of other companies ate American Express's lunch."

"It's true that they aren't so great at communicating with the Street," said the longtime Nike analyst Josie Esquivel, who covers Nike for Shearson Lehman Hutton. Esquivel once figured out for a 1990 report she was working on that Nike had come to dominate twenty-one of the thirty-seven footwear and apparel segments she could find to measure. Esquivel was one of the only analysts who regularly came to the World Campus and stayed long enough to soak up the intense corporate scene. Also present was Maggie Gilliam, the retail and apparel industry analyst for First Boston, who hobbled around the booth with a large cast on one leg. "I don't tend to complain about them," she explained, "because I bought the line when they were turning around in 1986 and took positions at seven dollars a share."

On the Friday following the last day of Super Show, Nike investor relations manager Ron Parham would announce that most of the Nike analysts who'd estimated the company's final numbers when the fiscal year ended in May would be wrong. The company would continue to grow rapidly and would easily show several hundred million dollars in annual profit, but it might not be the profits the Street was expecting.

The problem was largely the deepening recession in Europe, particularly in France, Germany, and Spain, where unemployment was pushing up toward 22 percent. Sales were ever more sluggish on the Continent, and with the value of the U.S. dollar up 10 percent during the quarter against the currencies Nike used in key European markets, repatriated money translated into lower values.

The first day the markets were open after the Friday announcement, the price of Nike's shares would fall by over nine dollars, though the stock was still up by 20 percent over the previous summer's price.

Many analysts considered the fall-off a chance for Nike bulls to get in on the coming ride. "I believe Nike is the Coca-Cola of high-performance footwear," said Willard Brown of Dean Witter. "This is a buying opportunity."

Others were less sure. "This 'revelation,' " complained Kidder, Peabody analyst Gary Jacobson in a written report, "came only one week after the Atlanta Super Show, where Nike presented an upbeat showing of new products."

Jacobson intimated that the "surprise" news might be due to Nike's traditional disrespect for professional investors. "We believe," he wrote, "that Nike is managing the Street lower only to have artificial, positive surprises later in the year. This was in line with what the company did in last year's fourth quarter and numerous times over the past several years. Therefore we are staying at our $4.80 [annual earnings per share] estimate."

Gary Jacobson said that Nike was way overvalued at over seventy dollars per share. He said a price just under fifty dollars was more realistic—once the glamor was replaced with pragmatism. "Besides," Jacobson said after Super Show. "Nike's been number one for a long time, and this industry is always looking for something new."

Knight—who would lose $275 million during a week of price declines—would view the Wall Street reaction as more of the same. "We're not an industrial company to them. We're not listed on the *Fortune* 500. And we're not a sales company either. Then again, we're not strictly a marketing company either," he said. "And we're not just the largest shoe company in the world either. We're an apparel company, a sports and fitness company, a marketing company. . . . We're a company that Wall Street's never known how to analyze."

It was true that most of the securities analysts covering Nike were veterans of the traditional fashion or specialty retailing sectors. Gary Jacobson used to be a toy-business analyst, and it was often said that Jacobson had made a name for himself by riding the price of a company called Coleco into the stars during the early 1980s—until the Coleco fad ended and the stock disappeared altogether. Flash-in-the-pan glamor businesses now tended to make Jacobson nervous.

For all of their willingness to ride along on Nike's success, Knight felt that many professional investors were never serious about understanding the company he'd built. It was as if they were all waiting for the whole "Nike thing" to suddenly go out of fashion and fade away.

"I'll never forget our first dog and pony shows when we were about to go public in December of 1980," Knight recalled one morning after the disappointing quarterly news and subsequent stock slide. "There was one analyst from a big Wall Street house who literally spent hours getting into really interesting details about the business. The guy just crawled inside the company, analyzing the impact of certain accounting procedures, trying to understand the structure of our costs. He was really into it, the most sophisticated kinds of questions.

"I was so impressed that I wanted to see what he did. I found out that he bought two hundred thousand shares at the opening, at nine A.M. on December third, 1980. The stock went out at twenty-two dollars and went to twenty-four dollars that afternoon—when the guy up and sold out. He made his $400,000, and I was taught something about certain kinds of investors.

"I'll never get used to investment bankers who exaggerate the positive and the negative data in order the churn the stock—just to do a lot of trading. But could we do better with Wall Street? Sure—and over the last five years we have gotten better. But the truth is, they just don't like our industry. As it gets bigger and better, the industry will gain respect. We'll just have to wait until this business is truly defined."

. . .

Guests sitting on the turntable inside the Nike booth watched the last of the elaborate pitches by the young marketers. Then the lights went down and the loud, penetrating strains of Nike's own anthem began to penetrate the occasion. The song, "Through the Storm," is a soulful, quasi-gospel number with lyrics that proclaim that while it is "easier to walk away . . . through the tears . . . through the day . . . through the night . . . we can keep it alive . . . we can keep it alive."

As the song blared with extreme fidelity from the expensive sound system surrounding the carousel, Michael Doherty's latest video creation appeared on the huge screen in front of the crowd. The sports highlights were immediately choreographed with the emotive music, and the thrall created by the sight of the artless mastery demonstrated so very slowly on the screen became, for each viewer, an experience that made the nightly sports reels and hundreds of sports videocassette efforts seem completely amateurish.

It was during the first-ever Nike marketing presentation—watching himself play basketball to music—that Michael Jordan says he first understood what was so compelling about the sight of him playing the game.

Now, in vivid, slow motion, Jordan flew again across the curved screen, his tongue moving in the air like a very slow pink fish; Sergei Bubka flew up to one of his thirty-four world records, and you could see and even feel his complete happiness when he was only halfway back to earth, with a huge crowd braying hysterically in the background. The cavalcade of Nike talent continued: The great long-jumper Mike Powell flew; the stylish pass-catcher Jerry Rice high-stepped; and Rice's quarterback, Steve Young, threw the ball, his eyes jacked wide open with anticipation of what might be done. Deion Sanders ran for a touchdown and did his little dance of joy in the end zone.

The noise of every crowd watching the original events rose up and surrounded the experience, sending a thrilling, nervous pulsation through the small audience; a hundred private explosions of feeling could be observed, as at the most frenzied of high school pep rallies.

And then there was again heard the deep, flat, Northwestern phrasing of the coach. "I've been blessed," Phil Knight said above the music. "During the past twenty years I've watched a **125**

lot of sporting events and come to know a lot of athletes. I've
been thrilled and surprised, elated and inspired. Because they are
not only great athletes, but good friends. . . ."

Now Charles Barkley fed a blind pass back to a soaring Scottie
Pippen during the Barcelona games. Next was the pathetic
grimace of the injured British runner Derek Redmond, his father vaulting from the stands to help him around the Olympic
track. The drama played out on the screen in excruciatingly slow
motion, the vivid prolonging of the runner's physical and emotional pain causing the viewers to squirm in their seats.

Runner Gail Deavers tripped in similarly slow motion before
the finish line and desperately reached out for the tape as others
ran past her. Sid Bream slid into home and the Atlanta Braves
pulled off their miracle victory in the previous year's play-offs,
and again, the music gave way to the keening of the crowd.

Announcer Dick Enberg's voice rose above the cheers as
Andre Agassi fell to the grass at Wimbledon, humbled, perhaps,
for the first time: "Twenty-two-year-old Andre Agassi," Enberg cried, "in tears!"

"I've worked with people who share these emotions for the
game," Knight could be heard to say again in voice-over.
"We've seen sports change—a lot—but our attitude at Nike remains the same. We understand the athlete—those who battle
the odds and battle the system. Those who crave the bell lap, the
last inning, or the final seconds of the season. . . ."

And a shiver ran through the crowd inside Nike's circle of
power in a way that made this moment inside a round, black
room completely alive and memorable. There wasn't a dry eye
in the proverbial house as Team Nike's collected heroes performed in perfect syncopation, each of them floating above the
reality of time and space in a subtle and quite beautiful ballet that
made everything about the moment seem instantly, if fleetingly,
profound.

BEAVERTON II

April 1993

Poised atop a tall stool in the middle of his colorful enclosure in the Jordan Building, thirty-two-year-old Nike designer Bill Worthington held his latest invention high in the air before him, staring hard at the object in his hand as he spoke. "It took nearly seven months to occur," he said in his even, somewhat affectless voice. "It took a lot of screaming and yelling and team-building inside the matrix. It took a lot of refusing to give up. I worked hard to build alliances and to counter internal skepticism over whether the consumer would be able to appreciate the technology inside this shoe or understand its . . . personality.

"This shoe," Bill continued on a breezy morning, soliloquizing to the prototype held at eye level, "is like an animal. It's like a living, breathing thing instead of an inanimate consumer product. I'd already played around with a shoe inspired by dinosaurs before this came together. Dinosaurs are very cool. I imagined a shoe called the Air-Odactyl. But then I came up with this"—he was still speaking to the shoe—"the Air Carnivore."

Deep, snaking grooves subdivided the complicated black and purple topography on the bottom of Worthington's shoe, cleaving the sole into separate "pods." The pod concept came up from the techies down in the Nike labs, as did the purple, black, and silver velcro "anti-inversion" strapping device running vertically along the outside of the shoe, which was designed to help athletes and nonathletes resist turning their ankles inward while in the air—and so to avoid breaking bones or straining ligaments **127** if they hit the court or pavement on the outside edge of their feet.

Another adjustable strap enclosed the "anti-inversion support collar" that braceleted the ankle, and Bill demonstrated a third strap, this one a huge Velcro fastener over the top of the foot designed to obviate the need for shoelaces. He caressed a "high-rebound" Phylon midsole ringed by a black-and-white zebra-print pattern, and he palpitated the "Dynamic Fit Sleeve," or "Huarache-Fit system" as it's also known, that employed the spongy neoprene/Lycra spandex material out of which Gordon Thompson had once made his noxious purple room.

Several arrangements of advanced designer polymers—variously rock-hard, malleable, breathable, or "high-memory" substances designers have borrowed from chemists, NASA scientists, sail-makers, and women's girdles or cooked up themselves—were glued or sewn to the "oxidized-green," black, gray, and purple shoe. The green "upper," the soft, outer foot-covering of the Air Carnivore, was made of a lightweight, leatheroid Nike material called Durabuck, which was cooked up when the lab guys made a prototype Nike Batboot for actor Michael Keaton to wear in the movie *Batman,* and which is now made for Nike in Japan by the world's best component makers.

Worthington, a former Los Angeles–based industrial design student and current holder of one of the most coveted of all design job titles, continued to slowly rotate in his hand the strange and rather beautiful object he'd wrought. As it turned, the Air Carnivore appeared to be leaning forward into the wind, like an object that was indeed, as its creator contended now without irony, just a heartbeat shy of being alive.

All around Worthington's work cubicle were images and storyboards that had helped inspire his new shoe. There were photographs from movies, notably from the *Alien* series, some of them depicting various creatures sucking away people's faces. One storyboard displayed a cartoon character Worthington had created to help him sell the image and market position of the shoe inside the combination organizational format, marketing mechanism, and cultural labyrinth known as the Nike matrix.

Worthington pointed to his drawing of a wild-eyed young man. "Bert Starkweather, here, is an average kid until Air Carnivores transform his personality. In the shoes he becomes the antisuperhero Bolt Stingwater, who wins drag races on foot and steps on people's faces."

Worthington pulled out a wanted poster on which the dangerous Stingwater was accused of "terrorizing slow-moving salad bar patrons, destroying basketball rims, and mocking L.A. Gear executives."

Like most of the shoe designers who work for Nike, Bill Worthington accepts the occasional classification of his creative cohorts as Nike's "cultural pirates." The designers tend to watch more nonsports TV than the others and read more nonsports magazines in search of ideas. Most of them spend weeks on the road, hanging out at playgrounds, at professional team practices, and—of course—at hundreds of regional malls. Gordon Thompson even likes to watch people in museums when he's in need of a creative kick.

Though the Air Carnivore was "inspired by nature" and, to some extent, related to a shoe that Tinker Hatfield had worked up for the people running around inside some of the dinosaur getups in Steven Spielberg's *Jurassic Park* (Tinker called those shoes Air Dinos and had since encouraged an "animalistic" design motif), Worthington admitted that his new shoe, due to debut in stores during the coming August, had drawn its distinctive attitude and attendant Bert Starkweather–Bolt Stingwater character from the real-life Nike Ekin and former hockey pro, Duke Stump.

Worthington had gone to visit Stump in Southern California for five days in search of some culture to pirate. They stayed at Duke's place in Manhattan Beach and went surfing. Worthington noted Duke's ability to become extremely serious and competitive around his sports. He seemed to change into someone else. Worthington was inspired by Duke and even drew pleasure from the simple, staccato pronunciation of the young Ekin's name: "Duke Stump."

People often inspired Nike shoes. The Air Diamond Turfs were meant to replicate Deion's fashion sense, and Tinker Hatfield had come up with the first high-tech cross-training shoe tethered to the marketing firestorm surrounding Bo Jackson after considering Bo's hyperbolic cartoon of a strong man's form and deciding he should have a big, strong, cartoonlike shoe. The resulting shoe even had oversized, fat bladders for tongues.

As automobile styles have tended to replicate certain dominant modes of transportation over time—the Model T looked like a train, the heavily finned '57 Chevy like an imagined rocket ship of that time—artifacts that captivate Nike designers have also turned into shoes. Tinker's fifth-generation Air Jordan was based on the P-51 Mustang fighter plane that seemed so romantic to the minds of a generation of boys raised on Landmark books about the great fighter pilots of World War II—not that boys old enough to remember the books were the prime consumers of the product. Hatfield also designed a Porsche-like shoe—"If this shoe was a car, what would it be?"—to help others inside the Nike matrix understand the inspiration of his new Air Huaraches.

"I do see our shoes as unique and uniquely American contributions to contemporary design," Hatfield said from behind his drafting table in April. "Adidas certainly pioneered the development of athletic footwear, but to this day they regard these shoes as equipment. They still don't understand how to go beyond that and design in romance and imagery and all of those subliminal characteristics that make an object important to people in less utilitarian ways."

Nike designers often point out that the standard issue that comes with their jobs includes a "license to dream." The Nike designers who create the look of the nine thousand different units of apparel and nine hundred footwear items for sale at any given time work in partitioned lairs that are mostly covered with drawings, strange postcards, old toys, prototype sports equipment, weird Arabic or Dutch shoes, lots of homemade signs, and a general ambience of youthful, free-associative creativity that is invariably tempered by some flavor of sophisticated wit. A huge print of the Rice-A-Roni box near one designer's desk had been refitted as a "Rice 'N' Ronnie" pastiche with images of Nike football players Jerry Rice and hard-hitting defensive back Ronnie Lott. The designers and various other creative types within the matrix have managed to so often wittily match new words with the utterly Nikeized noun "Air"—Air Revaderchi, Air Conditioner, Air Apparent, Air Assault; the list goes on for pages—that former talk-show producer Mike Doherty has observed that the near-daily repetition of the task reminds him of the trick of thinking up new questions for Merv Griffin to ask his perennial guest Zsa Zsa Gabor.

Because a shoe like the Carnivore must begin to wend its way through the creation process fifteen months before it appears in stores, Nike employs special consulting organizations based in Europe and Hong Kong to help them predict changeable consumer color tastes. The color gurus assess certain advanced, high-fashion trends, and they even look into coming automotive color trends to foretell the "in" hues of seasons to come. But Gordon Thompson and the other keepers of the official Nike palette distributed each season mix the consultants' intelligence with their own observations made in locker rooms and gyms. Though the technological projection of "global imagery" was homogenizing certain consumer preferences, especially among teenagers around the world, there were still regional predilections toward certain colors.

There had been jubilation inside the marketing camps at Nike when it was learned through the Asian factory grapevine that the Reebok "Shaq Attaq" shoe due to appear in stores in just a few weeks would be mostly white. Nike trackers were quite sure that the urban preference of the season—especially in the American Northeast—would be black.

Despite the statement made by the bright color of the Air Carnivore, the paramount enticement of the shoe was still its fully loaded technological package. As with many of the newest top-of-the-line models, the Carnivore incorporated recent developments passed along to the design teams from the Nike Sports Research Lab and the Advanced Product Engineering group.

The pod structure of the sole was based on lab work indicating that the forefoot and heel of the human foot actually have separate tasks and tendencies when called upon to perform athletic movements. A design that treated the foot as separate quadrants, or "pods," the research showed, might allow the twenty-six bones, three arches, and innumerable ligaments and muscles inside the foot to perform more naturally.

The anti-inversion strap was based on data showing that almost all ankle injuries suffered while playing basketball were "inversion-type" sprains. The data led to Nike lab tests that required stalwart subjects to strap their feet into shoes glued to stainless steel slabs inside the Nike Sports Research Lab. The slabs were connected to various ominous-looking steel gears and gauges and to an electric power source capable of pronating, inverting, and generally twisting a foot and ankle well beyond levels of simple pain—though test subjects reported no lasting effects from the experimental tortures.

The Sports Research Lab on the ground floor of the Jordan Building is dominated by a large open space filled with lots of computers on trolleys, automatic treadmills built into the floor, *131* exercise bikes, closed-circuit camera systems pointing at the treadmills and bikes, a full-sized human skeleton of the sort occasionally discovered inside closets during bad movies, assorted weight plates, and piled boxes of shoes made by Reebok and Asics as well as by Nike.

One of the many Victorian-looking machines in the lab is designed to rub the outsole—or very bottom—of a shoe for hours on end across surfaces that simulate clay tennis courts, wet boat decks made of teak, or the most porous of cement basketball courts. Another machine calls for test subjects to run without shoes across a steel "pressure mat" that, within seconds, causes a nearby computer monitor to light up with a color-coded map of the subject's foot, each hue representing a different pressure exerted upon distinct parts of the foot during landing.

The easygoing head of the Nike Sports Research Lab, Tom McGuirk, was a mechanical engineer who worked on a "coring system" designed to retrieve sediment from the floor of the Arctic Ocean before he came to Nike. McGuirk's lab, with its twelve biomechanical and physiological research specialists, was set up in 1980, when external support for sports medicine research projects was pulled inside. The allied Nike Advanced Product Engineering group, called APE inside the company, is more of a problem-solving unit than a leading-edge research group. When wearers of the first generation of all-purpose off-road-style cross-trainers complained that the soles of the shoes wrapped around the pedals of their mountain bikes, APE technicians quickly came back with the Air Revaderchi, a shoe with a thermoplastic shank inside that will allow the sole to bend only one way.

"Our job here in Sports Research is to define human movement in terms of biomechanics and physiology," Tom McGuirk said, his Nike passion comparatively sublimated by academic reserve. "Our job is to translate activities into a set of performance-enhancing and injury-reducing needs. And we do a lot of work to improve end-user perception. The Carnivore, for example, has only limited ability to physically prevent the ankle from turning in, but it will telegraph information to the user that will help him or her resist turning the ankle while in the air."

Because of the constant flow of data sent up from the Nike labs, Nike designers know that Michael Jordan ran about two and one half miles during a typical basketball game, and that he landed after an average leap at a peak force three times his body weight. After a test conducted at the University of Delaware, the techies learned that Charles Barkley, because of his size, jumping ability, and landing style, came down with a force seven times greater than his weight.

The technicians know that the average professional soccer player runs more than ten kilometers during a match in his cleated shoes, and after many visits to the lab by John McEnroe, Jimmy Connors, Mary Joe Fernandez, and other tennis players, the specialists studying the habit of so many players who drag their toes while serving were able to develop a material that can be placed against an abrasion wheel for three thousand cycles without wearing down.

"We do stuff with materials that they're only thinking about putting in the space shuttle," said Henry Chriss, a one-time pro football prospect who became a Nike chemist and then director of the Nike Environmental Action Team that is at work on a "green," completely recycled shoe. "There's some very serious polymer science being practiced around here," Henry said.

In a few weeks, when everything was totted up, it would turn out that Nike had spent some $22.6 million on research, product development, and product testing during the previous twelve months.

Nontechnical Nike executives seem to enter the world of product research in the Jordan Building with the bemused respect of James Bond being outfitted at headquarters by the ever-humorless Q. Wearing "what will they think of next" looks, they walk around the measuring equipment, huge shoe mills, and blocks of steel where test molds, customized shoes for college and professional athletes, and the all-important samples for the factories in Asia are made.

"We put so much into the technical side because you can't create an emotional tie to a bad product," Knight often says. "It's just not honest. People will eventually find out if you try to sell them a dishonest product."

Knight seemed pleased by a new full-page color ad running in spring issues of various national magazines. A pair of $120 Nike Air Max running shoes sat in front of a $70,000 Range Rover, the Rolls Royce of the utility vehicles now in vogue. "Now there's an air suspension system for every size budget," read the **133** ad copy, which then descended to smaller print, boasting that the very same technology that created a "revolution in running shoes" was, finally, available in a serious car.

Little ribbed, amber-colored Nike Air gas bags are visible on desktops all over the Beaverton campus. Brown cardboard boxes full of the famous bags lie open in corners all over the Jordan Building, and passersby can occasionally be seen to grab the bags and squeeze the firm little breakthroughs like state-of-the-art worry beads.

The material used to form the air bags is manufactured by a Missouri firm called Tetra, one of only three smaller companies that Knight has acquired—along with the dress shoe manufacturer, Cole-Haan, purchased in 1988, and a small Southern California sports hatmaker call Sports Specialty, purchased in January 1993. The bags and even the gas inside were invented by a fellow named Frank Rudy, a former aerospace engineer who first took his gas-cushioning idea to Adidas and was turned away. Rudy is said to record each and every one of his thoughts and his interactions with others in a journal, so obsessed has the extremely wealthy inventor become with somebody ripping off his inventions. If Rudy is coming to the campus, Nike lab and design employees know to mark off several extra hours in the little Nike Filofax-style "Just Do It" appointment calendars everyone carries around, because Frank always has a lot to say.

When Rudy arrived with his rough, air-cushioned shoes in 1977, Knight was still taking very long daily runs. He set out in one of the prototypes and was amazed by the "ride" the cushioning offered. Rudy and Nike's early Air-Sole technology was first built into a running shoe in 1979, and the bags were laid into a basketball and tennis shoe three years later.

But the cushioning innovation was buried inside Nike's shoes for years, and the customers didn't really seem to care. The invention was available while millions of Americans subjected their aging joints and tortured ligament encapsulations to high-impact jumping up and down in those flimsy Reebok Freestyles during the early 1980s.

The elevated spirit of Nike innovation was for some reason being left behind on computer screens and workbenches. The emotional power that inspired the products—all that romance, Nike heritage, and the swelling fantasies of authentic athletic possibility—was hidden inside the separate society of a company that seemed to have lost touch with the way people outside their world thought and felt and acted when it came time to buy a new pair of shoes. Famous Nike athletes were everywhere on fields and courts, excelling in the carefully made products, but that didn't seem to be enough to grow the business.

"We were in complete disarray," Knight recalls. "We had gone from never having an unprofitable quarter to having two back-to-back unprofitable quarters. We were . . . just so naïve. We had simply lost our way."

After the first round of layoffs in 1986—with the stock price falling under ten dollars—Knight had got up in a Portland warehouse to convene a meeting of all the employees. "Well," he said, without a hint of pleasure or pride, "we just crossed a billion dollars in sales. But I have to tell you that I would rather be the president of a great five-hundred-million-dollar sports and fitness company than the head of a badly run billion-dollar sneaker company." Knight seemed to have it in mind to stop being a shoe company. Nike had to be reconceived as something else, something more inspiring.

Nike still dominated the running-shoe market at the time, but that market was shrinking as the running boom continued to fade. The new Air Jordan line had opened with a bang, but it was suddenly slumping badly in 1986, in part because Michael Jordan had broken his foot early in the season and would miss sixty-four games. Old Converse seemed to be coming back from the dead and was cutting into Nike's sales, and Nike shoes were still relatively invisible in health clubs and on the aerobic dance scene.

The designers were laboring to address the latest fitness vogue, cross-training, based on the theory that participation in a variety of sports and exercises would enhance performance and lower the incidence of injury. Tinker Hatfield was working on a cross-training shoe that would wed enough air cushioning to allow someone to run a few miles in safety and comfort with enough structural support to also allow the quick lateral movements required by tennis or basketball. The idea of an all-purpose shoe that crossed dedicated sports boundaries harked back to research Tom Clarke had conducted when the Nike lab was still located in Exeter, New Hampshire.

In the fall of 1986, John McEnroe played in the Volvo Tennis Tournament in Los Angeles in a grayish, relatively high-sided shoe with a big strap across the top. Tinker Hatfield called his latest invention the Air Cross-Trainer, and customers immediately began to come into stores to ask about the unusual new tennis shoe they'd seen John McEnroe wearing on TV.

They were told that the shoes weren't tennis shoes. They were cross-trainers, but as with too many Nike innovations on behalf of athletes, the shoes failed to take on a more graspable public meaning out there beyond Nike, in the "real world."

"You know, I've been thinking about these next cross-trainers you want to move out next year," a young ad copywriter named Jim Riswold mentioned to Tinker Hatfield during a meeting in mid 1987. "If you're thinking about hooking the shoes up with a guy, this Bo Jackson kid's a natural."

Jim Riswold was thirty at the time, and his friends and colleagues often claimed that they were still waiting for Jim to turn thirteen. Riswold's house in Portland was cluttered with a collection of toys and various other artifacts connected to Warner Brothers and his childhood hero, Bugs Bunny. Riswold was also a bona fide sports nut in the manner of a somewhat hyperactive adolescent boy. One of his earliest memories was the sight of another boyhood hero, Mickey Mantle, actually weeping on television because he wanted his gelatinous breakfast cereal, called Maypo.

Firmly committed to protracting the experiences of a boy's life, Riswold managed to remain an undergraduate at the University of Washington for some seven years. He received a bachelor's degree in history before chickening out on "the idea of law school." Then he went back for another BA in philosophy, because he wanted to go on to advanced graduate research on the work of certain nineteenth-century German philosophers. But after graduation, when Riswold discovered that his inability to read or speak German might seriously impede this particular career route, he went back to college again for a third BA, this one in communications.

In 1979, Riswold had a part-time job working for the Seattle SuperSonics basketball team, which led to a full-time job with the Seattle ad firm the Sonics employed. Riswold figured he'd stick with advertising until he figured out what he really wanted to study during his next pass through school.

But then he heard about a tiny ad agency in Portland that was looking for a writer. Riswold submitted his résumé and soon moved to Oregon to work for Wieden & Kennedy. He thinks he was the sixth employee of the agency.

Advertising was always a touchy subject inside Nike, because

Knight was known to believe that the whole process was phony. Athletes were the real ticket. Real athletes in authentic shoes would draw the public to the goods because of the honesty of the process. Bowerman still referred to advertising and marketing with the turn-of-the-century term "salesmanship"—which he uttered contemptuously. In 1986, Nike job applicants were warned that if they ended up being interviewed by Knight, they should omit the words "advertising" and "marketing" from their conversation.

Nike began to place a bit of its advertising business with Dan Wieden and David Kennedy's company in 1980. Knight's first words to Dan Wieden when they met were "I'm Phil Knight, and I hate advertising."

But by the late 1980s, the relationship of Nike and the by-then much-decorated and annually awarded ad shop in Portland was the stuff of Madison Avenue legend. Nike had actually transferred its national advertising business to the much larger Chiat/Day Agency in 1983. A Chiat/Day creative team had created the first Air Jordan commercial. But by 1986, Nike and W & K were again a team, and soon thereafter the Wieden & Kennedy offices in Portland sported a basketball court replete with bleachers. The Nike model—or antimodel—became the basis of the philosophical and managerial culture of the ad agency and helped Nike out of a period of decline, doubt, and introversion by gleaning what was noble and cool about the tribal Nike style and worldview and then packaging their temperament and sports-lust as television commercials, magazine ads, and billboards. The customers, with W & K's help, would finally understand that Nike meant something more than shoes.

Around the time Jim Riswold mentioned his fascination with the multitalented kid named Bo, a new class of air-cushioned shoes were ready to debut. Tinker Hatfield and Mark Parker had been wondering if perhaps the customers would become more excited about the Air technology if they built them a little window in the side of the heel through which to actually "see" the gas.

After discussions with Wieden & Kennedy staffers, it was agreed that Tinker's new Air Max running shoe could be a way to resubmit the air bags to the public. The new shoe would be cast as the technical revolution it really had been back when Frank Rudy showed up years earlier. And the shoe would be portrayed as indicative of a much larger revolution now at hand. **137**

Knight was now saying that perhaps the running boom had been only the advance wave of a much larger health and fitness revolution to which Nike had never attached itself in a fundamental way.

Many members of the generation that came of age to the sound of the Beatles song "Revolution" were shocked and offended by the cooptation of that sacred piece of postwar culture to the cause of selling shoes, but few Americans also failed to see or hear the new commercials. A lawsuit on behalf of the Beatles increased publicity for the ad, and after the initial shock, the artful juxtaposition of black-and-white film showing nonfamous people swimming, biking, and weight lifting with shots of Michael Jordan and John McEnroe (in the cross-trainers he now wore during every tennis match) doing their respective sporting things seemed to captivate viewers and project an attitude that was absent from other TV ads.

The message seemed designed to diminish the distance between the greatest athletes and people who play and exercise for fun. Though Nike dogma would have previously precluded the potential muddying of a great athlete's image, the carefully contrived commercial ennobled every kid, pro athlete, and duffer who appeared. With the Beatles in the background, the commercial was like a ninety-second celebration.

And the new shoes moved out of the stores.

Shortly after the "Revolution" commercials aired, Jim Riswold's boss, Dan Wieden, was giving a presentation to advertising director Scott Bedbury and the other managers on Nike's ad board. Wieden spoke of a generalized strain of guilt shared by Americans who had let health and fitness issues slide or had managed to so complicate their lives that exercise and health had never become part of their routines. Wieden said Nike ought to address the powerful sense of ennui he perceived in the culture. He said that the "Revolution" spots showed that the right ads could get people out of their chairs and into the shoes.

"What we need to convey," Wieden said, "is just go ahead, just fuck it."

But the card that came up on the projection screen displayed a different way to say the same thing.

Everyone in the room looked at the words—"Just Do It"—and most of them were impressed.

Riswold was finally assigned the job of creating a way to connect Bo Jackson—who would never actually play his sports in cross-trainers—with the new category of shoes. Riswold's first attempt was a photographic concept for billboards and walls that depicted the powerful bare-chested torso of the athlete clad in football shoulder pads. Bo also held a baseball bat across the back of his neck like a yoke.

Bo had gotten married the day before the photo session, and a close examination of the billboards revealed the face of an endorsement athlete who would have preferred to be on his honeymoon.

Bo Jackson had mellowed considerably since his days as a troubled and fatherless child in rural Alabama. He was so tough and fierce as a kid that he been given a nickname derived from the local vernacular for wild boars. He was called Bo-hawg for a while, and the name was eventually shortened to Bo.

Jackson won the 1985 Heisman Trophy as a senior football player at Auburn, but Knight was less than pleased when he discovered that a Nike functionary had, without his approval, agreed to a $100,000 endorsement deal with some kid from Alabama who could have played high-profile pro football but had opted instead for a backwater minor league baseball career. But a year later, Jackson was playing major league baseball with the Kansas City Royals, and he'd committed to playing at least part of the next football season with the Los Angeles Raiders.

Riswold wrote a series of commercials that featured Bo exercising like crazy—which Bo really did every single day. He rode a bike like a madman in one and worked out furiously in another. Here, the commercials clearly implied, was the ultimate cross-training athlete. Bo was ready for anything. He was "intense" and "hungry," as the sports clichés have it, and yet the commercials made from Riswold's scripts also conveyed a certain irony. The commercials hinted that Bo had been allowed to understand that his depiction approached perceived limits of mortal capacity. After pedaling the bike like a powerful machine for all but the last few seconds of one of the new commercials, Bo turned and asked with a pregame determination, "Now when is that Tour de France thing?"

The ironies were complex and submerged. Bo was the omnibus athlete of ancient contests, but he was also the American John Henry, dwarfing his bike and ready to vanquish all comers.

The ads were judged quite good inside Nike and Wieden &

Kennedy, but everybody involved knew that the combination of the cross-training innovations and a Bo Jackson who played two professional sports could be made much bigger. And with Nike now drifting as the number two athletic shoe power, an explosive sort of success was all that would be accepted. "They have to be woken up!" Knight would say. "What we need is a way to wake them up all over again."

Jim Riswold had always believed that the "unique selling proposition"—the famous USP, which, according to standard advertising and marketing practices, was that feature or design of a product that distinguished it from the competition—could, under carefully crafted circumstances, be a guy . . . or at least the image of a guy. But while plenty of baseball mitts had been sold over the years because the local Johnny Peskys of a particular time and place had signed their names in the pockets, the massive portion of the general public that a corporation of Nike's current size needed to address did not, as a whole, understand the heroic qualities of great athletes in the way Knight and Riswold did. The trick would be to find a way to cause an athlete to rise above the mire of sports platitudes, the ersatz homilies and the canned emotions that the public had come to expect. A new perspective on the sports hero would have to come through some kind of creative incongruity.

In February of 1988, with the Bo-on-a-bike and other cross-training spots due to premiere that coming spring, Riswold was sitting in McCormick and Schmick's, a bar and restaurant on the corner of First and Oak, a few blocks from the Wieden & Kennedy offices. Nike and W & K personnel often retired to McCormick and Schmick's to cogitate together after meetings at the agency.

"We've got to ignite the category," Nike VP of marketing Tom Clarke told Riswold. "Bo's gonna be making the national highlight reels all the time. It's time for us to really light the fire."

Riswold already knew that Nike was prepared to risk a significant portion of the company's total ad budget on an inspired cross-training campaign.

"Yeah, thanks for reminding me," Riswold said to Clarke, staring into his local beer. "Bo," he said, squinting with fatigue. "Bo . . . Bo . . . Bo what?"

It was almost ten P.M. by then, and several rounds of beer had already come to the table.

"Beau Brummell," somebody said.

"Bo Derek," said Nike ad director Scott Bedbury.

"Bo Schembechler," added another, naming the football coach at the University of Michigan, a member of the ever-growing fraternity of Nike guys.

"Bo Diddley," said Tom Clarke.

A brief discussion about the rock-and-roll performer ensued. Diddley was a godlike figure to many of the most famous British and American rock stars of the past thirty years, but the Chicago-based singer and guitar player had never risen to rock-and-roll stardom himself—in large part because he seemed to regard his songs and all of life in general as a somewhat bitter and, usually, dirty joke. Bo Diddley was one of those underappreciated American originals, a legend few Americans would be able to identify because he simply refused to be anything but himself.

Bo Diddley stories were told, and the names of his old songs were tossed back and forth for several minutes, until Jim Riswold suddenly said, "We have to change the subject. Now."

And everybody at the table knew Riswold had an idea.

Later that same night, celebrating like crazy, Riswold hacked the phrase "Bo knows" out of "Bo, you don't know Diddley," the latter phrase having come to him back in the bar.

As the commercial evolved in his mind, Riswold combined "Bo knows" with the cavalcade images of Nike stars hailing from different sports that had looked so good in the "Revolution" ads. Inside a sixty-second commercial, the cross-training implications projected by Bo really "knowing" football and baseball could be overtly ironized through testimonials to his limitless powers from other Nike stars. Jordan could testify that Bo knew basketball. McEnroe could say that Bo knew tennis, too.

Several years earlier the sports marketers had signed ice hockey's reigning genius, Wayne Gretzky. It was thought Gretzky could help the Nike Canada division, and Knight often said it was imperative that an athlete statistically and visually more superior to his peers than even Jordan was turning out to be—better than other hockey players the way Hank Aaron was better than the rest in baseball—become part of the Nike team.

Riswold figured that the Great One, recently moved into the American marketing spotlight provided by his trade from Edmonton to the Los Angeles Kings, could contend that Bo knew hockey, too. A bunch of outsized weight-lifters on Venice Beach would attest to Bo's knowledge, and, finally, Bo Diddley

141

himself would appear . . . with Bo Jackson in a Bo Diddley hat
. . . wearing spandex workout pants and hacking at a guitar at the
other Bo's legendary side!

By now Riswold was jumping up and down on his bed.

The commercial was designed to open with the words
"Cross-training by Bo Jackson" set against a black background.
The next shot would be another printed message—"Music by
Bo Diddley"—which would identify the sound track for those
millions who couldn't remember the guitar riffs from the 1955
hit "I'm a Man."

The spot would be shot by the commercial director Joe Pytka,
whose powerful, if saccharine, Hallmark commercials belied
Pytka's macho, often ranting pony-tailed presence. Pytka always
traveled with a basketball and liked to take on all comers at one-
on-one—especially the star athletes in some of his commercials.
A huge man—much taller than Bo Jackson—Pytka would once
scream at Bo for not charging close enough to the camera during
the filming of one of the many commercials they would do together over the years.

During the next take Bo ran right directly over the director
and his camera and sliced up Pytka's nose.

The Bo-and-Bo part of the first "Bo knows" spot was filmed
in a nightclub near the Kansas City Royals spring-training facility in Orlando, Florida. The other athletes were shot wherever
they could be found. In Vero Beach, Florida, Pytka filmed LA
Dodgers star Kirk Gibson saying "Bo Knows." Riswold turned
to Nike ad guy Scott Bedbury. "This is gonna be the best fuck-
ing commercial you guys have ever done," he said.

It was on the set with McEnroe that Riswold came up with
the idea of McEnroe turning his "Bo knows tennis" proclama-
tion into a question; and before Gretzky skated up to the camera,
Riswold told Wayne to just stop, shake his head at the thought
of Bo Jackson knowing one of the whitest and most specialized
sports of them all, and say, "No."

By the time Bo Diddley was shown in the commercial—at
first to tell the younger and far more heavily muscled Bo that he,
in fact, knew diddley about music, and in the next shot, "six
months later," to admit that perhaps he did know diddley after
all—the musician's ironic smile and laconic "I'm good but I
don't really care" demeanor provided a near-perfect fillip to the
compressed whirl of jarring cultural, artistic, athletic, personal,
generational, racial, and ironic juxtapositions.

Endorsed inside a minute by the most overtly talented athletes of the time, and begrudgingly accepted by one of the coolest of all the characters from the era when cool was born, Bo Jackson—who had not a single line in the commercial—was about to become, as Michael Jordan would later put it, "a dream."

And Nike was about to ride that dream into what was often referred to as an extended "marketing orgasm" that would continue for another two years.

In June, the commercial was shown to a thousand Nike sales reps in for a massive sales conclave in Beaverton, and they all jumped to their feet at once and applauded and cheered and whistled for five minutes after the last note of Bo Diddley's guitar was heard.

Scott Bedbury went to Knight and proposed that it was time to take one of those old-fashioned Knight-like risks. Knight agreed to double the media investment in the "Bo Knows" spots, from $6 million to $12 million—which was a lot of money for a company not making much money at the time. All running-shoe advertising was put on hold, as was ad support for the burgeoning basketball category. No money would be spent on test groups or focus groups that might help measure the power of the commercial. All the money available and the entire back-to-school selling season would be hung on Bo.

On the morning of the July 1989 baseball All-Star game, a full-page ad in *USA Today* announced that Michael Jordan, John McEnroe, and Wayne Gretzky would all be joining Bo Jackson for the big game that night. A line on the bottom of the page said that anyone who missed the top of the fourth inning—when the Nike spot was scheduled to premiere—would be sorry. This, too, was something of a risk, because commercials during sporting events are often reshuffled; but more than that, promoting your ad—instead of your athlete or your gear—could easily be perceived as cocky . . . and that only if the ad was generally judged as particularly good.

Bo hit a homer his first time at bat; the plane flew over the stadium with the "Bo Knows" sign; smaller "Bo Knows" signs and "Bo Knows" hats were unveiled in the stands by Nike people spaced throughout the crowd. And then the commercial aired in the "A" spot just as planned.

Because of the big inning the American League team had just had, when the game recommenced, there was Bo again, standing at the plate. He singled to the right and went on to win the game's MVP award.

"God," Jim Riswold said as he watched everything fall into place from the stands, "is a Bo Jackson fan."

The commercial wasn't scheduled to run again for almost three weeks, timed to kick off the back-to-school season, but it was shown close to twenty times during those weeks anyway. It appeared on evening news spots about Bo and his brilliant new commercial. It ran on the network morning talk shows and on *Entertainment Tonight.*

The commercial immediately became the talk of the entertainment business, the ad world, and the sports scene. The wit and intelligence of the commercial was widely applauded by critics and various elite observers of popular culture. Nobody complained about Nike denigrating one aspect of popular culture by spiriting into another just to sell shoes—as many had after the "Revolution" campaign—because most viewers who might have felt that way tended to believe that Bo Diddley had always deserved to be more famous, like so many of the lesser-known athletes whose visages Knight had ordered chiseled into the walls along the Walk of Fame.

By the time all the critiques and news features were done, Scott Bedbury figured that Nike had received close to $20 million worth of free exposure.

As soon as the selling of Bo's shoes began, Nike quickly dominated 80 percent of the new cross-training shoe market. Sales of the shoes rose from under $40 million after McEnroe strolled out on the court in his strange-looking grayish shoes, to more than $400 million at the height of the Bo frenzy.

And Bo Jackson, who made around twenty-five cents from every pair of the top-of-the-line cross-trainers sold, became much richer by the day. Jackson was not the best football player or the best baseball player, and very few members of his new following would ever know that he tended to stutter painfully at times, or that he often growled at the sports reporters and columnists who usually form the public perception of most athletes' personalities. In 1988, Bo had even alienated many serious football fans by describing football as a mere hobby—though he had distinguished himself that year as an NFL running back while playing only a half a season with the Raiders.

But the Bo Jackson of the "Bo Knows" commercials had transcended all of that. By early 1991, Bo Jackson was the second most famous athlete in the world. He owned, by then, an "athlete influence rating" of 4.22—to Michael Jordan's 4.46. The hip and irreverent intimations of Bo's athletic superpowers and his happy, self-effacing flailing at the electric guitar and knowing glances at the camera had conspired to make Bo "real"—or at least appear knowable in a way that famous people almost never are.

Bo's image was full of warmth and cool and physical power. In 1988, Riswold's first campaign implied that Bo could do anything. By 1990, he simply "knew." Compared to a more traditional product-endorser—a monolithic white-bread presence such as Bob Richards, the Ward Cleaveresque prototypical letterman and Olympic hero of Wheaties box fame for much of the 1950s and 1960s—Bo was everything.

A *New Yorker* cartoon claimed that "Bo Knows Fiction." T-shirt one-liners appeared on boardwalks and beaches promoting the arguably racist and clearly sexual expansion of the cultural assumption: "Bo Knows Your Sister."

Bo had quickly transcended Kansas City and Oakland and gone national, and when the campaign was rolled across Europe, where soccer star Ian Rush and the cricket legend Ian Botham were inserted as Bo-endorsers with a local flair, viewers in France and Italy who would never see Bo Jackson play or ever be able to describe the basic rules of his games began to walk into stores to buy Nike cross-trainers because they were the shoes preferred by Bo.

By then most Europeans also understood the English phrase "Just Do It," and they knew about the company connected to the words.

The first "Just Do It" ads in 1988 featured the wheelchair racer, Craig Blanchette, who was shown competing ferociously at racquetball and basketball before a shot of his chair was shown. Another starred Priscilla Welch, the marathon champion, who had been a sedentary urbanite not long before winning the New York City Marathon at age forty-two. Another ad starred an eighty-year-old runner named Walt Stack, who ran seventeen miles a day up and down the streets of San Francisco. "Some people ask me how I can keep my teeth from chattering in the wintertime," Stack said during the commercial, puffing along. "I leave them in my locker."

In 1989, very few commercials contained anything like a lingering silence during which a few words in simple type were **145** shown against a black background and left unspoken. At first the idea was intended to address all the rapid channel-surfing and sound-track muting that was being done by television watchers during commercials because commercials were so loud and unpleasant. But something about the starkness of the presentation of "Just Do It" was important to the phrase's elevation as a modern war whoop.

Most members of the educated classes were closed to the suggestion that a television commercial, rather than a book or brilliant doctrine, could actually change people's perception of themselves. A "hot" commercial might add a passing nuance or recognizable line—"Where's the beef?" being a famous case in point—but somehow "Just Do It" managed to evoke countless previously impeded visions of personal possibility. The phrase entered popular discourse like some consumer-age variation on the old revolutionary interrogative, "What is to be done?"

Thousands of Americans felt moved to write letters to or call Nike, and millions of others began to loathe their own lassitude enough to buy a new pair of shoes and hit the road again or visit a gym. A *Time* magazine story about the baby boom generation would quote a social historian saying that the ethos of the largest American generation could be summed up in three words: "Just Do It."

Posters went up in health clubs and many workplaces: "There are clubs you can't belong to. Neighborhoods you can't live in. Schools you can't get into," read text above a runner on a country road. "But the roads are always open. JUST DO IT."

JUST DO IT said a T-shirt worn by students at the Ingham-Okoboji Lutheran Bible Camp in Northwestern Iowa, "Live for Jesus." JUST DO IT read a blaring November 1992 headline in the *New York Post*—by which the newspaper referred to the democratic duty of casting a vote in the general election.

The historical compression of Nike's earliest purposes and the subtle but massive selling mechanism of the phrase was so attractive that Scott Bedbury told Knight that "Just Do It" had to be protected from overuse. "We can't put it on pencils and key chains," he said. "This thing has become much more than an ad slogan. It's an idea. It's like a frame of mind."

In 1991, after Nike had returned to the number one slot in terms
of sales, the American superhero Bo Jackson was very seriously

injured on the football field. His dire medical prognosis inspired the Kansas City Royals to cut him from the team.

During a meeting in Beaverton, Tom Clarke told Knight, "I think we have to accept the fact that Bo's never coming back. Bo's gonna be a lucky man if he's ever able to tie his own shoes."

"I am gonna be back. I'm gonna play baseball again," Bo said to Phil Knight on the phone.

"We're with you," Knight told him.

By 1991, Nike also had several basketball superheroes on the payroll alongside one superhero who transcended the term—"the greatest player in the universe," as one tongue-in-cheek Riswold commercial proclaimed "Air" Jordan.

During 1988 and 1989, Jim Riswold had written one commercial after another—writing twenty-three Nike commercials during one twelve-month stretch. The Air Jordan line hummed along with sales of $200 million each year. Jordan showed himself capable of dominating almost any basketball game he played, and Riswold and his cohorts worked to twist and rotate his heroic athletics in ways that made Jordan "come to life" differently every few weeks.

Riswold was enchanted by the character a little-known filmmaker named Spike Lee played in a film, *She's Gotta Have It*. So essential were Mars Blackmon's Air Jordans to his sense of identity that he refused to take the shoes off while making love.

Riswold badgered his Nike contacts about hiring Spike Lee for months before they finally agreed to let Riswold begin his "Spike and Mike" series of ads. Jordan flashed goofy smiles and toyed with Lee's Blackmon character in some of the funniest commercials seen in years. Riswold and Wieden & Kennedy collected awards every time the award-conscious ad industry celebrated itself, as Michael Jordan felt himself disappearing into a world of other people's fantasies. One of the "Spike and Mike" spots didn't even show Jordan on the screen, but he was there and everywhere by then (and his technical absence allowed the commercial to circumvent an NCAA rule prohibiting the depiction of pro athletes during NCAA tournament broadcasts).

Just before the reinvention process began at Nike, during the fall of 1987, Michael Jordan was on the verge of leaving Nike to form his own marketing company in association with Rob Strasser and designer Peter Moore. During the first of several **147** extremely tense meetings held to discuss Jordan's future with the company, Jordan remembers Knight saying, "Michael Jordan without Nike won't mean anything," though Knight doesn't remember the conversation that way. Knight feels sure that Strasser was trying to manipulate Jordan and turn him against Nike at the time.

Eventually, Jordan agreed to a seven-year contract with Nike that was designed to track the balance of his career. He would get $18 million as a guarantee over that time, though the annual guarantee would be far surpassed by his 5 percent royalty on the net wholesale price of every Air Jordan shoe (a $5–7 million per year, ten-year "total buyout" of Jordan's marketing relationships was discussed and dropped—though it would have quickly played out in Nike's favor). Everyone was happy in the end except Strasser and Moore, and the powerful association of Jordan, Knight, and Nike resumed at full speed.

The larger marketing strategy sustaining Air Jordan now involved creating a "segment," a package that connected the shoes, colors, clothes, athlete, special Air Jordan logo, and other visual images, and the television advertising that would set the other elements of the marketing onslaught into motion.

The Air Jordan basketball segment, or sub-brand, was eventually lined up beside the Air Force segment, shoes designed for players who hit the court hard, players like Charles Barkley and David Robinson (Riswold helped Robinson to become the cuddly, piano-playing "Mr. Robinson" in several successful commercials). The Air Flight segment for which Jordan was originally signed on (and for which he continued to receive royalties despite the association of the shoes with other players) was now pegged to players who imagined themselves as deerlike leapers, those players who dreamed of flying across the lane like Scottie Pippen.

By 1991, a visitor to any playground in the world could find hefty young Charles Barkleys and towering David Robinsons playing Charles-style or Mr. Robinson–style in their Air Force shoes. Lean and aesthetic Scottie Pippens flew in Air Flights; little Bo Jacksons pumped iron in thousands of gyms, and, by then, miniature Andre Agassis lit up tennis courts in their peacock-colored Nike clothes and shoes. "Sometimes I'd stuff my hair up into my hat and go to parks, and I'd see the kids pretending they were me," Agassi recalls. "They'd be ripping balls into the far fence, pounding the balls over the fence. And I'd think, 'what have we done?' "

During 1988, Reebok had launched a $25-million television campaign around the slogan "U.B.U."—as in "You Be You"—which was widely judged throughout the shoe, apparel, and advertising industries to be as much a complete flop as the "Bo Knows," Air Jordan, and "Just Do It" campaigns were blowout successes. The Reebok endorser Miloslav Mecir, the pro tennis player, was overheard at a match around the time of Reebok's last campaign at the top of the heap, asking "Yes, but what this mean? I read it—U.B.U.—but what it mean?"

In 1954, a silhouette of a cowboy smoking a cigarette was just the outline of a cowboy smoking a cigarette, but six years later, after a historic blanketing of all available scenery with a specific set of visual images, that same silhouette meant Marlboro cigarettes to most Americans—and Marlboros, in turn, had become implicit of that romantic, lost possibility of individual expression, solitude, and freedom, the time when a man could really be a man.

The modern cultural process often called "branding" bore only a passing connection to the searing of a proprietary mark on a perambulating steer. Marking a product is only part of an ostensibly American art and science that can transform brownish sugared water into a commonly desired fluid called Coke. The most powerful brands have, for several decades, employed marketing techniques to enhance products with some of the compelling characteristics of people. Well-marketed products become brave or sexy.

For much of the post–World War II era—in particular, since the late 1950s—the culture of marketing has had something of a civilizing effect on businesses, since a company centered on marketing worked to create customers. Profit became less an end in itself than the reward reaped from customers who were satisfied—the state of satisfaction being, according to orthodox theory, finding a balance among the Four "P"s: product development, price determination, place of distribution, and promotion. In some companies marketing was subsumed in the management process, but in others—except during the 1980s, when company financiers had their moment out near the corporate footlights—the inspired marketers became the company's resident stars.

The marketing and advertising specialists who serve the most powerful brands are quite often the most intellectually aggressive and culturally conversant members of a given business. Though descendants of American sellers of a rich vernacular tradition often connected to P. T. Barnum, they tend to be the company employees who read books. American marketers, in particular, have taken this original hybrid of economics, psychology, sociology, statistics, and a bit of old-fashioned tell-ya-what-I'm-gonna-do and moved the discipline in the direction of some elevated, Platonic ideal of marketing.

Knight—who was featured in *Harvard Business Review* as something of a guru of state-of-the-art "High-Performance Marketing" during the Olympic summer of 1992, remains ambivalent about the characterization of Nike as the consummate marketing organization. Since 1990, when he became satisfied that Nike was no longer a shoe company, he'd always preferred "sports company."

"Marketing's just getting people to buy things," he said one evening, by way of succinct definition.

"One thing about bullshit," Bill Bowerman observed before a board meeting in 1993, "it's fertilizer, too."

Bowerman is old enough, and Knight is entrepreneurial enough, to believe that in certain bedrock ways, true economic success is won by those who place something in the world that wasn't there before. The two men are sure that they have done that in creating Nike, but intimations of undue "persuasion" as part of the selling process make both men squirm.

Sometimes Knight says he looks into the business environment modern marketing has made—where the gleaning of perspiration from certain country-and-western stars is sold as perfume, where one county's coroner division markets T-shirts bearing an image of the chalk line the police draw on the ground around murder victims—and he doesn't love what he sees.

"I think that the term 'marketing'—just the processes of bringing resources to bear on selling something—isn't necessarily all that wonderful a thing," Knight said one afternoon in his empty conference room. "The way I relate to marketing is as sociology. What Nike does well is interpret what people are doing, what they are interested in, and we've been lucky enough to align ourselves completely with what we perceive. In this day and age, the act of trying to sell somebody something they don't need is a wickedly difficult proposition. For us, marketing is building awareness around the products and reminding people what we do."

Narrowly defined behavioral segmentation is not part of the Nike marketing process, though a calibrated "psychographic" view of the marketplace—"boys who love soccer," "women who would prefer to walk"—had, by the beginning of the 1990s become part of the process of identifying the need for new product and marketing segments. One internally circulated cross-training market analysis depicted a large triangle in the middle of a chart. Down one side of the chart, Nike products were divided into "Max" (top-of-the-line technologies), "Perf" (for performance), "Core" (the middle zone, or "kill zone," as retailers say, where the lion's share of shoes would be sold), and "Entry" (the bottom of the category). Across the top was a far more abstract "consumer spectrum." In the thinnest segment, in the middle where the apex of the triangle crossed the Max product category, a column read "16–26—Young—Hardbody—Sports Driver." At the edge of the page, at the far end of the same spectrum, was the column reserved for the "Peer-driven," "Price-driven," and "Advertising-driven" acolytes of the brand. It looked like market research, but then the document also resembled something found in the appendix of a New Age self-help text.

"You know, it never appeared to me as part of some grand strategy," Jim Riswold added. "I mean, it's not nineteenth-century German philosophy. What's so great about how we do things with Nike is that it all just kind of flows, like a bad case of the runs. It's not like working with General Foods or Procter and Gamble. The shoe industry still isn't carefully studied like the packaged goods industry. There aren't a lot of surveys and test runs—and that's the way I like it."

In 1993, a year in which Nike was one of the first three companies to be inducted into the American Marketing Association Hall of Fame (with Coke and Absolut Vodka), Nike spent $250 million promoting products and the Nike brand. Brands considered for the Hall of Fame had "to show sustained success, represent innovative and trailblazing marketing, and have had a dramatic impact on our lifestyle, becoming enshrined as American icons."

"We determined that we wanted Nike to be the world's best

sports and fitness company and the Nike brand to represent sports and fitness activities," Knight told an interviewer working for the *Harvard Business Review.* "Once you say that, you have focus."

One of the greatest challenges to both the breadth of the Nike brand and the company's internal way of life was the decision in 1987 to muscle into the women's sports and fitness market.

A hard-edged, performance-oriented athletic approach to a larger population of women was tried at first, and the results were disastrous. In August 1989, a commercial showed the tough-as-nails female triathlete Joanne Ernst doing her athletic thing, as "Just Do It, Just Do It" repeated over and over in the background. Ernst comments at the end that "it"—complete physical freedom and the body of the goddess Nike herself, the commercial implied—would be more attainable if viewers could stop "eating like a pig."

The ad was pulled after two weeks of offending the less-athletic women Nike needed to attract. Eventually, a cadre of nearly forty women, hailing from various Nike and Wieden & Kennedy quarters, were drafted to the cause and set up shop inside the boy's club in Beaverton. From the beginning, the women of the new team realized they would have to succeed inside a society of men and women that had largely conformed to the jock and old-Oregonian knack for sucking back feelings.

A new "dialogue" print ad campaign from Wieden & Kennedy copywriter Janet Champ and art director Charlotte Moore addressed athletics as a personal experience of growth rather than a path to glory and physical power. Nonathletic themes abounded in the campaign. Marilyn Monroe was depicted with text that read: "A woman is often measured . . . by all the outside things that don't even add up to what she is on the inside." Another dialogue ad addressed the relationship of mothers and daughters, and another depicted the emotional confusion of a girl in gym class. The male Nike managers in the room grew pale at plans to discuss acne (in fact, to ask the reader to recall when her acne produced protuberances larger than her breasts). The women's team wanted to discuss PMS, hardly a marketable phenomenon in most of the men's estimation—but the members of the women's team held their ground.

152   Fifty thousand calls requesting the *Women's Source Book* of-

fered in the ads came into the 800 number during the first eight weeks of the campaign.

There were calls from therapists asking for reprints, and hundreds of mothers called to ask for copies of the ads for their daughters. Reporters called, and once again, Nike ads were treated like new plays or books.

Two hundred and fifty thousand calls inspired by the "dialogue" ads were fielded during the first two years of the campaign, and two months before Bill Worthington held his Air Carnivore aloft and spoke of it like Hamlet clutching that skull—in mid-February 1993—the Nike "women's dialogue" phenomenon moved to national television. Twelve million dollars was invested in air time for three black-and-white spots, with the actress Sigourney Weaver doing the voice-over.

During 1992, Nike had passed Reebok-owned Avia to become the number two aerobics shoe. New shoes and programs aimed at the one out of every three schoolgirls now playing on an organized sports team were launched at regular intervals. By the beginning of the year, when the often-interviewed trend watcher, Faith Popcorn, coined the term "female think" to describe a new trend that companies with brands to promote must learn to understand, Nike had been on the case for quite awhile, and sales had grown by 20 percent during each of the preceding three years. In response to the marketing challenge presented by shopping patterns that don't tend to bring women into the kinds of sports specialty stores where Nike things are usually sold, the women's team was actively exploring dedicated Nike women's shops, Nike CD-ROM shopping, and even a Nike interactive television channel with a women's tilt.

In the middle of March 1993, another Nike category made possible by the opening of new marketing segments—the outdoor stuff—also began to appear in national television ads. New high-tech fibers had been developed for the all-weather apparel, and a huge line of new shoes and boots was designed to be the four-by-four utility vehicles of footwear.

Nike employees had been hired away from retail stores in Denver and Boulder, Colorado, where the most exacting outdoor "technical gear" customers like to shop. The marketing manager for the category, Ann Wiper, had been both a specialty outdoor retailer and a senior executive with Lowe Alpine Systems, Inc., maker of some of the best camping equipment.

Specialists working for Black Diamond Equipment, Patagonia, the North Face, and other manufacturers of state-of-the-art gear were approached and sometimes hired, and the relatively tiny fraternity of outdoor companies shuddered as Nike bulled into their purview.

The category grew by 100 percent during the year leading up to the spring of 1993.

"There are no hiking referees. No hiker has ever asked to have his hiking contract renegotiated," read one Nike outdoor print ad, apparently contradicting the team athlete focus of other sub-brands and categories. "There are no loud or obnoxious hiking fans . . . no hiker has ever been picked last . . . no hiker has ever won, and no hiker has ever lost."

To each sporting dream a product; to each product a discernible state of mind.

Tom Hartge stood in front of a blackboard in his office one morning, trying to explain the company's latest version of the matrix, a rangy structure of Nike corporate governance designed—and constantly redesigned—so as to retain the romance and collegiality of an entrepreneurial past within the context of a big corporation forever being chased from behind.

Nike's running-shoe category still dominates the American market, but it was now the fourth-largest category at Nike, behind basketball, cross-training, and kids. Because of the nature of the matrix, however, the Nike running-shoe business was an extremely difficult entity to find: Along the top of the blackboard Hartge listed Footwear, Apparel, Advertising, Sports Marketing, and Retail. He drew cylindrical "silos" that descended below each function. "You see, I'm out here as the divisional marketing manager for running. My job is to influence everything that goes on across the matrix," Hartge said, drawing a thick and aggressive line into and through each silo. "I'm an influence broker in terms of the matrix."

The Nike matrix doesn't correspond to any standard matrix most organizational historians would recognize, or even to the more recent "network" corporate forms. Some Nike-watchers have contended that the informal system of getting things done is some Oriental hybrid that Knight adopted from his long association with Japanese companies. After watching Japanese businessmen aver from negotiations in English to chat among themselves, Knight once decided to quietly learn Japanese. He spent two years taking lessons, and yet he found himself still unable to comprehend private conversation during a day of negotiating at a factory. "They figured out that you were listening," Knight's Japanese ally Tom Sumeragi explained, "so they switched to an older style of Japanese."

Knight quit his lessons. "Sometimes you have to acknowledge there are some games you can't win," he says now.

Suppositions about Knight's essentially Oriental management style were made by the veteran sportswriter Frank Deford in a mid-1993 article about Nike published in *Vanity Fair*. "I knew about Japanese companies before a lot of people because I was doing business there and took certain lessons away," Knight said. "But the dominant culture at Nike comes from the playing field. The world of sports marks the way we talk to each other and how we relate. It's not like the imagined sports team in typical corporate parlance, but like a real team. Anyone can step up and make the play."

Conversation about management mechanics as such runs counter to the antiorganization ethos. Nike employees go to great lengths not to reveal their corporate titles. "Oh you want to know my *bureaucratic* title?" they will say if asked to identify their jobs. The idea of "reporting to" another employee elicits a similarly disdainful response, and the very word "supervisor" is as absent from the Nike vocabulary as the word "fashion."

"Structure is necessary, bureaucracy is not" reads one of the many slogans listed in a draft of the Nike "values" and "brand mission" circulating during the spring. "Perfect results count . . ." began another oft-repeated line from the statement of company values, ". . . not perfect process."

Visitors who "bounce around the matrix," as they say at Nike, soon realize that the capacity to influence others is a key to intracorporate success. Hartge talks about "lobbying" various internal constituencies to get things done. People who don't "like to get in other people's faces," as one executive put it, don't do well inside Nike. A certain force of personality and basic competence at Nike gamesmanship are essential.

Bill Worthington finished the colorful drawings of his Air Carnivore during the winter in early 1992, after he surfed in the Pacific with the inspirational Ekin, Duke Stump.

The process of gaining acceptance for his radical-looking shoe began with an informal alliance-building process. Worthington won over Kevin Paulk, the young "developer" who works in the cross-training realm of the production and development silo. It would be Paulk's job to figure out how to make Worthington's design become a shoe. Kevin was the former Reebok guy, though he had actually become a Nike-lover twenty-one years earlier, at the age of thirteen, when a Nike guy set up a table near a track where Kevin was competing in Tucker, Georgia, and began to tell him romantic stories about his shoes. If the Carnivore got the green light, Kevin would help select materials and figure out a price, and would coordinate a schedule that would extend to the production phase and the factories in Asia.

Because making an athletic shoe so often seemed absurdly laborious, the Nike internal development group decided to write down all the steps taken during the fifteen months required to produce a new Nike shoe. The resulting document left out a lot of details, but when it was tacked up to a wall, someone measured the step-by-step map of a shoe and found that it was sixty feet long. And yet a Nike developer working in "a zone" can glance at the drawings for a new shoe and know in thirty seconds what it will cost to make well.

Bill worked hard to win over Tom Phillips, the category marketing manager for cross-training. Phillips liked the audacity of the Carnivore. It was the kind of shoe that would help the cross-training category "mean something again."

Various representatives from different parts of the matrix sat down to listen to Bill Worthington present his "product brief" during the summer of 1992. Tinker Hatfield, who designed almost all of Nike's "statement-level" gear, was there with Sandy Bodecker and Tom Wolff from design and development. Andy Mooney, the lean young Scotsman who oversees marketing by day and goes home to play rock guitar in his own studio at night, was in the room, as was Ron Hill, the former Brigham Young University baseball star, who hails from Nike merchandising and is therefore charged with balancing the retail mix of a line.

Worthington's written brief began with photographs of competitors' cross-trainers. He wrote that the overall size of the cross-training shoe market would be $575 million during the 1992 fiscal year, and that Nike's 69 percent of the market would come out to $396 million in sales. The brief didn't mention that category sales had recently fallen by more than 30 percent after Bo was hurt or that some people inside the matrix were saying that cross-training was over—but then everyone in the room knew that.

Under a heading that read "Confusion," Bill had written that confusion was being "injected" into the marketplace, largely by Reebok, which held 17.2 percent of the market. Reebok had a "cross-trainer for tennis" and another for basketball—which had muddied up the consumer perception of shoes that were supposed to be suitable for both those things.

The brief said REDEFINE in huge letters.

A concise history of cross-trainers began, ending with Riswold's image of Bo with the bat across his shoulder pads. NO LIMITATIONS, the brief said. "Bo Jackson's commitment to athletics provides the most focused definition of Cross-Training's maximum level of product."

Worthington noted some of many new lab innovations that could be worked into the new shoe, but he also posited that what had been missing in other high-tech Nike cross-trainers of late was "visual excitement." Since the reintroduction of Nike Air in 1987, 75 percent of all the shoes contained air bags, instead of 25 percent, as in the past. But air alone was no longer enough.

Certain Nike products were designed and marketed as "brand identification tools," as statements. They existed to reorient, promote, or define a segment of Nike. The Air Carnivore would clearly assault and capture the eye and so support the mystique.

Tinker Hatfield's new Air Max Plus, a running shoe and cross-trainer with an air bag literally bulging with extra cushioning, was selling out all over the country by the late spring. The shoe was a "see it, want it, buy it" kind of Nike sell. But the Carnivore was a shoe with ideas.

Worthington talked about his antisuperhero, Bolt Stingwater. The Carnivore was a wild beast of a shoe. It was clearly part of the answer to the cross-trainer malaise in the wake of Bo's problems.

"This is a niche product. It's not the answer," said Ron Hill, the merchandiser.

Someone asked if this wasn't perhaps the right shoe for Bo in rehab.

Few people thought it was.

"The sellers will be able to romance this shoe. It's unique. It has its own history," Tom Phillips argued.

And so the battles continued.

The 1993 version of the matrix—with all the designers and advertisers together in their own silo—assured a level of consistency that had clearly helped redefine and project the meaning of the Nike brand. But many of the employees inside the web found that good ideas too often died when development, marketing, or design representatives couldn't agree. "It's easy to not be as knowledgeable about how your decisions and actions impact across the silos," Tom Clarke stated in the flashy and often revealing new company newspaper, the *Nike World Record*. The problem was called "silo-blindness" inside the berm.

Even the sub-brands that had helped propel the company out of the abyss of six years earlier were being scrutinized and reassessed by the spring. "We missed the outdoor basketball piece that Reebok jumped up and down on before we did because we couldn't figure out where it fit," complained advertising manager Scott Bedbury. "Was it Force? Was it Flight? We got handcuffed."

Criticism of the absence of a more coherent organizational form inside the company could also be heard regularly over coffee and healthy lunches. Some employees thought the matrix was too "political." Several of the go-aheads Tom Hartge had secured on new products and plans recently were widely thought to have resulted from his long, breathtakingly fast training runs with Tom Clarke. Others—notably Tinker Hatfield—were considered classic matrix "cowboys," employees who were so good at "finessing the matrix" that they had figured out how to get things done by circumventing the web altogether. The cowboys thought of themselves as "creative" and "entrepreneurial"—like Knight in the old days. Others disdained instinct-driven actions as the cause of the troubles of the 1980s.

"I fear that we no longer make quick decisions based on personal insights," Tinker Hatfield declared. "It's true that I'm fed up with the corporateness of this culture. Some creative work must be done outside the matrix."

Few visitors to Nike from companies half its size would perceive a "corporateness" inside the berm. But then everyone from the outside who has ever sold Nike for a few years or bought from them or even spent a long time hanging out inside Nike, realizes that the culture—arrogant though it is so often accused of being—includes a ritual stream of self-criticism. The image-meister, Gordon Thompson, was stunned one day when Tom Clarke asked him to redesign the Swoosh, the ubiquitous Nike logo and symbol. But Thompson was nonetheless well into the work at hand when Clarke told him that it was merely an exercise in "parallel thinking" designed to keep him sharp for the good of the matrix, to keep him on his toes in the way an employee should be at a loose-jointed and iconoclastic, risk-taking, hypercompetitive association of youthful would-be entrepreneurs . . . of a company that is forever—at least in some ideal sense—at play.

"Write the book. Don't follow it," one of the repeated sayings goes.

"Think outside the box."

And everything must happen fast. Though a process might have sixty feet worth of small-print steps, that process will run along in overdrive at Nike. "It's been running at such a high and fast level for several years now through this time of renaissance," Tinker Hatfield said. "Sometimes I don't know what could rev me up again, but then I realize I'm addicted to the process. I'm completely addicted to the pace. And—like so many other people around here—I just can't live without the chase."

For half a year Bill Worthington and his allies among the pro-Carnivore forces fought inside the matrix. "Seven months of screaming and yelling and team-building and refusing to give up," Bill remembered, fondling the Durabuck softness of the sample Carnivore's green upper. "The question now was whether the consumer would be able to appreciate the technology inside the shoe, or to understand its true personality. There are no compasses inside the matrix. We ride on our gut feelings.

"I designed the Carnivore for serious athletes. When it comes out in August there won't be much advertising, and there won't be a statement athlete to help promote it. The shoe will have to sell on its merits," Bill said in his cool way, turning his invention pod-side up. "People will tell each other about the Carnivore. They'll say, 'Here's a shoe that represents the aggression of sports.'"

PUSAN, REPUBLIC OF KOREA

June 1993

Toes pointed forward and trundling quickly along a conveyer belt through a factory known by its nickname, T3, the Air Carnivores in progress looked like the result of some terrible accident involving an athlete team and a moving sidewalk. At the far end of the long production line, the green Durabuck and Velcro-strapped uppers sat bulging and bloated to one side, as ineffectual and unaggressive-looking as those tea cozies old ladies in England place over the top of weathered, ceramic pots. Women working shoulder-to-shoulder along line number four, up on the second floor of the Tae Kwang Rubber factory, would grab the lifeless uppers and attach them to the Carnivores' soles through the rapid application of sharp knives, skivers, routers, glue-encrusted paintbrushes, and a lot of manual dexterity.

By the time the Carnivores motored past the gaze of a twenty-one-year-old T3 inspector named Yoo Hee Jeon, all the aggression Worthington had built into his conception of the shoe had been cemented into place—often under the weird, anachronistic glow of 1960s-style black-light tubes that allowed workers to see the luminants mixed into the cement that had to spread completely over the surfaces to insure a perfect bonding.

Yoo's eyes would barely move as she studied one shoe after another. Every so often, she'd see an imperfection—a wayward stitch or a crooked connection between soles—and she would grab the offending shoe, putting it aside without ever taking her eyes away from a day's run of Carnivores that would yield two thousand pairs of shoes.

Above the loud whooshing sounds and variously pitched buzzing noises emitted by the belts, lights, and pneumatic machines, Yoo said that the complex shape of the soles surrounding the Carnivore's front and aft air bags made it a challenging shoe. "When I first saw this shoe, I thought—wow—this is different," the inspector said, as translated through the agency of Mr. T. H. Lee, a tall and refined second-generation South Korean shoe man who has worked for Nike in Portland, the Philippines, and most often here in his hometown—the classic Asian "shoe city" of Pusan, South Korea.

More than eighty women worked the line with Yoo Hee Jeon, most of them dressed in simple, hospital-green dresses covered by aprons made of cloth or plastic garbage bags. Ceiling fans above their heads casually mixed solvent vapors with the steam rising from machines that pressed materials together. Bare fluorescent bulbs cast a penetrating white light above the lower, black-light tubes. Some of the black-light tubes were shielded, this since an American study released six months before the June run of Air Carnivores reported evidence of long-term eye damage resulting from constant exposure to the purple light. Some of the old-fashioned glue pots sat under protective roofs of glass reminiscent of the sneeze guards over suburban salad bars. Exhaust vents hung above the stock-fitting line, installed before it was realized that the solvent vapors are so heavy that they fall to the floor rather than rise to the ceiling.

"Inside the business," said T. H. Lee as he shook hands with the Nike-employed production managers who watch the stock-fitting lines of T3, "we talk about the three 'D's that characterize this kind of work. It's dirty, dangerous, and difficult. Making shoes on a production line is something people do only because they see it as an important and lucrative job. Nobody who could do something else for the same wage would be here. It's less dirty, dangerous, and difficult than it was in the past—but it's not an easy way to spend a day."

Yoo Hee Jeon, who was dressed in an inspector's blue shift instead of the general worker's green, said she had come to the big city of Pusan from a rural village in the northern provinces because she couldn't imagine spending her life on the tiny and hardscrabble family farm. Like most young Koreans without privileged childhoods, Yoo was quite proficient at reading and math. She was taking classes after work four nights each week, and though the comment inspired no apparent emotion when she spoke, she said she liked to hit the dance clubs after class.

Ever since 1990, when the "sunset" began as so many of the shoe jobs and shoe factories of Pusan began to move on to other Asian locales—one third of all South Korean production had disappeared in less than three years—the famously lengthy South Korean work week had been reduced for the shoe workers. Yoo and her colleagues began work at seven forty-five A.M. and left at five-thirty P.M. during these last days on the line at T3. On Saturday, the plant cleared out at four P.M.—which Yoo likened to working "half a day." Most of the workers on the line, a population clearly divided between young women Yoo's age on one hand and women who were fifty or over on the other, said they knew that the Carnivore would be among the last shoes they would ever make.

"Things change," T. H. Lee said in his slightly British accent. "Shoe empires in Asia rise and fall very quickly. The great Sam Hwa, my first employer, expanded until it was the second largest shoe corporation in Korea with over twenty thousand workers. It was the largest silk maker in Korea. Now it is bankrupt."

T.H. stopped on an exposed cement landing and pointed over the rooftops. "Over there was Kukje Corporation, where twenty thousand people worked in one factory. Now it's being converted into apartments and condominiums. Kukje ran one hundred and thirty production lines and was the largest Nike- and Reebok-maker in the country."

From the landing, a street vendor pushing a handcart full of watermelons was visible through a thick fog of dust. The man called his customers down to the street with a battery-powered megaphone. He slowly navigated a thin, truck-filled thoroughfare beneath looming Victorian-looking factories, corrugated steel fences, acres of filthy windows, and many signs that were too worn away to read.

Not long ago, the T3 factory was located in an outlying industrial sector of the old southeastern port city of Pusan, but as the South Korean economy boomed and joined Singapore, Hong Kong, and Taiwan as one of the "four little tigers" of the Asian economic scene, the city of four million slowly grew around and then beyond the factory. As with most of Pusan, the neighborhood became constantly congested and gridlocked by traffic.

From the landing, parts of the mountain ridges surrounding

the city could be seen cradling Pusan's ever-present cloud of befouled air. The city is bisected by a strangely colored and fetid river called the Naktong. Although the South Korean Bureau of the Environment has inaugurated a program to heal the destruction of the city's ecology—much like Pittsburgh's successful program to cleanse its rivers—Pusan has a long way to go.

A fifteenth-century city that didn't open to the rest of the world at all until the late nineteenth century, Pusan briefly became known to Americans during the early 1950s, when the Korean conflict went so badly for Douglas MacArthur and the allies that the city at the lower right-hand tip of the Korean Peninsula became the general's headquarters before a counter-offensive moved the war north again.

When Korea was partitioned, all of the power-generating capacity and most of the heavy industry was located in North Korea. Most South Koreans believe that the early governmental attempts to build a viable economy upon the South's ravaged, agrarian base was not consonant with the new leaders' efforts to build a new democracy at the same time. The old Hermit Kingdom quickly descended into a state of constant corruption, economic failure, and finally, to the military coup of 1960.

The young officer who took charge, Park Chung Hee, reasoned that an impoverished, mostly mountainous nation without many natural resources—and yet one possessed of a literate and famously hardworking polity—might emerge from its ruined state, despite a long history of economic isolation, as an export nation. A series of controlled five-year economic master plans was launched, and exports tripled in less than five years during the second phase. During the early 1970s, the low-tech shoe factories—harbingers of an advancing economy in Japan and Taiwan some years earlier—began to appear in the special economic zone set aside in Pusan.

In 1974, Phil Knight made his famous South Korea visit, an event that T. H. Lee and many others who watched the Korean economy take off soon afterward regard as something like MacArthur's return to the Philippines or the arrival of Commodore Perry in Tokyo Bay.

"I was there," T.H. said, climbing into one of the late-model town cars that spirit Nike expatriates, or "expats," and the travelers from the World Campus who arrive every few days through the untenable traffic of Pusan. "I was the director of sales at Sam Hwa when he came. We could only make typical canvas and rubber sneakers at the time, Converse Chuck Taylors and the like. But we knew that Mr. Knight and Blue Ribbon Sports were doing their business in Japan, with Nippon Rubber and the others. We had a relationship with Nippon Rubber, so we knew that the footwear industry was beginning to transfer away from Japan—to us.

"In 1977, Sam Hwa sent out the first shipment of performance athletic shoes to Phil Knight. The factories began to appear everywhere, almost overnight."

By the time Knight hired T.H. in 1982, Pusan factories were turning out millions of athletic shoes by the month, and South Korea had become the fastest-growing economy in the world.

"It's hard to imagine how strange the comment seemed at the time," said Whanil Jeong, the articulate president of the Dae Shine Trading Company, one of the six high-tech shoe operations in Pusan with which Nike was still doing business in June of 1993. "But in 1975, when I went to work for Sam Hwa, the manager running my orientation program warned us the Korean shoe business would not last long. I was younger then. I thought the man was crazy."

"A plant like T3," T. H. Lee said as the black sedan pulled away from the factory that was churning out Carnivores, "it just didn't keep up. So soon we will stop doing business with T3 and there will be only five Nike factories in Korea."

T3 is owned by one of the many industrialists and leading politicians in South Korea known as President Park. Y. M. Park never went to college and worked his way up to his own factory from the stock-fitting line. His forty-eight-year-old brother, Y. C. Park, is the multimillionaire founder and president of T2—the Tae Gwang Industrial Company—a more technically advanced facility where most of the Air Jordans are still made. Another Park brother, Y.K., runs a factory that supplies Adidas and Asics, and two other Park brothers also had their own shoe factories, both of which went bankrupt in 1991.

The Park brothers are extremely wealthy, though they live modestly by the standards of the internationally well-heeled, most of them still dwelling in apartments in Pusan. The Kims of Sam Hwa are extremely rich, as are the members of the Yang family that controlled the great Kukje plants. Several of the Taiwanese families that own Nike factories established after the Japanese passed along the production of athletic shoes are among **164** the wealthiest families in Asia.

Political liberalization, burgeoning economic growth, and the rising cost of increasingly organized labor that often sends wages up 20 percent a year are usually pointed to as reasons that the Korean shoe industry is disappearing. "Some of these guys whose factories have closed put their profits in their pocket," however, as Nike's thirty-eight-year-old VP for production, a company rising star named Dave Taylor, has put it. "Some of them shut their own doors during the 1980s and now only the most high-tech Korean shoemakers have survived."

By early fall, the writing would quite literally be on the walls at T3. According to an article by Paul Blustein in *The Washington Post*, some of the thirty-five hundred workers laid off would angrily spray-paint the walls with complaints such as "We want to be compensated for working our brains out!"

But the unemployment rate in Korea would still be just over 2 percent. Over the past six years, as the economic shock troops working in light industry like shoe- , toy- , and apparel-making were laid off, the service sector of the Korean economy has grown by a third, encompassing half of all extant jobs. Exports from the heavier, less labor-intensive and better-paying auto and machinery industries—the jobs more attractive to South Korean men—were up by over 50 percent.

Some of the older women on the line at T3 were making close to a thousand dollars a month, enough to have cable television and expendable income for other indices of an elevated standard of living.

Fifteen percent of the $29.50 Nike would pay Tae Kwang Rubber for each pair of Air Carnivores went to paying the workers on line four. Roughly 60 percent of the price Nike paid to make the shoe went to purchase components such as the synthetic leather uppers. Another 5 percent went to "indirect" labor costs and handling, 10 percent to the factory's amortized costs (largely the making of expensive molds), administration, and overhead. And 10 percent—around $2.95 per pair—was built into the formula as T3's profit.

Developer Kevin Paulk had figured out that the Carnivores could be "landed" in Nike's far-flung warehouses for $36.80 per pair, this after paying $1.40 in shipping costs and $5.90 to U.S. Customs in duty charges. (Though the final results wouldn't be made public for several weeks, Nike would report $365 million in profit during the fiscal year that had ended on May 31, 1993. Over the course of the same year, the company paid $175 million in customs charges—over and above other taxes—to the Federal government.)

Retail stores would pay a top price of $70 for their Carnivores—though most of the stores would get some kind of discount for ordering in advance as part of the "futures" program, or by ordering close to fifteen thousand pairs in one fell swoop, as the cross-training buyer at the Foot Locker chain chose to do. Around $4 of the $25 or so separating the landed cost to Nike and the cost to retailers was apportioned to taxes, and another $15 to running the business in Beaverton, to paying Knight and Bo and Bill Worthington and all the others on the team.

A final profit of $5.50 per shoe was close to industry standards, but over the past two years—because Nike was on top, connected to sports, and perhaps a bit self-satisfied in ways critics had often noticed—the process by which Nike produced and reaped profit from its Asian-made shoes had become the subject of widespread, if cursory, scrutiny.

Nike's offshore practices had been consistently criticized in the press since 1991. Labor conditions in Chinese and Indonesian factories were questioned in some of the reports, pay scales of Asian line workers and famous athletes were compared, and Nike was even blamed for abandoning the American shoe manufacturing industry of which it was never a significant part.

A few days before the November 1992 U.S. presidential election—in the wake of much public discussion about Nike's power in the wake of the Dream Team affair and Alonzo Mourning's novel, all-encompassing management contract and subsequent holdout in Charlotte—a forthcoming "million-dollar ad campaign" against Nike was announced by a foundation supported by labor unions and domestic manufacturers called Made in the USA. American consumers, a Made in the USA press release said, would soon be asked in magazine and newspaper ads to send their "dirty, smelly worn-out sneakers to Nike chairman Philip Knight."

"Friends, Runners, and Countrymen," a page inside the press kit began, "Send Phil Your Shoes. . . . Tell him that other companies, like New Balance and Saucony, make high-quality athletic shoes in the United States."

A Made in the USA spokesman said that Nike was chosen as the target of the campaign because of its fame and "Just Do It" slogan. "That's what we want to put in Nike's face," said Made in the USA chairman Joel Joseph, "to just do it and bring it [jobs] back to the United States."

The envelope prepared as an example of a future Made in the USA mass mailing bore a huge LET'S JUST DO IT banner and a bold-typed "Phil Knight, Spike Lee, Michael Jordan, and Bo Jackson are millionaires thanks to thousands of Americans who lost their jobs. . . ."

National television reports immediately picked up on the campaign, which included accusations of exploitative wage scales and poor working conditions confronting workers making Nikes abroad. Eventually the Made in the USA campaign generated so much publicity from the mere announcement of its intended campaign that the organization never bothered to run more than one ad.

Nike responded by pointing out that, out of the more than three hundred American shoe factories that were shut down during a general exodus during the 1970s and 1980s, only two ever made Nikes. Those were the company's own factories in Exeter, New Hampshire, and another in Saco, Maine, which were opened during the mid 1970s, when just over a million pairs of Nike shoes were ordered in a year instead of the 1.5 million pairs required every week in 1993.

It was true that there never was a high-tech athletic shoe infrastructure in the United States. Knight's earliest vision involved addressing the lack of innovation and will to invest in the domestic industry by designing shoes for athletes in Oregon and having them made in Japan. Few of the departed 65,000 American shoe manufacturing jobs the Made in the USA campaign's anti-Nike rhetoric referred to in 1992 were ever connected to Nike.

Adidas was the only large company in the business that had retained a domestic production, and part of the German company's decline was attributed to efforts to keep production in Europe. When Adidas did begin to import shoes from the Far East and North Africa, the company was immediately accused of "delocating," as it is called in European Community parlance, at the expense of European workers.

Knight, Liz Dolan, and other Nike officials argued that most of the 6,200 American employees of the company have the kinds of white-collar marketing, design, computer, and other jobs that are valued and desired in an advanced economy. One thousand two hundred others were directly employed in domestic manufacturing of shoe components—largely at the Tetra air bag membrane factory and Cole-Haan—more, they noted, than any other American athletic-shoe company.

Nike employees fumed when Maine senator George Mitchell took potshots at Nike for absconding with American production lines. By virtue of its Cole-Haan subsidiary, Nike was the largest employer of shoe workers in Mitchell's state. It was certainly true that the athletic-shoe empires had prospered at the expense of traditional makers of athletic footwear, but this was an indirect competitive phenomenon—and never part of the anti-Nike rhetoric to which Mitchell was responding.

Nike managers would point out that Barbie dolls came out of the chute in Singapore for a buck or two, and a billion-dollar empire now rested upon Barbie's sharpened, Asian-made, low-cost hips. Compact discs cost less than eighty cents apiece to musicalize (not including royalties), and they went out of stores at $15.98. A $6 lipstick cost the cosmetic manufacturer a quarter, and certain pesticides that cost $2 to make are sold to farmers for close to $100. The total production cost of most prescription drugs usually represented less than 10 percent of the retail price.

"And how much do you think a seventy-five-cent can of Coke costs to make?" Dave Taylor occasionally complained. "The Coke inside costs less than the can."

Taylor was perfectly willing to admit that the difference between making the Air Carnivores at T3, where the average line worker took home $800 or so each month, worked out to about $4.50 per pair of Nikes. And Taylor said it was the prospect of reducing that $4.50—perhaps by using the new factories in China and Indonesia where line workers take home the equivalent of $100 per month—that has created the propensity of athletic-shoe companies to "follow the market" into nations farther down the developmental ladder.

"Taking three dollars or four dollars out of the cost of the shoes makes a big difference to the bottom line," Taylor, who bears a passing resemblance to the actor Tom Hanks, said. "But we don't actually get four dollars back in margin. The cost of getting the best components to Indonesia and China from Japan or Pusan is a lot higher than if they drove the parts down the street. The Korean factories that acted like so many American industrial companies when global competition became part of the economic vista are dead or dying now, and yet we're still making millions of pairs of shoes in Korea, because some of those factories are just so good at it. Very few of the Taiwanese factories Nike employs have closed down. The Taiwanese plants stayed on top of technological advances. They were willing to keep up with us as we forged ahead."

"It's all happened so fast," the Nike vice general manager for Korea, T. H. Lee, said as the company car sat still in the kind of heavy traffic residents of Pusan have come to expect. "It seems like only yesterday that Phil Knight came here for the first time."

T.H. talked about his children—the one attending high school outside of Portland, and his other son, currently a student at the University of Chicago. He said he could never have dreamed that his children would be raised in the United States.

"I guess the only thing you can be sure of," T.H. said, "is that things will always change."

Michael Donaghu, a twenty-six-year-old Dartmouth grad, former five-thousand-meter runner, and rising Nike developer of running shoes, laid his chest down on a huge conference table and moved his face to within a few inches of one side of Tinker Hatfield's latest creation.

Three pattern engineers employed by the Sewon Company of Pusan leaned in from the other side of the table to get a closer look, too. One of them even crawled up on the table to study the strange, mustard-colored shoe the powers-that-be back in Beaverton had told Donaghu they wanted out in the marketplace by the middle of 1995. Michael began to draw lines on the side of the sample shoe built back in Beaverton, but each time he made a mark, he would wait for C. L. Lee, the Sewon engineer, to nod before he continued. The men jackknifed over the table didn't say much, but they were clearly communicating on a variety of levels via the arcane markings on the shoe.

The conference table beneath them was gray, the linoleum floor was gray, and the old-fashioned fans whirring atop high poles were the same shade of gunmetal gray. The only bright color in the room was Tinker Hatfield's prototype "harvest gold" (in official Nike palette terms) invention.

Michael Donaghu had led a typically youthful intermatrix Nike team to Pusan from Beaverton knowing that only Sewon—and perhaps two other Pusan factories—possessed the technical capacity and experience to make the revolutionary shoe Tinker called the Air Loom. **169**

DONALD KATZ

Sewon was one of the Korean companies that had invested in machines with microchips inside, and they offered lower costs because of building dedicated chemical facilities where they could make their own polyurethane—called "PU" in shoe circles—and the softer, lighter, superior cushioning compound Nike helped invent called Phylon.

In a room next door, a Brown & Sharp three-dimensional digitizer displayed the schematic image of a shoe on a computer screen. A powerful Silicon Graphics machine beside it displayed the contours of another shoe, and yet another machine against the wall drove a blue laser around the top of a smoking piece of leather.

"They know they have to be better and much faster than the cheaper producers," Michael Donaghu had said during a gathering the previous evening. "They're really under the gun."

Donaghu had joined the table full of Nike expats and the members of his Beaverton team for yet another "dinner with a factory" in a bar called O-Kim's, located just a few hundred yards down Pusan's hotel-lined Haeundae Beach from the Pusan Hyatt, where the teams from Beaverton arriving almost every week in Pusan tend to stay. Warm beer was served at O-Kim's, and a jukebox played a Korean singer's rendition of "The Yellow Rose of Texas" to the accompaniment of a lone organ.

The Beaverton contingent included a thirty-one-year-old developer named Rachel Speth, and Ed Kinnaly, a twenty-five-year-old product-line marketing manager who worked in "running" under Tom Hartge. A shoe designer with long hair, Bob Lucas, was the employee who said that working at Nike was not unlike "surfing down the face of a wave" in one of Mike Doherty's videos.

Two of the 183 American expats stationed abroad for Nike were also there. Mark Sheehan used to be a member of the Ekin cult—with a Swoosh tattoo on his leg to prove it. Now he was a shoe developer working out of the Nike liaison office in Pusan. When new prototypes were presented at a factory, Mark liked to put the shoes on and run ten miles across the polluted and hilly expanse of Pusan to test them out. Knight used to test shoes this way in the old days.

A soft-spoken Canadian developer named David Jones was also at the table. A pair of the prototype hockey skates the Nike sample-room cobblers once built for Wayne Gretzky sits in David's office overlooking Pusan harbor, where one hundred

Korean nationals and twenty-two Nike expats work on the six-
teenth floor of the Kukje Building. The Nike office also houses
testing machines that beat up shoes randomly selected from the
lines.

Like all Nike expats, Sheehan and Jones were given a six-
meeting preparatory course before they took off. Subjects included the do's and don'ts of living offshore, with special
sections on the culture of the country where they were bound.

The conversation at O-Kim's turned to "shoe dog" talk and
the kind of American storytelling that can be heard all over Asia,
tales of economic adventure having replaced the storytelling of
soldiers and explorers over time: "I liked it, all right, but Thailand was just too hot and just too weirdly formal," the former
Ekin Mark Sheehan said. "But I hear Indo makes Thailand seem
loose. I hear you can't even get mad at people down there."

"In the Philippines, there were power problems every day,
customs nightmares, and corruption everywhere you looked,"
T. H. Lee recalled of his Philippines years.

After coming to study South Korea's economic miracle himself, Philippine president Ferdinand Marcos went home and
vowed to turn his nation into a shoe paradise, too. American
managers who had the power to open factories with big orders
were greeted by well-orchestrated public demonstrations—lines
of cheering villagers waving flags would fill the roadways.

"Aside from having no electrical power much of the day, in-
surgents were running around in the countryside near some of
our factories," T. H. continued. "One time I was driving from
Manila to Bataan when men with assault rifles and masks lined us
up outside the car. They let us go when we said we worked for
the shoe factories."

The Philippines were eventually judged a quagmire by Nike
production managers, and the company pulled out. Though no
shoes are made there now, a vibrant door-to-door shoe-selling
network that used to move Tupperware still retails a lot of Nike
product made by factories in neighboring nations.

It was acknowledged among the Nike Asia hands gathered in
Pusan that Thailand—despite its low wage base—would be receiving decreasing numbers of Nike orders. The sewing operations in Thailand eventually had become proficient, but the shoe
factories didn't measure up. The aspect of the shoe life in Thailand that seemed to come up most often among expats was the
cultural differences between local workers and the shoe experts

imported to tell them what to do. The term "culturally challenging" is often used by the expats and the Nike visitors who regularly make the sixteen- to twenty-four-hour flights to the shoe capitals from Portland.

At first, Korean managers were sent to Thailand and Indonesia by the Pusan factories to set up early operations, and the Koreans were notable for having set new standards in deficient industrial diplomacy. Cross-cultural sensitivity had never been a prominent characteristic of Korean society in general, and humane personal relationships were definitely not among the strong suits of a Korean military order geared to domestic repression of troublemakers and the looming possibility of invasion from the North. The proud Thai religious traditions and the devout Muslim faith practiced by most of the workers who came to the new factories in Indonesia after 1988 were of little interest to the former Korean military officers often sent in to manage the plants.

"Koreans are, well . . . trained to work hard and late," T. H. Lee said in his soft voice. "I grew up expecting to work hard from seven in the morning to eight at night, Monday through Saturday, and if delivery schedules were behind, on Sundays too. What happened in Thailand and then in Indonesia was that many of the supervisors sent in were former lieutenants and captains, the kind of men who only understood our way of looking at work."

Management by terror and browbeating led to strikes by Indonesian workers who were fed up with former South Korean Tiger Division types yelling at them. It was suggested that some of the authoritarian managers from Pusan might have been acting out frustrations with Korean line workers whose demands for better pay were chasing the domestic shoe scene away. "They yell at us when we don't make the production quotas and if we talk back they cut our wages," one female line worker at an Indonesian factory making Nikes told a reporter for the *Far Eastern Economic Review* in 1991.

The stories of foreign postings told by Nike employees in Pusan during June often segued into conversation about the dire economic scene in Europe that summer, where a lasting recession was being called the worst in Europe in thirteen years. "Italy is dead. Germany is dead. France is dead. The U.K. is picking up." It was acknowledged that all of the athletic-shoe companies were taking fewer pairs of shoes out of Korea. It was noted at one meal that L.A. Gear's apparent hit with its flashing light shoes would be little more than a flash in the pan, because their Korean shoe-builders weren't making many new ones.

Most of the expatriates working for competing shoe companies tend to ignore the chauvinism that characterizes intercompany relationships back home. Many of the Asian-based shoe hands have worked for several different companies over the years. In cities like Pusan, Jakarta, or Bangkok, the expatriate shoe community is simply too small and too far from home to worry about the philosophical differences separating Reebok and Nike. Most of the Asian factories make shoes for several athletic-shoe companies, so it was easy to get hold of intelligence on other company's orders. Sixty percent of the production of the Sewon plant where the Air Loom would eventually be made goes to Nike, and 40 percent to Asics, Onitsuka having farmed out its own production to other Asian nations for years.

Michael Donaghu's stop at Sewon to discuss the "Loom" was one of four stops he would make with his team. Michael said a good developer becomes "a little cynical" after awhile because he is "the guy who always ends up holding the bag when something goes wrong." Somebody had to make sure that every size seven women's version of a shoe is just as comfortable and serviceable as the size ten version for men. Before the sales force ever waltzes out beyond the berm to sell the line, a developer and a production specialist or two have suffered through months of trial and error, through the slow test runs, when the line crawls along at one-tenth speed, and through laborious weeks of fine-tuning.

The Air Loom project was originally set on the typical fifteen-to-eighteen-month production track, but with sales and future orders faltering for the first time in years, pressure was being applied on Michael Donaghu to make it happen much faster. The Air Raid basketball shoe, after all, had been created in ninety days—and its commando shoe-making process was immediately institutionalized as the Quick Response program.

At the Sewon factory, Donaghu studied the series of extremely slender parallel ribs that rose up from computer-stitched attachments along the sole of the Air Loom. The fingerlike projections were the only firm components on the top of the shoe, rising like the uncrossed warp on a weaving machine. Minimalist in the extreme, the new shoe was little more than a mustard-colored exoskeleton, and absurdly light. Each of the ribs, like the *173* soft neoprene sock, stretched a bit, so the shoe could be snug but never tight.

For much of the past year, Tinker Hatfield had encouraged the other designers to imagine the next generation of Nike shoes as providing protection while also allowing the foot a freedom not unlike running barefoot on very soft and dense grass. The Carnivore's hooflike pods were wrought in this spirit, but the Air Loom took the minimalization process further.

The shoe was an obvious descendent of the Nike Sock Racer, a bright yellow and—as Knight often suggested himself—famously ugly minimalist design from the transitional years of the mid 1980s. The Sock Racer didn't sell well, and the fact that its innovative design was completely obscured by a bumblebee yellow hue that nobody wanted on their feet had helped frame the redefinition of aesthetic purpose during Nike's time of reinvention.

Yet the Sock Racer led to the Aqua Sock, the amphibious Nike footwear recognizable on beaches all over the world; and it led to the Nike Dynamic Fit neoprene liners that added so much comfort to athletic footwear. The theme had now permutated into the wild yellow specimen being prodded, twirled, and drawn upon with pens by members of the Beaverton and Sewon teams.

Speeding up the production process was a significant challenge in that making shoes was still as laborious and technologically unenhanced an industrial process as any other production process in any industry. No matter how inspired a new technical design, style statement, or marketing campaign, the entire industry's productive processes were still based on how fast the women in Pusan, South China, and Indonesia could glue together by hand up to twenty-five pieces of a single shoe.

The laser cutters and computerized stitching machines that made a shoe like the Air Loom possible took time out of the process, but now that true technical innovations seemed harder to come by and more of Nike's competitors were copying aspects of Nike's marketing methods by the day, a new concentration on what could be done to speed up shoe making had become an essential, if somewhat secretive, priority inside the berm. For two years there had been discussion and research applied to the idea of an "automated" shoe. Nike was seeking a proprietary advance in process that would, once again, allow the company to leap way ahead of the pack.

Prototype shoes were still sent out to hundreds of "wear-testers" all over the country, and the development process often paused for months before the well-worn shoes and technical reports came back from the field. For over a year a group working out of the lab had been developing a way to streamline the testing process by replacing the wear-test program with complex computer simulations based on Nike's huge database about the mechanics of the human foot in relation to movement and shoes. The final goal was a shoe that could be fully imagined in digital form, pretested as a "virtual" shoe, and then loaded directly into machines that made parts as a fait accompli.

"The real issue is information," the lab director Tom McGuirk had explained. "Once we can feed the proper information to machines, the whole process—from conceptualization to commercialization—can be automated. We're already close to taking the wear-testing phase out of the process via simulation." Other Nike technicians talk of "stereo lithography" technology, a "bath of liquids on a tray and a laser building shoes in digital slices." Once total automation was achieved, as everyone involved in the project knew, the era of occasionally controversial Asia "out-sourcing" would be over.

"Developing a new way of making shoes is a very high priority at Reebok," Paul Firemen would say later in the year. "We can't keep chasing wages around the globe forever like we do. There has to be a better way."

Knight and the other senior managers were closely watching the automated shoe project's progress by midsummer, and Knight had made it clear to the lab-dwellers and development specialists that if any company was going to revolutionize the production process of making the shoes, that company had to be Nike.

"We keep changing and working hard to keep up with Nike," said Michael Ku, the managing director of T2, who stopped in to say hello to Donaghu and the others during their visit to T2 later in the day. "The domestic situation is certainly changing around us," he said. "So we will continue to invest and study the new technologies. And during the spring of 1994, we will open our first joint venture factory. We will finally begin to make shoes for our friends at Nike in China."

• • •

DONALD KATZ

The once-verdant countryside visible from the roads running west out of the South China boomtown of Guangzhou looked like some massive strip-mining operation had occurred—or perhaps an aerial attack by planes carrying defoliants. Rice paddies were drained of water, and all hint of color had been bleached away by the sun. Fertile black bottomland that was very recently covered by deep green vegetation for all of a twelve-month growing season lay cracked and whited and covered over by hundreds of construction sites stretching out to the horizon.

Workers in traditional conical straw hats stood atop fifteen- and twenty-story-high scaffolds made of hand-lashed lengths of bamboo. Great cement struts marked bridges to be. In several villages, where the road had to be widened so that the endless cavalcade of trucks could bounce along the pitted thoroughfares—occasionally in both directions at the same time—the fronts of entire buildings had been simply sheared away, the villagers, still at home, discernible inside.

"Even in ninety-one this was some pretty turf," said the Nike general manager of China, Charlie Brown. "It's just unbelievable what they've done. . . . Look, this company must be building a little soccer stadium for the workers," he said, pointing into the swirling, sunlit dust. "A Mead Johnson factory is going in down there. . . . Colgate's over there. . . . The Wrigley plant's there. . . . And there's H. P. Fuller, the chemical and glue company."

Charlie Brown had "run China" for Nike for the past two years. At thirty-five, Brown was a twelve-year Nike vet—a lifer—with stints behind him at the Exeter, New Hampshire, R and D facility in Bangkok, Pusan, Beaverton, and then the Nike China office in Guangzhou. While based in Thailand and still a single guy, Charlie once took Phil and Penny Knight to see a live sex show in Bangkok's Pat Pong district ("Predictable," Knight recollects). Knight, along with others in the company, call Charlie "C.B."

As the Mercedes meandered along clogged and tortuous roads more suitable to Jeeps, Charlie put the back of his neck on the top of the backseat and stretched out his long legs. The easygoing ex-athlete out of rural West Virginia was dressed for a factory day in elegant wool twill slacks, a woven soft leather belt, and decidedly nonathletic designer loafers. Charlie Brown conformed to a certain archetype of the fair-haired all-American at work in the developing world. Ten years earlier, any journalist with half a notion about the players working the geopolitical outer postings would have wondered if Charlie Brown was a CIA station chief.

In Nike terms, Brown's somewhat sardonic and to-the-point style would have been recognizable in Beaverton or Pusan as typical of the development and production subculture inside the company. A penchant for both irony and pragmatism is in part the result of working with the nuts and bolts of making shoes. But the style also tends to emulate the ironic asides and no-bullshit pragmatism of Dave Taylor, the production VP.

"Let's just talk for a second about how some of our designers *look*," Charlie Brown blurted out one day in Tayloresque style. "You walk through the Jordan Building and you see those wild-colored clothes on some of these people and sometimes you just gotta ask, 'Do people really dress like this in the world? I mean, what a damned show.'"

As we neared the town of Dongguan, only forty miles from Guangzhou but more than two hours away, ancient black locomotives with old-fashioned smokestacks puffed along through withered banana plantations. Peasants swung scythes in the intense tropical sun near huge pipes that disappeared into the many creeks and rivers that flow through the southern delta region. Other pipes spat tons of brown sand and dirt into the ancient, hand-carved irrigation ditches. Shanty shops lined the slowest parts of the road, and at certain bottlenecks, local tough guys had set up ersatz toll booths.

"Bandits," Charlie Brown scoffed as Linda, his driver from the Guangzhou office, a quiet young woman with a blunt haircut, handed over a coin. "Entrepreneurs one and all," Brown said, smiling through the window without sincerity at the young men working the makeshift gate.

Near a tiny village outside Dongguan called Gao Bu, just beyond a gutted former cement factory where red dust was piled six inches high on every remaining wall like russet snow, the Mercedes cruised through a guarded gate and up to the four-story, two-year-old, 35,000-pair-a-day Yue Yuen Factory Number Two. The façade of the factory—one of twelve inside the Yue Yuen complex—was adorned with huge red-lettered Mandarin characters and an equally lofty and bright red NIKE atop a Swoosh.

The Yue Yuen factories—"the biggest shoes-industry kingdom in China," as a Yue Yuen circular boasted—make athletic shoes "with partners" such as Nike, Adidas, Converse, and Reebok-owned Avia, and one of the buildings housed lines producing shoes for the "made in America" running shoes favored by jogging president Bill Clinton: New Balance. (The president had given up his Asics shoes as the Made in the USA sensibility became more widespread.) "We'd rather put our money into our factories than into the hands of celebrities," the New Balance president would proclaim during the coming fall, apparently referring to the fact that most consumers remained unaware that New Balance did business with offshore factories, too.

The shop floors of the Yue Yuen factories are much cleaner, brighter, and better ventilated than the older factories of Pusan. A nineteen-year-old worker named Wong Shu demonstrated a Japanese-made high-speed embroidery machine that powersewed the Nike logo into one piece of soft, gray leather after another.

Wong worked in a pair of extremely tight stretch-pants and a bright and gauzy floral-print blouse. There was a bright blue ribbon in her hair. A few years ago, only the infants of China, aglow at all times in their colorful split-bottomed pantaloons and bright ribbons, demonstrated the Chinese love of color and style that for thirty years was sublimated by the edict of the regime in Peking. The shimmering lipstick Wong Shu wore would have been judged a punishable bourgeois corruption in more fiercely revolutionary times. When Wong was a little girl, most Chinese women's haircuts looked like they'd been administered with scythes, but her dark hair—as with many of the young women working beside her in the great amphitheater of the factory—was feathered and cut at a stylish angle.

"I grew up in a little village in Szechwan Province," she said. "I heard about the jobs in this area from friends and came on a bus. I was very lonely at first, but now I have friends. We all exercise together in the morning at seven A.M. I read. I play badminton."

Theater groups perform along the stale-smelling river beside the factory complex, and there is a very serious basketball league—the up-and-coming world sport having become a local passion in urban and coastal China. A Yue Yuen pamphlet with photographs of the superior life available inside the factory gates showed runners in official-looking togs breaking a tape at the finish line ("Making a sport"), and a picture of a young man clutching a microphone and so clearly lost to after-hours revelries that he looked very close to tipping over ("In the state of being crazy and drunk, at a song and dance party," the caption in the Yue Yuen pamphlet read).

A high wall of clean windows lit the work areas along the production lines at Yue Yuen, and some of the lines had been fitted with ventilation systems below the belts, a response to the solvent fumes having been found to be heavier than air. Supervisors in Nike armbands strolled the broad aisles, and huge posters exhorted workers in Mandarin and English to make great shoes for the good of the national and company cause. One sign in English near the hot and odorous chemical plant proclaimed that Yue Yuen–made soles WILL MAKE YOU HIGHER FASTER AND 3TRONGER. JUST AS THE ARABIA CARPET.

When she first came to work at the new factory, Wong Shu was paid around 350 yuan a month—the rough equivalent of $50. A new bicycle over in the old-West-style village of Gao Bu can be had for 250 Yuan. Now Wong made around 400 Yuan each month, and she said she earned extra money for "bonus work"—overtime pay for hours put in beyond her nine-hour-a-day, six-day standard week, and other payments for "rational use of materials" and producing at a high rate.

She also got a bed in the huge cement dormitory full of hundreds of metal bunk beds, three meals a day, medical care in a clinic staffed by twenty doctors, and two weeks of vacation.

Wong said she spent half of her wages every month and sent the other half home to her parents. Workers in the Yue Yuen post office report that around 70 percent of the twenty thousand workers at the factory send money home every month. As every plant manager, political official, and American executive working the economic eruption in South China will repeat, the shoe workers making Nikes at Yue Yuen and the other factories are paid a higher wage than most Chinese doctors and university professors. More than a few of Wong Shu's colleagues at the factory have college degrees.

Ninety percent of the workers at Yue Yuen are women, as are 80 percent of the supervisors—a much higher portion of female managers than in the older factories back in Pusan. The average age among workers is twenty-one, and applicants must show government documents indicating that they are at least sixteen. The women and girls live in segregated dorms and must obey a long list of rules concerning fraternization with men and curfews. Several recent American reports of worker exploitation in athletic-shoe factories highlighted the fact that workers inside the compounds needed permission to go out at night. "These people have never been away from home or had any unsupervised time before. Without the rules this place would become a maternity ward," Charlie Brown said as he went into a sitting area for tea and cookies with a group of local managers. "Their parents expect them to be protected here."

After tea was served, Charlie and the Nike production manager assigned to the factory, Jarmo Vahtervuo, a burly Finn who came to Nike when Finnish shoe production migrated to Asia, began to tease Taiwanese Yue Yuen manager Frank Lee, who was apparently hoping that the child his wife was expecting would be a boy.

"It's true," Jarmo was saying, "I've read that the sex of a child can be controlled by changing technique at conception. If you just increase the . . . depth, you get a boy."

"Well Frank," Charlie said, "guess that means you're having another girl."

Frank, a soft-spoken and meticulously polite man, began to belly-laugh.

Frank Lee is a third-generation Taiwanese. He is old enough to remember Chiang Kai-shek and the time of constant tension dividing the tiny island-based Republic of China and the People's Republic across the Formosa Strait, a country over 270 times larger than Taiwan in terms of physical size and home to more than 60 times the number of people.

A militaristic rhetoric of return and revenge was an aspect of daily life in Taiwan for most of the post–World War II era, but Frank Lee is part of a return home that has occurred without the aid of the Nationalist army. Chinese leader Deng Xiaoping told his people to get rich over a decade ago, and after attempts to do so without regional assistance failed to find success, Taiwanese industrialists who had become extremely adept at accruing wealth were invited to do business in the Motherland.

A day earlier, Charlie Brown had been in Hong Kong to have dinner with a member of the Tsai family of Taipei, Taiwan, owners of the shoe production empire called Bao Chen and of the new Hong Kong–based Bao Chen subsidiary called Yue Yuen. Bao Chen is the largest athletic-shoe factory empire in the world—its lines producing sixty to seventy million pairs of shoes per year—and its patriarch, C. J. Tsai, is among the richest of all Taiwanese.

The Tsais' man in Guangdong Province, Frank Lee, does not see his labors five hundred miles from home as part of some victorious return. He says he doesn't imagine his job as a colonial posting either. Because of a singular vision of ethnic community among the dominant Han Chinese, Frank Lee and a third-generation Chinese-American valley girl from Southern California are imagined by more than a billion people as members of the same "overseas Chinese" family. Even at the height of China's isolation from the rest of the world under Mao Tse-tung, it was still widely believed on the Mainland that some day people like Frank Lee would return.

"It is said that we are so advanced in Taiwan, so far ahead of the people of Mainland China," Frank said. "But for five thousand years, the people of China taught the rest of the world everything. For only forty years did the others move ahead. I'm proud of being part of this culture. We are the same people. A lot of intelligence and human power was wasted here for too long. I'm just happy the reunion has finally occurred."

When Deng Xiaoping first decreed that what was left of the Chinese economy was open for business again, he said China would grow and prosper through decentralization. The Communist Party would remain intact, along with its authoritarian political control, but—like South Korea and even the renegade society of Taiwan before—China would flourish and grow rich.

Nike managers immediately began negotiations pursuant to setting up production facilities in China. Phil Knight was always fascinated by China, and he was charmed by his first visit in 1980. For a while after Knight got back from China, it was erroneously rumored inside the company and shoe industry that Knight was spending his long hours behind closed doors writing a book about China.

The early Nike visitors from Portland often slept on cots in the dilapidated German embassy buildings in Beijing. Only the state-run factories were available for contract work at first, and nothing ever went right inside the plants. Five years after Nike began to order Chinese shoes, not one of the twelve Chinese plants had yet managed to make a white shoe. Everything was so dirty and poorly maintained that the shoes came out gray. Running water, electricity, and phones were always in short supply.

But then a new set of revisionist economic policies decreed that new facilities could be built through joint ventures, and others could be foreign-owned if located in certain development regions. The same light-industries shock troops who had served at the front in Japan, Korea, Taiwan, and Singapore immediately rushed in. The Taiwanese athletic-shoe companies had already transferred production facilities to Thailand and Indonesia, countries considered next along the Asian developmental pecking order. Japan resided high atop the economic list (and in many ways Richard Nixon's "cutting loose the yen," as Knight puts it, began the modern low-wage labor tango across Asia). Taiwan, Hong Kong, Singapore and South Korea—the Little Tigers—came next. Then Malaysia, then Macao, the Philippines, Thailand, China, Indonesia, and on down to Vietnam and Burma. When Burmese cities coursed with citizens wearing Walkmans and Nikes, the Asian "out-sourcing" hands tended to agree, then the stock-fitting lines and lasting machines would probably show up in South Asian nations like India and Sri Lanka . . . and in Africa after that.

Some of the same seasoned shoemakers who taught Charlie Brown and other Nike expats the tricks of the trade in Pusan and Taipei were now working in China. As Frank Lee strolled the line, he said that he tried to think of himself and the eleven other Taiwanese managers less as incarnations of the owners than as teachers.

The technical expertise of the Taiwan manufacturers was judged such that Nike maintains an APE—Advanced Product Research—lab in Taipei. "Technically, most of the ten factories I'm using in China are already better than the ones in Taiwan. And we're moving right up on the best Koreans," Charlie Brown said with palpable pride. Chinese factories have stitched the uppers for the last three Air Jordan basketball shoes, and his plants were churning out the miniature, children's version of the Deion Sanders Air Diamond Turfs that would arrive in stores in June 1993. In a glass case behind his desk back in Guangzhou, Charlie kept a pair of the retro, 1994-model black and white Air Jordans, made at one of the Chinese plants as a personal demonstration project.

More than three thousand Taiwanese companies had set up shop in the special economic development zones in China by the early summer of 1993. Nearly twenty thousand factories owned by investors and companies based in Hong Kong—some of them Taiwanese holding companies—were estimated to be up and running just in Guangdong Province, a veritable economic free-fire zone where investments from Hong Kong, Japan, Taiwan, and the United States constituted half of all foreign investment in China during 1991.

Factories representing hundreds of industries in need of fast, efficient, inexpensive, "dirty, dangerous, and difficult" work had galloped into China, and the Chinese economy surged all at once. During 1992, the domestic economy grew by nearly 13 percent, making China the third largest of all the world's economic orders.

In January of 1992, Deng Xiaoping made what most observers assumed would be the aged leader's last trip through the south. Deng said that China's Pearl River Delta should rise up to join Taiwan, Hong Kong, Malaysia, and Singapore as the "Fifth Dragon." Others perceive Hong Kong, Taiwan, and the delta provinces of South China eventually merging with the Yangtze Delta development regions as a much bigger economic powerhouse, as a reunited economic community that will grow so quickly that it will achieve the stature of one of the dominant "Triad" economies of the United States, Europe, and Japan.

China's economic rise startles even longtime students of economic development because of the speed of the change. For most of the century, the change from a subsistence economy to a consumer-based economy took many decades to achieve. But the torrential fluidity of capital, the flow of cross-border expertise, hard work, external corporate lust inspired by a vision of the size of a consumer marketplace in China, and the sheer desire of the average Chinese to collect new things have all conspired to supercharge the development process. By some estimates, the Chinese economy will achieve in a decade what the miracle economy of Taiwan took twenty-five years to accomplish.

"Things have actually cooled down a bit for us," Charlie Brown said as he took his long, easy strides through a room full of sewing machines. "I was pushing two million pairs of shoes a month outa here not so long ago, but it's down to around one point seven million right now—times being what they are in the business, especially in Europe."

Brown said that he felt assured that Nike was set up in the very best of the Mainland factories, though he admitted to coveting a   **_183_** "little factory" Reebok kept tied up with orders in Fuzhou. The current Nike master plan included moving about 30 percent of all Nike production to China, with only political uncertainty restraining the company, as Knight put it one evening over dinner, "from just taking the whole thing into China and letting them make 'em all."

The political risks of doing business in China emanate from sources other than the impenetrable halls of power in Beijing or the coming return of Hong Kong to Chinese rule in 1997. In October 1992, George Bush vetoed a bill that would have placed restrictions on the most-favored-nation status that regulates U.S.–China trade. Proposed quotas on shoes and other imports—despite the athletic-shoe industry lobby's constant protestations that Taiwanese and Hong Kong companies actually make most of the shoes—arise regularly in response to news of human rights violations perpetrated by a regime with a long record of brutality.

"The Communists are still here with us," Frank Lee said. "Yue Yuen employs a party cadre we call a manager. But he doesn't know anything about making shoes. He deals with our relationship to the local government. He has an office and some assistants."

Charlie Brown studies the daily news of political shifts in China, but he tends to accept local belief that Guangdong and the other southern regions are becoming insulated by distance and success from the political struggles of the north. " 'The mountains are high, the emperor's far away,' " he said, quoting an old proverb.

On the short car ride between the Yue Yuen factory and the nearby village of Bao Gu, the *Ping-jing* problem—the constant transportation bottlenecks that choke almost every route throughout China—was easy to see. "We're going to clean up that river," Frank Lee said, passing the time while several sedans idled behind two trucks that were too wide to pass by one another.

In Bao Gu Frank pointed out the town square, recently rebuilt at Yue Yuen expense. "The population has doubled to thirty thousand. We're building a hospital over here," Lee said.

Six new dorms were also being built near a pig farm at the edge of the village. The completed cement-block residences included huge and extremely spartan dorm rooms for unmarried line workers, tiny cement-floored one-bedroom dwellings for supervisors, and bigger apartments for the senior managers from Taiwan—which were identifiable from a courtyard below because air-conditioning units hung out of the windows.

A bus pulled up near a lot filled with thousands of bicycles, not far from the gate outside Factory Three. Several young women climbed down with small bags. One teenaged girl said she'd made the two-day bus trip after reading an ad about job openings in a local newspaper in a village west of Chengdu, a thousand miles away. Another new arrival said her sister was working inside and had written her to come apply for a job at Yue Yuen.

Of the 1.2 billion citizens of the People's Republic, three quarters of the population still live an entirely rural life—usually in a place a long walk from the nearest road. But most of them know about Deng Xiaoping's desire for the people of China to get rich. Rumors of the South China boom times have reached well into the Chinese interior and out toward the deserts of the northwest. Estimates of the numbers of unemployed Chinese workers run as high as 300 million. Everyone has heard about the millionaires of Guangdong Province, where Yue Yuen and Guangzhou are located. So every day hundreds of young Chinese citizens travel to the nearest bus stop and head south or east in search of a new life.

Indonesia's nepotistic leaders also sought to jump up the Asian pecking order when the shoe factories were chosen to be among the light-industry facilities to receive assistance in the development process. Over three years some $350 million in foreign investment poured into Indonesia, and a billion dollars of foreign exchange revenue was expected to be generated. The value of athletic footwear exports rose from $4 million in 1988 to $1.5 billion in 1993, but the amenability of most Chinese workers to slogans, epigrams, and expectations that were part of both a recent political and much older Vulgar Confucian tradition was not shared by Indonesian workers. The premium placed on extremely hard work, rigorous discipline, and a sincere respect for hierarchy present in the traditions shared by workers from Korea to Greater China was simply not part of the cultural infrastructure in Indonesia or Thailand.

A thin line separated images of economic development assisted by foreign capital and expertise, and overt exploitation. The perceptual difference between development and oppression was not made easier to discern in Asia by the fact that the reigning models of fast-track emergence from poverty included an authoritarian approach to internal politics and the management of daily life—as was the case in South Korea, Taiwan, Singapore, China, the Philippines, and the rest. And the wage scales set at the beginning of an industrialization process were horrifying to anyone who hadn't experienced daily life in the rural hamlets the new factory workers had left behind.

In June of 1991, the *Economist* magazine reported that "a pair of Nike sports shoes that sells for $150 in the United States is made by Indonesian women paid the equivalent of 58 cents a day." The British weekly noted that though women on the line seemed glad for their jobs, the Indonesian government manpower minister had admitted that the nation's official minimum wage was below what was needed to make a living.

Knight and others in Beaverton realized that the wage estimate was a bit low because various incentive bonuses were not considered, but they also knew how hard it was to explain the situation in light of the stark comparison of the retail price of Nike shoes and the hourly wage of a woman on the Third World line.

Subsequent articles posited that Nike was part of a progression that included not only exploitation, but abandonment, too. The term "footloose" was applied to Nike and the rest of the industry, because workers in Pusan were being left without jobs. The Korean economy's superior capacity to absorb the workers in a burgeoning service and heavy industry sector—the latter fed by the export of sewing machines and trucks to China and Indonesia—was rarely mentioned in the spate of bad press. The shoe dogs had "abandoned" New England, Spain, Italy, and Japan, and now they were turning their backs on South Korea and Taiwan.

Neither Dave Taylor or Phil Knight ever argued that working in a shoe factory was a pleasant way to spend a day ("We're a company of contrasts," Taylor said. "And there's no doubt that I work at the edge of Nike opposite all the glamor"), but Knight, in particular, believed that his company had been a small part of the emergence of several national economies into the modern age.

During the summer of 1993, Knight was spending a lot of time thinking about Vietnam—a country where he wanted to make shoes. He talked of the satisfying symmetry of shoes coming out of Vietnam "instead of body bags." "Hanoi's been punished long enough," he would say.

Charlie Brown had gone off to Vietnam to visit Hanoi and Saigon in February. He came back and reported that people along the streets of both cities knew all about Nike products. "The place is ready, like a horse in the paddock," he told Knight.

But by the middle of 1993, the internal company perception of Nike's role in the Asian economic boom as relatively benign was being regularly obscured by its public portrayal as an imperialist profiteer. In a few weeks, a young CBS news producer named David Hawkins would finally see the feature spot he'd made about Nike's exploitation of Indonesian factory labor on TV. Hawkins had despaired about his piece ever running when the "news magazine" show for which the spot was made, *Street Stories,* had been canceled. One night Hawkins had turned on his television set to see CBS correspondent Ed Bradley—who introduced the features on *Street Stories*—sharing a round table on the Charlie Rose talk show with his friend, Nike-guy Spike Lee. Hawkins wondered if the "influence-peddling operation" at Nike might kill his story off.

What intrigued Hawkins about the story was the "marketing hypocrisy" indicated by the distance between "a one-hundred-dollar pair of sneakers and a worker making those sneakers being paid a dollar-fifty a day." Hawkins had approached Reebok (which actually made a larger percentage of its shoes in Indonesia) about the story, but officials there had agreed that the situation in Asia was not good. " 'Oh yes,' they said, 'isn't it terrible?' " Hawkins reported several months after his feature aired. " 'We are committed to changing the production scene in Asia.' But Nike wouldn't apologize at all."

The segment would finally run—opening with images of Michael Jordan and Andre Agassi, athletes who "make millions" while others, in China and Indonesia, make "pennies" so that Nike can "Just Do It." "Prepare yourself for a shock," Ed Bradley would tell the audience tuning in during the July 2, 1993, showing of *Street Stories.*

The image of undernourished-looking Indonesian peasants plowing fields with filthy rags on their heads was quickly replaced by a shot of healthier, well-dressed line workers in a "factory called Bao Chen" (though Bao Chen was in fact the gigantic Taiwanese holding company that operated the Yue

Yuen plant). Ironically, the factory looked so clean and well-appointed that it made T3 in Pusan—and most of the shoe factories still operating in New England, for that matter—look like something from Dante's vision of the inferno.

An American labor activist named Jack Ballinger appeared on screen to talk about Nike's exploitation of labor. Two years earlier Ballinger had been quoted in a *Far Eastern Economic Review* article as having said that Nike pitted "six Korean-run factories against each other and [has] them compete for orders based on which produces the cheapest shoe."

The *Street Stories* spot reported a strike at a different, unnamed Indonesian factory and the subsequent suspension of twenty-two workers. Wage stubs were shown that indicated a daily wage below the official minimum—which, the Hawkins report continued, was purposely set below the poverty line in Indonesia by a government afraid of the "footloose" shoemakers going away.

Some benefits of working at a factory like the one owned by Bao Chen were mentioned, but little was made of the dormitories, meals, staff doctors, factory mosque, or the cleanliness of the plant. The dorms in the inevitable worker compounds were depicted as little better than worker prisons, where young employees had to get permission to leave.

The domestic press also weighed in during the summer with similar reports. A Portland *Oregonian* reporter named Nina Baker went to Asia and wrote about glue and paint fumes and about workers standing unprotected near hot molds. The cost of the wine Dick Donahue was depicted drinking in Paris was contrasted with the wages on the line. A young worker was followed home to a hovel and a bamboo mat that served as a bed. A columnist writing in the *San Francisco Chronicle*, Dick Meister, claimed that the fourteen cents an hour paid workers making Nikes was "typical of the 35 plants sprinkled through Indonesia, China, Thailand, South Korea and Taiwan." Meister's column appeared with a cartoon showing an hourglass with an overfed fellow in a bathing suit floating happily in the top of the hourglass, from which tiny drops of water fell down to an impoverished-looking woman, on her knees, who was trying to catch the drops in her upturned mouth.

The *Street Stories* segment would be particularly infuriating to Nike PR director Liz Dolan. After less than four days in Indonesia, Dolan would wonder aloud to Knight—who wouldn't watch the show—had Hawkins of CBS and his crew inquired of the wage scales and working conditions of the pool boys who served them in Bali, where she understood the crew had stopped off to vacation after filming at the "factory called Bao Chen" outside Jakarta? And why had "the human rights company," Reebok—producer of many more shoes in Indonesia than Nike—not been included under the spotlight?

"This comes with the territory. It's like John Thompson likes to say," Knight counseled Dolan. " 'If you want to have a lot of friends—lose.' " But Knight also seemed to appreciate Dolan's energetic defense of the company. At one point during the Operation PUSH affair in 1990, Knight was told of a request from Jesse Jackson in Chicago. "Just do me one favor," Jackson had apparently passed along. "Get that bitch Dolan off my back."

Knight reminded Dolan of the characterization regularly.

Subsequent research by Nike in the wake of the *Street Stories* segment indicated that the much higher wages paid workers in a nearby Indonesian factory making shoes for Bata were the result of the factory opening eight years earlier. Wages had risen with the seniority of line workers. One of the workers the CBS report said was fired for being part of a strike, had actually been fired, Nike officials contended, for destroying documents at another factory, Sung Wha, where Nike no longer did business—though it did at the time of the strike.

But the questions about Nike's offshore relationships continued to flow over the berm, and by the middle of the summer, many employees at the World Campus had begun to wonder if it was indeed possible that Nike was in the wrong in Asia. They were assured by company officials that the Korean martinets assigned to Thailand and Indonesia were long since back home. They were told about the hospitals factory owners were building, and that the Hasi Corporation and Bao Chen joint ventures in Indonesia had built their workers mosques.

Anyone who had spent time in a shoe factory knew at a glance that the spotless, air-conditioned, state-of-the-art Bao Chen plant featured on *Street Stories* was a veritable industrial paradise compared to older factories—though the work being done was still typical of the numbing, repetitive, and physically taxing work of building sophisticated shoes by hand. But most Nike employees working in Beaverton had never been in a shoe factory. The only lasting machines and glue-making procedures they'd seen were in the sample room in the Jordan Building.

In a long interview published in the company newspaper, Dave Taylor argued that the $1.50 per day earned by workers making Nikes in Indonesia—not 14 cents per hour as some of the press reports claimed—"was not $1.50 per day." The pay rate was in fact 3,000 rupiah, Taylor said, enough, relative to the cost of living in Indonesia, to buy clothes and even save money. Indonesian labor policy did allow for a ninety-day training period during which workers were paid below the minimum wage, Taylor admitted, but after a year, employees in the plant were paid well above the allowable minimum.

"We're not gouging anybody," Knight said after the *Street Stories* spot aired in early July. "Our gross profits are published every quarter, and at around 39 percent we're right on the industry standard. We make our profit on the volume. A country like Indonesia is converting from farm labor to semiskilled—an industrial transition that has occurred throughout history. There's no question in my mind that we're giving these people hope. I've seen the change for decades, and this happens to be the way countries move ahead."

A letter sent by Nike PR to hundreds of news organizations and companies doing business with Nike pointed out that the 2,800-rupiah-per-month entry-level wage in Indonesia was five times larger than the monthly wage of local farmers—a not particularly valuable comparison, however, in that farm incomes in poor regions like Indonesia are only in a very small part represented by cash payments.

But brief public lessons on comparative costs of living or the historical course of economic development—or trying to explain the cost of molds, packing, freight, warehousing, hefty duty charges, and the fact that all the other athletic-shoe companies were in the same boat—would forever be difficult to reconcile in the minds of sports fans and shoe customers informed of the disparity between a Third World hourly wage and Michael Jordan's gathering a yearly income almost twenty thousand times larger than that of the former peasants making shoes.

Nike sent its own film crews to Indonesia to produce a rebuttal reel to send out to news organizations. Several Indonesian workers appeared on the screen to say that they liked their jobs—one woman reporting that she had left a job at an insurance company to make better money on the line. Boxed personal financial data appeared on the screen, like the boxes of personal financial information in the middle of issues of *Money* magazine. The boxes indicated a high savings rate, though the take-home pay was still startlingly small from an average American's perspective.

Knight appeared in several sound bites, referring in one take to Taiwan and Japan's huge gold reserves in the wake of development. "Twenty years from now," Knight quipped, "one of those workers you say is so abused will be your landlord."

Over the years, Knight and the Nike managers on the production side of the business had adopted something akin to a "Who are we to say?" anthropologically neutral position that complemented their macroeconomic view of Nike's role in development. Nike did not own the factories in question, nor did the company dictate the labor and wage laws under which the factories operated. "We don't pay anybody at the factories and we don't set policy within the factories; it is their business to run," Dave Taylor told the interviewer from the company paper.

This official cultural relativism was also reflected in a Nike document called the Memorandum of Understanding. Every factory manager at every supplier company and every subcontractor had to sign a written certification that "all applicable local government regulations" regarding minimum wage, overtime, child labor laws, pregnancy and other kinds of leave, retirement, safety, insurance, and environmental practices had to be honored. Forced labor was forbidden no matter what local rules applied, as was "discrimination in hiring, salary, benefits, advancement, termination or retirement on the basis of gender, race, religion, age, sexual orientation or ethnic origin."

Inspections of plants and pertinent documents were part of the deal if you wanted to do business at Nike. But if minimum wage was artificially suppressed by an authoritarian government looking for light industry, then it was not Nike's job to dictate a just wage. "You sound like you are proud of what we are doing there," the Nike interviewer grilling Dave Taylor observed after he laid down the company line.

"Let's put it this way," Taylor said. "I don't feel bad about it. I don't think we are doing anything wrong. To say that Nike can go into a country like Indonesia with 170 million people, or to China with 1.4 billion, and make a huge impact on what happens there, in labor or human rights or industrialization, is ridiculous."

Only when foreign labor issues come up can a Nike manager **191** be heard to say, "We're not good enough to change that system."

"Does the difference between a dirt floor and no bathroom, and a cement floor, toilets, and running water, mean you're really living well?" Charlie Brown asked as he walked away from the stark, vertical pavement of the *Clockwork Orange*–like living quarters thrown up beside the Yue Yuen plant. "No way," he answered himself. "Saving that twenty percent or sending money home makes a big difference, but no, this doesn't meet American standards or the standards of the richest Chinese or Indonesians, but then chasing our standards is what this whole deal is about."

The work of relatively pliant and extremely industrious Asians—and the attendant fear that their capacity to work hard would take jobs away from Americans—was essential to American economic development from the time of railroad building and frontier taming. The moral neutrality of the Nike position is well within historical tradition, but then bucking tradition has been a larger part of Nike's history than has falling in line.

Quietly, some Nike managers concede that when the leap is made from a high-wage country to a lower one, the increased profit margins created do leave some room for the setting of examples. Given the publicity generated by the combination of Nike's rise to public prominence and the foreign-wage-scale status quo, it was hard to imagine that shareholders would mind some kind of required minimum-wage safety net—which competitors were sure to be forced to copy.

But then again, young Wong Shu and the other women making baseball shoes along the line at Yue Yuen had parents or grandparents who had spent winters eating the bark off trees because of the famines brought on by the absurd economic policies of China's recent past. The young job applicants getting off the bus at the Yue Yuen factory gate said they had left behind villages where ownership of an ox meant that you were privileged. The ox was the difference between standing up straight all day and crouching over to break up dirt with a sharp stick.

There are indeed very strict rules involved in living in the Yue Yuen dorms, but then the China of 1993 was still a place where public protests in the name of a greater personal freedom could be grounds for the administration of jolts from cattle prods.

Back in Pusan, some of the members of the generation largely absent from the shoe production lines—between the grandmothers on the line and the young kids beside them who come off the farm—were among the students who rampaged through the streets of Pusan in 1978, waging full-scale war against South Korean troops and police. The next year the eighteen-year-old military dictatorship of Park Chung Hee ended with Park's assassination. In 1988, when the quadrennial Olympic festival came to Seoul, the regime was still efficient enough to pull 260,000 people off the streets as part of a "social purification" program. But the liberalization process had been set in motion. Wages had risen radically, and everything about the opportunities, materials, and general tenor and freedom of everyday life had changed. The difficult light-industry jobs were disappearing to more repressive nations, where workers spent long days in the fumes so that their children could go to college or, like so many Koreans, could save enough money to move to North America and open a small grocery store that was open day and night. The shape of the changes that follow economic development is not the same from nation to nation, but the Indonesian dictatorship and the authoritarian regime emerging from a totalitarian one in China do resemble the Little Tiger governments of not long ago.

Meanwhile, the course of world economic change at the end of the century has turned areas of Northern England back into low-wage regions well-suited to assembly lines again. The global disaggregation of business functions that once caused Nike to be called a "hollow" company had coalesced with the globalization of consumption. Now Honda's Alabama-made automobiles were shipped back for sale in Asia. Japanese producers so recently promoting "quality circles" and "zero-defect" processes in order to control and retain domestic manufacturing were now farming out production to other Asian countries. New Balance had shoe components made in Asia and glued them together in the United States. Nike made air bags and other shoe parts in the United States and had them built into shoes in Asia. ("Our way is much better in terms of progressive quality control," Liz Dolan would argue.)

Standing next to German, Korean, British, and Japanese high-tech sewing and cutting machines, a few feet from boxes of component shoe parts made in Thailand, Japan, China, Korea, and Missouri, a daughter of inland Chinese peasants—wearing lip gloss and stylish slacks—chatted shyly with managers from Mainland China, Taiwan, Hong Kong, Finland . . . and with a fair-haired boy from Nike named Charlie, who was dressed in

Italianate threads, who was indirectly responsible for more than 25,000 desirable Chinese jobs, and who, if economies were not among the most fluid of all human creations and possessed of the power to change everything about peoples' lives over time, would probably have been spending six days a week blasting coal out of a deep hole under West Virginia.

Near the end of the long ride back to Guangzhou, Charlie Brown pointed across the Pearl River to the tall office tower that houses the Nike China office. "The ad agency J. Walter Thompson, Motorola, and Standard and Charters are all in there with us," he said. Then Brown pointed out the window at a billboard displaying a huge ad for Camel cigarettes. "Good old U-S-of-A," he sighed. "We'll export death anywhere."

The Mercedes, secured for official Nike use by one of the factories, crossed over a broad fork of the Pearl. At the height of the murderous inversion of Chinese society two decades earlier—the Cultural Revolution—the Pearl River was on occasion observed to be so full of the corpses of property owners, entrepreneurial rich peasants, factory managers, intellectuals, and representatives of every other facet of authority or bourgeois success, that residents of Hong Kong, eighty miles downstream, could look out and see bodies heading out toward the South China Sea.

But now bourgeois attainment had become an expression of patriotic duty in China. The promise of personal wealth had been quickly reconnected to the long Chinese tradition of hard work, and for the first time, a vision of attainment was being defined for the Chinese masses by access to externally invented consumer products. "First the young women in the Nike office began to wear matching clothes," said Charlie Brown. "Then the makeup appeared and soon the application of the makeup got more professional-looking. Then everybody talked about getting TVs. And then you stopped seeing the same outfit very often. Every month you see another change."

Nearly 40 percent of China's rising gross domestic product emanates from the coastal regions. *The New York Times* would soon report that, in the southern Guangdong Province village of Haotou, the mania surrounding becoming rich had inspired local peasants to kidnap girls and women and force them to work in brothels that had formerly been the peasants' homes.

As young people left rural villages and headed for Yue Yuen

or one of the thousands of other new factories, others embarked on foolhardy, occasionally fatal one-hundred-day boat journeys in the general direction of North America. Thousands of young Chinese citizens—largely natives of Fujian Province who were looking to earn more than the two hundred-yuan average monthly income in that province—made harrowing boat trips across the Formosa Straits. The Mainlanders would sneak into Taiwan in search of short-term work. And they would come back to talk less of the wages available in Taipei than of the *things* people had there: the goods . . . the stores, the jeans, the TVs, the Walkmans, and the shoes.

News of an internal Chinese savings rate of close to 40 percent in no way conveyed consumer desire so completely "pent up" over the years of enclosure that, during only a few days of the summer of 1993, some 6 million pairs of old-fashioned canvas sneakers had been bought in Peking just because the word "Pepsi" had been printed on the side.

"The first Lamborghini was delivered in Peking the other day," Charlie Brown said. "And there's supposed to be around thirty Rolls Royces now. Less than a half of one percent of the Nike product we're making here is sold in China," he said. "But the awareness of brands is absolutely amazing."

During the summer, Nike sales in China would top $1 million in a month for the first time (when that fact was reported in a subsequent issue of *Fortune,* the article pointed out that Nike sells a million dollars of shoes every three hours or so in the United States). In Beijing and in Shanghai—near Nanjing Road and a little Nike shop—young Chinese consumers-in-training wore imported sunglasses with the price and information tags still attached. Makeshift basketball rims were discernible in the thriving alleyways between the Beijing and Shanghai airports and the downtown centers. More than 800 million Chinese citizens were now estimated to have access to television sets, and over 5 million of those sets residing in the households of Guandong Province were able to capture Hong Kong's Star TV satellite broadcasts—with Asian MTV, the BBC, a special Mandarin language channel, and a consistent display of Nike imagery just as vivid and evocative as anything available in the United States.

Athletes like Michael Jordan and Charles Barkley were Asian icons by 1993, and Nikes were desired by global citizens who had previously never owned shoes with laces.

"When I talk about two billion dollars in sales just waiting out there for Nike to become the first truly global company in this industry," Knight had said, "I'm extrapolating our thirty percent of the market in the parts of Europe, Latin America, and Asia where we are already strong. But China? Well, China's a wild card. There's no telling what can happen to the business if China truly catches fire."

If brand consciousness is just beginning to invade the psyches of aspiring consumers in southern and urban China, then it has arguably been installed as a civic religion in the tiny nation of Hong Kong. A two-hour train ride south of Charlie Brown's current home in Guangzhou, Hong Kong is a veritable holy land of retail possibility and acquisitive fervor. The famed crown colony stands out from the ever-globalizing world of purchasable things as a clear test tube—backlit by bright neon—in which a pure strain of consumer culture is unadulterated by any other nuance of culture save a surfeit of Cantonese food.

Hong Kong's state-of-the-art capitalism is practiced in the soaring office monuments that fill the skyline of the colony founded by the nineteenth-century British trading firms known as the Taipans, while, down below—along streets where every other male pedestrian either speaks into or conspicuously carries a cellular phone swaddled in glove-soft leather—the consumers of Hong Kong dart in and out of shops that alter their store-window displays up to three times each day. The designer boutiques mix Asian brand names with Paris and Manhattan's finest, and roving gangs of very wealthy ladies called *Tai-tais* can be seen buying trunkloads of goods on the shopping streets crisscrossing both sides of Kowloon Harbor.

Not far from the crowded Mongkok subway station in northern Kowloon, a different kind of Hong Kong shopping street— Nelson Street . . . though nobody in the district recognizes the old English name—turns into as crowded, urgent, noisy, smelly, and extremely colorful a marketplace as any of the great bazaars in the world. Pedestrians must turn sideways to move along past huge tanks full of black, yellow-bellied eels of every imaginable length and circumference. Immense bamboo cages full of frogs complained into the day on one side of Nelson Street, and butchers cried out over long slabs of meat on the other. Open trucks full of chickens sent feathers into the air, and vendors chopped at giant watermelons with sharp axes. Rats, dogs of indistinguishable heritage, and any number of other creatures were all offered for sale as future meals.

On the other side of the subway stop, to the east, an entirely different retail effluvium clogged Nelson, Shan Tung, and Fa Yuen Streets. From one end of each street, the sky was completely obscured by a riotous wall of outlandish neon signs thrusting up to twenty-five feet away from the storefronts. Descending low to the truck tops and rising high above the tops of the buildings in a dizzying competitive frenzy, the signs said NIKE, JUST DO IT, REEBOK, MAX SPORTS, ADIDAS, PONY, L.A. GEAR, and on and on, for blocks and in several directions.

The Mongkok sportswear district consists entirely of shops selling athletic shoes and related gear. Most of the fifty or so shops are open to the street at one end, so that the effect is a single unrelenting sports-and-fitness-goods fiesta. Posters are plastered on each of the slender bits of wall separating the shop openings: Charles Barkley glowered, and Michael Jordan grinned. NBA's NEW STAR WHO WEARS REEBOK were the words on the top of a huge poster of Shaquille O'Neal.

The shoes on display in the crowded shops—particularly the famous brands—were all shrink-wrapped like so much iceberg lettuce in a produce department. The packaging stood in interesting contrast to the fly-covered meat a few hundred yards away. At 899 Hong Kong dollars, the latest Air Max running shoes, under clear wraps in the shop a woman named Sarah Wong has run for six years, were priced similarly to the American retail price—just as boosters of the coming global marketplace for all things say all the world's prices will soon fall into line.

Reebok and Nike goods dominated the selection, and Sarah Wong confirmed that the obvious division among her customers—the younger shoppers in oversized shorts, Nike T-shirts, and huge shoes gravitating to the Nike shelves; and the somewhat older and less flashy customers gazing through the plastic at Reeboks—was par for the course.

Young people on motorcycles passed by the shops in a dazzling display of American team paraphernalia—down to regulation NFL helmets that had become hip alternatives to regular motorcycle headgear in Hong Kong. The kids all over the streets of Mongkok looked precisely like the kids on Asian MTV—who are Asian kids dressed precisely like kids in American high schools. The kids also looked like the kids in the Nike ads carried via the Eurosport network into Eastern Europe, and like the kids on the MTR subway system below the street who resembled Asian Jordans—all of them the ubiquitous "universal teenagers" of so many product marketers' passionate dreams.

Asian MTV and the other stations and television commercials sent skyward by Star TV landed not only in Hong Kong and China. The same signal was received in Australia, Thailand, Japan, India, Sri Lanka, Kuwait, and the seventeen other nations now served as a result of Hong Kong–based Star TV's quadrupling of viewership between the summer of 1992 and the summer of 1993.

For much of the post–World War II era, a tremendous time lag had separated the arrival of contemporary fashions and the material ingredients in American consumer culture and the slow penetration of cutting-edge information and related goods in other countries. As with the delayed arrival of the black-and-white television set and, eventually, color TVs, the lag time between the introduction of information in American markets and the arrival of the same imagery in Japan and Europe was estimated—well into the 1970s—to be around twelve years.

But now Asian rappers jerked about on MTV in the same way and in the same clothes and shoes as American rappers. "Just Do It" was projected everywhere in its untranslated simplicity, and was recognizable and even pronounceable in deepest China. By the middle of 1993, there was barely an information lag at all.

Hong Kong remained a relatively small if rapidly growing market for Nike products. Of the billion dollars in non-American sales in fiscal 1992, only 15 percent came from the Asian-Pacific region of which Hong Kong was a part. Seventy-five percent of sales occurred in Europe, and 10 percent in Latin America and Canada combined. But everything about the Hong Kong selling scene—from the obvious retailing differences, as exemplified by the shrink-wrapping of shoes, to the palpably enhanced power of those goods and aesthetics connected to sport—attested to the "global power brand" Nike had become. The Nike style was now everywhere on display in developed and developing economies. Anywhere there was the faint possibility of a growing middle class, Nike—in accordance with Knight's edict—was there, at least to be understood and desired even in those places where the goods were still hard to find.

During the fall of 1990, Knight had driven through what was

left of the Berlin Wall to visit a sporting-goods store in East Germany. He discovered a huge JUST DO IT banner hanging down over all four stories of the Haus Fur Sport, which Knight found to be indicative of the tendency of those reclaiming political and economic freedom (Knight tended to write the word "Freedom" with a capital F) to entwine the exercise of that freedom with sports: the freedom to be healthy; the freedom to be beautiful and expressive of the joys of being young, the freedom to generally embellish daily life with props and niceties. As the Victorian promoters of the first international Olympics envisaged sport as a metaphor for otherwise bloody nationalism and imperialist aspirations, Knight saw sport as a common medium of an unleashed global desire for things. "Sport already *is* the culture of the United States," he would say. "Soon it will similarly define the culture of the world."

"They're out there like ready-made consumers," Knight said after a new Nike office in Vienna was set up to service Eastern Europe in the summer of 1993. "We have to fight through the currency issues, the distribution and customs issues, and the corruption issues in some places, but the consumer is already out there, just waiting."

The biggest battles in the shoe wars during the summer of 1993 were still being fought in Europe, where Nike battled for what Knight called "our rightful share" of 280 million more potential consumers than there were in the United States. But Europe's larger population still bought less than a third the number of athletic shoes purchased by Americans. Despite all the Nike-conscious global teens in Europe, the Nike addicts of Holland, the Nike-crazed working-class youths observable in the suburbs surrounding Paris, and all the others, Europeans owned, per capita, only two pairs of athletic shoes. Americans owned an average of four pairs, with American boys owning around twelve.

But selling Nikes in Europe was not the same as selling them in the United States. For one thing, costs were significantly higher due to internal duties and fees, so the shoes were more expensive. The means of displaying Nikes and retailing them to customers was also much different. The street-corner athletic-shoe specialty shop was not a significant part of the European retail tradition. This fact had been underscored by the recent attempts of Nike's largest single retail customer—the Woolworth Corporation–owned Foot Locker chain—to drop their cookie-cutter, Nike-lined stores all over Western Europe, pausing only in 1993, when it became clear that the stores were losing a great deal of money.

Knight observed that Foot Locker management "didn't think through the process of truly lighting up the European customer." Certain retail-theater-style "Nike concept shops" were doing very well in Munich and London, but the best way to bridge the gap between the High Street emporia of upmarket European tradition and a Foot Locker store was not yet forthcoming.

Another impediment in Europe—particularly in Germany—was that retailers often balked at Nike's "futures program," the early ordering system in which Nike offered its domestic retail customers a 5 percent discount for ordering their shoes six months in advance. The futures program was an essential aspect of the reinvention years in that it allowed Nike to rationalize planning and production schedules in the Asian factories, guard against inventory buildups, and all but guarantee on-time delivery.

But German retailers envisaged the program as a risk-transfer mechanism that would only curtail their own freedom to make traditional "at once" decisions based on the state of the marketplace at the moment.

This list of obstacles was significant and still didn't include the simple preference for leather shoes among so many Europeans. And yet Nike's share of the European market climbed steadily through the recession summer of 1993. In January, Nike had controlled 20 percent of European sales. By midsummer, the company held 22 percent of the market—and Reebok had 14 percent, a rise from no more than 12 percent in the wake of heavy advertising.

But both companies were battling over a pie that was expanding very slowly, and general growth of the Nike brand outside of the United States had by late June slowed down to a third of its pace two years earlier.

Knight was extremely dissatisfied with the $250 million in sales garnered by the distributor controlled by Nike's longtime financial partner, the famous Japanese *sogo sosha*, the trading company Nissho Iwai. Back in the early 1970s, when Knight had no money left in the bank and his last American source of credit was being closed down, the Japanese trading company had stepped in to bail the young company out. To this day, Nissho

Iwai provides much of the capital Nike requires. Wall Street company evaluators sometimes criticize the extra cost of the financing partnership, but then Nissho was part of the Nike family. But now Knight said he wanted to lead a consumer revolution in Japan, a rich nation where consumption as a percentage of gross output was more than 12 percentage points below the U.S. If taking the retail operation from Nissho Iwai was necessary to secure Nike's position in the Japanese market, then that would simply have to occur.

Knight, Nike International director Dave Kottkamp, and other strategists would often gather to discuss the precise means by which the company's non-American sales could quickly reach half of total sales. The dialogues often concentrated on the distinction between a Nike cast as a global company serving a homogenized marketplace with universally accepted images and products, and a Nike that becomes the consummate global company through careful customization of its images and products in accordance with local preferences and conditions.

The controversial "homogenization" of global consumer desire was articulated as marketing theory by Harvard professor Theodore Levitt during the early 1980s. Levitt's work suggested that a common marketplace of shared consumer perception was ushering in an era of standardization for all products. Technology, Levitt posited, had created a single scale and common field for all selling activities.

According to the homogenization view, certain brands—Coke as a prime example—were preferred for the same reasons on Baffin Island in the Canadian Northwest Territories as "Coke-Ah" was desired in the cafés along Rue St. Germain.

But it had taken years to create a universal desire for Coke (if the eight ounces of Coke consumed per capita over a year in Asia, as compared to nearly fifty ounces in the U.S., can be called universal), and Nike had gone global in a fraction of that time.

Knight felt assured that Nike "meant something to everyone in the world by 1993," but in terms of planning the future global presence, questions about whether Nike meant the same thing to everyone persisted. Scott Bedbury's ad staff had secreted the very successful spring 1992 commercial called "Instant Karma" within a long "clutter reel" full of all sorts of TV ads shown to test consumers in Japan and Australia. The "Instant Karma" spot used John Lennon's song of the same name to evoke an emotional connection between the "superstars," as the late Beatle sings it on the sound track and—as in the "Revolution" campaign—anyone else who loves to play and compete. The commercial had been made in both thirty- and sixty-second versions for the domestic market, with one variation that showed a preponderance of basketball imagery and another loaded with women's fitness imagery.

Men and boys tested in Asia universally picked the Nike commercial out as by far the most "meaningful" message on the clutter reel. Many of them didn't recognize John Lennon's voice and some were young enough to not know who John Lennon was, but the ad still invited the viewer to become part of an emotional experience created by Nike's sports imagery and Lennon's wonderfully affecting song. "Instant Karma" was soon rolled out in seventy-five different countries, with interesting icon-oriented subtitles, and sales trekked up when it appeared.

Wieden & Kennedy opened an office in Amsterdam in February of 1993, less because of the "homogeneity of markets" theory of action than the countervailing "think globally, act locally" tactical plan. W & K soon debuted three European Nike commercials that were heavily customized for European viewing. A hefty $1.5 million was spent just to produce the three "opera spots" starring Quincy Watts, Sergei Bubka, and Charles Barkley, and a typical Nike extravaganza was staged to introduce the campaign at the Bastille Opera House in Paris, with Bubka—who had set another new world record a day earlier—and seventy-five members of the Paris sports and fashion press in attendance.

The idea behind the commercials was to take a particularly European cultural item—opera—and juxtapose it ironically to American cultural items: superstar athletes and their beloved shoes.

The "Barkley of Seville" commercial in particular was an immediate sensation in Europe, with attendant press coverage reminiscent of other Wieden & Kennedy campaigns. The commercial looked every bit as elaborate as an operatic staging in Milan or Paris, with Charles appearing to vocalize quite professionally in Italian, prancing through a basketball cathedral, killing the referee after being called for a foul, and then having his shoes taken away as punishment by a looming figure cast as the image of Death. The thought of the loss causes Charles's voice to crack into a falsetto—"La Scarpes" he begs. "No!"

Quincy Watts appeared in his complementary "Don

Quincy" spots, and Sergei Dubka starred in a commercial called "The Magic Shoes." Inside the company, the opera commercials were widely judged the best Nike television ventures of 1993. By NBA play-off time in June, "Barkley of Seville" could be seen all over the United States.

"Charles clearly travels well," said Scott Bedbury. "His Godzilla spot was a hit everywhere too."

But Bedbury also believed that local and regional heroes were essential to driving sales. The first Wieden & Kennedy print ad in Europe proclaimed, in English, "Protect the Future of Football." The photograph showed schoolboys, shoulder to shoulder, with their hands folded in front of their genitals. The image was immediately recognizable by any European as a humorous play on a particular defensive strategy during the free kick, in which the receiving players must remain immobile and thus very vulnerable, but nobody at Nike would have ever suggested that the promotion of Nike's sponsorship of Under-fourteen European soccer be exported to other markets.

The local versus global conundrum was constantly underscored by Nike's struggles with the soccer market. The very first shoes that bore the name Nike—the ones that quarterback Dan Fouts had worn on the football field—were actually soccer shoes. Though basketball was clearly on the move, soccer was still the most popular sport on earth, and even according to Nike's vigilantly self-critical internal analysis, Nike made the best soccer shoes. But the market was still owned by Adidas.

Technical aspects of soccer boots were less than essential within the largely working-class and tribal football culture in Europe. The better young players were told by their fathers, older brothers, and coaches to buy their boots several sizes too small, wet them, and then force their feet inside. Back in the lab in Beaverton, the problems of deformed "soccer feet" were the subject of various studies, even as the marketers looked to the World Cup in 1994 and an ongoing effort to break soccer's secret global code.

"The biggest reason we can't break open soccer is a domestic problem," Howard Slusher observed. "The problem is that Phil doesn't get soccer like he gets the other sports. He didn't really get Europe until fairly recently, and I had trouble getting him into the football grounds in Germany. For things to operate at their best around here, Phil must be emotionally involved."

"We can build a certain market share upon American icons

alone," the corporate brand-master and general manager, Tom
Clarke, said in the Boston Deli between training runs and work
one afternoon. "But that won't sustain us. We can blast a lot of
business with Barkley or Jordan spots, but the staying power will
come when we truly connect at the grass roots."

Nikes and even wraparound sports-specific sunglasses could
be found all over the world, on clerics and even terrorists, but
the sociology of accoutering a product so it becomes an essential
part of a culture was not a simple thing. Knight had recently
finished reading Kenichi Ohmae's book *The Borderless World,*
and he had told several associates that he considered Ohmae, a
McKinsey & Company consultant, former nuclear engineer, and
Japanese management guru, "something of a genius."

Ohmae wrote about a global economy driven by global companies that had each given up a "headquarters-driven management style" in favor of "local, market-driven decision making."
He exhorted companies in his books and in-house lectures to
"relearn the art of invention," which he perceived as lost to
modern business civilization because of too much copying of
others and too much buying and selling of businesses. In the
ILE—the interlinked, deregulated, billion-person economy of
the future—Ohmae argued, national trade statistics would
become as meaningless as the outmoded nationalist imperatives
most governments exist to protect.

"What he also says," Knight would tell those to whom he
recommended Ohmae's book, "is that there is no value in making things anymore. The value is added by careful research, by
innovation and by marketing."

"Global localization," a term Ohmae borrowed from Sony's
Akio Morita, was one way to create a truly global company that
was as much "an insider as a local company but [that could] still
accomplish the benefits of world-scale operations." Ohmae
contended that at a per capita income level of $26,000, consum-
ers went global. They would then want quality and value and no
longer care where an item was made. And at that point, the very
axioms of traditional macroeconomics would become meaningless, and everything, Ohmae augured, would emanate from the
will and global reach of a powerful new breed of world consumer.

Knight believed that recalcitrant Japan and others as yet un-
Nikeized on the global scene would see the light only when they
understood the concept of the brand. He talked now about ex-

panding the brand with "constraint" so as to retain its integrity. "We've already got something very powerful in place, but to succeed globally we've got make sure we truly stand for one thing. A certain amount of localization is important, but in every market we have to be the same brand, the same thing. We have to take a single set of values and transform them around the world. And I don't think we're very far along in that."

During the spring and early summer, the Nike stock price had continued to decline, in part due to the aura of "brand crisis" or "brand demise" palpable in business-press and Wall Street circles. The apparent crisis had begun in late April when Philip Morris announced a 40 percent price reduction on Marlboros in response to the rising popularity of generic, nonbranded cigarettes. Kellogg's was also widely sold off by investors in light of the company's similar competition from generic cereals.

Managers in Beaverton scoffed at the idea of a pair of Air Carnivores or Air Huaraches being portrayed as fungible indications of a threatened brand. The brand crisis was largely the result of companies making both branded and nonbranded goods and thereby creating price compression at the top of their own line. Sales statistics confirmed that Nike's balance of sales wasn't slipping to lower-priced shoes, even as anxiety rose in Beaverton over the sluggish holiday-season orders that had surfaced during the spring.

An early July article in *Footwear News* began "All's well in the house of Nike, Inc., as U.S. sales of footwear increased 21 percent in the fourth quarter ending May 31, finishing off a record year for sales and profit."

But orders for the 1993 holiday season were lower than the previous year's pace for the first time in years. Knight talked of consumer confidence levels as low as he'd seen them since the launch of the Nike brand. The disappointing projections for the coming quarter would knock the price of Nike shares down below $55, from over $72 a share at the beginning of June.

But despite indications that the European recession and general retail environment would get even worse before it got better, Knight declared the globalization of Nike would continue apace. China would be targeted for new advertising, with particular investment in the tennis, soccer, and running lines. Mexico, Chile, Argentina, and Brazil would be targeted with buildup marketing programs.

The Korean managers of T2 would open their factory in China in 1994, and two thousand workers would begin to make 350,000 pairs of shoes per month—under much more diplomatic Korean managers and the scrutiny of Nike's Charlie Brown.

"I'd say we're only halfway to being truly global," Knight said.

"The globalization of Nike will certainly continue, in part because Global has become a Nike state of mind," Tom Clarke declared. "We've been moving the finish line that says 'truly global company' out into the distance in front of us for five years now. The completely global Nike will look much different than we look now, but we're closer all the time."

KANSAS CITY

June 1993

The unveiling of Project Victory, the joint Nike and Creative Artists Agency plan to revivify college football, was scheduled to occur at five P.M. on June 29. But it was already nine minutes past the appointed hour, and the Most Powerful Man in Hollywood sat close to his new friend and ally, the Most Powerful Man in Sports, waiting for their scheduled opportunity to pitch their idea to the committee of university presidents that ostensibly governs intercollegiate sports.

Mike Ovitz and the two other members of the CAA team milled around in their Italian suits alongside the members of the much less tailored Nike team, Knight and Howard Slusher, who'd flown in on the company Gulfstream from Portland. Once the twenty or so academics who represent the 106 big-time sports-oriented, Division I NCAA universities finally showed up, the Victory game plan was to energetically convey the emotional resonance, business logic, and nigh patriotic service to sports fans of an NCAA-sanctioned national championship football tournament—a seven-game extravaganza concluding in January with a college matchup that would immediately dwarf the appeal of the Super Bowl. Project Victory, they were prepared to argue, would create an American game of games.

No longer would fans be asked to accept a "number one in the nation" football ranking derived from the polling of sports-writers or from the almost random possibility of the two best teams meeting in one of the nineteen annual bowl games. The **207**

Nike and CAA alliance would tell the Division I presidents that the national tournament would generate no less than $106 million in varied revenue—a sum representing a tenth of the total football revenues colleges realized over the course of the season and a number not uncoincidentally divisible evenly among 106 institutions. If the Presidents Commission voted to take the proposal to the entire NCAA later in the year, a million dollars could be filtered through the NCAA and into the beleaguered athletic department budgets of each Division I school by January kickoff time in 1995.

The plan addressed recently flagging interest in and revenues from college football, and it addressed the dire financial state of all but a handful of university athletics programs. Though most members of the general public believed that college basketball and football programs had made the independent athletic departments of high-profile, widely televised schools rich, standardized accounting procedures would show only a few of the multimillion-dollar departments operating in the black. Athletics departments all over the country were under duress from constantly rising costs, falling television and ticket incomes, and—according to representatives of many of the big football and basketball powers—the exigencies of providing equivalent sports programs for women according to the mandates of the Title IX educational amendments of 1972.

Beyond the financial expediencies, Knight envisaged the tournament as something incontrovertibly "good for sports." It was part of Nike's history to assist the emergence of the best of sport from bureaucratic entanglements. The plan didn't even call for Nike or CAA's name to be attached to the tournament. The Victory alliance was willing to run the show for a set fee, or they would do the work in exchange for insider marketing rights. The CAA and Nike team was also prepared to own the events outright and simply fork over the $106 million—in which case Knight did admit he would want to "get out the sharp pencil and do the numbers again."

Howard Slusher looked over at Knight as he chatted with Mike Ovitz at the front of the room, and he sensed that Knight was feeling confident. As much as it frustrated him at times, Slusher admired the innocent passion of Knight's bedrock belief in the existence of some ultimate and tangible good when it came to the athletic pursuits he loved. Former professor of the philosophy and psychology of sports that he was, Slusher was endlessly captivated by Knight's ability to perceive athletes as heroes of the oldest and most noble order and to then work day and night to help—or make—others embrace the best players of games in the same way.

But Slusher was getting more concerned by the minute that the presence of Knight, a man who had made so very much of sports, and of Ovitz, who was not unconnected to movie stars being paid $8 and $10 million for a single movie—might inadvertently bring to the surface some of the ambivalences and hypocrisies intrinsic to the relationship of academics and sports, and of sports and entertainment. As Slusher watched the microbiologists and historians file noisily into the room to dictate the course of a college athletics system only a few of them understood (he remained unaware that some of the academics had already noted among themselves that "one of the original sports agents, a man of varied reputation," was a member of the Nike team), he wondered if Knight or Ovitz could possibly imagine the small-minded, superpoliticized, and consummately vindicative interplay of egos that had so often turned the most innocuous weekly faculty meeting into a display of muscle-flexing and grandstanding that caused the machinations of billionaires and superagents to appear halfhearted and entirely tame.

"I come from their cloth," Slusher had tried to warn Knight. "You never know when the holy and mighty game is about to begin."

The NCAA was born back in 1906, after a particularly savage season of college football—played by various thugs and "tramp" players assembled as "student" teams—had accounted for no fewer than eighteen deaths. The new institution was supposed to clean up college sports, but though the organization's relatively tiny enforcement division still exacted punishments for infringements of an endless list of rules, the latter-day NCAA and its highly paid staff were far more concerned with packaging the big games.

On one hand, the NCAA appeared to be yet another powerful marketing organization protecting and promoting a variety of local brands. The billion dollars the NCAA was being paid by CBS for the right to cover the annual March Madness college basketball tournament over seven years was something of a sports-marketing milestone. The basketball tournament had become as essential to the business of sports as any other series of games. "In terms of launching a new shoe," Knight had said before leaving for Kansas City, "the final game of the NCAA basketball tournament has become better than any runway in Paris. Kids will climb right up next to the screen to see what the players are wearing."

But on the other hand, the NCAA also included an antibusiness and antisports strain that was less a discernible constituency than a rhetorical line that almost any academic involved could seize, as needed, with moralistic fervor.

The NCAA included college presidents who sometimes argued that big-time athletics was overshadowing learning and should therefore be cut down to a reasonable scale. There were others who sometimes argued that the big sports schools should break off and form a more professional sports association.

Aware of all the philosophical ambivalences and Byzantine politics involved, Howard Slusher had spent much of the previous six months on the road, waiting in the anterooms outside university presidents' offices and jawing with coaches and athletic directors from Tulane, New Mexico State, Purdue, and many other schools. Steve Miller had also weighed in to help lobby Nike's intricate network of coaches and athletic directors. The NCAA's executive director, Dick Schultz, had flown his plane into Portland several times to talk to Slusher, Miller, and Knight about the tournament.

Schultz had become extremely enthusiastic about the idea, and it was Schultz who suggested that a formal presentation be placed on the agenda for the June 1993 meeting of the Presidents Commission. A vote of confidence from the commission almost always carried the day when the rest of the Division I members voted on a proposal at the annual general meeting, though Schultz didn't realize until the night before the presentation in Kansas City that one of the hundreds of obscure amendments to the NCAA rules meant that a majority of the schools in all three NCAA divisions—893 institutions—would have to approve the plan. Schultz had called Slusher at his Kansas City hotel to break the news, though he did cite precedent to assure Slusher that the smaller schools would not stand in the way of Division I—especially since they already had their own championship tournaments.

In his dogged way, Slusher had personally pitched all but two of the commission presidents in the powerful IA subdivision of the Division I schools. One president, the University of New Mexico's Richard Peck, had come out of his office to inform

Slusher that pressing personal business meant that their meeting would be postponed. Slusher pursued another meeting, but Peck never seemed to make much of an effort to reschedule. By the time of the meeting in Kansas City, Slusher figured only Peck of New Mexico and Wake Forest President Thomas K. Hearn, a philosophy professor, would probably vote no. The president of the University of Alabama, E. Roger Sayers, had even offered to second a motion to take the proposal to a vote of the larger body, but President Sayers, a geneticist, said this was dependent on the commission chairman, Chancellor Charles E. Young of UCLA, proposing to vote on the matter.

Slusher went to see the UCLA athletic director, Peter Dalis, who—Slusher said—had indicated that Young was in favor of the Nike and CAA college Super Bowl idea, but personal contact with Young had been left to Mike Ovitz. Ovitz was an extremely active UCLA alum, a major benefactor of the university, and a friend of Chuck Young's. Less than six weeks before the meeting in Kansas City, Ovitz had helped assemble Bette Midler, David Letterman, and other stars as part of a gala black-tie fund-raiser for the UCLA Medical School, which had raised over $1.2 million.

Ovitz's personal involvement had clearly put Young in a difficult position. Young knew many of the details of the Project Victory proposal from his ongoing conversations with Ovitz, but he had decided not to get involved in the substance of the Nike/CAA presentation because, he said, "they were so good at that."

With the presentation finally about to begin, Slusher noticed unfamiliar faces in the back of the room. As Young attempted to bring the meeting to order, Slusher turned to look at the laughing and boisterous crowd in the back. He had expected only the Division I presidents, but he saw representatives of schools from other divisions, which would not benefit from the payout structure of the Victory plan.

Dick Schultz and Charles Young finally introduced the visitors from CAA and Nike, and Knight got up to talk for just over two minutes about the good sense of the plan. Howard Slusher had been moved to tears by Knight's oratory over the years, but he was disappointed by the cursory opening. Slusher had noted before this that Knight seemed slightly jumpy around Michael Ovitz, less centered than usual.

Knight sat down as the lights went off. Music began to play,   **211** and quick-cut images of Bo Jackson and Michael Jordan flashed along with pictures of Barbra Streisand. The images pulsed and quivered on the screen as a stentorian sports-moment voice thundered out information about Nike and CAA. The joint tape was no different from the video extravaganzas that entertained thousands of businesspeople by the day in 1993, but as Slusher looked at the academic faces behind him, he wondered if the visual marketing tool hadn't, in this case, been a mistake.

Chancellor Young would later talk of the "unfortunate MTA-style music they used," apparently meaning to refer to the rock video network MTV. "They clearly expected to light a California wildfire," Young would say. "But they were dealing with people who are very conservative when it comes to their institutions. You can't set fires with university presidents using the same fuel that would be good for a Madison Avenue meeting. With all that glitz, they couldn't have come up with anything more perfectly designed to turn these people off."

"I feel dirty," one lower-division president said to an NCAA official when the video ended. Then the man stood up and stalked out of the room.

Then Slusher got up to talk about the proposed package and began by saying, "I'm sure that the first section of the newspaper you all look at in the morning is the sports section. . . ."

Charles Young and many of the others in the room cringed ("I think he forgot who he was talking to," Michael Ovitz would note some time later). By then, there was a lot of noise coming from the back of the room. Lower-division presidents joked and rattled their coffee cups.

The CAA agent Rand Holston got up and talked of a powerful new revenue stream that could address the gender equity issues all the universities faced. He also mentioned the global marketing possibilities the project would create.

Charles Young could tell that Mike Ovitz was irritated by the lack of attention as he rose to speak, but Ovitz soldiered on through an artful dissertation on a technologically altered future in which every collegiate league might have its own channel. "The best teams in the country will probably have their own channels," he said. The possibility of some five hundred channels meant that the marketplace would create a de facto tournament, because the customers wanted to know which college football team was best. In light of the inevitability of the tournament, Ovitz argued while trying to suppress his ire at those members of the audience who were clearly inattentive, the Presidents Commission should seize the day. "Your choice is between being dragged along or being masters of your own destiny," Ovitz warned. "This is going to take on a life of its own whether you address it or not."

During the pause before Chancellor Young began to respond to the presentation, Slusher quickly considered his six months of legwork. He found himself thinking back to a day, years earlier, when, as a young sports agent, he was having lunch with cigar-chomping Boston Celtics coach Red Auerbach at Duke Zeibert's restaurant in Washington, D.C. Movie stars and famous political leaders occupied every single table in the restaurant.

"I can't believe how glamorous it is," Slusher gushed to Zeibert when he came to the table.

"Come with me," Zeibert said.

Slusher followed the restaurateur into the kitchen. Food was piled everywhere, and workers in stained clothes sweated in the steam. "This is what my life is really all about," Zeibert said. "What's out there is just the show."

After a long pause, Charles Young of UCLA thanked the members of the Nike and CAA alliance for coming to Kansas City. "Of course, this is just an exploratory session," Young said, ignoring the Nike wing of the Victory team's expectation of a vote. "The simple truth is, we're not much interested in portraying ourselves as being so very . . . commercial," Young said when a group of presidents gathered after the presentation. "There is already too much commercialism in sports."

Other Division I and lower division presidents joined in when the proposal was discussed.

"How Barnumesque," one of the academics said to some of the other presidents.

"Do they think everybody's as starstruck as they are?"

"This Hollywood glitz is precisely what we have to protect against."

"It was sleazy," said another.

Dr. Judith Albino, president of the University of Colorado, a former professor of psychology, and the incoming chairperson of the Presidents Commission, said, "Well, I do think we need to look at this."

The other previously enthusiastic respondents to Slusher's proposal stood by silently as several presidents vociferously criticized Albino's suggestion. It was even noted that Albino's imminent ascension to the chair of the NCAA body might be jeopardized by her comment.

"That was the devil coming to tempt us!" one of the morally offended presidents declared, glaring at Albino. "We must send those people away."

Knight considered the Kansas City experience part of an "interesting" spring and summer for the Nike sports-marketing team. Howard Slusher, Steve Miller, Howard White, Ian Hamilton (manager of Nike's tennis sports marketing) and many other Nike managers had spent most of May and June shuttling around the world on Knight's behalf, like senior diplomats during times of geopolitical tension—or like the mergers and acquisitions specialists of the previous decade, a time before sports marketers and entertainment agents became such prominent wheelers and dealers of the newsmaker scene.

Nine days before the NCAA meeting in Kansas City, the 1993 NBA play-offs had ended with a stunning victory for Nike. Michael Jordan and three of the other victorious Chicago Bulls starting players were prominent Nike guys, as were Charles Barkley and three of the other starters playing in Nikes for the cofinalist Phoenix Suns. The stark, black-and-white Nike commercials run during the breaks in the action had featured Jordan, Barkley, and the lesser-known Phoenix player Dan Majerle. The controversial commercials had once again drawn extra media coverage on the sports pages and in the local and national news, and Nike shoe and apparel sales had spurted in response.

During the play-offs, the World Campus in Beaverton was abuzz over rumors linking Charles Barkley with the pop singer and serious student of modern marketing techniques, Madonna. The blond singer, who had not—for some reason—been observed in the stands when Charles and the Suns were playing the Minnesota Timberwolves or the Dallas Mavericks during midseason, was now shown at courtside during breaks in the action. As with earlier rumors linking Andre Agassi and Barbra Streisand, the gossip, from the Nike "always-cause-a-ripple" perspective on things, was just fine.

Before the Bulls' championship game victory on June 20, Jordan had laced up a prototype pair of Tinker Hatfield's elegant new black and white Air Jordans, scheduled to pour out of the Sewon factory in Pusan for delivery during the late fall. Jordan bounded around the court in the new shoes during a single morning practice in suburban Chicago, and from a lone, extremely murky photograph of the shoes in one local newspaper, nearly four hundred people called the Chicago Nike Town store to ask when the shoes would be in. The 800-number operators in Beaverton fielded phone calls about the new Jordans, too.

During June, Steve Miller and his staff worked to close a deal that would take away the longtime Converse college basketball coach, Dean Smith, Michael Jordan's college mentor, at the University of North Carolina. Smith became a Nike guy in the wake of the sports marketers' equally controversial signing earlier in the spring of Mike Krzyzewski, the basketball coach down the road from UNC, at Duke.

A few weeks before the Kansas City meeting with the NCAA Presidents Commission, Nike marketers had watched the company's latest tennis star, Mary Joe Fernandez, time her ascent to the finals of the French Open tournament in perfect synchronisation with a new package of signature Nike commercials. Fernandez, the seventh-ranked player in the world, was signed up after Ian Hamilton and his tennis specialists had invested months trying to work out a deal with Monica Seles. But Seles twice walked away from deals with last-minute requests for more money, so the tennis group had gone after young Mary Joe, an attractive, onetime child prodigy.

Until the fiasco in Kansas City, June had generally gone well along the sports front, helping to make up for a wild May.

It was at the beginning of May that Deion Sanders had let it be known to his Nike contacts that he was no longer much interested in being a professional baseball player.

Deion had become extremely distraught over scant playing time with the Atlanta Braves, despite a .308 batting average during the first few weeks of the new season. Sanders said he believed that he was sitting on the bench so often because of salary negotiations with the Braves that had been stalled for weeks. Deion had wanted to sit out the beginning of the season until his contract issues were resolved, but Nike's Fred Schreyer had successfully convinced him that he had business responsibilities connected to Nike that necessitated his presence on the field.

But at the very end of April, Sanders had lost his fifty-one-year-old father to a malignant brain tumor. Deion had occasionally observed that he and "Mims" Sanders ("like me, a class dresser, real cool," Deion once said) had somehow reversed the roles of father and son. Mims had recently toured the world as **215** part of the entourage surrounding the rap star Hammer. Deion said he was happy his father had remained strong enough to make the trip with him.

The Braves gave Sanders permission to leave the team on April 28 to attend his father's funeral, but the Nike sports marketers discovered a few days later that Deion had become so depressed and angry that he now refused to return to the team. The immediate problem this posed from the Nike perspective was that several hundred thousand pairs of the nifty black-and-gold-meshed Air Diamond Turf cross-trainers—each shoe bearing both Deion's football and baseball uniform numbers—were due to arrive en masse on the American retail scene in mid-June. During the week after Deion said he was through with baseball, he was scheduled to star in a Nike commercial for which a director, crew, and various props had already been contracted.

The Nike reps in the field reported that the big order for the new Sanders shoes was a sure sixty-day "sell through." But without the commercial and Deion playing with the Braves, a bottom-line debacle was at hand.

During the same week in early May, the comeback of the Nike cross-training category was set back by Bo Jackson's uncharacteristic refusal to appear in the new Bo ads Jim Riswold had cooked up.

Bo had called Knight a year earlier when the pain in his injured hip had become so intense that he couldn't continue his comeback attempt with the Chicago White Sox. "I'm going in for a hip replacement," he said. "But I promise you that I'll be back."

Not unaware of both the uplifting pathos of a successful comeback and the pathetic sight of a comeback that fails, Nike took a chance on national commercials that specifically addressed Bo's injury and rehab work, and in early April of 1993—when it looked like Bo and his new hip would actually make the cut with the White Sox—Scott Bedbury had jumped out of his hot tub to call Jim Riswold with a thought that became a full-page ad in *USA Today* two days later. With numerous Nike colleagues in the stands on opening day at Comiskey Park, Bo hit a home run his first time up. Hats suddenly appeared with the same line that ran in bold letters in *USA Today:* BO KNEW.

But Bo didn't know about the new commercial scripts he saw in May.

"Enough with the hip," Bo said.

"But I love this stuff. This stuff is hysterical," Jim Riswold argued.

Bo had once refused to appear in another commercial that would have shown him at first deciding to knock the lights out of the Comiskey Park scoreboard and then proceeding—Babe Ruth–like—to do so. Bo said the spot was arrogant.

Riswold's new scripts and storyboards focused on a few ancient bleacher bum characters who'd clearly come to watch Bo sprinting around atop his bionic hip and taking batting practice. Watching the scene, the old codgers would talk about their own thoughts about getting hip replacements. Would it cut down on their mobility? Would it be a durable fix? They would then turn to watch Bo run and hit, fantasizing aloud about pro ball and even the shoe deals that would come their way after surgery. But in light of the hard work of rehab suddenly appearing on the screen (the entire narrative progression of Riswold's plan, typically compressed into thirty seconds of film), the old guys would decide to forgo the hip operation and get hair weaves instead.

In a related Bo spot, the same old coots would watch Bo in the field: "That Bo has a heart of steel," one would say. "And Bo, he has a hip of plastic," would add another.

Suddenly a grounder would hit Bo between the legs and he would double over. "But best of all," the third old-timer would observe, "Bo has a cup of reinforced polyurethane."

"Now that is funny," Riswold complained. "Every male in America who's ever played sports will relate to that pop between the legs."

"Too much with the hip," Bo said. "No more."

So Riswold was sent back to the proverbial drawing board, and Fred Schreyer, still trying to remain sensitive to his precarious emotional state, appealed to Deion's "business sense." Deion, after all, fancied himself something of a hands-on entrepreneur. He was very involved, for instance, in the new Deion Hair Design shop in Atlanta. Deion might even be reminded that a Nike endorsement athlete was expected to show up and perform.

In Atlanta, where huge numbers of the new cross-trainers were expected in the one hundred local retail stores Nike serviced in the greater metropolitan area, Deion's absence was interpreted as something other than a psychological episode. "He appears more preoccupied with his shoe contract and clothing line than with his role on the team," one letter to the editor of the *Atlanta Constitution* complained. "His selfish and juvenile antics and publicity stunts have been an embarrassment to his team and the city of Atlanta. He runs away and hides when things don't go his way, all the while claiming betrayal by those he runs away from."

Beyond the problems of commercials and shoes, Deion's retreat from baseball was once again being interpreted as a case in which Nike was managing a commercialization process that was bad for sports.

"It's not Nike's fault that this strange and emotional connection between the public and the company has been formed," Steve Miller observed while waiting for a table one evening at Zefiro, the Portland restaurant Gordon Thompson designed. "We're drawn in because of the nature of sports and the way sports imprints our society. If someone makes a terrible mistake during a piano recital, you don't hear people in the audience suggesting that the pianist ought to die or have his house burned down. But you sure do hear it in the world of sports."

Miller stood among the lean and well-attended Portland loft-dwellers at the copper-covered bar like an anachronism in a sport coat . . . like the high school coach he used to be, as if searching out his truant quarterback at the pool hall or local saloon. The *Chicago Tribune* had recently named Miller the "second most powerful man in sports," behind Knight—which had made the old coach wince.

At fifty, Steve Miller was one of only a handful of Nike managers old enough to have dedicated his career to sports before an era commenced in which a brilliantly executed maneuver on the playing field could elicit from a television commentator—as it recently had—the ejaculatory observation, "Look at the move! How'd you like to be that kid's agent!"

"The business has clearly changed, but the passion is constant," Miller said. "People have brought all of their passions and frustrations to sports for a long time, and as long as two children run between two trees to see who's the fastest or toss stones into the water to see which one skips the farthest, they always will. Nike is part of a much larger emotional equation, and all we can do is be honest and fair to our customers, to our athletes, and to ourselves."

But the weary look on Miller's face indicated the toll of the pace required and the passion he invested in the day-and-night process of directing more than sixty-six Nike sports marketers (there were only twenty-three shoe designers at the time). It was Miller's job to oversee the drafting, managing, positioning, and constant reorganizing of the Nike stable of athletes so that Nike was always there on the cover of *Sports Illustrated,* always in the television close-up, and always present as a part of every daydream in which the greatest athletes of the day appeared. And at the end of a day, Steve Miller sometimes wore the strain.

Thousands of hours of managerial time are spent merging the "personalities" of consumers, athletes, and products. Though the advertising component of the $250 million Nike was in the process of spending in mid-1993 exceeded the cost of endorsement guarantees, Steve Miller's job description included the maintenance of a dominant Nike connection to every sport, match, and award ceremony, and to the top players of any game connected to the brand.

Celebrity endorsement is an accoutrement of consumer culture harking back to the time when the imprimaturs of kings and queens were attached to products during the late eighteenth century. But Nike has turned the endorsement relationship and the marketing processes emanating from it into an extremely expensive art form. Observers of the hero machinery inside Nike occasionally wondered what popular culture would look and sound like if Phil Knight had grown up obsessed with classical music or poetry instead of sports.

Knight had warned Steve Miller that he would be looking over his shoulder, and Miller now understood that Knight perceived the landscape of potential sports heroes by force of processes that were difficult to anticipate.

During the summer, Knight told Miller and tennis manager Ian Hamilton he had an idea that might help reignite the Nike tennis category and perhaps light a fire under the flagging professional tennis scene in general. "What would you guys think of adding Pete Sampras to the mix?" Knight asked.

Back in the fall of 1990, as Nike tennis guy Andre Agassi began to miss tournaments, Knight had sent Howard Slusher out to bag young Sampras, but Sampras had signed with the Italian company Sergio Tacchini instead. Slusher then went to Germany to pursue Boris Becker throughout the Christmas holiday of 1990, and when that deal didn't work, Nike had—only ten months before Knight brought up Sampras—finally reeled in Jim Courier, now the number one player in the world.

DONALD KATZ

To address a "tennis slowdown" felt internally since the end of 1991, Nike marketers and advertisers had worked overtime to "give Jim Courier a personality," as many tennis and industry insiders put it. Courier was widely perceived to be something of a machine, and the marketers worked to adjust that perception. The $4 million paid up front to Courier, against a complicated $26-million potential payout over six years, seemed reasonable in light of the $20 million the company would spend on supportive advertising at the end of 1992 and the beginning of 1993 (through control of marketing rights, Nike could actually end up recouping $2 million). The investment also addressed the $100 million in sales lost since the Nike tennis category reached its reinvention-era apogee atop the Agassi- and McEnroe-led, anti-country-club, "rock-and-roll" tennis surge.

Courier had been welcomed into the stable as part of the elaborate Nike brand segmentation formula. "The people in the Nike sports-marketing family must represent all the various dimensions of sport," Steve Miller often said. "Sports touches all the things society is about—calm versus anger, exciting versus collected, even tall versus short and fat versus thin. It's much more complicated than simply finding the best players and signing them up."

As the presence of Charles Barkley protected the Nike Air Force basketball category from public confusion with Michael's Air Jordan line and Pippen's Air Flights, the youthful image Deion Sanders projected was part of the positioning of Deion and his related products in relation to the image projected by the venerable Nike guy Nolan Ryan—and to Seattle Mariners star, Ken Griffey, Jr., too.

Jim Courier was taken into the stable because Andre Agassi's image and affiliated Nike Challenge Court line of shoes and apparel left older and somewhat more conservative players without an immediate Nike identification point. Neither Miller nor Hamilton saw where Sampras would fit in to the mix. Words like "bland" and "robotic" now came to mind more readily when Sampras was mentioned than they had with Courier. How would another retiring and superserious American athlete be refitted as a Nike-style star?

If Nike marketers were going to spend millions "presenting athletes as whole people," as Knight often put it—taking the time of dozens of well-paid specialists from various parts of the matrix to hang out with athletes and get to know them, to build them flashy shoes that conformed to everything from their automotive fantasies and taste in jewelry to their personal sports obsessions (as Courier's fascination with baseball had recently become the basis of his signature Nike tennis clothes); if many Nike teams were then going to work to weave the packaged imagery surrounding the athlete into "the very fabric of daily life," as so many of the Nike sports marketers tended to put it; then that player had better come equipped with hooks upon which to hang the bundles of Nike allure. The Nike guys had to mean something way beyond the simple capacity to win.

"When I scout and draft a Nike basketball team," Howard White had said during a recent basketball category meeting convened to assess the new crop of college players about to turn pro, "I'm looking for a special attitude. If I was pulling together a competitive basketball team instead of a Nike team, I might need a great center, a player like Brad Daugherty—somebody who'll get everybody involved and help you win.

"But when we go after somebody for Nike, that player has to represent something more. There are elements of style to consider. Does he excite anyone? Does he get up real high on his dunks? Cause if he can't move people and offer an attitude we can work with, then he just won't do much for us as an endorser."

Long and often metaphysical debates ensued inside the Nike hero machine when it came time to assess what an athlete will "mean." There was a great deal of contentious discussion before a champion triathlete named Mark Allen was selected from the stable to run elegantly through the spring and summer commercials introducing Tinker Hatfield's overstuffed Maximum Air, Air Max running shoes, because some running-shoe marketers feared that their pure, sports-specific running customers would be offended by the lack of authenticity implied by connecting a triathlete to a pure runner's shoe.

Both Hamilton and Miller told Knight that, on top of all the other good reasons to let Pete Sampras stay with the company whose shoes and apparel he now wore, signing him would cost millions of dollars that might be more profitably deployed. Only ten years earlier, John McEnroe's $100,000 windfall package with Nike was widely thought to be a scandalously large sum, and when David Falk negotiated a $3-million, five-year Nike contract with Michael Jordan two years after that, the deal looked like the endorsement coup of the century for the Bulls' rookie and an indication that the whole endorsement game was careening out of control. But now Pete Sampras could expect a $25-million multiyear package like Courier's, and both Miller and Hamilton—once they realized they were in agreement—began to argue aggressively to Knight that Nike could put the money to better use elsewhere.

Knight listened to his sports-marketing specialists offer their opinions. Then he leaned forward toward Hamilton and Miller. "You guys are nuts!" he growled. "Sampras could mean total domination for Nike. You're both nuts."

Howard Slusher was thrilled when Knight told him to pursue Sampras and try to wedge the young player out of his long-term contract with Tacchini. Slusher knew that a certain constituency inside Nike would not appreciate Knight's unilateral dictate. To many inhabitants of the matrix, the suppression of raw and untested instincts in favor of procedure and process was an indication of Nike finally growing up. The untempered passion route to corporate decision-making was thought to have been one of the problems leading to the morass of 1985–87; Knight had said as much himself.

But Slusher was enthused by the sight of the matrix jangled by this instance of management by entrepreneurial hunch. "This is the old Knight," Slusher said after receiving his new orders. "Never toe the line."

With the help of gentle pressure from Beaverton, the Deion Sanders–Air Diamond Turf crisis had eventually passed on June 1, when Deion signed a $10.75 million three-year deal and returned to the Braves. The new deal included Deion's agreement not to play football until the baseball season ended, and Sanders had endeavored to grant a few interviews after his return, in which he tried to assure his fans that his sadness and disappearance had not dampened his love of his games.

Jim Riswold had come up with a variation on his "old fogies talking about Bo" theme. In the new scripts, the old guys were shown sitting in a barbershop elaborating the legend of Bo, while Bo exercised like mad on the television screen in the corner of the shop, commenting on their screeds or rolling his eyes.

Miller and the sports-marketing managers assigned to Bo were relieved when Bo said he liked the new spots just fine, and in June the NBA play-offs and French Open were graced with unavoidable Nike imagery.

But Steve Miller got home typically late after listening to

Knight make his case for Sampras, and Suzanne Miller noticed he seemed down. "I'm not feeling so secure in my job," Steve said. He told his wife the story of the day's meeting. "I'm the director of sports marketing," he concluded, sounding like the gifted player who missed a catch. "But the truth is, I think he was right."

If Slusher managed to land Sampras for Nike, the tall Southern Californian would enter a pantheon of Nike players who'd help change the fundamental image, substance, and sociological positioning of the venerable game. Nike's first tennis star was the gifted "bad boy" of his day, Ilie Nastase, who agreed to wear Phil Knight's products back when the company was still Blue Ribbon Sports. In 1977, Knight sat in the stands at Wimbledon and watched a florid-faced eighteen-year-old play the game of tennis like even more of a maniac than Nastase. Knight realized that the kid—John McEnroe—exuded an iconoclastic attitude that both conformed with the Nike view of things and abutted strikingly the subdued norms and conventions of a tennis establishment that had effectively packaged the sport for elite consumption.

Tennis and golf celebrities were actually the first modern sports heroes to be glamorized and fitted out as players in elaborate marketing dramas. But the endorsement stars of the late 1960s projected imagery implicit of the sporting aristocracy—cardigan knits and crocked cheese at the club locker room. The pro shop mystique, Knight and others at Nike realized, could be in every way contradicted by this young McEnroe kid's penchant for racquet breaking, apoplectic stomping, and inappropriate language and style on the tennis court in full view of the television cameras.

McEnroe became a Nike guy and proceeded to stomp and swear his way to the top in a game still under the control of an establishment that would have, on the whole, preferred tennis to remain a rarefied and familial pastime restricted to backyard courts and private clubs. "Remember that this is the sport with a scoring system that was specifically designed to keep the commoners from understanding what was going on—'deuce,' 'love,' and all that—it was elitist code," the longtime Nike tennis maven, Ian Hamilton, would say. "Mac broke the tennis code everywhere he could."

During the Master's tournament of 1985, McEnroe had appeared in center court in a pair of *black* tennis shorts . . . and a dark blue shirt. By then the sport was already drawing many young and less privileged players to tournaments and local courts, and the great rivalries of professional tennis were between players who *looked* like kids. Tennis had suddenly become an arena in which young players could act out the glory of rebellious youthfulness—at least from a youthful point of view.

Nike's tennis sales exploded during the mid 1980s. At one point, after stepping on a ball and turning his ankle, McEnroe appeared on center court in a three-quarter-high Nike racquetball shoe, only ten thousand of which had sold the previous year. Less than a year later, over one million pairs of the same shoe had been sold.

But by the end of the decade, a reading of the market indicated that McEnroe was no longer appealing to the antiestablishment tennis crowd. Everything about Nike's lack of marketing focus was being assessed during the late 1980s, and it was decided that McEnroe needed to be allowed to grow up. He would therefore be repositioned as a more mature draw—"resegmented," in the language of the new Nike marketing vision—which meant that the Nike Challenge Court line of goods required a new "kid," a new "horse."

Ian Hamilton had already been courting and collecting younger tennis players under the auspices of the Nike Junior Team, a selection of promising, high-profile teenaged stars who were clad in Nike tennis stuff for free. In October 1988, three of the best amateur players in the world posed together for a photograph later reprinted in *Sports Illustrated* and other publications, some of them in John McEnroe–style Nike gear. One was a then-much-ballyhooed player named David Wheaton; another was a much less flashy and more emotional kid from Florida named Jim Courier; and the third was an utterly out-of-control teen phenom with long hair growing out of only one side of his head, Andre Agassi.

Shortly after the picture was taken, Ian Hamilton kicked Agassi off of the Nike Junior Team for screwing around with his shipments of Nike goods and for being a general embarrassment everywhere he went. But Hamilton, a world-class player himself for many years, had been around the game long enough to know—and to often say—that all the great players of an individual sport like tennis "have an 'ism' of some sort. None of the great ones are what you'd call balanced."

So Hamilton kicked Agassi out of the junior program and told him to call him in Beaverton as soon as he turned pro.

Agassi called. Hamilton knew that none of Nike's competitors or even any of the top tennis agents wanted any part of the kid, but Andre was clearly the Nike guy required at the time.

The Nike vision of rock-and-roll tennis was quickly conceived and soon made unavoidable, whether Agassi was winning his tournaments or not. A 1990 commercial began with grainy, 1950s-style instructional footage in which a stiff, clean-cut man in all-white tennis attire described "proper tennis." His lecture—"Maintain proper body position. . . . Tennis is a civilized sport"—was intercut with color shots of Agassi and McEnroe, dressed in wild attire and pounding tennis balls with complete abandon. Another spot ended with Agassi taunting the status quo: "That ought to shake 'em up at the country club."

"After that one, I could see and hear the typical, avid tennis fan booing me when I went out on the court," Agassi recalls.

As sales boomed, young Andre would report to his Nike design and sports-marketing contacts that other players were constantly coming up to him in the locker room to say that his clothes and jewelry were embarrassments. Agassi had complained that his hips tightened up in cold weather, and the designers had come back with Lycra shorts that stuck out under his tennis pants. "They say they wouldn't be caught dead in my clothes," Agassi reported during his frequent World Campus stays. "Keep it up, guys," he'd say.

Andre wore dangling earrings. He alienated thousands of grown-ups and had a fan club with thousands of teenaged girls as members. From the time McEnroe appeared in black shorts through 1991, the Challenge Court Nike tennis category grew from $50 million a year in sales to $300 million.

But the Nike marketers figured that the Challenge Court focus concentrated on only 5 percent of the total market. The Nike-Agassi tennis attitude was not suited to the traditionalist market, and it was clear that McEnroe—moving toward official retirement not long after the Barcelona Olympics in 1992—would not bring in those of less flashy tastes.

The answer was another "horse" and another segment.

Ian Hamilton had thought that young Jim Courier was all but signed up with Nike five years earlier when Ian was told that Courier would be wearing shoes and clothes made by the relatively obscure Diadora company. Hamilton figured that tennis **225** superagent Bill Shelton of IMG, one of only three agencies that all but control everything that goes on inside professional tennis, had steered Courier away from Nike in an effort to guard against too much power accruing to the Nike machine.

But Hamilton had kept up with Jim Courier, who had been Andre Agassi's roommate back at the Nick Bollettieri tennis star training outpost in Bradenton, Florida. Courier—a far more introverted individual than Agassi, who was given to darker moods and court play that were less than entertaining on TV— didn't care for his former roommate at all. After a match against Agassi in the 1990 French Open, Courier stormed up to Hamilton's seat in the stands. "I saw you cheering for Andre," he yelled. "That's just not right, Ian."

"Hey Jimbo," Hamilton yelled back. "It's all about the shoes on your feet."

But by the fall of 1992, after Slusher had failed to land Sampras and Boris Becker, Hamilton was pursuing Courier, then the number one player in the world, with millions of dollars in hand.

Courier was reportedly a "wreck" after coming to Beaverton to sign his huge Nike contract. The deal distracted Courier from his training regimen—which included slamming one tennis ball after another for most of a day. Andre Agassi was extremely upset when he heard about Courier's deal, and it took a lot of managerial time and diplomatic effort by Ian Hamilton to explain to Agassi why his old nemesis was required—and why he would be paid more than the $2-million-per-year guarantee (plus royalties) that Andre got.

"It wasn't so much that they signed him," Agassi claims. "It was that I wasn't a part of it. I deserved that respect. I might have said, 'Yeah, go for him. He might not be what you're hoping for, but take the risk!' But I was just not . . . I don't know, *informed*. I had to answer questions about it in the press conferences. I'm Nike's guy. I grew up with this chemistry they can create. We grew up into a personality we made together. We'd made an experience together. We had a history, and I should have been a part of that decision."

But before Agassi was mollified, the Nike tennis team had set to work crafting a solid but warm projection of Courier and his new line of goods that would use Courier's recently discovered emotional maturity to display a monogrammed Courier genre of spirit replete with the mortal attributes Jim Courier had often been thought to lack. Looking toward 1993 and January Super

Bowl ads that would once again pair Michael Jordan with Jim Riswold's childhood nonsports hero, Bugs Bunny, Scott Bedbury and Wieden & Kennedy writer Jamie Barrett decided that it was time for some "substance"—a return to that aura of authenticity that Nike had progressively twisted and tortured to comedic effect during the time of "Bo Knows" and the "Spike and Mike" series.

Since Courier's idea of fun was hitting ground strokes, the athlete's "work ethic" would be the key to the commercials and general image. And baseball would be woven into the new image too. Baseball was one of Courier's off-court passions—along with his electric guitar—so the designers began to work pinstripes and intimations of the grand olde American pastime into the look of the new Supreme Court line.

Jamie Barrett came up with an a-day-in-the-life, at-home-with-Jim documentary concept for the new commercials. The spots would show him powdering tennis balls, playing his guitar—badly—and one spontaneous moment in the black-and-white series would even catch Courier staring at photo of himself as a five-year-old: "It's impossible," Courier would say, but then, after a pause and a smile, he'd think again and add, "It's possible."

The tennis ads debuted during the Australian Open broadcast in January. Courier won every match he played during the tournament, and during almost every break in the action, a catchy new Nike commercial was there to explain who Jim Courier "really was." Nike Australia's sales doubled immediately, and domestic sales also responded.

"This is how it should always work," Hamilton crowed on the phone to Knight from Australia. "This is why we do it."

"If they want to think Jim Courier got his personality from Nike," Knight said in the company newspaper in response to the widely repeated supposition that Courier finally had a personality, thanks to Nike, ". . . well, I can live with that."

When Agassi was contacted to set up shoot dates for a similar series of black-and-white, "real-life Andre" ads, Agassi said he wanted nothing to do with the cinema verité approach to tennis commercials. "What the people want is the Andre Agassi who's in Nike commercials," he told Hamilton and Bedbury. "What they want me to be is the kid leaping around the court, the guy gunning around in cool Nike ads. The real Andre Agassi is a boring kid. The real Andre hangs out with his friends in Las

Vegas and goes to the movies. The last thing I want is for people to see the real me."

At first, Hamilton and Bedbury found it difficult to argue with Agassi's position. Agassi was one of the only Nike stars who sat at a table and talked about himself as if he were somebody else. "This is the reality of the life I have," Agassi had said when he was only twenty-one years old. "What people want to see and need to see is separate from what is. The Agassi in their minds—not me—is the thing that motivates them . . . to play and to buy."

Because of the gift of eyes like an eagle's and the uncanny ability to hit tennis shots within inches of where he aimed them without the slightest physical restraint, Andre Agassi had effectively been spirited away from home as a young child and sent to special training camps for children with gifts like his. Because he was so very good at the game, Agassi didn't finish high school and didn't go to college, but Ian Hamilton and the others inside the sports-marketing realm of Nike had to acknowledge Andre's singular perspicacity. Unlike Michael Jordan, who had for more than a year now seemed ever more psychologically unmoored because of the way he'd ascended from everyday life and entered millions of unconscious fantasies as other people's dreams, Agassi—son of television and Las Vegas, Nevada—had somehow figured out early on that a dream was the very best and most profitable thing a young man could be.

"I mean there's an upside aside from all the money," Andre would say. "You can make somebody's day. You can make someone's week, and a few times I'm sure I've made a whole childhood. I don't ask to become two people because of the images Nike and the coverage made for me, but the way I look at it, the kids didn't ask to look at me this way. They don't have much choice."

Andre "got it" in a way that Michael—for all of his understanding of gunslingers and global markets—never had. But there were still Nike commercials starring Andre Agassi to be made, and over the past year, Phil Knight had made it quite clear to every individual even faintly connected to sports or sports marketing that he—and not agents or philosophical athletes—intended to control the flow of images that came up and over the berm.

Agassi listened to Scott Bedbury and Ian Hamilton argue that the new spots would not undermine his charismatic flair. One thing that the real Andre loved to do, they said, was play golf. Of all the nonprofessional golfers among Nike athletes, Agassi was probably the best. Michael Jordan got a lot of press for his five handicap, but Agassi rarely shot over par. "What if you could change the rules of golf?" the Nike guys asked him. "What would Andre golf be like?"

The Agassi "rock-and-roll golf" commercials were finally completed, with Ian Hamilton and some of the other Nike guys pictured in films of Agassi running full speed at a golf ball on a tee with a golf club, tomahawklike, in one hand. Employing his stunning hand-eye coordination, Agassi smacked the ball nearly 250 yards.

The Agassi "rock-and-roll golf" commercials aired, but the slump in the tennis category persisted—despite the popularity of Courier's Supreme Court line. One of the problems was that the McEnroe- and Agassi-style wear-anything-on-the-court mystique had inspired thousands of players to come to the game in basketball shorts and general fitness apparel. On top of that, sporting a tennis look away from the court was no longer in. On the spectator and television viewing side of the game, the sport had lost some drawing power because the young tennis powers of the day, including Courier and Sampras, failed to inspire as had the young McEnroe and Connors.

This last issue was one of the problems with tennis that Knight had in mind when he ordered Slusher to bring Pete Sampras into the fold. As Nike's wild growth-spurt of the previous six years finally seemed to have slowed by the middle of 1993, it was occasionally wondered inside sports and shoe industry circles if perhaps Knight's acuity and insight into the far-flung company was no longer congruent with his control. Knight didn't show up in the places most CEOs would naturally be, and it seemed that many of his top managers didn't really know what he thought or did. Besides, the line of conjecture continued, Phil Knight was an honest-to-God billionaire, and how was it possible for him to continue to truly care? How could he muster the energy to continue to embody Nike's high-minded, must-win company culture?

People inside the berm wondered these same things time and again. Knight's perceived distance made those times when he swooped in close all the more unsettling. Steve Miller and Ian

Hamilton knew that Knight was ready for a debate on the Sampras issue, but they were both shocked by the certitude of Knight's position.

After Knight told them they were nuts, he went on to argue that the pin-striped Courier segment still left an even more traditional "tennis whites" crowd outside the Nike circle. "And a Sampras, Courier, and Agassi triumvirate would mean dominance of the game for Nike and America too. They could be the Americans in the tradition of the Aussies when they owned the game." Knight claimed the three players—the "three Nike amigos," who happened to hate each other—could be recast in a way that could revive the entire sport and reimbue the game with its former vigor.

"This is what we are supposed to do in sports. We elevate the game. We add to the whole," Knight said instructively. Agassi was the marketing phenomenon, Nike's crazy tennis child; Courier was the don't-ever-quit player whose triumphs were the result of so much concentration and desire that his play often transcended the bounds of his natural capacities; and Sampras, if Nike could manage to help him out of his current contract, was the tennis "man-of-war," the introverted natural, the pure athlete who played the game like some invincible machine and was hell-bent upon becoming the best player of all time. Sampras had even studied the great players of the past, and had been compared to the straight-shooting Australians of tennis legend.

"And that the boys don't like each other isn't half bad either," Knight added.

"I'm not big on this rival theory." Agassi, the professor of image argued when he heard that Slusher was out gunning for Sampras. "Rivalries are not created. Not even Nike could have created the Magic and Bird mystique."

But Knight wasn't so sure of that.

Andre Agassi's public contention during his 1990 Canon commercials that "image" was "everything" and David Falk's addition of Hanes to Michael Jordan's portfolio of endorsement deals were only among the several final straws that had led Knight to launch Nike's sports-management division a year earlier.

After watching the images of too many athletes become no longer "clean," as sports-marketing lingo has it, largely, Knight thought, because of their agents' greed, his first instinct was to simply buy a sports agency.

Though the legendary agent Howard Slusher dwelled in the Nike shadows, most Nike regulars would have been shocked if they'd known about Knight's discussions with Mark McCormack of the huge International Management Group, since Knight had so often complained that the extant class of professional sports agents was "inherently in conflict with the interests of athletes at every turn—in conflict with athletic performance, with the creation of a public image, and in conflict when it comes to the way payouts and deals are structured." But if Nike stepped hard into the agenting business, Knight figured all of this could be made to change.

Early in 1992, Knight sought to redress the imbalance posed by agents capable of diffusing the impact of Nike's athlete connections by flying to New York City, where he asked McCormack, the sixty-five-year-old founder of IMG (once said to stand for "I Am Greedy" by sportswriter John Feinstein), what a Nike and IMG merger would entail.

Mark McCormack had become famous for launching the modern sports-marketing business when he packaged and marketed Arnold Palmer, endorsement king of the pre–Michael Jordan era. McCormack's broadly based company garnered more than $700 million in sales representing a fractional portion of the deals IMG made.

But when McCormack explained to Knight during their meeting that he dreamed of leaving control of the business to his three sons, Knight didn't press. He was not interested in unfriendly takeovers. When his interest in buying the respected Boston-based children's shoe company and owners of Keds, Stride Rite, had been met with assurances that the acquisition could not be friendly, Knight had immediately backed away.

In 1992, Knight had also made an offer to buy the Starter Corporation of New Haven, Connecticut, makers of the licensed apparel worn by many professional and college teams. Knight considered Starter the best-run company in the nearly $12-billion licensed sportswear realm, but the entrepreneur in charge, David Beckerman, decided he wanted to remain independent. (Starter finally went public in the spring of 1993.) During the fall of 1992, Knight tried to buy Apex One, the licensed apparel company that had muscled in on Nike's control of pro football shoes displayed on autumn Sundays, via an exclusive three-year deal. But the owner of Apex, Joseph Kirchner, proved too mercurial and difficult, so Knight had again backed away. Knight was currently interested in buying Oakley, the makers of his beloved sunglasses, but Oakley's chairman seemed hesitant, so Knight was biding his time.

Knight considered internal start-ups outside the basic business to be potential quagmires for a company dependent on corporate focus and spirit, but after the meeting with McCormack, Knight returned to the idea of a Nike sports agency—a concept that had been kicked around inside the company for quite a while.

Before Steve Miller left Kansas State and came to Beaverton, then sports-marketing director, Fred Schreyer, had come into Knight's office to report that he feared that the same kinds of deals that had obscured Jordan's Nike connection might soon muddy Nike's association with Bo Jackson.

"Bo's still clean," Schreyer said, "and we should try to keep him that way."

As a partner in a Hollywood entertainment law firm, Schreyer had seen the tremendous authority that accrued to the big Hollywood talent agencies like Mike Ovitz's CAA and CAA's archcompetitors, International Creative Management, largely because of the way the agencies had learned to control and combine the careers and images of their talent roster. The agencies helped control access to the stars and tuned their public presences by steering them into various projects. CAA and ICM packaged entire television and movie projects from their own rosters—much as the "Revolution," "Instant Karma," and "Bo Knows" commercials displayed the tour de force assemblage of athletes who played for Nike.

Schreyer, Slusher, and Knight looked at the pro golf scene in 1992, and they were hard-pressed to discern a name or a face that meant anything outside the game. This, they believed, was because each golfer had sold bits and pieces of his or her image to equipment firms or even to accounting agencies. There was no Nike presence to manage the image bank, and no young Arnold Palmer capable of transcending the game by force of personality and flair.

Knight had judged golf as ripe for Nikeization during the mid 1980s, but the sport had proven far more inured to hipper or radical imagery than tennis. Nike's golf business continued to be relatively weak—representing just $50 million of the $4 billion in sales. Michael Jordan didn't like to wear Nikes on the golf course, he said, because the shoes looked too much like sneakers. Jordan said his friends in Beaverton didn't understand the formality of the golf look.

In 1992, Knight had launched an effort to take Nike into the professional golf establishment when Nike bought the cash-strapped Ben Hogan golf tour, one of the less prominent PGA circuits but the one known for nurturing many great players. The Hogan would henceforth be known as the Nike Tour.

Knight didn't enjoy playing golf nearly as much as he liked tennis ("He's what you call a very competitive tennis player," Agassi, whom Knight challenged whenever Andre was in town, observed). But he did consider pro golf to be, along with basketball, one of the only "well-run sports" from an institutional perspective. During a mass conference call with golf writers, Knight had bristled at the implication that Nike's purchase of the Hogan Tour was an effort to bring in the carriage-trade types who gravitate to golf: "That's like saying we go directly at inner-city kids with our basketball line," he snapped. "We do these things to be in the sport. We're in sports—that's what we do."

In late 1989, when Fred Schreyer said he thought Bo's marketing purity should be protected by a new kind of endorsement deal that exchanged control of his other marketing relationships for money, Knight agreed to launch a Nike sports agency initiative inside the sports-management program. Schreyer recruited Bo to the program and he was soon joined by San Francisco 49ers star Jerry Rice, Scottie Pippen of the Bulls, Deion Sanders, Ken Griffey, Jr., and the young basketball player Tim Hardaway. Nike paid a yearly guarantee against marketing income in exchange for control of all the athlete's endorsements and nonteam marketing-related activities. Schreyer negotiated deals with Pepsi and AT&T on Bo's behalf ("Bo Knows Long Distance"), taking a relatively small percentage of the endorsement fee against the guarantee. And the new department set up AT&T, Coke, Montgomery Ward, and even a Scottie candy bar deal for Pippen.

Michael Jordan was approached to join the new management program. "But I told them that while I understood their feelings about control, they'd have to compensate me for what I could lose in the process," Jordan recalled just before the June 1993 NBA play-offs began. "That ended the discussion."

The more controversial "full representation" program, Nike Sports Management—as opposed to the original "marketing **233** only" plan—was launched with the 1992 pro basketball draft, when Nike agreed to pay Alonzo Mourning a guaranteed $16 million over five years for total control over most aspects of his career. The same long-term "total career management" relationship was offered to USC star Harold Miner, and during the spring of 1993, the college football star Rick Mirer was signed, too.

As the NBA season was drawing to a close, the Nike sports-management client Alonzo Mourning began to get nervous about his Nike commercial. "All I have to do is go out and work hard on the court, and Nike will just take care of the rest," the rookie center had said during a shoot-around practice session with his team, the Charlotte Hornets. Mourning's teammate Larry Johnson was already appearing in commercials, slam-dunking in a wig and a dress on behalf of Converse. Alonzo was more than ready to taste the rarefied air of a public ascension he perceived as not attainable by professional performance alone.

To Alonzo, Nike taking care of "the rest" involved the catapulting of Nike-tuned images of Alonzo Mourning into the upper tier of sports celebrity, of making him "a household name" like Michael Jordan and Andre Agassi and Bo Jackson.

"It's as if there are now two levels of attainment in sports," said the director of the nascent Nike sports-management program Mourning had joined, Fred Schreyer. "There's accomplishment in the sport itself, and accomplishment in the world of marketing. And the latter part is like an ordination right now. It's as if you're not truly a member of the elite until you have a marketing organization to take you higher."

Alonzo spoke regularly to Howard White—who called him "Zo"—and he stayed in daily contact with another Nike sports-marketing executive. When Alonzo said that he was thinking of buying some new televisions for his house in Charlotte, Nike arranged to have them brought in. But there was still the not small matter of the Nike commercial.

Mourning was indeed doing his part by working very hard on the basketball court, and members of the Nike rank and file duly tracked his rebounds and points and compared his stats every day to those of Reebok's rookie sensation Shaquille O'Neal. Alonzo would finish the regular NBA season fifteenth in the league in scoring, fourteenth in rebounds, and fourth in blocked shots. Except for the fact that he was constantly being overshadowed by the thundering, backboard-smashing marketing festival called Shaq, Alonzo would surely have been the rookie of the year.

Basketball cognoscenti—like Mike Ovitz and some of the other CAA jocks—were already willing to fly across the country to see Alonzo-versus-Shaq match-ups that were being compared to the titanic Wilt Chamberlain versus Bill Russell contests of years past. After slamming into Charles Barkley over and over again one night, Barkley told an interviewer, "Alonzo's got the worst attitude I ever saw in a rookie. . . . Alonzo's going to be great. I love his game."

By the late spring, young boys who lived hundreds or even thousands of miles away from Charlotte, North Carolina, were wearing the Hornets' trendy teal (colors picked for the team by fashion star Alexander Julian), and many of them wore jerseys and jackets with Alonzo Mourning's number on the back. Mourning's youthful and exciting Charlotte team was sure to make the play-offs—which, Alonzo figured, would dovetail perfectly with the TV commercial he pondered throughout the spring. The play-off berth would mean that millions of people could see what he could do near the basket, and when the action stopped, his Nike commercial would mean that the millions could see who he really was.

At twenty-three, Alonzo Mourning—like Andre Agassi—was a Nike man young enough to have grown up a Nike child. He attended the Nike basketball camps the company created; he played in Nike high school tournaments, and when Alonzo blocked twenty-seven shots in an AAU tournament when he was only fifteen—doubling a record set six years earlier by his hero, Patrick Ewing—Alonzo did so in Nike shoes. Still a high school sophomore, Mourning was befriended by Nike's then-grassroots talent scout, the infamous basketball character Sonny Vaccaro, and Alonzo still considers the controversial and always-entertaining Vaccaro to be one of the most important people to ever enter his life.

Sonny Vaccaro is regarded by more than a few gifted basketball players in the same way successful heavyweights mythologize the back-of-the-yards trainers who nurtured them at the corner gym. But to many others involved in the nurturing—or exploitation—of young high school and college basketball talent, Vaccaro has become a living metaphor for the subordination of modern sports to the profit motive.

In 1978, around the time Knight first saw basketball and tennis as growth categories for the coming years, Nike hired Sonny Vaccaro to establish a grassroots basketball presence for Nike. National television was still an expensive proposition, but there did seem to be a connection between the shoe preferences of the local college and even high school hoops star and the shoe preferences of the kids who screamed from the stands during home games. Converse, in particular, seemed to have established a loyal following at the grassroots level.

The drafting of Nike college teams and a network of high-profile Nike coaches immediately followed, and the early Nike coaches, like UNLV's Jerry Tarkanian and Georgetown's John Thompson, were soon being paid six-figure yearly sums. Not long after that, Georgetown and UNLV became coveted brand names, too.

Sonny Vaccaro had argued in favor of signing the young Michael Jordan in 1984, though Howard Slusher—who had argued that Knight should draft either Akeem Olajuwon or the "fat kid from Alabama," Barkley, instead—also told Knight that he didn't trust the neutrality of Sonny's opinions. Knight and Slusher were aware that Vaccaro's hold over the best young high school stars was widely thought to emanate from some under-handed relationship with the young man or his parents. Every time a promising player chose a Nike school, someone inside the basketball scene or the basketball press publicly assumed that Vaccaro had manipulated the situation. Knight would ask Vaccaro if the deals were all straight, and Vaccaro would say that they were. Knight told Slusher and other doubters at Nike that he believed Sonny didn't lie. Besides, Howard Slusher didn't trust anybody.

In 1985, Vaccaro brought Michael Jordan down to a high school "All-America" camp he was running in Princeton, New Jersey, and Vaccaro watched the way personal contact with Jordan affected the younger players: "They clawed at Michael. They fought just to touch him. I remember thinking then that this is how the whole game will work from now on. The kids will become the messengers." Vaccaro was early in predicting what Jordan would eventually mean to Nike.

As marketing initiatives began to connect the reinvigorated NBA and companies like Nike with the basketball courts next to junior high schools, some two hundred different summer basketball camps for young amateur players appeared. The glamor and the increasing sums of money also drew hundreds of non-players who wanted to be agents some day. These "runners" haunted playgrounds looking to endear themselves to future stars. "It became very sleazy at the bottom," Knight says now. "There's no doubt about that."

Some of the Nike summer camps were billed as Life After Basketball camps. John Thompson, Senator Bill Bradley, and specialists in career and financial planning would come to talk to "the kids." But Nike and Sonny Vaccaro—whose penchant for colorful friends and Las Vegas evenings led to constant speculation about underworld ties—were still depicted every so often as running a less-than-subtle recruitment system predicated on creating loyalty among young rising stars and a sense of Nike cool on the streets.

As with so many entrepreneurial initiatives Nike began in the spirit of the underdog and upstart—as a friend to the great athlete and to the athletes who were not great—the company soon came to dominate the college and high school basketball scenes. "We had the run of the mill!" Vaccaro recalled during the late spring, twisting the aphorism as of habit.

Vaccaro and, by association, Nike were widely criticized when Alonzo Mourning decided to attend Georgetown University. It was assumed that Vaccaro's long relationship with Mourning and Nike's relationship with Georgetown and its coach John Thompson had influenced the decision.

"Give me Alonzo Mourning and I'm right there for the national championships," Georgia Tech coach Bobby Cremins had been quoted as saying when the college recruitment derby surrounding Mourning began. "He's the last piece of anyone's puzzle."

But Alonzo went on to attend not just a Nike college, but the premier Nike flagship college; and he was mentored there by Thompson, who was a Nike coach and a member of the Nike board. Alonzo says that he'd wanted to attend Georgetown from the day he watched Patrick Ewing and the Hoyas play North Carolina in the 1982 NCAA finals, when Mourning was twelve—which at that point happened to be Alonzo's shoe size.

By 1988—Alonzo's freshman year—Nike colleges had taken four of the last eight NCAA basketball championships. Three years later, Vaccaro's dispensation of contracts to college coaches and creation of formal connections to high school coaches through various summer leagues—and his dispensation of shoes and T-shirts to thousands of amateur players—garnered him the title of "the most powerful man in college basketball" from *USA Today*—"which was when Nike got rid of me," Vaccaro claims. "I didn't fit in with the new corporate image up there in the McEnroe Building. I never dreamt in my wildest dreams that I wouldn't be with Nike all my life," Vaccaro said in May, 1993. "But as I told Phil when I saw him after I left—and he didn't disagree—I was like the gunslinger brought into Dodge City to clean up the bad people. In this case the bad people are the other shoe companies. Once I got rid of them, the good people realized they don't need a gunslinger anymore."

When Alonzo Mourning graduated from college, signing up with Nike seemed no stranger to him than a military career would seem to an army brat. Mourning, who was not raised by his parents, came with John Thompson to the World Campus for his tour and presentation. He and his coach listened to Steve Miller, Howard White, and Fred Schreyer describe the total management idea and he says the whole thing seemed "like a steal."

The $16-million, five-year guarantee that would shock the sports world was apportioned to coverage of his NBA contract, his shoe deal, and his other marketing arrangements. Any money Alonzo would get from his NBA team above the proportionate guarantee was his to keep. The money earned above the marketing guarantee would be split.

Alonzo listened carefully. "Experiment with me," he said.

The same deal structure was applied to Harold Miner's Nike sports-management deal, but in Harold's case, the guarantee Nike offered was predicated on Howard White and Fred Schreyer's estimation that the player often called "Baby Jordan" or "Mini-Mike" would be drafted sixth or seventh overall. The Miami Heat took Miner as the twelfth draft choice, which meant that his salary could not approach the Nike estimate or contractual guarantee.

Contentious internal debate ensued in Beaverton, after Knight decided that Miami Heat owner Lewis Schafel was playing fast and loose with the negotiation process by throwing things into the contract that he knew the league would later disallow. Knight hated this particular bargaining strategy, because its success was predicated on the league barring "the kid" from playing in exhibition games and practices at the last minute.

By then a rookie is immersed in becoming part of the team and would often tell his agent to give in.

Knight wanted Miner to leave training camp and renegotiate the whole deal, but eventually Miner signed without missing a regular season game. The deal would cost Nike $800,000 over each of the next five years because of the difference between Harold's salary and Nike's guarantee.

Knight was still fuming about the rare endorsement setback when the sports press picked up on the controversy in Charlotte over Alonzo Mourning's holdout for a better contract. Sports insiders wondered aloud if perhaps the new Nike management deal was part of an elaborate Nike plot connected to the company's ongoing power struggle with the NBA. Maybe the new NSM deals were designed to get around the NBA salary cap, perhaps by trading future promotional and ad space for services.

"All these people are getting mad at me because of who I worked for," Alonzo said at the time. "I wouldn't do that to anybody else."

Just before the NFL draft in April, the new coach of the New England Patriots, Bill Parcells, had phoned Beaverton. "I heard that either Drew Bledsoe or Rick Mirer is going into your full management program," the coach said, referring to the two most promising college stars. "Which one have you got?"

"Well, Bledsoe is on board for product, and Mirer is with Nike Sports Management," one of Steve Miller's guys replied.

"Thanks," Parcells said, "I'm drafting Bledsoe."

When it came time for an agent to negotiate Rick Mirer's contract with the Seattle Seahawks, talks became contentious, but, for once, the sporting press failed to pick up on the Nike connection.

"Overall management just isn't smart for Nike," Mark McCormack commented after the dust had settled and the NBA season began. "Phil's killing an ant with a machine gun here. The Jordan and Agassi problems could have been solved with contract clauses. I endorse his desire to be more involved in marketing Nike superstars and controlling what they're doing, but taking it to the extent he has will be complicated down the line. Agents and managers are going to be less inclined to sign athletes with Nike just to keep them away from the web."

• • •   **239**

DONALD KATZ

The spinners of the Nike web were all present during the early spring of 1993 for one of the largest annual sports-marketing orgies of them all: the Atlanta Super Show of sports events called the Final Four weekend. Even Knight had joined the large Nike contingent in New Orleans for the last games of the NCAA men's basketball tournament. The Nike entourage included several young Ekins, whose elite access to the relatively inaccessible tournament was a reward for services rendered and general loyalty to the cause. Inside Nike—as was also true inside a very long list of American companies with no working connection to sports—a free, company-acquired ticket to see one of the Final Four match-ups in New Orleans and the attendant tickets and passes required to get past the security lines into the many parties held all weekend long was an acknowledged measure of status and standing . . . like a new pair of Air Jordans on almost any inner-city street.

The Nike advance team in New Orleans had set up a basketball court near the New Orleans Superdome where passersby could try to sink a basket from the same spot from which Michael Jordan launched his game-winning shot as a North Carolina Tar Heel during the 1982 NCAA finals. Jordan's face was projected several stories high onto the side of one huge building near the arena, and the requisite airport and highway billboards hurled Nike images into every vista.

One of the young Ekins graced by the opportunity to join Knight and the rest of the Nike army for the weekend, Brian Clare, said he felt part of "some amazing force" when he beheld Nike's presence. But from another perspective, Nike's traditional presence at the finals was subdued. This year, it was Gib Ford's Converse—still a relative fossil among competitors, from the Nike perspective—that took out a full page in *USA Today,* boasting that the feet of three of the final four teams would be clad in Cons.

"That was our game," cackled Sonny Vaccaro when he saw the ad. "We had all four teams one year and Nike laughed at the world."

Twenty-three of the sixty-four teams that made the NCAA men's tournament wore Nikes by contract, but only the University of Michigan squad would be sporting Nikes during the finals weekend—and for some reason of his own, one of the Michigan players had invoked an NCAA rule that no player can be forced to wear an endorsement shoe, and "the white kid," as all the sports insiders called him in New Orleans, ran onto a stage "better than any runway in Paris" in Adidas shoes. The comparative absence of Nikes on display suggested, once again, the requirement of vigilance and the ever-present question of control.

Knight had recently said that while the sight of local college stars in Nikes seemed to require the methodical shodding of as many amateur players as possible, he thought that the brand presence was such that if Nike could simply stop paying any college coaches or teams, the impact on sales wouldn't show up for quite awhile. But this was not what Knight and his team had in mind in light of the relatively minimal Team Nike presence between the baskets in New Orleans.

Knight believed that Nike's demonstrated success had by now instructed the rest of the industry as to the whys and wherefores of turning the heroism of great athletes into a general desire to own certain shoes.

Converse was doing well with a very funny Larry Johnson "Grandmama" campaign, and students of the sports-marketing scene wondered if not grabbing the happy-go-lucky Johnson when he turned pro was—along with passing on Shaq—another of Nike's rare marketing mistakes. Adidas had built an interesting campaign around Dikembe Mutombo, the seven-foot, two-inch center for the Denver Nuggets, and the marketing teams that had gathered in the McEnroe Building before leaving for New Orleans had shared industry intelligence reports indicating that Fila, Puma, Pony, British Knights, and even Asics were garnering resources to bag a signature basketball star when the NBA draft occurred in late June.

The group of potential stars that might be drafted as pros at the end of June was judged comparatively thin on future superstars of Nike aptitude or attitude. Fred Schreyer and Howard White liked little Bobby Hurley, the feisty senior guard for Duke University, and they were watching Kentucky's Jamal Mashburn and Michigan's Chris Webber. Hurley's dad, a well-known New Jersey high school hoops coach, not uncoincidentally would soon be the honorary coach at a Nike-sponsored high school All-American game in Chicago.

While the sports-management program was one response to competitive replication of Nike's methods, there were passing suggestions made inside the berm that perhaps Nike should simply gather in the entire crop of college seniors this year. Sonny Vaccaro says that in 1985, a year in which Nike had all four final teams under contract, Knight sat him down and asked, "How much would it cost to get all 227 top level teams?" ("It's true," Knight verified. "I was euphoric.")

But if Nike lured all the best players into the stable, what would the public reaction be to a Nike "corner" on the NBA draftees? Besides, the Nike basketball stable was already full of talent—as Shaq had astutely observed during the previous drafting and signing season.

Sonny Vaccaro was back in the talent chase during the Final Four weekend in New Orleans. Vaccaro held forth from the Adidas suite, located one floor above the Nike suite in the same hotel, alongside his new boss, Rob Strasser. The reunion of the ex-Nike guys was the talk of New Orleans—at least among the shoe armies and those on the weekend's sports-marketing cocktail circuit. Coaches stopped by the Adidas suite, and several mentioned to Vaccaro—in passing—the date that their Reebok and Nike contracts would expire.

Strasser and Vaccaro sat not far from Knight at a dinner to honor the extremely ill North Carolina State and Nike "Walk of Fame" coach Jim Valvano, but by then the ex-Nike team now working for Adidas was no longer the subject of insider gossip.

Before the Valvano dinner began, a rumor had coursed through the hospitality suites and VIP lounges that told of Phil Knight making another move. Mike Krzyzewski, the respected and successful coach of Duke University's basketball team and an Adidas endorser for years, had apparently agreed to nurture his famous teams as a Nike guy. The coach would agree by contract to give clinics for Nike and to offer input about the shoes, but the deal was really about getting his team into the right shoes.

The piece of the rumor that shook the national sports grapevine as it was reported as news around the country, was that Krzyzewski would get a million dollars as a signing bonus, a $375–400-thousand-per-year multiyear contract, and lots of Nike stock options as part of the deal. The yearly compensation was actually a bit lower than reported, and the stock options were restricted in a way that meant they might not factor in, but the contract would still rank among the largest ever struck between a shoe company and a coach.

It appeared that the Adidas camp had actually leaked news of the Nike raid after Krzyzewski told Strasser about the million bucks up front. The timing of the Nike deal was for the most part predicated on a long back-and-forth negotiation process, but what mattered was the general reading of the timing: Phil Knight had decided to send a message to Vaccaro and Strasser, his old friends and current nemeses—just as they set out upon their Nike-style revival of Adidas USA.

"Knight signed Mike because he's a great coach and has a great program—and because he's a Nike kind of guy," David Falk observed when he heard the news. "But at the same time," Falk continued, "Phil was sending a signal to Rob: 'If you want to play in the big leagues, then be prepared to play in the big leagues.' "

"Hell," Sonny Vaccaro complained. "I'm not gonna have a million dollars to spend on promotional deals all year. . . . Adidas is like a pimple on Nike's rear end. Only Reebok can go head to head with Nike right now. I just think Phil Knight doesn't want to see Rob or me even make a dent in this industry."

Steve Miller admitted that the timing of the Krzyzewski announcement in New Orleans was indicative of the Nike proclivity for public orchestration, but he endeavored to point out that what was being called the Krzyzewski deal would really be part of a deal between Nike and Duke.

The new thrust from the sports-marketing department was to hook up "near exclusive" sponsorship deals with entire universities—as Nike had struck with the University of Miami in 1989, and was in the process of working out with USC and the University of North Carolina at the time of the New Orleans extravaganza. As contracts with competing manufacturers ran out, the University of Southern California's football, basketball, tennis, volleyball, and track-and-field teams, for instance, would be prominently clad in Nike gear. The money would first pass through university administration and then go to the team coaches. "If the institution ends up keeping some money for itself, then we think this is the way it should be," Steve Miller explained.

But the general reading, as with the million-dollar bonus to Krzyzewski, was that the blanket agreements were yet another aspect of Nike's desire to vertically integrate all of sports.

As the value of contracts for college coaches increased radically during the later 1980s—while sports purists pointed out that coaches were only paid because it was against NCAA rules to **243** pay the athletes who really filled the stands—the cultural status and media prominence of the coaching establishment was also on the rise.

Sports continues to occupy and preoccupy ever-greater portions of the collective popular consciousness, and coaches who might have been sainted inside various undergraduate quadrangles have been suddenly elevated and decorated on a more visible plane. The machinations of Indiana coach Bobby Knight became the subject of a best-selling book, and several college and professional athletic coaches became highly paid speakers on the inspirational corporate pep-talk circuit. A longtime college coach like Dean Smith of North Carolina, Michael Jordan's college coach and an avuncular deity in the state of North Carolina (the basketball arena at North Carolina is called the Dean Dome), was now featured on television talk shows. Nike coach Joe Paterno was called "Saint Joe" in Pennsylvania.

In Nikeworld, the prefix "Coach" had carried a particularly honorific gravity since Bowerman and Knight had installed the locker-room esprit de corps. Inside the berm, "Coach" easily eclipsed titles like "Chairman" or "Senator" or even the ecclesiastical "Father" or "Reverend." "Part of it is that Knight is much more the coach than the owner. He's not just a gatekeeper," Howard Slusher noted. But now millions of nonathletes outside the berm regarded coaches with a similar reverence, and politicians seeking office wanted a winning coach beside them on the stump in the spot once reserved for Billy Graham.

Those closer to the college coaching scene knew about the seasonal groveling and glad-handing, and even rule-breaking coaches felt they had to partake of each year to recruit winning teams. But to a general society bereft of other more traditional authority figures, the coach appeared worthy of celebration in the way of generals during and immediately after wars. This was particularly true, it seemed, of the coach of a culturally diverse team that included men from backgrounds often feared to be inimical to traditional order.

And in such a time formal public association with a newly prominent coach would carry a rising price in the marketplace. As the intensity of the need to be entertained brought Oprah Winfrey her $50 million per year and Michael Jordan his $40 million, the need to believe in the capacity to lead was beginning to make a bunch of unlikely sports fanatics—who had, by and large, come to their jobs as a calling—wealthy.

"Rich as Coaches," read the report on Krzyzewski's deal with Nike in *Forbes*.

"Krzyzewski's Deal With Nike Really Worse Than Prostitution," read the headline representing another point of view in the Portland *Oregonian*.

Knight—ever partial to the individual athlete—was less energetic than usual in his defense and support of Nike's habit of paying coaches in order to get shoes on the kids. "The first coach we ever paid was Dick Harter of the University of Oregon," Knight said as the Krzyzewski news appeared under headlines on the business and sports pages all over the country. "After two or three years of trying to get shoes on the school, we heard that Harter had a deal with Converse for twenty-five hundred dollars. So we said, 'If that's how it works, we'll pay him the twenty-five hundred.' Then the whole March Madness and the Final Sixty-four phenomenon took off on TV and the numbers for coaches just started going up from there."

News of the money involved in the Krzyzewski deal was received with variable degrees of enthusiasm inside Nikeworld. In the Jordan Building and in the liaison offices in Pusan and Guangzhou, developers and production employees heard about the deal, and some of them had to wonder once again what the well-dressed, well-paid sports marketers in the McEnroe Building were doing. Here the people who actually made the shoes busted their butts to shave a few tenths of a point off the cost and price of the goods, and a contract worth up to $15 million over seven years is handed out to a coach who put his team in Adidas for years. Many Nike employees on the shoe-making side of the business (the linemen, the unsung play-makers) had felt for some time that the sports marketers (the running backs, the slam-dunkers and shooting guards) were overpaid. An executive compensation firm had been brought in a year earlier to address those complaints, but a subtle skepticism still separated the sports-marketing team from elements of the rank-and-file employees—and many of the old runners and other members of the small coterie of "originals" also entertained their doubts about the size of the endorsement deals.

Back in 1973, a year after the Nike brand was launched at the Olympic Trials in Eugene, and two years after the word "Nike" came to Jeff Johnson in a dream, Knight sent Nelson Farris out to hang around the gyms at UCLA and USC to try and give away a few pairs of Nike shoes. This was what was thought of as **245** athlete promotion twenty years ago. In 1993, Nike would give away over $7 million worth of shoes and gear to noncontract college athletes alone.

"It's the numbers involved in the Krzyzewski thing that are painful for some people around here. It's certainly the kind of show of force we like to see, but it's just so much money. It makes you wonder," Nelson Farris said.

But Farris joined everybody else on the World Campus as they monitored the results of every March Madness game. When Nike's Michigan team lost during the last seconds of the finals to Dean Smith's North Carolina Tar Heels, Farris felt connected to the defeat in a way that made him really want to win next year.

And when still-young longtime Nike coach Jim Valvano finally succumbed to his cancer just before the NBA play-offs, Farris was part of the general mourning that overtook all of Nike. Employees placed bouquets beneath Valvano's image along the Walk of Fame, and others made signs and cards to tape onto the pillar below it.

By the time Valvano died, Dean Smith had agreed to put the proposal that he break his twenty-three-year association with Converse in favor of a new deal with Nike to a vote of his senior basketball players.

"Nobody can win a vote among players now except Nike," Sonny Vaccaro commented from his home in Los Angeles. "Adidas will win that vote some day, but right now it's all Nike. Let's face it, they're still too damned good. They'll get their six billion dollars in business and more."

Nike easily won the vote. Twenty-four of North Carolina's twenty-six intercollegiate teams would receive shoes, equipment, and apparel from Nike. (The men's and women's soccer teams voted to stay with Adidas.)

Kidder Peabody analyst Gary Jacobson said that Nike's pursuit of Smith was "consistent with their ongoing strategy of trying to outfit every athlete in the world."

Knight watched Dean Smith on an ESPN documentary one evening after the coach entered the fold. "You know it's just amazing," he said with perceptible irony. "I used to think the man pontificated, but now I think he's entirely sincere. Must be the shoes."

But whatever the coaches were suddenly getting paid to suggest which shoes their players wore under the lights, those inside the berm never doubted that the remuneration was but a by-product—like the huge success of Nike—of their loyalty to their games.

It was Jim Riswold's job to come up with an Alonzo Mourning commercial for the NBA play-offs. Riswold was also supposed to come up with a new Harold Miner, Dan Majerle (the hard-working Phoenix Suns three-point-shot specialist), Michael Jordan, and Charles Barkley commercial, too.

The Barkley commercial was the one everybody was talking about inside the ad and marketing sides of the company, because the whole serious-minded conception of the spot entailed a significant risk.

The marketing and positioning of Charles Barkley's public presence had changed significantly over the nine years of his basketball career and Nike deal. Charles had come into the league from Auburn as a talented if overweight and belligerent young man—the latter quality being often attributed to years of being teased about his weight during high school and then in college, where he was known as the "round mound of re-bound." Barkley was known to call people he didn't know "knuckleheads" out of habit; he punched opposing players and various civilians in the nose on occasion; and as Phil Knight seemed to enjoy pointing out to Barkley now and again, he once claimed that he was misquoted by the ghostwriter of his own autobiography. It was hard to forget the time a throatful of spit Charles had lofted into a crowd landed on top of a little girl, and Barkley had constantly whined to reporters when he played in Philadelphia that if he could only play with a team of contenders, he would surely soar.

Shocks and "offense to the community," as the Nike endorsement contracts phrased it, were Charles's stock-in-trade, and while he was more than welcome to occupy one of the bad-boy slots in the Nike stable, his year of soaring with a team of contenders had helped take the hard edge off both his personality and his image. Since Barcelona, the gentle joker inside Charles Barkley had modified the ugliness, and Charles had stepped up, from the Nike perspective, at a time when Michael Jordan—for a variety of reasons—was stepping back.

The basketball marketers had always thought David Robinson, the towering and articulate San Antonio Spurs center, would be the number two basketball endorser. Barkley had once appeared in a "Mr. Robinson's Neighborhood" commercial. Charles blew down the door to Mr. Robinson's house and Robinson, in a singsong, kindergarten teacher's voice, asks Barkley if he can tell the boys and girls how you get fined. Several video clips of on-court violence appeared, including a vicious encounter between Barkley and the brutal Detroit Piston Bill Laimbeer that nobody in Beaverton could believe the NBA ever allowed them to use.

Then Charles reappeared with a halo on his head and generally stole the show.

Now Barkley was on one of the two or three best teams in the league, and his signature Nikes were moving out of the shops faster than Air Jordans. Knight, who thought long and hard about such things, said that playing with Phoenix certainly played a part in the sudden Charles mania—as the disappearance of Magic and Larry Bird had opened up two senior statesman and superstar slots in the NBA firmament. But Knight also thought that in the wake of their Dream Team association, Barkley had ascended through association with Michael Jordan. Charles was perceived as Michael's big buddy or big little brother, even though Barkley and Jordan were the same age.

Now that Charles was a certified Nike hero and part-time comedian, opinion was mixed inside the Nike berm about a serious commercial. The new play-off commercials were supposed to be leveraged off the success of the black-and-white, documentary-style Courier and Agassi spots, but the Barkley conception went much further.

Ever since the Olympics, Barkley, who grew up in a fatherless home, had privately expressed his frustration with society's expectations of him as a contrived role model. "The thing is, parents should really be kids' role models," Barkley would say to his many Nike contacts. At one point, one of the many internal film crews that conduct interviews with the Nike stars caught Barkley saying, "Because parents don't do their jobs in America anymore, people like me have become role models instead.

"Real role models are people you can talk to at breakfast, but people can't really come up and touch me," Barkley would say. "I'm a famous basketball player.

"Besides," Charles would add, "sports isn't even that important. Sure, somebody might have died or the kids were giving somebody a hard time at home, so they come to the game. I give 'em two hours of pleasure. It's something, but it's just sports."

Jim Riswold thought Barkley's role-model hobbyhorse should be taken to prime time—the commercial as social criticism. Here was a chance to return to authenticity. Such spots would serve as an antidote to what Knight perceived as the recent corporate projection of too much fantasy, of "too much hype." But could the same Charles who leapt onto the scorer's tables, dumped beer on fans looking for an extra autograph, and lobbed spit onto the young fan be taken seriously as a proponent of parental responsibility?

Eight of the ten men on the floor during most of the NBA finals between the Chicago Bulls and the Phoenix Suns were prominent Nike consultants, and between basketball and Madonna moments the new Jordan, Barkley "Role Model," and even the Dan Majerle commercials were ready to roll. During game six of the series, a huge 18.6 rating for men between twenty-five and fifty-four was achieved. This meant that 20 percent of all American men in that age range were present and accounted for in front of the game.

Now called the "Nike unplugged" series, the package of five black-and-white "message" spots received immediate follow-up press coverage. The Barkley "Role Model" ad had aired during the first round of the play-offs. Charles was heard to say that he "isn't paid to be a role model. . . . I'm paid to wreak havoc on the basketball court." And, as he had wanted to say for years, he concluded, "Just because I can dunk a basketball, doesn't mean I should raise your kids."

A *New York Times* editorial called the pairing of Barkley and talk of role models "ingenious irony. . . . This is the most subversive sneaker commercial of all time. It shows a sneaker salesman telling us that sneaker salesmen can't save us." The Chicago columnist Mike Royko wrote that Charles was undoubtedly right about parents being proper role models, but "today," Royko continued, "when the male parent leaves the house in the morning, it isn't certain that he'll be back within a year, a decade, or ever." This was what had happened at the Barkley house when Charles was little—which was why he wanted to say his piece.

Barkley's message was joined by a far more self-involved-sounding soliloquy from Michael Jordan: "What if my name wasn't in lights?" Jordan mused woozily as he stood in an empty gym, shooting one dead-center free throw after another. "What if my face wasn't on TV every other second? . . . Can you imagine it? . . . I can."

Everyone at Wieden & Kennedy and inside Nike sports marketing knew that Jordan as a rule did not participate in commercials shot just before the play-offs, but when Jim Riswold sent him the script for this more serious sort of ad, Jordan told him that he thought the message conformed with his encroaching ambivalence about the oppressive weight of his own celebrity. After talking to Riswold, Jordan felt that the ad conveyed the message that "If people didn't know me or see my face or even know who I was, I would still be happy in a gym shooting baskets—even happier—just playing the game like I used to before everything changed."

But many viewers thought the commercial simply said, "Just get off my back"—a sentiment underscored by Nike star Ken Griffey, Jr.'s "I am not a role model" pronouncement in a magazine interview a few weeks earlier.

The apparent ingratitude some perceived in Jordan's message was complicated during the play-offs by Jordan's furious reaction to reports of his gambling habits and gambling losses. Two months after Barcelona, Jordan had testified in a federal court in Charlotte, North Carolina, that he gave a check for $57,000 to a man called Slim Bouler, who was then on trial on drug charges. Jordan said the check covered losses on golf bets.

While the Bulls were playing the New York Knicks in the NBA play-offs seven months later, the sports media played up a late-night trip Jordan and his father had made to the casinos in Atlantic City. The trip once again called attention to the previous gambling debt, and the public discussion continued into June, when a new book written by a San Diego businessman alleged that Jordan had at one point owed him $1.25 million from lost golf bets.

Jordan was sometimes devastated by the charges and at other times enraged. He began a personal boycott of all media representatives during the play-offs, but he eventually agreed to a taped television interview with his friend sportscaster Ahmad Rashad that was shown during half-time. To the chagrin of viewers in Beaverton, Jordan chose to wear Phil Knight–like dark glasses—which made him look like a gambler. Though Jordan denied the $1.25 million figure, all he could do was explain to his public that while it might be hard for them to imagine how rich he was, losing ten thousand dollars here or there was like someone less fortunate losing twenty bucks.

As with the general interpretation of the Nike unplugged commercial, Jordan's public presentation lacked the precision of imagery, script, and professional play that had caused the spotlight to become so focused over the years that it seemed Michael Jordan was always bathed in ethereal light.

"Let's just say Michael Jordan is clearly not as good a golfer as he is a basketball player," Knight joked when the subject of Nike's public comments about the gambling accusations first came up. Knight did not think Michael Jordan had a gambling problem. He'd watched Jordan bet a hundred dollars or more on golf holes before, but Knight had never seen or even heard about Jordan betting at the levels now being widely discussed. "And if Michael wanted to drive to Atlantic City with his dad and get to bed by one, then he was also up at nine and at practice. That's plenty of sleep, and in my view the trip was an acceptable way to get ready for a game," Knight added.

But Knight also seemed concerned. Ever since the Summer Olympics, he had watched Jordan in retreat. Jordan talked often of the burdens of the game and his discomfort with the weird religiosity of his image. Several times he'd talked to Knight and Howard White about his thoughts of retirement.

One day, after hoisting a heavily loaded barbell up from the floor, Jordan had turned to Howard White with the weight still hanging below his waist. "Ya know what? With as much money as I got, there's got a be a real big reason to continue to do this. Because I really don't have to."

On Halloween night, Jordan had been known to invite local suburban kids inside his house, but now ground was being broken for a new twenty-nine-thousand-square-foot house that was already surrounded by a twelve-foot wall. The grounds were to include a three-hole golf course, and the house would contain a full basketball court. Jordan was building the kind of fortress one would never have to leave.

Jordan's friends at Nike had long been aware of the way he could lose himself to everything but the flow of a basketball game—to the arc of the shot. Playing the game was the way Michael Jordan escaped the dream he'd become for others, but at least three times since Barcelona, Knight had heard him say that this wasn't as true anymore.

251

"If we back off Michael in terms of advertising a bit, we certainly won't back away very far," Knight said, as Jordan's public agonies and private ambivalences persisted through and beyond the Bulls' third NBA title. "Whatever happens in the short term, whenever Michael announces his final year, he will be enormously popular—there will be a huge surge."

But as Knight assessed the living hero scene in the middle of 1993, he sometimes wondered if, once again, the business of sports was about to change. Sports, after all, had not always been so much at the cultural forefront as it had over the past decade. The cultural and political whirlwind of the late 1960s and early 1970s had certainly overshadowed the pull of sports for millions of Americans. Lately, the antics of team owners and the constantly rising ticket prices had alienated certain kinds of fans, and statistic-obsessed sports regulars divided contract values by home runs hit averages and yardage gained without pleasure.

At the top of the various sports-marketing establishments, there had been growing concern about a decline for some time. The estimated half-billion-dollar loss suffered by CBS on a four-year-long, $1.06-billion contract with major league baseball was the main reason the sports-marketing boom was being cast as a bubble that might burst. The vulnerability of the economic sector was more recently indicated by the fact that while the Barcelona Olympics and Seoul Olympic television rights had been bid out nearly four years in advance, no television deals had come together for the Atlanta games in 1996, with only three summers to go. (NBC acquired the rights in July for a record $456 million, though fears of a market lapse were only mildly assuaged by this.)

Internally, Knight had noticed less of a tendency to connect Nike's symbiotic relationships with big-time sports with the reinvention-era term "marketing." But he figured this was largely the result of a growing feeling inside Nike that the sports-marketing ventures and related advertising during 1993 weren't quite measuring up to the stellar standards of the past seven years.

When Jim Riswold had presented his creative package for the play-off spots, he included a commercial in which Alonzo Mourning appeared with a miniaturized Charles Barkley standing on one shoulder and a similarly Lilliputian David Robinson on the other. Charles would be dressed as the devil, and David, appropriately for the ever-serious and born-again athlete, would be dressed as an angel. Both players would whisper advice in the rookie's ear.

But the spot was rejected by the Nike ad department before Mourning even heard about the script. It was thought unhelpful to a future Nike superstar's formative image to present him in the shadow of more well-known stars.

The idea of coming up with an "unplugged" commercial for Alonzo also foundered when Riswold and others working on the project couldn't come up with an angle.

Knight was told that Alonzo was crushed when he heard that there would be no debut commercial during the play-offs. Alonzo was particularly upset when he heard that fellow Nike Sports Management client Harold Miner would have an unplugged commercial in which he claims his separateness from the constant comparisons of his play with Jordan's. Harold, Alonzo pointed out, wasn't even on a play-off team.

Alonzo performed brilliantly on the court—particularly when Charlotte met the New York Knicks during the second round. But he would have to wait until the next season for those magical thirty seconds when the Nike hero machine would take him up and away.

Jim Riswold and others involved said they didn't really know who Alonzo was—not really—so Riswold vowed to spend some time with the young center during the off-season.

"All we'd have to do is take the money we're using to advertise Charles Barkley and Michael Jordan, put it into Alonzo, and a lot more people would be talking about him," Knight said. "And there will be a time when that will probably happen."

Near the end of summer, Knight heard that due to a $900,000 shortfall in the UCLA athletic department budget, the university would soon kill off its men's swimming program and both the men's and women's intercollegiate gymnastic teams. The decision was made by UCLA chancellor Charles Young and athletic director Peter Dalis, who commented that "soaring costs and flat revenues"—in particular a drop-off in ticket and television revenue from football—had led to the painful decision.

"He drops a program that provided half the 1984 gold medal Olympic gymnastics team, a program that produced Mitch Gaylord and Peter Vidmar!" Knight raged. "And the UCLA swimming team must have turned out twice as many Olympians and national champions as the gymnastics team. They're closing down a swimming program—in Southern California—for the want of the million dollars the university could have had from us. These are the guys teaching our children! And I'm the guy in all the newspaper articles who's bad for sports!"

Two weeks later, UCLA was forced to hold off on closing down the women's gymnastics program because of a threatened gender equity lawsuit.

Around the same time, the Disney Company announced publicly that it would approach the NCAA with a gala plan to stage the "Disneyland Classic," a national college football championship to be held in Anaheim, California, in January of 1995. The elaborate weeklong festivities would conclude with a visit from Bill Clinton, though when contacted by reporters, Clinton's scheduler didn't know what the reporter was talking about.

"They're just trying the public route," Knight said with a smirk. "We tried to do it quietly . . . and we did it first."

Howard Slusher figured that a deal would eventually be struck between the NCAA and one of the networks, and by the time the tournament commenced, Slusher believed that Ovitz's vision of some kind of interactive technology component to the event would have become real.

During the fall, pursuant, in part, to Judith Albino of Colorado's favorable comment after the Nike/CAA presentation in Kansas City—and in part to Charles Young's sense that several months needed to pass before the effects of the "setback" caused by the Nike/CAA presentation had dissipated—an NCAA Presidents Commission committee had been formed to look into a national college football championship. The committee had been formed to collect facts, and NCAA-watchers were predicting a late summer 1994 vote and a 1995 kickoff.

"There is still no enthusiasm for a play-off, but there is a feeling that this is something that must be pursued—with or without enthusiasm," Young commented as the fact-finding committee began its work. "We need to understand what the problems would be, and we need to determine the reasons for proceeding with a tournament despite the problems—financial reasons included."

"This event will happen because it's the right thing to do," Knight said. "In a way it doesn't matter who organizes the games, because it will be good for the sports—and because when it finally happens, we'll be right there."

NEWARK

August 1993

Du4ing the middle of a very hot afternoon, fifty pairs of
Air Carnivores designed in Beaverton, Oregon, and built in
Pusan, South Korea, arrived—via the big Nike warehouse in
Exeter, New Hampshire—at the veritable metropolitan mu-
seum of athletic footwear called the Essex House of Fashion.
The hallowed, urban shoe emporium is located not a half mile
from Shaquille O'Neal's birthplace in downtown Newark, New
Jersey, close by a corner where the broad thoroughfare called
Market Street crosses Halsey and is suddenly abloom with star-
tling colors and noise and urgent whorls of shoppers.

Along the sidewalk across from the hulking, empty shell of an
old Macy's, the crowds along Sneaker Row mill constantly in
front of the overstuffed display windows of the Essex House of
Fashion, Bros. Sneakers, the Sneaker Room, 108 Sneaker, the
Sneaker Joint, and the thirty-thousand-square-foot monster
shop called Dr. Jay's Sneakers.

On Market Street, news of the backroom unpacking of a new
long-awaited model from Nike, Reebok, Adidas, Converse,
K-Swiss, Fila, Pony, or one of the others can inspire frenzy.
Almost every jock in Newark knows that the new Air Jordans
arrive during the NBA All-Star game break, and during some of
the big runs on Air Jordans over the years, some of the stores in
downtown Newark raised the selling price of the coveted shoes
well above Nike's suggested price as a way to allow the market
to control the shoe-hungry crowds.

Most of the regulars on Sneaker Row are young. In a city **255** where truancy rates can run up to 49 percent, the Newark shoe stores are often bursting with kids in the early afternoon.

The boisterous vernacular of the street corner immediately gives way to softer tones when the young shoppers come inside the stores. Some browsers clutch one hand in the other below the waist, and they tend to walk very slowly, almost piously, stopping in front of Lucite slabs that protrude from the walls bearing shoes. The kids will patiently wait to move closer to the little shelves, bending forward from the waist with studious expressions.

"Yo. *Check* out these new Scotties."

"Look, dere he is," whispered a Haitian woman scanning one of the many Nike "personality posters" forming an entablature along the top of the long walls of the Essex House of Fashion. "Dere's Bo!"

Both circular and waterfall-style stainless steel racks near the front of the store displayed hundreds of examples of freshly minted Nike apparel, and a large display case next to the centrally located checkout counter offered for sale rolled posters of Charles Barkley ("Say What?"), of Bo lifting weights, and of Deion Sanders crouched like a bird of prey in his Atlanta Falcons uniform.

The owner and curator at the Essex House of Fashion, a beleaguered-looking man of thirty-eight named Steven Roth, was somehow able to scan the shop floor and carry on conversations while also ringing up sale after sale from behind a long counter set in the middle of a quarter-acre of shoes, athletic apparel, and so many balls of crumpled white paper pulled from the toes of the new shoes that they moved back and forth across the floor like little tumbleweeds with the constant rush of customers. Roth's employees would quickly pick up the paper, but it would immediately be replaced as dozens of pairs of shoes were tried on all at once.

Roth wore a white tennis-style polo shirt with a Reebok emblem over the left breast. Beside him, working the next register, stood a much larger man who wore three gold chains adorned with heavy gold medallions and a bright green sweatshirt. The sweatshirt was heavily "strapped"—the black, nine-millimeter pistol ensconced in a black shoulder-holster assemblage was held tight to the clerk's broad chest with straps. The jet-black Velcro straps were even thicker than the Velcro locking system on the

Air Carnivores, five cases of which had just been delivered by UPS and unpacked in the back of Steven Roth's store.

"Not what I'd call a huge order," Steven said. "Especially when you consider that I can sell fifty pairs of a new Air Jordan model inside an hour."

Roth set one of Bill Worthington's new shoes down on the counter and considered it with a skeptical gaze. "Some print advertising starts next week. A shoe as different as this won't take off unless there are ads. It's harder to sell a hundred-and-thirty-dollar pair of shoes right now than it was last year."

Steven Roth is a second-generation Market Street merchant. His father's tailor shop around the corner served Newarkers of modest means for years before the term "inner city" came into popular usage. When Steven Roth opened the Essex House of Fashion eighteen years earlier, the shop was a haberdashery. "Sharkskin suits by the truckload and very funky wide-brimmed hats," Steven said, still ringing up sales. "But then he came along"—Roth pointed up at one of several posters depicting Michael Jordan—"and him"—he pointed at Bo—"and all of a sudden fashion meant shoes."

Steven conversed easily with one young customer after another, often in a blend of street argot, the shoe-tech spoken by the Nike Ekins, and local shoe slang. He seemed to know many of the young customers he served the day the Air Carnivores came to Newark—if not by name, then at least according to their aesthetic preferences.

"Everyone knows me around here," Roth said. "They know who I am and they know what I am. There's a guy in New York who plays up the 'Jewish-merchant-in-the-black-neighborhood' bit by calling himself and his store 'the Jew Man.' I'd say that's a bit much. I'm white and I'm Jewish and there aren't any black entrepreneurs in retail around here at all. Those are all facts. Most of my employees are black or Spanish, and the fact that I've never had trouble after all these years indicates how I'm regarded in the community—but then somebody always wears one of these."

Roth pointed at the gun.

"Nice try," Steven said in a weary voice to a very tall kid who was trying to "return" an LA Raiders windbreaker. "You know as well as I do it's not from here. Best take it on down the street."

The young man looked down and shook his head sheepishly, **257** trying unsuccessfully to look irritated. He turned and trudged away atop huge black high-topped basketball shoes, his baggy blue jeans bunched so heavily around the bulbous tops of his Nike Air Force Max shoes that he walked like someone wearing leg irons.

Once out on Market Street, the kid turned left and quickly disappeared into another sneaker store.

As part of the refocusing of the Nike brand and sub-brands accomplished in recent years, Knight ordered the retail distribution specialists to streamline the system. The number of official store outlets was reduced from fourteen thousand to twelve thousand during the reinvention years, and only two of the nine or ten retailers on Market Street made the cut. And yet all of the stores on Sneaker Row carried some "Nike" shoes and related apparel—this as the result of overt counterfeiting and a related, industry-wide phenomenon called "diversion."

Diverted goods come to market when retailers or wholesalers order more shoes and apparel than they need and then profit from diverting the gray-market wares to other stores Nike either doesn't or will not sell in the quantities the stores desire. Internal complicity is occasionally involved. In June, two Nike sales reps were fired for allowing diversion to occur inside their territories.

Factories found to have contributed to the huge gray market by continuing production runs past the bounds of Nike's orders—or found not to have destroyed shoes that didn't make it past inspection—are summarily dropped, but the threat has made barely a dent in a parallel marketplace endowed with internal economic structures no less elaborate than the drug trade.

"There are these wandering minstrels!" Dick Donahue fumed after a meeting about counterfeiting in Beaverton one day. "They scour the Orient. They promise a producer or a distributor they'll drop the shoes in darkest Africa and then they turn up in New Jersey."

After years of pressure—mostly from Nike—Korean export laws were changed in July 1992 so that bills of lading must indicate the contents of closed shipping containers. Efforts to crack down on factories has meant that gray-market Nike shoes and strange-looking shoes made from bits and pieces of Nikes, Reeboks, and other brands cobbled together from stolen or diverted components—"Mr. Potato Head shoes," as they're known in the industry—are less readily available on the streets of South Korea than in years past. But even after a series of Nike-inspired police sweeps, a $10-billion counterfeit branded goods industry still thrives in Korea, and the fact that so many of the merchants on Sneaker Row selling Nikes without official accounts are also Korean nationals is not thought to be coincidental.

In Chicago, Nike conducted a spot-check of Air Jordan apparel—which is much more easily copied than high-tech shoes. Two thirds of the stuff on display turned out to be phony.

It's hard to spot fake T-shirts until the images come off in the washing machine, but almost every one of the fifteen hundred advanced students of athletic shoes who entered Steven Roth's store every day could pick out a counterfeit Nike basketball shoe at ten paces.

Roth can spot phony goods from much farther away.

"Very nice," Steven said, holding up a pair of ex-Nike guy Jim Moodhe's top-of-the-line Guess Athletic basketball shoes. The sixteen-year old who planned to purchase the black shoes, Rockean Sanders, leaned over, closer to Roth, to once again admire the lines and contours of the shoes.

Rockean had just completed ninety minutes of analysis in front of "the wall." Rockean thought that some of the new cross-trainers on display were so hot-looking that he had wandered from his usual concentration on the basketball shoe display. Rockean spent several minutes checking out the Deion Sanders Air Diamond Turfs, which—as with all the new cross-trainers—were moving well as the back-to-school campaign shifted into gear. The weekly "push" on the Deion shoes—the percentage of the total number of shoes delivered that were sold during that week—was running at close to 30 percent in the retail chains and most of the bigger stores. A 30 percent push was a slam dunk in shoeworld. Within eight weeks, 60–70 percent of a big shoe disbursement needed to be sold for a profit to be achieved, and the Air Diamond Turfs were already there.

Tom Phillips and the other cross-training marketers were surprised to learn that the red, white, black, and gold shoes were a hit with young, inner-city high school girls. In Atlanta the Air Diamond Turfs were the hottest shoe on the street. The whole cross-training line was way up—sales would jump by 34 percent by the end of the quarter on August 30—though elation inside the cross-training segment cutting across the operational silos would be mitigated by conjecture over whether or not the soft sales in the basketball segment were in some part due to basketball customers switching over to cross-trainers.

"Gotta be black," Rockean said, putting the Air Diamond Turfs down with care and shuffling over to a specially designed platform displaying a pair of Nike Air Raids, shoes designed for outdoor basketball to which Nike designers had attached a fancy permanent tag meant to replicate the tags being left on urban court shoes in the cities as a style statement—as the tags were left on sunglasses and blouses in Shanghai.

"Too much money," said Rockean, who said he had a dozen other pairs of basketball shoes at home, most of them Nikes.

By far the majority of athletic-shoe buyers do not spend $130 for the shoes that catch the eye in store displays or on the feet of superstars on TV. Only 10 percent of Nikes retail for over $100. The "middle price points" or "kill zones" as retailers often call the lucrative center of the market—in Nike's case, $60 to $80 shoes—account for a huge majority of total sales. The single most popular Nike basketball shoe in the summer of 1993 was the $80 Air Magnum Force.

Rockean strolled over to a pair of Reebok Shaq Attaq shoes. The $140 Shaq Attaqs premiered along with a major television ad campaign, and retailers reported that the shoes moved well at first. But by August, Rockean Sanders and the other young mavens coursing through Steven Roth's store reported that they didn't approve of the bits of vinyl attached to Shaq's signature shoe. Vinyl was not a material the seasoned shoe-buyer expected to find on a top-of-the-line shoe. And the Shaq shoe—unbelievably, the reviewers along Sneaker Row agreed—was white. The color of the moment was black, a fact reflected by now in the spread sheets available at Reebok headquarters in Massachusetts.

"But considering that it's not black, it's doing okay," Reebok manager John Morgan noted in August.

The boys wanted black in 1993, and it was the boys who moved the market.

More than half of all the athletic-shoe customers in the country were now young men under eighteen. The average American boy was estimated to own twelve pairs of athletic shoes. Americans under twenty-five accounted for more than half of

Nike's sales, and Nike marketers estimated that 70 percent of the money spent on footwear by American boys between thirteen and eighteen was spent on Nikes.

Everything about the shoes, the shoe ads and the athletic images "bolted" to the product, as is often said on the World Campus, read "boy"—young boy . . . testosterone-soaked, freedom-loving, tough as Charles, strong as Bo, outrageous as Deion, and cool as Mike.

The boys were called, and the boys surely came to the shoe walls when the shipments arrived, carting their vivid and multifaceted fantasies of the best vision of themselves inextricably connected to shoes. The shoes were beauty. The shoes were sublime. The shoes were how the boys felt about life, and they had magically been ingrained with their secret aspirations. As cowboys had their tooled boots in the days when brands were the hammered configurations at the end of red-hot irons, the boys had their shoes.

Just a few miles away from downtown Newark, along a suburban roadway that cuts between Ground Rounds and hair salons bearing names such as Hair & Beyond and Hair We Are, the boys surrounded the Air Diamond Turfs and Air Carnivores inside the local agora called the Willowbrook Mall. The eight-hundred-store Foot Locker chain had ordered twelve thousand Air Carnivores, skewing the order to upmarket malls like Willowbrook—and with a 10 percent push during the first week, the shoes were doing pretty well.

The suburban boys trundled into the store on the enclosed Main Street of the mall in jeans so oversized that they had no logical reason to ride above their knees. They wore customized sweat clothes that would not have been acceptable in locker rooms a few years ago. Stretchy workout pants and sweatpants were often pulled tightly into every crevice of their loins, their baseball caps turned backward and sideways like the hats meant to denote a dullard in Elizabethan comedies.

The mall-based shoe scholars were more often joined by young women, some of them sporting hair that rose high above their heads with the aid of acidulous processes. Some of the young women looked in a perpetual state of comic-book fright underneath their hair, and some of them had paid specialists to have miniature still-lifes ascribed atop fingernails grown long as trench knives.

The mall kids in Nikes looked slightly rougher than the global teens of Hong Kong's Mongkok district but not a bit less street-worthy than the kids on Sneaker Row.

Each available silhouette—from head to toe—could be located within a one-minute perusal of the cable TV selection available in most parts of the world. The looks were original, but not too original—which was one reason why a company like Nike had grown so large.

Further south, in the Philadelphia Main Line suburb of Glad-wyne, a tall, blond nineteen-year-old university student named Michael Haines reverently parted the doors protecting shelves bearing his beloved collection of Nikes. The nearly forty pairs of shoes were all perfectly aligned, like carefully selected, stored, and sheltered bottles of the finest wine.

"They have to face backward on the shelf," Michael explained, "because they're just so much more . . . beautiful from behind."

Michael became a true connoisseur of Nikes when he was thirteen, when a modest fascination with athletic footwear became a full-blown mania the first time he glimpsed that window of air built in the heel of the first Nike Air Max. His collection includes earlier mid-1980s models, but most of the shoes Michael carefully extracted from the shelves were purchased in concurrence with Nike's rise as a marketing power. The collection included early Air Force Ones adorned with a silver Swoosh and silver buttons. There was a pair of maroon and silver Air Stabs, and in the special, futuristic carrying case designed for the shoes, Michael even owned a mint-condition pair of the awful Air Pressures thrown together in response to the Reebok Pump—the $170 Nikes that came with nozzles and a hand pump, an experiment that most employees in Beaverton would prefer to forget.

Every Air Jordan vintage was represented in Michael's closet—several pairs of which had never been worn and won't be, if Michael remains true to his vows. There were new Air Huarache cross-trainers, some Air Revolutions, and a pair of Air Force Threes. "I got these black Air Max basketball shoes when I played in the Maccabiah Games in Israel," the former high school basketball and baseball player said, sitting down beneath a poster showing Michael Jordan with his arms spread crucifix-wide across an entire wall. "I wanted to look tough.

"Whenever friends came over during high school, we would

come up here and take out the shoes," Michael continued. "I was fifteen when I really went crazy. I was buying a pair of new Nikes every single month when I was at my worst. My mother tried to get me to see a psychiatrist. She said I had a fetish. She said I couldn't buy any more after awhile, so I started to spend my savings and bar mitzvah money. At first I could hide new pairs in the collection because there were so many, but after awhile I had to hide them around the house—like an addict.

"I could always tell my dad about a new pair, because he loved them too. Eventually, when I just couldn't buy any more, I convinced my dad to buy them. So this forty-six-year-old guy was walking around in black Air Jordans.

"It's like Michael Jordan says when he puts on a new pair before every game, there's nothing in the world like the feeling of lacing them up for the first time. The feeling I get when I put them on is like the feeling I get inside a gym or near a baseball diamond—but that feeling is starting to fade now that I don't compete much anymore.

"But still, if I could have a new pair every day . . . I still love to come home during school breaks and come up here to open the doors."

He paused and stared dreamily at the backs of the shoes. "I love them. I love thinking about opening the box for the first time. I love taking them out. Just talking about them gets me . . . I don't know . . ."

Michael has never gone out in the rain in a pair of Nikes. "Other shoes are for that," he explained. And so much the Nike guy is Michael Haines that his wing-tip dress shoes were made by Cole-Haan, Nike's nonathletic shoe company. "There's an air bag in the heel," he noted.

Though Michael had recently purchased the new Air Max running shoes, a pair of Scottie Pippen Air Flights, and the latest Air Huarache cross-trainers, he admitted to being somewhat concerned about the late 1993 vintage. "There's a sameness over the last year," the connoisseur said. "They just aren't quite as cool this year. But they're still cooler than any other shoe you can buy. I had an awful pair of Converse shoes once and a poorly made pair of Reebok basketball shoes. I'd never touch another brand."

Phil Knight would argue that the seismic sociological shift by which American children of the last quarter of the twentieth **263** century had been turned into ritualistically brand-conscious consumers was as much a function of television's grip as it was a change created by Nike and other companies with similar bottom-line desires. And yet for all of the provable truth in Knight's observation that kids will move their eyes within inches of the screen to see what an otherwise obscure college basketball player is wearing, other research indicates that six out of ten shoe sales are made because of something that happens between the eye, the id ("the craziness," as Michael Haines put it), the censorious combination of the superego and the amount of cash in a given pocket, and the shoe on the Lucite slab. The final scene at the end of a dream that began when Bill Worthington went surfing with Duke Stump and was inspired to design a shoe that was then built in Korea and then shipped to Newark and the Willowbrook Mall and onto the public stages inside twelve thousand stores—occurs inside the fifteen inches separating the customer and the wall.

And inside the Essex House of Fashion, the configuration of the wall during the late summer of 1993—as has been the case for six years—was dominated by Nikes.

The company's visual and economic presence inside Steven Roth's store was only in part a testament to the company's marketing prowess. The Nikeization of the Essex House of Fashion was also due to the fact that Roth is yet another Nike guy. "I get insomnia at night, so I get up and call Nike, just to talk about a shoe I need or get a question answered," Steven said, ringing up sale after sale into the late afternoon. "Somebody who knows what's what is on call for me in Beaverton twenty-four hours a day. Nike has even equipped all the sales reps with these unbelievable computers that can show me a whole line of shoes on the screen. The rep can spin the shoes around, change them into all the colors they'll come in, and he can even show me the commercials that will run to support the shoes on TV."

A few months earlier, a trade publication, the *Sporting Goods Dealer News,* published the results of a survey of five hundred retailers. Nike was universally judged to be the proprietors' favorite brand, and the article attending the data noted that since the dealer survey began in 1988, Nike had been ranked first in each of a dozen or so categories such as delivery, product profitability, promotion support, returns, and packaging. Only one top ranking—for quality, to Reeboks in 1989—had ever been awarded to a company other than Nike.

Store managers could have their Nike orders overnighted to anxious customers by Federal Express. On-time delivery had become an essential aspect of the selling process since the streamlining of the system began during the late 1980s, and the round-the-clock access was welcomed by Steven Roth and the thousands of other in-the-trenches retailers who never stop thinking about their stores.

"I can call Nike up on a Wednesday and tell them I need fill-ins of a hot model, and by the weekend they'll come in. No other company can do that," Steven said. "I've sold thirty percent more Nikes each year since they went into overdrive back in 1986—except for last year when things were a bit flat. The kids started buying a lot of those boots toward the end of last year."

Roth pointed over to a slender display case that he had placed at least twenty feet away from the athletic-shoe walls, behind the long rug-covered benches where customers tried on shoes. The case was filled with all-weather boots and shoes made by the Timberland Company of Hampton, New Hampshire. Known on the street as "Tibs" or "Tims," the Timberlands—along with the old combat-boot-like Doc Martens and several other brands—had become desirable in certain advanced realms of the urban marketplace two years earlier. From his watchtower along the front, Steven Roth recognized a trend that would grow like so many styles and fads now emanating from the inner city, so Steven had purchased Timberland stock at $5 a share in 1991. At the end of the first week of August 1993, Roth watched the price of the shares jump another $6, to $66 per share.

In late June, *USA Today* had run a cover story about the rugged boot fad: "New Fashions Slam-Dunk Sneakers," read the headline of an article that reported the downturn in Reebok and Nike's stock price. The sneaker giants were described as "out of step" with current fashion and at the mercy of "more nimble" competitors like Timberland.

Steven Roth—whose loyalty to the Nike brand is understood inside the berm to be as essential to Nike's power and continued success as all but a few of the professional athletes on the payroll—said intimations that the current slump meant that Nike was in serious trouble were typical of the overstatements made by those outside the industry tribe.

"It's true that I was very disappointed in the spring 1994 stuff I was just shown, and it's also true that Air Jordan's been taking a big hit," Roth said. "It's not just Michael's erratic play this season and the gambling stuff either. The kids talk about Michael's problems, but for two months now the heat's transferred to Barkley. The Air Force Max is very hot, and from this level it looks like Air Jordan might be finished.

"But then Michael," Roth said, waving up at the photographs of Jordan flying and smiling and spreading his arms as if from sea to sea, "he created this whole amazing thing over the past seven years. No athlete ever made the customers come to the shoes like that. It was almost too easy to do what I do for the last seven years. Everyone who came through that door wanted a hundred-twenty-dollar pair of shoes, and you don't have to be a great merchant to show increases with price points like that. When most people want sixty-dollar shoes, then this store turns into a very solid business instead of an unbelievably lucrative one."

Roth buys 80 to 85 percent of his Nikes through Nike's "futures" program. At the February Super Show in Atlanta, the futures structure allowed Nike to inform analysts and retailers that orders for the fall of 1993 were up over last year by 18 percent. Lately, a fall in futures was telling Knight and other close observers of the company that Nike's double-digit gallop over the last few years might stall for much of the coming year. Steven Roth's spring 1994 order from Nike would be off by 25 percent.

"A lot of the sluggishness is macroeconomic," Knight observed in early August. "But very recently I've seen a certain predictability that's crept in to our line. I've seen people compare the shoe wars to the cola wars, but in the cola industry they don't change their products more than once in three or four years. We have to change everything about our shoes several times within a single year, and a few of the recent turns simply haven't been aggressive enough."

A July issue of *Sporting Goods Business* still placed Nike at the top of a list measuring retail level growth in terms of both percentage of total shoes sold and their dollar value. Nike was judged the "hottest" brand of 1993 in the report, with Converse taking the "comeback of the year" laurels and Rob Strasser's Adidas highlighted as "the brand to watch."

Knight was watching Strasser's strategy and tactics closely in August, and he was becoming concerned about the possible relationship between Nike's falling urban basketball sales and reports that Sonny Vaccaro was rewiring his "collection of weirdos," as Knight called them, on the urban basketball scene. Knight believed that Sonny's Rolodex included the names of inner-city YMCA managers and playground superstars all over the country. Because of the dense concentration of the urban basketball-conscious public, a well-wrought grassroots initiative could quickly become a powerful low-cost display mechanism for Adidas. Knight had also heard that Vaccaro had ingratiated himself with Felipe Lopez, perhaps the best high school basketball prospect in the country. Word went around inside the berm that Adidas now employed Felipe's brother.

"The kid in the street," the number two Adidas man, former Nike designer Peter Moore, had said, "holds the key to the kingdom."

Phil's concern about Sonny is just "white, Hillsboro, Oregon coming out," Howard Slusher said. "Sonny's gone a lot more corporate than Phil thinks. We'll be fine in the city."

But one quarter of the nearly 80 percent of the basketball-shoe market Nike dominated was based in the cities, and at the end of the summer of 1993—as a new Adidas shoe called the Equipment Boot got hot in the stores—Knight told Tom Clarke and his basketball marketers he wanted them to react to Strasser and Vaccaro on the street.

Steven Roth had seen the hard-edged marketing wars along the urban fronts take on many forms over the years. He had seen new and late entries to the market use an ugly marketing maneuver called seeding to position their shoes. Free shoes would be given away to neighborhood "leaders"—the overlords of street gangs and the most prominent drug dealers—to garner influence.

Some of the names of new shoes brought to market during 1993—notably the Converse Run 'N Gun basketball shoe, a name the company changed in response to public outcry; and the British Knight Company's ad campaign for its Predator basketball shoe model: "Wear the Predator, or be the prey."—seemed designed to imply a level of aggression that had nothing to do with playing games. Nike sold shoes with more subtly aggressive names like Air Darwin and less subtle names like Air Magnum Force ("I like that one a lot," Knight admitted). The "aggression" Bill Worthington admitted he had designed into his Air Carnivores was obviously sports-minded, but it was ag- **267** gression nonetheless. When Converse chairman Gib Ford complained in *The Wall Street Journal* that his Run 'N Gun shoe was certainly no worse than competitors' shoes named Shooter, Assault, Marauder, and Slasher, it was hard to disagree.

When Steven Roth saw the first of hundreds of young men wearing the same gang colors come into the Essex House of Fashion in search of the Reebok Legend shoes and only Reebok Legends some years earlier, he immediately knew what was happening and reordered accordingly. Roth saw the street scene's appropriation of the decidedly nonurban Timberlands coming when gang leaders first asked for the boots.

Roth said he was at first quite shaken when a sudden wave of publicity in late 1989 indicated that American children had begun to injure and even kill one another over the shoes he sold. Numerous local newspaper articles set the stage for a report in *Sports Illustrated* in 1990 about urban youths who had been murdered for their Air Jordans and other coveted models.

Public outrage quickly focused on the shoe industry that had spawned such a surfeit of material desire that young people were willing to do violence to one another over something as utterly meaningless as a pair of sneakers. Some columnists suggested that while "Just Do It" might inspire some people to go to the gym, in other reaches of the social order, the phrase might inspire drug use and the commission of violent crimes. Phil Mushnick, the hard-line anti-Nike sports columnist for the *New York Post*, addressed a spring 1990 column to Nike commercial-maker Spike Lee and others at Nike. "It's murder, gentlemen. No rhyme, nor reason, just murder. For sneakers. For jackets. Get it Spike? Murder."

The Reebok Pump shoe was widely criticized for its $175 price tag in 1990—the higher prices having been cited as a reason that some young people in the cities turned to selling drugs. Paul Fireman was asked about "the lengths to which kids will go" to own the shoes in an interview published in *The National*, a sports daily.

Fireman replied that there was another way to look at a marketplace phenomenon that was being covered in the press via isolated incidents drawn out of context. "If we can make a product that young people are aspiring to, why isn't that the place where they go out and get the job after school—the paper route—things that teach them to aspire to have things that they want in life?"

The Horatio Alger bootstraps-tugging evocation was hardly satisfying to those members of the public beginning to reconsider the brief social history of the modern athletic shoe. Whether a paper route or a day's windfall profit from selling crack financed the shoes, the question of the moment was "Why shoes?" Magic had accrued to the most carefully made shoes, and this perception was clearly the result of a hundred intricate cultural signals—many of which had indeed been manufactured as a way to manipulate the shape of popular desire. At the heart of the critique was what sociologists call a "moral panic," the roiled state inspired over the question "Why shoes?" suddenly reminiscent of the "Why rock music?" of nearly forty years ago.

As sickeningly absurd as a killing over a pair of shoes or a leather jacket or a gold chain clearly was, certain members of a culture of constant acquisition that had, by and large, bypassed the absurdity and larger moral implications of stealing and killing over objects as apparently essential as cars were outraged when violence was done in the name of something as silly as a pair of shoes. Journalists and other assessors of an American public descended from a tradition of a great deal of stealing and killing over horses were suddenly stunned when poor people stole shoes or spent too much money on Nikes and Reeboks when, as one group of critics put it in 1990, they ought to be buying themselves books.

"When all that came up, I could never really get a handle on it," Bo Jackson said before a baseball game at Fenway Park during the late summer. "I'd always thought part of the whole deal was that kids might want to emulate me—to do what I do to get ready to play on the field. I always thought that if they emulated me instead of some street dealer—that was the idea."

"I guess I don't really understand it either," Alonzo Mourning said when asked about violence over the shoes. "I grew up seeing kids steal all sorts of things. I saw people hurt each other for all kinds of reasons. Was Nike supposed to make unimpressive shoes because some people can't afford the best products? The whole thing is hard to figure."

In one of the several books about Michael Jordan, a biography called *Taking to the Air,* author Jim Naughton pointed out that, at first, Michael Jordan said that he would rather "eliminate the product than know drug dealers are providing the funds that pay me." But within a few weeks, Jordan's comments had a different spin: "It's kind of ironic that the press builds people like me up to be a role model and then blames us for the unfortunate crimes kids are committing."

When the spate of Nike-related crimes was pointed out to Spike Lee, the filmmaker replied that the marketing of the shoes was hardly the point. "The real question that needs to be asked," he said, "is what is it about these kids' lives that is so bleak that they need a pair of sneakers or a Georgetown jacket to give them self-worth?"

Liz Dolan and the others in Nike public relations rejected implications that Nike scientifically targeted poor kids for marketing initiatives that capitalized on specific African-American aspirations or on particular dreams of material ascension connected to sport. "We don't target market to a demographic," Dolan would tell reporters. "What we do is sell to psychographic segments—people who love only basketball; people who want to walk for exercise instead of run. We sell to passions and states of mind, not by age, address, or ethnicity."

Nike had hit upon ways to glorify athletes and games that no other institution had imagined during the several years preceding the controversy over the urbanization of the shoes, but the company was not alone in the larger positioning of sports beside entertainment industry stardom, crime, or the more distant possibility of academic and meritocratic ascension as one of the paucity of means by which Americans growing up urban and poor could imagine grabbing a significant piece of the economic pie. But Knight and the others realized—especially after the Operation PUSH affair and the publicity connected to sneaker crime in 1990—that the company had indeed become part of a complicated urban equation.

A series of hip antiracism ads by Spike Lee followed in 1992—with profits from the related goods going to urban youth organizations—and by 1993 many of the successful "midnight basketball" programs in the country were Nike-supported. One Newark basketball program was even underwritten in a cooperative effort by Nike and Reebok.

Asked what the shoes really "meant" to them, most of the customers coming in and out of the Essex House of Fashion during the course of the warm August afternoon said they really weren't sure. "They're just cool," said a kid in Air Flights and a Charlotte Hornets jacket.

"They make me feel special," said another.

Most of the kids would think about the question for a while

before saying that the answer is hard to put into words. The shoes are expressions of feelings and impulses that are otherwise difficult to express, and the inability to come up with an immediate, anthropologically astute analysis of their larger meaning is shared with motorists asked to describe the deeper meaning of a new Lexus. That these shoes happened to become magical items in one realm of the economy in the way Apple Powerbooks possessed a particular aura in another might offer insights into the social and economic order of the moment. But the problem is much deeper than the fact of the shoes.

"What too many people who live in other places don't understand is that there's a part of America where a Big Mac is a celebration," Steven Roth said as he half-consciously opened and closed his cash register, sending one kid after another away from his counter wearing the same dreamy smile Michael Haines wore when he opened his closet full of Nikes. "Most of the people in this store, their lives are shit; their homes in the projects are shit—and it's not like they don't know it," Roth said. "There's no drop-in center around here anymore, and no local place to go that they can think of as their own. So they come to my store. They buy these shoes just like other kinds of Americans buy fancy cars and new suits. It's all about trying to find some status in the world.

"But the truth is," Roth said, pale and exhausted at the end of another day of selling, "I do get weary and worn down from it all. I'm always forced to face the fact that I make my money from poor people. A lot of them live on welfare. Sometimes a mother will come in here with a kid, and the kid is dirty and poorly dressed. But the kid wants a hundred-twenty-buck pair of shoes and that stupid mother buys them for him. I can feel the kid's inner need—this desire to own these things and have the feelings that go with them—but it hurts me that this is the way things are. I've been spending a lot of time lately wishing that the world was a better place than it is."

A week later, Gordon Thompson—just recently elevated to a newly created vice presidency of Nike image and design—strolled slowly through the Chicago Nike Town, staring at the displays, the shoes, and at hundreds of customers' and visiting tourists' feet with obvious concern.

Gordon's hair was still wet from a long morning workout and a run along the path set against the Chicago lakefront. He wore

shorts, Air Deschütz sports sandals (the best-selling Nike product of the previous spring), and a work shirt, and he carried a water bottle as he walked past walls loaded with Nike images of his own design. Nike artifacts were displayed like objects in a state-of-the-art museum, with museum-style display copy underneath. Gordon had coordinated the color of the fish in a twenty-two-foot-long tropical tank as part of the store's design. He'd ordered banks of television monitors, and sculptures hung everywhere in the air. Shoe boxes trundled along through Plexiglas "shoe tubes" from one floor of the open, multistoried environment to the other. The design reference to the futuristic *Jetsons* cartoon series was intended, Gordon said. Back in 1989, Gordon worked as a consultant on the movie *Back to the Future II*. The athletic-shoe store of the future he designed for the film became part of the inspiration for Nike Town.

Another Nike Town had opened in Costa Mesa, California, in the spring, and it was greeted with widespread praise. Watts Wacker, the retail trend tracker for New York–based Yankelovich Partners, described the store as a combination "museum and theater." Wacker noted that with Americans in 1993 spending half the amount of time in malls as they spent there in 1985, "retail entertainment" was becoming increasingly important.

Among the many retailers who were concerned and even overtly scared of Nike's foray into upscale retailing were many of the merchants regarded as members of the family inside the berm. If Nike Inc. grossed $25 on a $130 pair of Air Carnivores sold to the stores for $65 to $70, then it's not lost on the retail community that in a wholly-owned Nike Town, the company will make another $60 to $65 per pair, minus the cost of running their own store, on the same shoes.

But Nike sales managers assured the retailers throughout 1993 that the new Nike stores were brand-building, 3-D commercials that would benefit everyone inside the family circle. As soon as the first of Gordon's retail theaters opened in Portland, they would point out, sales of Nikes went up all over town.

The new Nike Town opened during the spring in Costa Mesa was followed by a hastily assembled version in Atlanta, which offended Gordon Thompson's design sensibilities. Plans for a dazzling Manhattan showcase at the corner of Madison Avenue and 57th Street had fallen through during the early summer when the landlord inexplicably backed away from the deal, but another building on the East Side was now the subject of negotiations. Fourteen different potential Nike Town sites nationwide had been identified by the late summer of 1993.

"But right now I'm obsessed with going beyond Nike Town. I have an idea that will take me a year or two to finish, but I think I'm stepping into a new frontier for retailing. We have to move hard into the next series of ideas to maintain our hold on what's cool—our hold on a market saturated by competitors."

Thompson went on to talk about creating hands-on sport environments inside new San Francisco and Manhattan Nike Towns that would boggle the mind. Sports bars would be set inside digitized environments that made customers feel like they were standing beside the pitcher during famous games. He mentioned interactive television technologies that would allow Nike customers to press their bare feet up against their home television screens to be measured for the digitally customized shoes being imagined in the Nike lab.

A group of young mothers pushing strollers passed by, half of them wearing Reebok Classic aerobic shoes. "Look. Their bread and butter," Gordon said, interrupting himself to point at a few of the 50 million or so pairs of Freestyles sold since they were invented. "Then as now."

Gordon watched a group of young boys in hip-hop apparel walk by wearing Fila basketball shoes. "Fila. Very hot," he said. "A company that made pastel duds for the country-club cocktail set not long ago. They just copied a few of our moves and now they're happening."

Fila outfitted Bjorn Borg in his heyday, but the company had experienced market vicissitudes ever since. The Italian company had made significant inroads with Foot Locker at one point, helping Fila move up to number three, but then the brand fell away again. Fueled more recently by a public offering in Italy, Fila had turned toward the same urban basketball-shoe customer Rob Strasser and Adidas were after.

Fila had just signed one of the recent NBA draftees the Nike sports marketers had also considered as an endorser. Jamal Mashburn, a twenty-year-old star at Kentucky who opted to go pro early, had appeared at a press conference convened on a basketball court next to the Booker T. Washington Junior High School on Manhattan's Upper West Side. Jamal stood beside a new $120,000 red Ferrari—a signing bonus connected to a $6-million multiyear contract. He said that even though he was leaving college for the NBA, his message that day was that kids should stay in school.

"He's not dropping out," his father told the crowd. "He's just temporarily not finishing."

Nike never had a chance to negotiate with Mashburn. The deal with Fila, assisted by Kentucky coach Rick Pitino, had been quietly made shortly after the Final Four tournament. Jamal, like Shaq, appeared to be yet another young athlete who was not awed by Nike. "They wouldn't have had a clue about what to do with a basketball star unless we showed them how," Knight grumbled when Mashburn went to Fila.

Gordon Thompson continued to stare at competitors' shoes, but he was clearly much more unhappy about some of the shoes and apparel being displayed by his own company.

"Part of the problem is that it's not very cool to be number one. It's harder to take risks," Gordon said. "I'm far from the only one inside the berm who's not happy with the spring 'ninety-four line that's being ordered right now. It's so . . . so safe. Too many innovations designed for the top-end shoes have been simply laid into the shoes all the way down the line.

"The divisional VPs are meeting regularly now because we all agree that it's time for another of our big changes at Nike. It's time to shake everything up again. There are some people who came on board during this hypergrowth of the last few years who probably shouldn't be there, and it's time to address the way the matrix serves the company. It's simply gotten too unclear how to get things approved and get things done. It's as if we're poised between a democracy and a bureaucracy. We tend to run in two gears—constant incremental change on one hand and big-time changes on the other. We need to move toward the big-time changes right now, and I really hope that this means that Phil is going to get more involved again."

Knight had made a brief public appearance in New York City a few weeks earlier. He decided he'd better personally address the analysts and institutional investors whose views had mired the Nike stock price in the $55- to $56-per-share range for most of June, July, and early August.

The official results of Nike's fiscal year ending on May 31 were announced in July. Sales had increased over the year by 15 percent, to just under $4 billion, and profits had increased by 10 percent, to $365 million. Knight reported that domestic sales had grown by 13 percent, three times the rate of the rest of the sports and fitness marketplace, and sales outside the U.S. had grown by 24 percent.

But the numbers were not what the Street had expected earlier in the year when official estimates had helped the share price ascend toward $90—when the analysts' bullish projections caused the stock sellers who depend on their reports to tell their clients to buy. The additional news that futures orders for goods to be delivered between June and November of 1993 were off by one percent had upset the investment community, and Knight's projection of flat sales in Europe and only single-digit growth during 1994 had once again infuriated some of the opinion-makers who followed Nike by the day. Analysts who had predicted a 15 to 20 percent growth in earnings for 1994 had to revise those estimates by close to 5 percent—which made few of them happy.

During presentations in New York, Knight admitted that the weakness of the European economies, the soft dollar, and cautious ordering by U.S. retailers had clearly slowed the company juggernaut down. But he proclaimed all of the negative conditions to be temporary.

The official Nike press release about the disappointing results compared Nike's global markets to the domestic situation in 1987, when "the experts"—the words in the usually unironic release of financial results were in quotation marks—said that the athletic-shoe and apparel run had reached its zenith. Now, the statement continued, Nike's sales totaled $2.3 billion domestically, nearly four times the "zenith" analysts had predicted six years ago.

Knight worked to explain the costs of setting up the Nike infrastructure in Europe and other global markets, but he could tell the investment community would have to be shown.

"The fact is, we can be a lot better," Knight said before a Saturday morning breakfast with the editors of *Forbes* magazine, "but one of our biggest problems is that Wall Street simply mistrusts the whole industry. Sony's earnings fall by 50 percent and their stock falls by 10 percent. We continue to grow and make $365 million in profits and our stock gets hammered. But the Street respects them—Japanese Goliath, technological innovation . . . all that stuff—we're still the fashion fad, the flash in the pan."

"They say the bloom is off the rose," added Paul Fireman, **275** who had seen Reebok's share value battered, too. "When I came into this business in 1979 the bloom was off the rose. The business is six times the size it was then and now the bloom is gone. Trying to figure out how to grow is what makes business exciting. You can only sell the same thing the same way so many times."

Knight, Tom Clarke, and Liz Dolan were offered a tour of the private *Forbes* museum of items collected by members of Malcolm Forbes's family over the years. Kip Forbes, one of Malcolm's sons, was particularly intent on pointing out the original copy of the famous letter Harry Truman had written in 1950 to a music critic for *The Washington Post*. The critic had given the president's daughter, Margaret, a terrible review after a Washington, D.C., singing recital, and Truman had promised that if he ever met the critic, the man would need a new nose, meat to put on his black eyes, and a "supporter below."

Tea was served after the tour, and an interview followed.

Back on Fifth Avenue an hour later, Knight pronounced the visit a "complete waste of time."

Knight read in the *Forbes* article that followed that he'd said it was a "big thrill" when Wall Street got skeptical about Nike, because it meant that the assured price comeback would prove the doubters wrong. But the article also observed that a 15 percent rise in sales and an 11 percent increase in profits was not the stuff of the "hot stock" Nike had so recently been. "It will take superhuman efforts and a lot of luck for Nike to continue the 20 percent-plus annual return on equity that has supported [Nike's] stock for so long," the writer had observed.

But Knight was pleased when he got to the end of the article. "Knight, a fierce competitor, says he looks forward to the challenge," the article concluded. "Grinning from behind his sunglasses, he recalls what he learned from his old University of Oregon track coach (and Nike cofounder) William Bowerman: 'Play by the rules, but be ferocious.' "

DUPLIN COUNTY, NORTH CAROLINA

August 1993

The tiny church in the middle of a cornfield was surrounded by television crews and strangers wearing Bulls and North Carolina Tar Heels regalia in mourning. Knight sat in the second pew in the middle of the Rockfish A.M.E. Church on the bright, humid morning of August 15, beside B. J. Armstrong of the Chicago Bulls. They listened to the heartfelt hymns and prayers, and after the preacher's cadent talking, they watched Michael Jordan rise from the row in front of them and stride slowly and deliberately to the pulpit.

"Maybe I shouldn't even go," Jordan had said to Howard White, Tinker Hatfield, and some of his other friends the previous evening. "It's just gonna cause a big stir if I'm there. I'll just . . . detract."

But White, Jordan's mother, and his buddies from back home all endeavored to convince him that the funeral of his murdered father and closest friend was, in many ways, for him. The friends had helped Jordan slip past the press entourage waiting across the street from the church and past the assembled locals by the front door, and now, as Phil Knight watched him intently, he squared the expansive shoulders of his dark blue suit and stepped to the lectern to offer a eulogy.

"As the youngest son and the one with the biggest mouth," Jordan began, his deep voice slightly strained, "it's my role to say a few things about my father. And the first thing I want to say is that I'm just so, so glad that they were able to find my father's remains so we could bring them on back home, to the town **277** that's still home to all of us, and to the people we always will remember here."

At this Michael Jordan looked out to the crowd of just over one hundred people—immediate family, the aunts fanning themselves in the heat, cousins, coaches, teammates, and just a few friends from almost every phase of his celebrated and lately troubled life—and he burst into tears.

Knight sat and stared as Michael Jordan stepped away from the podium, his bowed head moving up and down as he sobbed. Over the course of a decade, Phil Knight had watched the good-natured kid named Michael Jordan grow up to be an unusually sensitive and entirely special young man. Knight had often mused that Jordan was the kind of man who would have been acknowledged as different and special by the people who knew him even if he hadn't become a famous athlete. He was sensitive in the way of an artist, and Knight always wondered if he had been "knocked around" as a kid, because an amazing will to compete was always there to protect his softer side. Because of his physical skills and because, Knight would admit, of Nike's careful celebration of his athletic powers, Jordan had recently found he had to hide behind a constant flow of sports platitudes, behind his circle of lifeguards, and behind a fortress of real and psychic walls.

Knight knew a lot about the walls that can arise between your own feelings and exterior expectations so strong that they dwarf and obscure a sense of who you are. Phil Knight protected his own emotional life behind barricades that had grown more elaborate by the year, that rose and fell instantly as circumstances required. He competed at all things because of the nature of his family and life when he was young. And especially after "the wealth" became part of his life—Knight always said "the" wealth, or "the" power instead of "my" wealth or "my" power, like Andre Agassi pointing to the famous tennis player called Andre in the next chair—Knight had found that his guard was usually up before he'd even thought about the particular dynamic of the situation at hand. And yet for most of the past ten years of his own all-American story of success, there had always been someone connected to the legend of Nike who had to be more guarded and more unable to ever be natural and at ease outside his own house. For more than a year before James Jordan died, Knight had realized that Michael Jordan had been playing hurt—though his body was never stronger or more attuned.

Knight immediately understood that when Jordan had looked out into the faces staring back at him inside the country church, he had seen one of those rare situations when it was safe enough to come out from behind the wall. As Jordan sobbed in the front of the church, Phil Knight bowed his own head and began to weep, too. "Superman in tears," Knight thought as he cried.

Tinker Hatfield was sitting directly behind his boss, and when he saw Knight's composure break, he realized he'd never seen it before.

After a few moments, Jordan began to draw a long breath. Strength seemed to return to his bearing, and Michael raised his head, his eyes seemingly focused. He stepped back to the lectern and spoke in a much deeper voice than before. "I know I can get through this," he said. "It might take me time, but by God, I am going to get through it."

And for ten minutes, Knight heard Michael Jordan talk about his father. He said that from James Jordan he'd come to understand that life is an endless series of new lessons, and that even this tragedy was another chance to learn. At the end of every few sentences, Jordan would begin to cry hard again and step away. But then he would draw in a breath, right himself, and step back up to continue.

"Still the warrior," Knight thought, riveted by the exhibition of will. The man stepping back and forth through the pain of his loss was nothing like the hero on a string Jordan had imagined himself to be during the trials of recent months. Here, Knight reflected, still crying, is a hero, the hero from the best of old books. Here is that elusive capacity of special people to tap the best of spirits and draw greatness from simple moments.

When the eulogy was over, Jordan walked at his mother's side as pallbearers hoisted a stainless steel casket bearing the remains of fifty-seven-year-old James Jordan. They walked out of the church, as the choir sang "May the Life I Live Speak for Me."

By mid-August it was hard to find a Nike manager who didn't believe that big adjustments inside the berm were in order. The lack of enthusiasm over the spring 1994 line at retail and the diminished stock price had engendered a spirit of harsh self-examination that was never deeply submerged inside Nike. The managers working at the top of each departmental silo took the formal lead in articulating the deficiencies of the Nike process, the Nike matrix, the Nike point of view. But energetic discussions about what needed to be done could be heard everywhere in the hallways, in the cafeteria on the World Campus, and in the locker room inside the Bo.

Some managers seemed to take pleasure in the opportunity to offer overarching critiques; others seemed to repeat the "we're better than this" maxims, like political party regulars or players commenting on a slumping team. Managers partook of the dialectical self-examinatory debates, but they seemed careful to avoid the season's "in" jargon of corporate change.

The management buzzword of the summer of 1993 was "reengineering," a term referring to internal process redesign initiatives of the sort that theorists such as W. Edwards Deming had been preaching for years. But "reengineering" had been brilliantly packaged for general consumption by a Harvard professor named Michael Hammer, whose book *Reengineering the Corporation* had become *The One Minute Manager, In Search of Excellence,* and *Theory Z* of the season. Hammer was now advising companies and giving speeches about reengineering protocols at a cost of $10,000 for a day. Reengineering was difficult to distinguish from merely instituting significant organizational changes, but since company cultures tend to calcify and politicize in ways that make them resistant to change, new buzzwords and new protocols for remapping business systems were often helpful in cutting through the thick crust of custom.

"You just know that a spate of 'Why Reengineering Doesn't Work' articles in the business and academic press are just around the corner," observed David Rikert, the ex-Harvard management prof whose job entails studying Nike's internal business processes. "You can't just import a framework like that and follow the steps and have anything happen. Changing companies is hard work. You've got to first make sense of the need for change inside your culture and figure out how to apply new disciplines. But there are indeed times when dramatic change is needed, and I think we're seeing the time at Nike right now."

One of the ideas being tossed around by a committee of vice presidents was to turn the matrix on its side and have the silos of authority conform to business segments—like the outdoor business and the basketball business—instead of organizing beneath departments like advertising and design. Others wanted to get rid of some of the free-floating marketing managers, while still others wanted the marketers to take on more control.

One school of thought feared that Nike was backsliding into

the anarchic pre-reinvention mode of 1982–86 when management by hunch and introversion had almost brought the company down. Another constituency decried the rigidity of the reinvention processes and organizational forms. This was the "where's Phil" contingent, who lamented the absence of his entrepreneurial explosiveness.

Too many bright ideas die inside the matrix," the running-shoe marketing chief, Tom Hartge, complained during a quick lunchtime run. "We've got these gorgeous apparel designs based on the stuff we've made up for the Kenyan track-and-field team, but I can't get the goods out of the damned system. I'm told the line will have to wait until the spring of 1996. I'm told that Nike has bigger fish to fry. This isn't the way this place was ever supposed to work. This is the way big corporations squelch the best ideas."

"There are too many committees, there's too much talking, and there's too much input from retailers and focus groups," railed Tinker Hatfield. "The matrix is killing brilliant insights. As enlightened as this company is, a lot of people inside it are not. They will analyze you out of doing something that comes from the gut—though creating from gut emotions is supposed to be our specialty. I don't see much real risk-taking coming from the marketers here. I'd even say that the designers and Wieden & Kennedy have accounted for most of the risky ventures. Sometimes I think our structure is a formula for mediocrity."

Hatfield had recently made enough noise about leaving Nike to manage to formally exit the matrix. He said he had to get away in order to push through radical new ideas—like his wild yellow shoe, the Air Loom. So when Gordon Thompson got his new design vice presidency, Tinker had been given a free-floating officer's role, but he still criticized the restrictions of the system whenever the debate arose.

"We need an entirely new social form," said Gordon Thompson. "We just have to pick a form from out of this state of constant revolution. The systems by which changes are made are less important than the changes themselves. We need the kind of changes the customer can see."

"Three or four years ago we didn't have a marketing director," complained advertising director Scott Bedbury. "What we had was a very focused product management function headed up by Tom Clarke. We had a very focused advertising function that I headed up. Public relations was focused. And there were all these varied *disciplines* that added up to marketing—separate but equal, working across the matrix, shoulder to shoulder.

"But then, in the interest of time and the incredible pace we keep, we created all these product *marketers* and category marketers. There must be fifty people in the company with some kind of marketing title. But marketing is a verb. It's not a noun. It's process," Bedbury proclaimed, leaning toward the adherence-to-process school of thought. "It's not a place, and it's not a person.

"The way we've set things up, these marketers must be omniscient and visionary. They must be able to say, 'this is where we're going.' So the marketers are always in the face of designers, in the face of PR, and in my face too, talking about their own 'brand.' A new organizational web must reconnect us without getting in the way of making the brand more culturally intelligent. The generalists have to step back, and the wild-ass visionaries have to step up."

"Everybody in this company knows exactly how Nike should run its sports-marketing operation," said Steve Miller. "I sometimes can't believe how many people are in my face because I'm the facilitator for sports marketing. Everything is controversial and debatable because of the way the matrix is designed. This is a time when we can get better. We're too big now to make changes when everything is great. Now we're focused, and I wouldn't be surprised to see the matrix turned on its ear."

"What we have to do is improve all the processes. Nobody wants to admit it, but eighty percent of what we do is just generic business process. Maybe twenty percent is special," the reigning managerial protector of standing corporate form, Dick Donahue said. "But if we really are going to keep our competitive edge, we have to improve the manufacturing process. We need to take this next step in production quickly—this automation and computerization of the shoe-making process—and it must be a proprietary development. Unless the other bastards beat us to it, an innovation like that will allow us to leapfrog everybody once again."

"The structure has to change so we can continue to excite the public," said Liz Dolan after one of the meetings of VPs ended in late August. "If it's product categories or even progressive ideas about society that excite people now—instead of heroes—then maybe the sports-marketing structure has to change accordingly. The way PR, sports marketing, and advertising serve the com-

pany is completely antiquated. I think maybe organizing as a
'basketball business' and a 'running-shoe business' will help put
more creativity in front of the process. But we can't just go to
some traditional business unit structure either. For the kinds of
people we are, there are no text books. . . . "Besides," Liz added,
"a lot of what's going on around here is a complicated reflection
of what's going on inside Phil Knight's head."

"Here they go again," sighed Jim Riswold of Wieden &
Kennedy. "One of the most amazing things of all the many
amazing things about Nike," Riswold quipped as the self-im-
molation continued to the end of the summer, "is the way they
all just love to beat themselves up. No company in America does
it any better."

Over a period of weeks, a consensus had formed among most
of the aggressive young senior managers at Nike. It was time to
direct energies away from simply "feeding the beast," as the pro-
vision of sustenance to the business organism was usually called.
It was time to reconstruct again, and to most of the young directors of Nike's operations, this meant that Knight had to finally
anoint a successor—an Air Apparent.

Dick Donahue, who was never really accepted as being of
pure Nike blood and would soon turn sixty-six, had come to
symbolize communications patterns and an adherence to form
that many of the younger executives resented. Almost everyone
who had occasion to come up to the fourth floor of the
McEnroe Building wanted Knight to choose Tom Clarke as the
next president.

The odd mix of biomechanics scholar, very fast long-distance
runner, day-to-day manager of the brand, and general smart guy
was generally thought to have positioned Clarke as the next in
line. Clarke was seen as part manager and part geek; he was a
grown-up and also an eternal Nike kid.

When Knight had been on the verge of buying the Apex
Sporting Goods Company a year earlier, final price negotiations
were interrupted when the New Jersey entrepreneur who
owned the licensed apparel firm, Joseph Kirchner, announced
that he had one quid pro quo: "I won't work for Tom Clarke,"
he said.

"Then you won't be working here," Knight said, getting up
to leave.

But then Knight also seemed ambivalent about Clarke, and he **283** remained unaware of how strongly his young officers felt that Clarke's ascension was required to help break the internal log jam.

During the first few days of September 1993, word went around the World Campus that Knight had not been at all happy with Nike's annual show of force at the ISPO gathering of the trade in Munich, Germany. Knight had judged the Nike booth in Munich as good but not good enough. The "dominance" the company usually projected, he said, "was missing."

Knight sensed hostility toward the company from the German retail community during his visit, which was reflected so prominently in the local business press that he could only assume that residual loyalty to Adidas had something to do with it. Nike was depicted as attempting to dictate how German merchants should run their business by imposing its futures program on them. Rumors that Nike would soon pull out of ISPO altogether coursed through the large show.

"It's like we're the big bad Americans or something," Knight said to Liz Dolan.

Knight said he wasn't satisfied with the four mannered and evocative commercials designed for the European market. One of the spots shot by David Fincher, a filmmaker who had made some of Madonna's rock videos, showed people playing soccer in a beautiful European square. A man in glasses heads the ball, and the words "Find Something You Can't Live Without" appear on a black border before the "Just Do It" card.

Another spot showed children running in slow motion, and another presented women running to a brilliant Jimi Hendrix guitar moment. Wheelchair racers churned up and down a feudal-looking European hillside in the last of the four commercials, the words "Never Give Up" appearing three times before the black backdrop and the inevitable "Just Do It."

"I just hate these things," Knight said. "Where's the authenticity? Where's the Kenyans running? Those kids could be used by any company. The newer markets require images that can only be associated with Nike. Where are our heroes?"

Knight was equally displeased by the latest salvo from the aggressive women's marketing team. Twelve heavy and burnished pages had been inserted in various national magazines, the mélange of photographs of interesting-looking women and text was entitled "Falling in Love—In Six Acts—A Passion Play." The text included lines such as "Oh let us sing and dance and eat brown mushy foods low in fat! Oh joy! Oh rapture!" The document seemed to equate human love with the love of exercise, but it was hard to tell. "I don't have a clue what it means," Knight scoffed. "I wouldn't even want to guess."

"The black-and-white 'Nike Unplugged' tennis and basketball stuff and the opera spots from Europe were pretty good," Knight said when he returned from Europe. "But the fact is there hasn't been a barn-burner campaign in quite awhile." By then rumors were rife inside the ad community that Wieden & Kennedy—still reeling from the loss of their huge Subaru account—would soon lose Nike, too.

"No," Knight said. "We don't operate like that. They're pretty much vertically integrated with us by now. They're a great partner—a partner that can do better."

Scott Bedbury added that it was Wieden & Kennedy's job to come up with "the big and brilliant idea." "We can always bolt another athlete to another product. It's the idea we want. We have nine different commercials playing during the fall of 1993. The energy is diffused. And there are too many commercials because of the demands of the marketing orientation of the matrix. We're missing that call to action."

"A lot of what's going on with Nike—the European slowdown in particular—is environmental," Knight said. "But the fact is, when we're good enough, we can blow right through environmental factors. We've done it before. There's too much sameness of product, sameness of communication, and the formulas that have worked for us are necessarily old now because they've been copied by everybody else. Now you've got Converse ads that look exactly like Nike ads. . . . Fila goes out and pays millions for this rookie named Mashburn because they have 'discovered' that having NBA players on board will make you a success. Adidas and Reebok are suddenly trying to say they understand the kids on the street. We created all of these standards . . . years ago."

Nike employees working the booth at the ISPO event heard that the Adidas worldwide marketing and planning meeting held during the show had turned into a screaming match. Camps pushing for a performance and technical approach, for a more fashionable or retro campaign, and a group that wanted to go completely urban battled it out—with Rob Strasser yelling and debating the points all night. **285**

The industry seemed constantly abuzz about what Strasser would do next. He had recently hired Steve Liggett, the Reebok executive credited with creating the white Freestyle. At first, word was that Liggett would add a certain solidity to the Adidas team, but then Liggett left the company shortly thereafter.

Knight walked into a Munich restaurant and saw Strasser and his wife at a far table. Knight thought Strasser looked terrible, bigger than ever. Others in the industry who'd spent time with him in recent weeks said that Strasser would sit at his desk with sweat soaking through his shirt.

Knight nodded quickly in the direction of Strasser's table, and Strasser nodded back.

One week earlier Knight's face—half-covered up by a pair of Oakleys fitted with the interchangeable "Heater-style" sports lens—had appeared inside the famous rectangle usually reserved for the kinds of athletes Knight signs to endorsement deals.

Phil Knight was the first corporate executive ever to appear on the cover of *Sports Illustrated*.

Aside from the article about Knight and Nike filling up twenty of the seventy-four pages in the August 16 issue, a picture of a baseball player sporting Nike-Swooshed shoes appeared on page 4. Several basketball players in Nikes appeared on page 9, and Nike icon Nolan Ryan was depicted pounding on the head of another player on page 12. Nike's Bo was shown being bitten by another player on page 15, and Nike shoes and Nike logos were prominently visible during a baseball melee on page 16. Nikes could be spotted on some NFL players on pages 18, 21, and 22; and an ad for Modell's Sporting Goods carried a full-page photograph of a Nike hiking shoe on page 26. The Dutch tennis star Richard Krajicek wore flashy Nike Challenge Court items on page 45, and a baseball catcher showed off his Nikes on page 47 . . . which led up to the long portrait of the company's role in sports that began on page 54 and took up the rest of the issue.

By the time the magazine hit the stands, the general industry rush to be like Nike had complicated the sports-marketing department's seasonal pursuit of NBA draftees. First Jamal Mashburn went off to Fila. Then, despite Nike's connection to his basketball-coach father, David Falk engineered a deal for Bobby Hurley to endorse his own in-house line of shoes for Foot Locker. Nike and Falk had battled throughout the Final Four weekend for the right to represent Hurley. The sports marketers knew that Knight wanted Hurley on the team. But Falk won, and Hurley was also bound for Foot Locker. He would play far from the national TV limelight in Sacramento and then be taken out of play by a near-fatal car accident in December.

Howard White landed the number three draft pick, Anfernee Hardaway, a flashy guard who answered to the nickname Penny and who was bound for the Orlando Magic, where he would pass the ball to Shaq. Another deal to bring the number one pick, Chris Webber, into the total Nike Sports Management program was also struck, but just before Webber was due in Beaverton to sign up, his agent called to say he'd just received a fax from Webber's aunt telling him he was fired. Apparently a new advisor had come into the Webber family circle, and the future Golden State Warriors player's aunt was insistent on renegotiation.

When Knight heard what was going on, he told Steve Miller to pull the whole deal off the table. So Miller and Howard White began a new negotiation process that would continue to the end of 1993. Knight also became intrigued with the idea of signing the seven-foot, six-inch giant beanstalk of a center out of Brigham Young, Shawn Bradley. Ever mindful of the newer Nike markets, Knight said he could imagine young Shawn causing quite a stir in Tokyo, where the sheer size of some of the NBA players drew attention in the way of sumo wrestlers visiting the West.

Jim Riswold had played golf with Alonzo Mourning during the last weeks of summer, and he couldn't help but notice Alonzo was the worst pro athlete golfer he'd ever seen. But they had a good time together, and Riswold told Scott Bedbury and the basketball marketers he had some ideas.

Before the NBA season started in the fall, Alonzo was told that he would have his own sixty-second commercial to accompany the first Alonzo Mourning shoe.

In August, Phoenix Suns owner Jerry Colangelo announced that he was trying to draft Phil Knight to be a co-owner of a proposed major league baseball franchise in Phoenix. Knight said that the Colangelo entreaty was nothing more than a brief discussion, but he would not rule out buying a team or any other sports-related company—if promoting, protecting, and controlling the Nike brand and Nike images were the result.

A few days later, on August 17, the four-hundred-meter star **287**

Quincy Watts felt his customized Nike track shoe fall apart in the middle of his race at the World Track & Field Championships in Stuttgart, Germany. The midsole detached from the upper, and for the first time anyone at Nike could recall, Bill Bowerman's edict about shoes that had to go the distance was contravened in full view of the world's track afficionados.

Quincy angrily waved the shoe around at a press conference after the race, though when he finally calmed down, he sent the shoe back to the Nike sample masters for an "autopsy." They found the bonding process had either never been properly activated because of a lack of applied heat or the shoes had for some reason been exposed to extreme heat in the meantime. Quincy asked the sample-room workers to "take the jinx" out of the shoes. He said he wanted the shoes rebuilt so he could win in them the next time.

Before the World Championships, Jackie Joyner Kersee had joined the Nike track-and-field stable, and Butch Reynolds ran beautifully in Stuttgart—in Nike colors. Butch was still hurt by Nike's lack of support during the years of his battle against the IAAF, but when Steve Miller approached him about a new deal, Reynolds decided that Nike was the company he wanted to run for.

Besides, a U.S. district court judge in Virginia had recently ordered $691,667 to be paid by the Mobil Corporation to the International Amateur Athletic Federation as part of a Mobil/IAAF sponsorship deal, to be redirected to an interest-bearing account in the name of Butch Reynolds, pending the IAAF's legal appeal. IAAF kingpin Primo Nebiolo railed that Reynolds could live "200 years" and not see a bit of his $27.3 million judgment.

But now it looked like Nebiolo might have been wrong.

Reynolds took second place in the final four-hundred-meter race in Stuttgart, the time a half-second behind Nike and U.S. sprinter Michael Johnson's pace.

On the August Sunday evening the World Championships ended, Phil Knight raced around the tennis court behind his house in Hillsboro, Oregon. Knight was playing well, but his doubles partner for the evening—Pete Sampras—was playing even better. Ian Hamilton and Dave Larson, another very good player and a former Reebok guy out of the Nike tennis marketing department, were on the other side of the net, and when pressed for a point, it was clear to everyone watching that they weren't trying to hit the ball to the current number one player in the world.

Sampras and Knight eventually lost the match. "Guess I can't do my usual thing of blaming my partner's play," Knight said, slipping his racquet into its case.

At ten A.M. the next morning, Sampras, his father, his brother, and his lawyers took in a marketing presentation designed to offer a sense of what the Sampras "Nike Classics" segment would look and even sound like once the program got rolling. But Pete Sampras was already sold on the deal. When Howard Slusher had received word two weeks earlier that Sampras was about to sign a deal with Fila, Sampras had called Knight himself to say that he wanted to be involved in deciding where he ended up. A week after that, Slusher was informed that there was an "out" clause that had been inserted into Pete's long-term deal with Sergio Tacchini, and serious negotiations commenced from there.

Tinker Hatfield had gone to Indianapolis to go bowling with Sampras and show him some drawings indicating what Nike had in mind. Sampras, like so many other athletes, was entranced by Tinker's ideas. "This is really fun," Sampras said at one point. "How in the world did you know I love to bowl?"

Tinker shrugged.

After the marketing presentation on August 23, Sampras toured the campus and fell into a three-on-three basketball game in the Bo.

Slusher and Sampras's advisors waded into an extremely complicated deal that was predicated on Sampras being extricated from his Tacchini commitment at one of five points between January 1, 1994, and 1999—though Slusher and even the Tacchini representatives who were privy to the negotiations were set on Sampras appearing in Nike shoes and apparel at the 1994 Wimbledon Tournament.

Negotiations were complicated by the fact that the Sampras side clearly had a copy of Jim Courier's contract in hand—which didn't surprise Slusher but certainly intrigued him—but the deal was hammered out in time for Howard Slusher to take it over to an Italian restaurant in Portland called Perlina's, where Sampras signed while having dinner with Knight.

The sports machine became strangely quiet immediately after that, as the debate over structure and organizational ethos per- **289** sisted. But the lull lasted less than two weeks, when a Nike event so comparatively unimportant that it didn't even make the Nike World Calendar published on the back of the company newspaper turned into a full-blown fiasco that Knight would call "the worst thing that happened to this company in many years."

On September 10, the Nike Town Fab 40 Shootout was held at the World Campus in Beaverton. Close to forty talented high school basketball stars were flown to the campus to play in a series of basketball games in the Bo. The boys attended seminars on various subjects, and they visited the employee store. Since some of the high-potential kids the company was looking to impress were assumed to have come without much money, a hundred-dollar gift certificate was handed out to each player before the store visit.

But someone in the Nike events planning group failed to do his homework when it came to the gift certificates. Nike functionaries had checked with the NCAA about possible rules violations or eligibility issues arising from the new high school program, but they failed to check with all but one of the state high school athletic authorities. The gift certificates and various other Nike gifts turned out to be in violation of many states' rules. Knight conjectured darkly about former associates and current competitors who might have turned Nike in, as wire reports soon indicated that Illinois authorities had suspended, for four games, two Chicago high school stars who'd gone to Beaverton. Some Virginia players were suspended for three games, and in Tennessee, two players were suspended for all of the coming season.

The Oregonian followed with a lead editorial—"Nike Goofs Big"—and in a frothing screed published in the *New York Post,* columnist Mark Kriegel called Knight "a Yuppie gone mad" and proclaimed that "Nike is in the sneaker business the way the Gambinos are in the carting business.

"No one will take the sneaker gangsters to task because no one can—they own everybody," Kriegel ranted on. "Nike has become a corporate consortium of schoolyard flesh peddlers, replacing all the street-scam recruiters with thirty-something hustlers of good manners and the ethics of brothel keepers."

In *USA Today,* a Maryland high school sports official called the Fab 40 incident a form of "child abuse." At this, a writer for *The Oregonian* came to the company's defense: "It makes you wonder how idyllic life is in Maryland, that it makes giving kids a bunch of stuff classify as child abuse. . . . If a teenager creates marketable software, or sings a hit song or writes a book, story or screenplay, he or she can sell it and get paid. Nobody is saying that the millions of dollars Macaulay Culkin received for putting his hands on the side of his face and screaming is a form of child abuse. . . ."

The various state rules covering a wide range of high school sports are complex—in Oregon, for instance, the possibly more well-to-do tennis and golf stars from the high school teams can receive up to five hundred dollars in cash without consequence—but even after the Tennessee players' suspensions were cut to a quarter of the next season, Knight remained depressed about the terrible bureaucratic snafu.

"This is the worst thing a company like this can possibly be a part of," Knight told a group of department directors. "We harmed athletes! We all know that among the hundreds of basketball camps and all-star events out there violations occur all the time. But this was Nike . . . Nike hurting the players, hurting the kids! We've turned back upon ourselves this time. We've violated a commitment at the core of our purpose. This cuts right into our soul.

"The thing is, we do not cheat," Knight said, his voice strained. "Sometimes I think that some people want to believe that the whole thing—this whole rags-to-riches creation—was the result of cheating. It's as if they'd have an easier time with that."

During the summer, a Virginia high school basketball and football star named Allen Iverson was accused of hitting a woman in the head with a chair during a fight at a bowling alley. Iverson's case received national notice when *Sports Illustrated* reported that Nike had flown Iverson to a Nike high school all-star tournament during a break in his trial. The prosecuting attorney paced before the judge during closing arguments, arguing that the young athlete—bound for glory and wealth as he was—had already had his moments in the sun. "Now," prosecutor Colleen Killilea said, "it's our turn to just do it."

John Thompson of Georgetown told Knight about the wording of the prosecutor's address, and Knight was speechless when he heard the news. "Even if Nike had the noblest of intentions," a *Sports Illustrated* writer noted, "bankrolling Iverson only could have hurt him from a legal standpoint, making Iverson appear to be a spoiled athlete who didn't realize the gravity of his situation."

During the fall, the NCAA announced that a subcommittee was being formed to study "the relationship of apparel manufacturers to the intercollegiate athletic community." An NCAA spokesman said that overarching deals between shoe companies and universities and the "Nike basketball camp fiasco" would be subjected to inquiry—this as Charles Young and UCLA were wrapping up a blanket arrangement with Reebok very similar to the Nike university relationships that inspired the NCAA investigation.

After the Iverson sentencing and the Fab 40 disaster, Knight spent a lot of time alone. "There have been other times when I wanted to just dim the lights and stare at a blank TV," he said, wincing at the thought of the missteps of the early fall. "But there haven't been many. And you have to really think about them when they happen."

In the spirit of ongoing internal analysis and the recent bad news, Tom Clarke stopped Howard Slusher in the hall on the fourth floor of the McEnroe Building. "If you could do one thing to really upset everybody at Nike, Howard, what would it be?"

"I'd stop signing every star athlete in the whole world," Howard said. "We're good enough and the product is good enough to sell the stuff without personalities. We just need to shake off all this corporate shit and get back to being family. We're getting like the old Adidas around here. Pretty soon we'll have a board of governors. We have to get away from gesellschaft and back to gemeinschaft—to the old community. Then we'll figure out the next way to teach the beauty of play to people without superstars—and we'll save fifty million dollars while we're at it."

Slusher looked back at Clarke—expecting him to fight his suggestion. "Ya know, Howard," Clarke said, "I've been thinking along the same lines."

"I think we can tone down the hype and reorganize our relationship to athletes," Knight said, strolling the Walk of Fame a few days later. "But if we lose touch with the athlete we lose our center, and without that we'll lose our edge."

Howard White strolled easily at Knight's side. "What's a

building that says John McEnroe on it going to mean to people in ten years, when Mac's been retired for a decade? What will the Michael Jordan Building mean to people in ten years?

"Well here's what I think," Knight continued without waiting for an answer. "I think that in ten years it will mean a lot that Michael Jordan was the greatest basketball player in the world. And I think John McEnroe has put an imprint on tennis that nobody will ever take away from him. You might not like it, but it's there.

"I guess I believe that some things people do are there forever," Knight said. "Some things never really fade."

BEAVERTON III

September 1993

Charles Barkley loomed very large and foreboding in front of a much larger projected photo of his own most menacing glare. It was long past dinnertime by Barkley's reckoning. "I don't like memorizing lines," Charles said for the second time. "I'll do it better if I let the words kinda flow on outa me."

All around him, Nike employees were busily completing the conversion of the basketball court inside the Bo Jackson Fitness Center into the scene of the next day's annual meeting of Nike shareholders. The gleaming hardwood floor was already covered by a rug, and the back of each of the hundreds of folding chairs arrayed in broad rows was being carefully draped with a red and white T-shirt bearing a big orange Swoosh. A folder fat with printed material, rested on each chair—some of the documents pertaining to the comparatively gloomy sales and earnings numbers that would be made public the next morning.

Charles Barkley's oversized, S-shaped body was clad in a short-sleeved tennis shirt, black jeans, and a very long and thick belt embellished by a cowboy's silver buckle the size of a salad plate. When the six-year-old son of Ron Parham, Nike's director of investor relations, charged up to Barkley, he barely reached his thigh. Jake Parham thrust one of the Nike T-shirts above his head. "Sign this!" he crowed.

Charles slowly lowered his head and stared, squinting for focus—as if the little boy was so far away that it took him a moment to lock in on his face. "Sign this, huh?" Barkley growled. "How's about instead if I jus' toss you down on the floor and stomp on yo' little chest till your guts come out your mouth!"

Jake's jaw dropped. With his face fully horizontal and his neck craned backward so he could look up at the giant superstar's face, Jake's fully opened mouth looked like a hole on a putting green. After a moment, the famous scowl depicted on the oversized photograph near the temporary stage in the gym caved in and became a smirk. "Gimme that thing," Barkley teased, grabbing the T-shirt while Jake squealed with delight.

Phil Knight trucked quickly into the gym, looking preoccupied. He had just left a meeting with the personnel committee of his board of directors, and Knight was still pondering the members of the committee's suggestion that a fifty-five-year-old CEO of a major American company ought to be thinking seriously about succession.

Knight was wearing a dark suit that was so much more deeply wrinkled and disheveled than usual that it looked as if the creases had been pressed into the fabric with an industrial steam iron. He scanned the darkened gymnasium slowly until he saw Barkley, who was standing near the far wall. Knight beamed as he approached, though Barkley had marshaled a convincingly threatening expression. Before Knight shook his hand, Charles was already complaining to Knight about the half-million dollars in paper profits he'd given back as Nike's stock price fell from its ninety-dollar zenith to under fifty. Barkley had apparently exercised his option to buy up to twenty thousand shares per year at prices below market level. He had purchased a half-million dollars worth of Nike stock at forty dollars per share, and he'd watched with pleasure as the value of his holdings quickly doubled. When the stock hit ninety dollars, a few months after he played with the Dream Team in Barcelona, Charles had called Howard White to ask him if he should sell. "Put that stock in a drawer someplace, Charles," Howard had said.

Barkley called his financial advisor, who told him the same thing. Then Barkley called Knight: "These last two jokers I asked wouldn't know a million dollars if it bit 'em . . . don't even know what a million looks like. So I'm asking you, should I sell?"

"No way," Knight had said.

Since Knight had spent weeks imagining an army of angry shareholders surging forth from the crowd at the annual meeting, he'd telephoned Charles Barkley ten days earlier, while

Barkley was on vacation in Hawaii. "Now's your chance," Knight said. "Come to the annual meeting and you can be the most irate shareholder of them all."

"And I am irate too," Barkley reiterated in the gym. "But then I hear that you lost some money too," he said to Knight. "I hear tell you lost 'bout a billion dollars? Just how's that make a man feel?"

"Makes him feel happy that he had it to lose," Knight countered, grinning away.

Knight seemed happy but extremely jumpy in conversation with Barkley, though the public business he would conduct over the next twenty-four hours had nothing to do with it. Though Knight arguably spent much more time with a wide array of the world's finest athletes than anyone else, he still became the shy and nervous fan in their presence. Knight could remember in great detail the thrill of having Nike athletes like Sidney Wicks and Elvin Hayes come to his country house in Sunriver, Oregon. He remembered the day he realized that he and Rob Strasser were far more despondent over John McEnroe's loss at Wimbledon the year after he first won than were McEnroe's father or even McEnroe. "The most powerful man in sport"—which by now had become a standardized, ironic idiom inside the berm—got wired up around athletes because he saw them as modern saints. The empire-builder receded into humility and shyness, because he knew that he only had an empire because of great athletes and the way he perceived their greatness.

For all the excitement of Barkley's company, very early the next morning there would begin one of those public days that had always caused Phil Knight a modicum of pain. A week earlier Knight had summarily turned down requests for interviews from *60 Minutes* and *Good Morning America*. The latter appearance would have been part of a segment focusing on Nike as one of the best places to work in America. Knight even happened to be in New York when the show was scheduled, but he still said no.

In the morning, "the drill" would start as early as Bowerman's predawn training sessions. At six A.M., the announcement would be made to hundreds of investors and securities analysts all over the world that the first quarter of the Nike fiscal year had gone poorly according to standards set over the past six years. Expectations for the second quarter of the year weren't much better. Those who expected Nike to continue to rack up another year of huge increases and double-digit growth by the late spring of 1994, the morning announcement would convey, would probably be disappointed.

The annual meeting would convene after that, and in the afternoon all employees working on the World Campus were invited to gather in the gym to witness a mock reenactment of the morning shareholders' meeting.

This year—for the first time since the beginning of the great surge of the past six years—Knight dreaded this last and most familial of the day's public responsibilities most of all. During the afternoon session with the employees, Knight would tell them of an immediate round of company-wide layoffs. The cost of running Nike had risen by 5 percent over the past year, and the extreme profitability of the company would be modified in the near future. But the underlying reason behind the cuts was largely informed by a desire to make room for new talent and to selectively prune the Nike populace after a lengthy hiring binge.

The company remained the most profitable in the industry and far from the dire financial straits of 1985 and 1986. The traumatic layoffs of those years meant that 600 employees were culled from a community of 2,000. This time, fewer than 250 employees would be cut from a team of nearly 10,000, but the plan worried Knight and made him feel as if he and Nike had let the employees down. Knight had vowed when the process of reinventing Nike began that a measure of the company's greatness would be that layoffs never occurred again. When he made the pledge, Knight had never imagined coaching a company so large that it now rolled out far beyond his capacity to know or even see it. But he also understood that the high-strung spirit of the company was born of a complex and volatile chemistry.

Nelson Farris, the longtime company vet and director of internal relations, had argued vociferously against the cuts. "Let's step up," Farris said to GM Tom Clarke. "Let's say that we're here to cover you during the bad times, and let's add that the five percent of you who aren't 'getting it' have to change."

Clarke had replied that "emotionally" the idea sounded right. "But this is one of those Nike-business versus American-business dilemmas we face from time to time."

Knight had been sleepless, trying to calculate the psychic toll of the cost-cutting measure. He had become so preoccupied with what to say during the afternoon session that he had driven up to his house in rural Sunriver three days earlier to think and be alone—not that being alone wasn't a standard aspect of his days inside the berm.

Knight stepped onto the stage and huddled with Dick Donahue, Tom Clarke, and Ron Parham. Donahue and Clarke raised their voices during a brief debate over the proper way to depict the 3–5 percent work-force reduction if any of the analysts sitting in on the mass conference call scheduled for the next morning asked about cost-cutting. "We reported three hundred and sixty-five million dollars in profit three months ago. We have three hundred and sixty million dollars in cash on hand. Why should we play up a cost-cutting measure that's really a pruning operation anyway!" Donahue argued.

"Still, if anyone asks about layoffs in the morning," Knight said softly, backing Clarke's position on openness, "we'll just tell them."

A few feet away, Charles Barkley was handed a pair of the newly designed Air Max² CBs—for Charles Barkley—due to premiere during the early weeks of 1994, and for the first time in a half hour, Charles stopped talking. He picked up one of the black shoes that were dotted with silver circles, and he reverently turned the size nine prototype over and over. Barkley tried without success to thrust his hand inside the shoe, which was loaded with air bags that had been variously pressurized to conform with jumping and landing patterns. "It's real good," Barkley said. "When can I get a pair?"

Someone asked if Knight was concerned that Barkley had balked at the idea of planning what he would say during the shareholders' meeting the next day.

Knight briefly pondered some of Charles's other public performances, and he wondered if the Barkley stunt might backfire—as with a few too many plans of the last few weeks. Knight recalled that Barkley had recently gone to speak at the opening of an orphanage his Phoenix teammate, Kevin Johnson, worked to support. Charles got up in front of a large crowd of public officials and children and told a few inspirational stories that all proved, he said, that "You've got to just go and do it. You've got to just go for it. You've got to really believe if you want something." But then Barkley had paused, a twinkle in his eye. "Then again. If you really get to thinking about it, you come to the case of Jeffrey Dahmer," Barkley had mused, referring to the Milwaukee serial killer who ate his victims. "Now Jeffrey Dahmer really, really believed too. Jeffrey, he just went out 'n' he—"

Knight was told Charles was still talking when Kevin Johnson dragged him away from the microphone.

"Don't you worry now. I'll just get up there and wing it," Charles told Knight as he hoisted Howard White's six-year-old daughter above his head. "I'll just say what needs to be said. God will come over me, and he will tell me what to say. So don't you worry about that one little bit."

Deep blue and black bands of light arched across the sky as Knight's Acura roared through the opening in the berm at quarter to six. For all the things the leader of Nike has been called over the years, a "morning person" has never been among them. The conference call was scheduled for nine A.M. Wall Street time—six A.M. in Portland—so Dick Donahue had tried to convince Knight that the event would begin at five-thirty in hopes that the leader would be on hand when the hundreds of telephone connections were made.

Runners were already moving through the dark morning when Knight pulled into his parking place. Employees arriving early for long runs or workouts at the Bo pedaled by on mountain bikes. A blind employee speed-walked along in front of the marble fountain with cane in hand, brightly saying good morning as she passed.

Upstairs in the small and square Fenway Room on the top floor of the McEnroe Building, Dick Donahue was pacing back and forth staring at a key. "I can't get into my gawddamned office," Donahue roared, his Boston accent invariably more pronounced when he became agitated.

Knight shuffled in, blinking, and immediately asked Liz Dolan to make coffee. The gender politics joke was one Knight repeated almost every time he greeted Dolan in the early morning. As per their script, Liz rolled her eyes and Knight went off to find the coffee himself.

By the time he returned and put his sunglasses down on the small table in the Fenway Room, Donahue, Tom Clarke, Ron Parham, and Bob Falcone, the chief financial officer, were already in position. They all looked sleepy—except for Tom Clarke, who sat bolt upright and eager in a fashionable suit and tie, his hair falling well below his collar. The men all stared down at the middle of the table, at a low-lying gray plastic box with an undulating, perforated top.

"Gentleman," said a voice from the box. "My name is Pete. I will be your teleconference operator this morning. We have around a hundred and twenty people on the line, and more are signing in as we speak. We'll be ready to go in just a moment."

The audience would be largely composed of brokerage-house and investment-bank analysts. There were members of the financial and athletic-goods industry press on the line, some institutional portfolio managers who held Nike shares, and several would-be large holders of the stock who had been identified and contacted on Nike's behalf by one of the thousands of ancillary financial services firms created in recent years—this one a Chicago company specializing in identifying appropriate new investors for large corporations.

"Well, gentlemen," Ron Parham said in a hypothetical, press-conference voice, "do you expect to continue paying exorbitant fees to athletes in light of these numbers?"

"Why yes, as a matter of fact we do," Knight said, trying to rub life into his cheeks and eyes in a vigorous, circular motion.

Ron Parham picked up a phone and asked where Nike shares had opened. He grimaced and reported to the others that the quarterly news had hit the wires. Another two dollars had been peeled from the price.

Pete came back on the line and said the conference would begin in twenty seconds.

Tom Clarke leaned forward as if at the beginning of a race. "Let's be aggressive here, gentlemen," he said.

During the week after the shareholders' meeting, a *Wall Street Journal* article would posit that Nike was "racing" to remake its image. The feature did not mention all the internal soul-searching going on inside the berm, but the writer would suggest that the appearance of certain ads for the outdoor categories' shoes and apparel were indications of an entirely new corporate purpose. Tom Clarke would storm into Knight's office with the article in hand. "Why do we even talk to the *Wall Street Journal*! We spend five years building a constituency of tens of millions of people who understand that we're a sports-and-fitness company with a hundred different purposes, and the press and some of the analysts can only think we're junking everything because they think nobody wants athletic shoes anymore. Every fifteen-year-old boy in America gets it. Maybe we should just communicate with them!"

For Clarke—as with Knight—the business was definitely personal.

When board members had questioned Knight about succession issues, he told members of the personnel committee that "the next guy must come from within the company. But there's a lot of young talent around here," Knight had continued. "There are several people who are going to be getting a lot more responsibility in the near future. And I can watch what they do."

The conference call began, with Knight speaking first. "When we left you last," he said in a very flat voice, "we were optimistic about the coming fiscal year. Now we have an all-time record year in terms of revenue—if the same rules and scorekeeping system of last year could be applied." He went on to blame currency exchange rates and the new tax laws for bringing the earnings lower. "We're positioned well. We have more growth coming, but it will always come with bumps—as it has over the last ten years. Nike's value as an investment will be dictated by how well we chase the two billion dollars in untapped business we see out there, and by whether or not we become the first truly global company in this industry."

It was left to Clarke to report the worst financial news—that futures orders for the coming period were valued at $724 million, less than the $800 million worth of orders during the first quarter of last year.

Clarke also reported a decline in the basketball category. Nike had sold close to $150 million worth of basketball shoes in the quarter, and still controlled 50 percent of the market, but sales were 16 percent lower than the previous year, which included a huge, nearly 20 percent rise in domestic sales in the wake of the Dream Team Olympic Summer. Other categories were fine—cross-training up 34 percent, outdoor up 29 percent, women's footwear up 18 percent—"but," Clarke said, his voice trailing off, "we will be down in ninety-four."

During the question-and-answer portion of the conference call, several Nike-watchers on the line wondered why the company didn't buy up large blocks of its own stock at current prices. Such a stock "buyback" was typical of the kinds of maneuvers designed to support the price of shares that many conservative analysts and investors liked. After a past price downturn and stock buyback, the company's shares had appreciated by $80 million when the price went back up.

"But it's just not how I see Nike operating," Knight said as he walked across the campus toward the Bo. "I'm still a small businessman at heart, and I just can't imagine how a company that swallows itself will ever achieve greatness."

"Phil is a lot less comfortable than I am with the idea of stable growth," Ron Parham of investor relations said in the lobby of the Bo. "He will go out and satisfy his desire for fast-paced, entrepreneurial growth outside the United States, and much as I'd like us to be a stable company for the sake of Wall Street, Wall Street doesn't dictate what Nike will be."

Parham had seen the way Nike's times of hypergrowth were invariably juxtaposed to sorry numbers when the cycles Knight talked about dictated a lull. Parham talked often about his and Wall Street's desire for "several quarters of moderate growth in a row," but he knew that this went against the grain. From Knight's perspective, the company drew its vital energy from the extreme pace of the chase.

Penny and Travis Knight had taken seats in the back of the gym as the shareholders filed in for the annual meeting. Penny, dressed in a tailored suit and wearing very long fingernails, chatted with her running partner Howard Slusher. The two would both complete their first marathon in October. ("Penny did a four forty-four and Slusher—the dumb schmuck—he had to be taken to the hospital to be rehydrated," Knight would report after the race.)

Twenty-year-old Travis Knight, wearing an earring and very short blond hair, stood next to his mother, waiting for the meeting to begin. The younger of Phil Knight's two sons looked more like a football player than a runner, though Travis was more interested in music than sports. A new compact disc by "Chilly Tee" that had recently arrived in record stores around the country—featuring a single that was getting a bit of radio play called "Get Off Mine"—was in fact the work of Travis Knight.

A year earlier, Travis had been drawn into a discussion of his future by his concerned father. Phil Knight wondered if perhaps Travis's interest in drawing and design might indicate it was time for him to get a low-level job with an architecture firm. But Travis said he wasn't much interested in that scenario.

"Well, what do you really want to do?" Knight asked his son.

"I want to be a rap star."

Knight only helped out when it came time to hire an entertainment attorney. The CD was released by MCA, and Travis had already applied his advance to a new recording facility that was built into the family house in Hillsboro.

"It sure makes you think about the psychology of fathers and sons," Knight said. "I thought a lot about my father going on about my own crazy notion. I'm really proud of Travis."

Knight stood alone on the stage as the members of the Nike board of directors filed in, his hands in his pockets.

Doug Houser, one of the original board members and Knight's cousin, approached Tom Clarke on one side of the stage. "I've got an idea," the Portland lawyer enthused. "How about baby shoes . . . not just baby shoes, but baby shoes with different colored booties you slip inside?"

Tom Clarke nodded very thoughtfully, clearly thinking about something else.

Bill Bowerman, looking tanned and extremely fit, stood a few feet away, listening to the conversation and shaking his head from side to side. "Some of the guys on this board don't know which end of a damned shoe faces forward," Bowerman said, not bothering to lower his voice at all.

Bowerman said he'd made at least a half-dozen pairs of shoes over the past year, though he added he'd gotten rid of the old-fashioned n-hexane-laced glue.

"I find that some of my fellow board members have lost sight of the objective," Bowerman noted. "Are the shoes light? Are they comfortable? Can they go the distance? Those are the fundamental questions."

"One thing about Bowerman," Knight had said earlier in the year. "He has an amazing capacity to screw up all the facts at hand and still come to the right conclusion. That's a gift."

"I don't know how you ever got along with him," Bowerman's wife had said to Phil Knight one day when she'd accompanied Bill on a visit to Beaverton. "Nobody else ever did."

"I could say the same to you," Knight had replied.

Board member John Thompson, who looked much bigger than Charles Barkley, took his seat in the front. During a meeting of the board convened between the morning conference call and the shareholders' meeting, Thompson had been shown a good-looking new 1994 cross-trainer inspired by African runners. The shoe, he was told, was tentatively entitled the Black Massa.

"Just so it's not the white massa," Thompson had replied.

As the formal proceedings began, Thompson seemed to scan the faces in the crowd methodically, moving from row to row with his dark eyes.

Many of the shareholders who by now had filled all the seats in the Bo were among the oldest people to appear on the World Campus in months. As with most audiences attending the annual meetings of large corporation, the majority of the attendees were retired. Some of them lived comfortably because more than twenty years earlier they'd taken a flier on a little shoe venture started up by the son of a Portland publisher—one of Bowerman's boys. Four of the Oregonians sitting near the front of the room were among the original class of debenture owners who'd ponied up the $200,000 Knight needed to proceed in the Blue Ribbon Sports days.

During the question period after the various formal reports, film clips, and pep talks about the future, one of the multimillionaire original investors got up and began a long and rambling dissertation on the importance of "keeping 'the stripe' on the shoe. I mean we've got to see the stripe in the morning paper."

Knight smiled at the man and nodded in response to every point he made.

It was clear that the meeting would not be marred by investor rancor as Knight had feared. The audience seemed mesmerized by each numeric celebration of the corporate story and each promise of more of the same. "If you look at a graph you'll see that the ride in this industry has always been bumpy," Knight said. "But as in the past, we will continue to ride up."

Knight asked if there were any more questions, and a commotion ensued in the back of the room. A loud voice was heard to bellow, "I have a question! I have a question!"

Several hundred people turned around in their seats to see Charles Barkley in a gigantic purple suit. Looking for all the world like a 252-pound grape, Charles began to steam toward the stage, glowering and shaking hands along the way. He bounded up next to Knight. "I demand to be heard!" he proclaimed.

For a while, Barkley played the angry shareholder part he'd been assigned but eventually his tone softened. "You know," he said, looking out at the audience, "people are always bad-mouthin' Nike for some reason. But the truth is, as hard as I play, Nike has taken me to places I could never have got through basketball alone. Nike has made me a whole lot of money too.

"And you know, everywhere I go people ask me the same thing. They say 'What's that guy Phil Knight really like?' And I always say the exact same thing to them," Charles declaimed, as the corporate secretary duly recorded his words in the minutes and Phil Knight began to grimace slightly because he'd already guessed what was coming. "I say, 'Phil Knight is the only guy I know with a whole lot of money who's not an asshole.' "

The observation so entered in the corporate record, Charles hurried off to catch a plane to New York, where he was scheduled to host *Saturday Night Live*.

During a gala summer sales meeting, a Nike version of *Saturday Night Live* had been staged with Phil Knight in the leading role. Knight appeared in one skit doing a decent imitation of Marlon Brando playing the Godfather. "The most powerful man in sport" sat in his study like Don Corleone in the movie's famous wedding scene, supplicants approaching one after another to kiss his ring and ask for favors.

Mike Krzyzewski appeared on stage, though the new Nike coach had at first balked at making the trip because a Nike employee spelled his name wrong ("Not exactly a name that's easy to spell right," Knight observed when told of the coach's ire). But Krzyzewski came and appeared before the laughing and cheering sales reps, bowing before the Godfather of sport.

"Mikey, Mikey, Mikey," Knight rasped. "I have not always been pleased with you."

Joe Paterno pranced onto the stage to complain that *he'd* been a favorite Nike coach from the beginning, and now these new guys were muscling in on his territory. Then Andre Agassi, John McEnroe, and Jim Courier appeared behind Knight on film, bowing to the Godfather's demand that they play in the next Davis Cup tournament.

Later, during a skit spoofing the Village People's song "YMCA" ("N-I-K-E"), Knight appeared again—this time in a leather motorcycle jacket and a leather cap turned to the side. **305**

He was bare-chested except for heavy chains and an S-and-M-style harness ensemble.

He even sang.

Around the same time, the Nike video-maker Michael Doherty began to clown around during one of his Friday morning shows on Nike Free Radio—call letters KAOS—the World Campus radio station. "And next," Doherty said, "maybe we can get Phil Knight to come down here and tell us just what he does with all his money."

Within most large business organizations, the jest would have been regarded as an affront to propriety and inimical to the aura of managerial authority. In some companies, the kidding might have been viewed as an acceptable way to demythologize the leader for the good of morale. But at Nike, the ritual irreverence was essential. The recurrent injections of iconoclasm acted as inoculations against the encroachment of a bureaucratic and big-business style that would indicate that Nike had become no different from the gray and soulless monoliths beyond the berm.

Many of the employees who filed into the gym for the afternoon reenactment of the annual meeting would regard the high corporate formality as parody. The slightly ironic tone that Knight, Tom Clarke, and the others would adopt ("Then we got to the part where we tell them all . . . Then we read all this formal stuff. . . .") would serve to subtly undermine the nuts-and-bolts expediency of the annual rite. The Nike idyll, the message was there to be read for those who would see, was still not amenable to spreadsheets. The reductionist talk of dollars and cents was still as removed from the true ethos of their corporate experience as history professors lecturing without passion about the "youth culture" of the time when Nike was born.

Most of the employees still filing into the gym in the Bo were too young to have felt the dizzying historical compression of recent days, when a cook and restaurant-owner in Corvallis, Oregon, had revealed herself to be Katherine Anne Powers, the suburban-born radical who'd been living underground since taking part in a bank robbery and fatal shooting in the angry year 1970. The front-of-the-baby-boom Nike employees who felt the strange nostalgia of the event—the ones with graying hair or less hair than before, the ones who complained about their knees and hips in the locker room at the Bo before hitting the running trail—were also among those Nike employees who were startled to hear about the mail that came to Nike after the John Lennon

"Instant Karma" ad campaign began. Apparently young acolytes of the brand loved the commercial, but many of them wrote in to ask if the singer used in the commercial had made any singles or albums they could buy.

On one recent late summer day, when dozens of Nike employees had gathered around tables set out on a patio overlooking the seven acres of Lake Slusher, Michael Doherty had looked up to see Knight standing over him with his lunch tray. Doherty said he was finished with lunch and about to head back to work.

"Just stay awhile," Knight had said. "I don't know anybody here.

"I do miss the old days," Knight had said. "Those early entrepreneurial days, frankly, were more fun. There are only a few old-timers left that are friends of mine . . . and we were so footloose in those early days."

For half of a century, students of management have studied and debated the nature of the traumatic transition of the successful entrepreneurial enterprise from an inspired adventure to a multi-faceted organization run by managers. Those who remembered the early days would invariably regard the following generation of managers as mere bureaucrats, as caretakers who could at best perpetuate processes without passion, and at worst, would bury the animating sensibility of the original cause and close out the golden age.

Inside Nike, the entrepreneurial purity of the early dream was carefully protected, sanctified. The ethos of the upstart team on a roll was still regarded as the source of the culture's power. "The team on the run," Knight would say. "Everyone up to speed, everyone on the same squad."

So those who were invited to join the life inside the berm tended to remember how it felt to win games. The years they missed were compressed and conveyed via images of Prefontaine and other athletes of a Nike stripe in full glory—and by the presence of the old track geek and founder himself, the hip Walt Disney who's not dead yet—and by the contrived rituals of the tribe . . . covering up the laugh lines, like a big pair of high-tech wraparound shades.

Knight again stood alone on the stage as Nike employees filled up all the chairs. They filed five and six rows deep between the last rows of chairs and the walls, and they leaned against the railing from the oval running track suspended above the court.

Along the ceiling of the gym above them, so high in the rafters that they were easy to miss, were colorful banners hung like the pennants in sports arenas honoring bygone winning seasons and the retired numbers of former members of the team.

Dan Wieden and David Kennedy's names were on separate flags, as were the names of the Nissho Iwai executives Masaru Hayami and Tom Sumeragi, men who'd stood by Knight in the early days when American bankers pulled the plug. A few lower- and middle-level employees who had died had flags at the top of the gym, as did the compulsive Nike Air inventor Frank Rudy, and the first employee, Jeff Johnson.

As Knight looked out into the gym, he sensed the alarm and confusion in the room. The news of job cutbacks had spread electronically to employees in all corners of the global web by midafternoon. Knight pondered the fact that many of the employees staring up at him were too young to have known the times when Nike hung by a thread. Of every thousand Nike employees, some eight hundred of them only knew the incredible streak of the past six years. Nike was to them less a team than a dynasty. The sight of their fear made Knight think of the thousands of bright-eyed $200,000-a-year Wall Street kids laid off en masse after the stock crash of 1987. He remembered the interviews with some of them when the ax fell. They had all been lulled into thinking that bull markets could last forever. They didn't understand business dreams rode along atop cycles and waves.

Knight, Tom Clarke, Donahue, and Mark Parker walked the employees through a compressed version of the shareholders' meeting, then Knight asked for questions.

He seemed somewhat pleased by a woman near the front who asked about the general "response" senior management had gotten to one of the new commercials she had just seen as part of the presentation. The commercial featured the towering volleyball star, *Vogue* model, and rookie Nike endorser, Gabrielle Reese. The beautiful athlete was depicted lounging languorously across unkempt pink satin sheets in some shots of the commercials and viciously spiking volleyballs and diving through the air in others.

"Well, we try to work with our women athletes, to use them in our communication," Knight said, but then with a knowing smile, he asked, "What was your response?"

"She's a woman athlete presented as a sex kitten and therefore less seriously," the employee responded in a clear voice. "We wouldn't see Charles Barkley in that bed."

Next, Donahue talked about China ("It's so huge, and we don't have to have it all. We only need a bit at the top."), as a chart behind him showed that there were 11,812 people in China for every pair of athletic shoes sold there within a year— compared to the four residents of the United States per each pair of retailed shoes. Tom Clarke described the tragedy of Quincy Watts's broken shoe before someone asked Knight about the CAA and Mike Ovitz relationship.

"It's all overblown in the press," Knight said.

The layoffs were only mentioned in passing. Knight mentioned a 3 percent reduction, but then Tom Clarke referred to work-force cuts of 4 percent a few minutes later.

"Three!" hundreds of people whispered, as if on cue.

When there were no more questions, after a long pause, Knight stepped up to the microphone.

"Over the last six years Nike has added thirty-eight hundred jobs," Knight said. "If we had been perfect, we would have added thirty-five hundred. Or, basically, we were off by one and a half percent each year. If you are a professional manager, that doesn't bother you. But nobody has ever accused me of being a professional manager.

"I know that the average Nike employee will not be on the cover of *Sports Illustrated,* but I also know that without the average Nike employee I wouldn't be on the cover of *Sports Illustrated.*"

Knight stared up into the crowd.

"Without the Nike employee, I'm a rumpled suit and a pair of Oakley sunglasses. Without the Nike employee, there's no me. That is why these things are so painful. And that is why I personally hate Paul Fireman, Rob Strasser, and Gib Ford. I hope you can understand that at this moment.

"I wouldn't trade places with any company in this industry. I think our opportunities and challenges have never been greater. There is an opportunity to be the first in this screwy industry, to be a true global company. There's two billion dollars worth of sales out there. And I wouldn't say the opportunities are in the international division alone. It isn't enough to just win in Germany and not win in the United States.

"Nike is as American as Coca-Cola. Nike's opportunities have never been better. . . . Let's win."

With that, the strains of "Through the Storm" boomed through the high-efficiency speakers and a newly culled series of slow-motion ballets performed by Barkley, Pippen, Harold Miner, and Sergei Bubka appeared on a screen behind Knight's head. The new clips included shots of athletes hitting the floor and turf and ramming into the steel poles that hold up the baskets.

Some of the employees sitting in the Bo stayed in their seats to watch the film, their faces reflecting the pain and glory as the sports moments cascaded across the screen. But others had jumped up quickly and moved to the door. Many heads were bowed in the crowd waiting to exit the gym, and conversation was strangely subdued.

Knight stood on the stage looking out, his jaw clenched, until most of the employees had left the gym.

"I looked out at the end of that meeting and I could see it—a schism, a divide," Knight remembered over dinner near the end of 1993. "Some of them never wavered from understanding that Nike is special, not just a business but something more, something of which business is only part. But I could see others— particularly the ones who came on board over the last few years—thinking that after all they'd done and been taught to believe, it was just another business after all."

Not long after the Tae Kwang Rubber Company closed down the T3 plant in Pusan, several Ekins in the field, a lot of secretaries, the guy who coordinated the Ekin visits to the World Campus, the sports-marketing guy who was in daily contact with Alonzo Mourning, and other members of the Nike tribe had been asked to move on. As the employee cuts ran up over two hundred, most departmental managers saw that attrition would allow them to consolidate further.

The pall that settled over the World Campus after the September annual meeting lifted slightly when word of a more inspired and well-received fall '94 line went around. But then Michael Jordan retired in October, and the world inside the berm was rocked again.

When Knight talked to Jordan on the phone about his plans before leaving to join him for the retirement announcement in

Chicago, he told the star that he'd understood that his departure was coming for quite awhile.

When Jordan's entourage had arrived at the Bulls practice center on the morning of the press conference, Knight walked past the wife of the Bulls' coach, Phil Jackson, who was completely dissolved in tears. Knight shook hands with NBA commissioner David Stern, his ally and nemesis in the making of the dream of Michael Jordan and the remaking of an American game. The two men went into an empty office and closed the door.

"What do you think?" Stern asked.

"I have mixed feelings," Knight said. "I'm happy for him, but I feel the impact personally—the loss—and I'm concerned about the impact on the company."

"This is happy time," Stern said. "Magic Johnson retiring because he was sick was sad. We should be happy."

Knight stared long enough to make sure that Stern was being sincere. "Yeah," Knight said. "I think you're right."

Jordan was in Beaverton several times before the end of the year. A small casual line of Jordan shoes, shirts, and jackets was quickly designed and scheduled for the spring of 1994, and several NBA players known for the finesse and style of their play—Harold Miner and the Seattle star Kendall Gill among them—were told that they would henceforth wear Air Jordans as would the players on the University of North Carolina basketball team.

Jordan even had an office at Nike now—the only office on Knight's side of the fourth floor of the McEnroe Building, though even the hero down the hall didn't wander at will into the inner office with the dark wood.

Back in Chicago, Jordan began to spend more time outside of his private enclosure, chatting with other diners at Michael Jordan's Restaurant. He was spotted playing cards at various country clubs in the area. "I have a new goal now gentlemen," Jordan told a group of men at a card table inside a country club catering to a largely Jewish membership. "I plan be the first black man in the gin rummy hall of fame."

During the early weeks of 1994, Jordan began to pursue the goal of playing baseball for the Chicago White Sox, just as he'd told Knight, Tinker Hatfield, and Howard White he would do the night he retired. Just before he began watching major league fastballs and curves hurtle toward him, Jordan had gone skiing for the first time. He spoke with such enthusiasm about the experience that friends began to wonder if downhill racing wasn't next on Jordan's experiential agenda.

A few weeks after Jordan retired, Steven Roth, owner of the Essex House of Fashion in Newark, accepted a buyout offer from the largest retailer on Market Street and closed up shop. "From very different ends of the spectrum, I guess Michael and I did have similar philosophies about backing away," Steven said. "I've got three children at home I didn't get to see often enough. I'd made enough money, and I was just too overworked. I wanted to get back to a more normal life. The American dream includes not doing things you just don't have to do. Just like Michael says."

On the last Saturday in October, Rob Strasser died suddenly of a heart attack at the age of forty-six.

Knight and other veterans at Nike spent much of the following week reminiscing and wondering whether or not to attend the funeral. Some of the senior Nike managers who'd kept up with Strasser said that Rob's blood pressure had been up around 240/210. Others talked of the rigors of the seemingly impossible task Rob had set out for himself—saving old Adidas and sticking it to Nike along the way.

Knight seemed unable to separate his shock over the tragedy, the pleasure he clearly drew from recalling the Strasser of the halcyon days, and the injuries he'd suffered from things Strasser had said and done and claimed to have done in recent years. Knight's photograph appeared in *The Oregonian,* the caption offering a rare quote: "I knew Rob Strasser over twenty years in a variety of capacities including lawyer, colleague, friend, competitor and enemy. I was greatly saddened by his death and choose to remember the many grand adventures and good times we shared together."

On the Monday morning after Strasser died, Nike's stock rose by $3.50.

A subsequent article in *The Oregonian* described the funeral that Knight, Slusher, and many others from Nike did not attend: "While an image of Strasser's sunburned face smiled slyly down on them, most of the eight people who paraded to the lectern Monday spoke of war. There was discussion of the parallels between the generalships of Strasser and George Patton. There was talk of combat in the arena of sports merchandising. There were the inevitable warlike allusions to Nike, which plays the Death Star in the Adidas universe. . . . You start to wonder," *The Oregonian's* writer added, "just what goes on in the sports and apparel and footwear business, anyway. It's just a business about games, isn't it?"

"It was never a game to Rob," Sonny Vaccaro said after the funeral. "The mission killed him. He worked himself to death. And it's never been a game for Phil either."

Just before Strasser's death, Nike's jockeying for position on the grassroots urban basketball scene led some of his colleagues at Nike to question whether Howard White had fraternized inappropriately with Sonny Vaccaro and Adidas. At first Knight ignored reports from other managers that phone records indicated Howard had telephoned Sonny Vaccaro after having conversations with Knight. But when he was told that White might have set up a dummy company office in Portland, he agreed to further investigations.

Knight told Howard to take some time off, and by January, 1994, the industry coursed with news that the FBI had become involved in the investigation. Inside the berm, some speculated that before he died, Strasser had stepped up the level of the blood feud in an effort to buy off one of Knight's closest friends inside the company.

But Howard White was totally exonerated by the FBI and Nike. There was no dummy corporation, some of the phone calls thought to have been made to Vaccaro were in fact placed to White's old friend, the broadcaster, Ahmad Rashad.

"When Phil told me to take some time off, I said I'd done nothing wrong, but I told him to go ahead and do what he had to do," White said after the incident had passed. "I knew that being so close to Phil and Michael made people inside and outside the company want to take shots at me. I was surprised when it got to the FBI, but in a way that was a good thing because everyone knew they would bring out the truth.

"I knew that in the past people like Rob and Sonny have gotten real close to Phil, and then something happened between them and they were suddenly on the other side. I also know that this is a big-league corporation now and not the little intimate company I came to twelve years back. All I ever cared about was PK's take on it because to me Phil Knight and Nike are one— **313** like the same thing. Phil and I never stopped talking through the whole deal, and when he told me to take time off, he sent my whole family to the Bahamas. Tests like this go both ways, and I think Phil came through strong. We were all stronger in the end. In a way," Howard White said, "I was glad the thing came at me. Because I think there are others who would have lost their jobs."

Knight had told his troops gathered for the mock annual meeting in September that he hated Paul Fireman of Reebok, but some of the senior executives present took the statement with a grain of salt. By then they had heard about what had happened at the U.S. Open a few weeks earlier.

Paul Fireman was sitting in the Reebok box close to the court when a man in a black suit stepped in front of him and extended his hand. "Mr. Fireman," the man said, "I'm Philip Knight."

An ex-Nike Reebok executive Knight had always liked, Tom Carmody, had come over to say hello to Knight. "You know what," Knight said. "If I'm ever going to meet that son of a bitch, I think you're the one to introduce us."

Knight took an empty seat next to Fireman after they shook hands, and they chatted for ten minutes about tennis and the business environment in Europe.

A friend of Knight's, the Lehman Brothers banker Ken Tuchman, gazed over from a nearby box and referred to another historic reckoning of the same month. "First the PLO and the Israelis, and now Knight and Fireman," Tuchman said. "I really don't think I can take much more."

"He was gracious," Fireman reported. "After fourteen years, we've finally broken the ice."

"We had our picture taken," Knight told the others back inside the berm. "I was on a step so I look much, much bigger."

"Rob's dead and Fireman is a real person," one Nike executive commented when news of the fraternization spread. "Who are we gonna fight now?"

"The ferocity is still intact," Knight said over dinner at the end of the year. "But it's time to rethink certain aspects of the quest. Nobody in this company has been taught to be content to simply manage. We grew from a billion-dollar business into a four-billion-dollar global organization in just a few years, and we still managed to keep Nike special. Now we have to grow even larger without becoming formulaic.

"Seven years ago we struggled to figure out who we were," he continued, sipping at his white wine. "We resurrected Nike as a sports-and-fitness company, and our television advertising and our marketing triumphs were energized because—unlike most companies—we were sure about why we were here. We have to do something much less radical now—which is to look hard at the corporation, at the form. I honestly think some of the younger people at Nike might be able to balance creativity and organization better than I can. Maybe they'll be better able to mix the past and the future, the creative and the managed."

During the early weeks of 1994, Knight would seek the counsel of various management theorists. He would discuss issues of transition with Kenichi Ohmae and with Jeffrey Pfeffer, a professor of organizational behavior at the Stanford Business School. A local management consultant, Don Murray, would begin taking soundings among the young senior managers, and Knight was surprised by how dissatisfied most of them were with the current structure, and by how very much most of them felt it was time to change the corporate guard. Some said they were extremely concerned that Knight would not choose Tom Clarke to be the next president when Dick Donahue's contract expired in June 1994, and that Clarke would leave the fold.

Knight knew that the current business lull was not thought to be amenable to a fix generated by new heroes. In many ways the internal cult of sports authenticity had boxed the company in. Certain kinds of acquisitions and even products seemed to run against a Nike moral order that was in need of change.

Knight seemed energized by the soul-searching and external adversity. "There's an aura of challenge again," he agreed. "It does tend to concentrate your mind."

At the end of January, a few days before the annual Super Show in Atlanta and less than two weeks before the Winter Olympics were scheduled to commence in Norway, Knight surged briefly into public view when he came to the defense of the embattled figure skater Tonya Harding. In a letter to employees explaining his decision to donate $25,000 toward Harding's defense of her right to skate in the Olympics, Knight wrote that he didn't know whether or not Harding was guilty of the attack on rival U.S. skater Nancy Kerrigan. But he was sure that **315** a possible U.S. Olympic Committee move to force her to withdraw from the team before she was found guilty in court violated both his own understanding of due process and a venerable Nike tradition: "Twenty years ago, another athlete who didn't quite fit the mold, Steve Prefontaine, fought a battle with the AAU, the governing body that ruled amateur athletics in those days, and Nike was at his side."

Before announcing the donation, Knight had Liz Dolan phone Harding's attorneys to warn them of Nike's long history of antagonistic relationships with international sporting authorities. But the lawyers and Harding—a Portland native who previously had only received a free set of sweats from Nike—said they welcomed Nike's support.

Knight gave sharp interviews to ESPN, NPR, *Larry King Live* and *The Today Show*. He said that Nike would always argue the case of an athlete over an "athletic bureaucracy," and he posited that if Harding were eventually proven guilty, her medals could be taken away. "If in fact she is proven innocent and yet doesn't get to skate," he said during the ESPN interview, "you can never repair that damage, ever."

Knight was clearly fired up by the controversy, and everyone on the World Campus could sense the return of the old élan.

In February, with the stock price already 20 percent above the lows reached around the time of the shareholders' meeting, Knight would announce that Dick Donahue was stepping down. Tom Clarke would be the new corporate president. When Donahue had assumed the presidency from outside the berm four years earlier, he had said that his job was to help identify the next generation of managers—which he had.

Clarke would take over later during the year, around the time the stock price surged back above $60 per share, just before the basketball shoe business rebounded from its slump, and before Knight would pursue the idea of buying the New York Knicks and New York Rangers before deciding the price for the teams and an attendant television sports network was simply too high. By the end of 1994 the stock would rise above $70 a share with reports of increased earnings and orders for the winter and spring of 1995 that were up by 34 percent. Knight would also okay a promotional deal with the National Hockey League and the $385,000,000 takeover of Canstar, the largest hockey equipment manufacturer—though Knight would admit that hockey had never been a personal passion.

"Whatever happens, I'm still here," Knight said over dinner that evening in Portland. "I would like to stay around as a kind of senior presence, as a teacher, but I'll have to learn to find that middle ground. There's a side of me that goes in for relentless pursuit, and another side that tends to back completely away."

It was hard to back away as Michael Jordan had backed "away from games," because Knight knew he had guided the creation of an institution that transcended the games Nike celebrated. Nike now imprinted daily life in ways Knight never could have imagined when he started selling track shoes. He easily agreed that the recent hold of sports upon the popular imagination was in some part due to the way the fear of being blown up and other contemporary preoccupations had freed up emotions and peoples' time. But there were still competitors to fight, a few athletes still not draped in or performing atop his wares, and if people's closets were indeed getting full because Nike had helped make the shoes so remarkably essential, then there were other businesses and ideas connected to games that were still unexplored.

"Who knows," Knight said in the restaurant parking lot, "maybe I'll end up going off to open up a Taco Bell or something. People are coming into the company who do what they do better than I. I'm just a generalist, one of those entrepreneurs my college professor said would always eat lunch alone, off to the side. Sometimes I think there's only a few of us left."

Knight nodded and smiled in a way that indicated that only part of what he'd just said was true. Then he jacked himself into his sleek black car, gunned the engine, and drove off going fast—as if racing toward that finish line that isn't there.

Acknowledgments

A list of Nike employees who taught me important things about the company would take up many pages. The following executives—as much as they all hate that term—made themselves available time and again during my months inside Nike. My sincerest thanks to Scott Bedbury, Charlie Brown, Tom Clarke, Henry Chriss, Mike Doherty, Michael Donaghu, Dick Donahue, Nelson Farris, Ian Hamilton, Tom Hartge, Tinker Hatfield, Dusty Kidd, Dave Kottkamp, T. H. Lee, Tom McGuirk, Steve Miller, Ron Parham, Mark Parker, Kevin Paulk, Keith Peters, Tom Phillips, David Rikert, Fred Schreyer, Howard Slusher, Duke Stump, Dave Taylor, Gordon Thompson, Howard White, Anne Wiper, Glenn Wakefield, and Bill Worthington.

Liz Dolan, head of Nike PR, is the second corporate public affairs official I have worked with who naturally digs inside the company for the truth like a reporter, and Phil Knight is the second CEO who has allowed me to watch a large corporation in motion. He was willing to explain his thinking after making decisions, and he never shied away from a question, even after more than a year of fielding them. Though I could tell it sometimes shocked his colleagues, he always returned my phone calls. I will always be grateful for his cooperation.

Outside of Nike, many dozens of ex-Nike executives, competitors, journalists, athletes, sports agents, team owners, sports-marketing managers, network executives, and league officials were extremely helpful. Among those most generous with their **319**

DONALD KATZ

time and insights were Leonard Armato, Bill Bowerman, Len Elmore, Josie Esquival, David Falk, Paul Fireman, Dave Fogelson, Dave Gavitt, Maggie Gilliam, Bill Grant, Dave Graves, Michael Haines, David Hawkins, Arnold Hiatt, Rick Hinden, Brad Hunt, Michael Jacobsen, Gary Jacobson, Jeff Johnson, Mark McCormack, John McIntyre, Susann McKee, Mike Moran, John Miller, Jim Moodhe, Roger Noll, Michael Ovitz, Phil Patton, Jim Riswold, Steven Roth, Lisa Ukman, Sonny Vaccaro, Patricia Violante, and Charles Young.

Mark Mulvoy, Rob Fleder, Kelli Anderson, and others at *Sports Illustrated* aided my research and writing—and listened to my suppositions about sports and the marketplace—long after my *SI* article about Nike was published.

My talented editor at Random House, Jon Karp—and his boss, Harry Evans—were extremely supportive of my desire to put another book project aside for a time so I could write about Nike, and many others at Random House have enthusiastically welcomed me aboard. My agent, Amanda Urban, saw the potential of this project from the start.

Mark Padnos, Jean Kidd, Anna Maria Pineda, and Alvera Rivers all weighed in with research, transcription, and general paper management assistance. My friends David Blum, Paul Hawken, and Fred Smoler helped by reading and commenting on a draft of the book, and my uncle and friend, John Strauss, applied innumerable helpful and even witty Post-it note messages to another draft. My wife, Leslie Larson—not a fan of sports or business books—was still able to offer all sorts of good ideas after reading a typescript . . . as always.

Leslie, Chloe, Austin, and Dashiell—who was born around the time Deion Sanders told his Nike contacts he wanted to quit playing baseball—all put up with the very long absences that have come to mark the last months of all my book writing. I promise my wonderful family that the seven-day work weeks won't happen again . . . for a while.

Several months before completion, I became assured of the importance of a book about the dream-makers at Nike while tucking then four-year-old Austin into bed. Two weeks earlier Austin had conducted an extended phone conversation with Bo Jackson, and he was able to easily pick out various Nike stars from a televised image of a crowded basketball court. But on this night, something about the superstars seemed to perplex him. "Daddy," Austin said before I turned out the light, "is Michael Jordan real?"

320

INDEX

INDEX

INDEX

INDEX

INDEX

INDEX

329

INDEX

INDEX

INDEX

INDEX

About the Author

DONALD KATZ is the author of *Home Fires: An Intimate Portrait of One Middle-Class Family in Postwar America,* published in 1992 and nominated for a National Book Critics Circle Award. Katz's previous book, *The Big Store: Inside the Crisis and Revolution at Sears,* was a national bestseller in 1987 and winner of the *Chicago Tribune* Heartland Prize for nonfiction. A longtime contributing editor and columnist for *Esquire,* Katz is also a contributing editor for *Outside* magazine, *Men's Journal,* and a consulting editor for *Worth.* Katz's magazine work won a National Magazine Award in 1994, and his coverage of the Ethiopian revolution for *Rolling Stone* won an Overseas Press Club Award in 1978. He lives and works in Montclair, New Jersey, with his wife, Leslie Larson, and their three children.